M000211449

Claire Nahmad has published a numbe
South Yorkshire, England.

Margaret Bailey is a visionary and a practising Buddhist. She has worked in the field of mental health for many years before recently becoming a full-time artist.

The Secret Teachings of Mary Magdalene

INCLUDING THE LOST GOSPEL OF MARY,
REVEALED AND PUBLISHED FOR THE FIRST TIME

CLAIRE NAHMAD & MARGARET BAILEY

WATKINS PUBLISHING
LONDON

This edition published in the UK 2006 by
Watkins Publishing, Sixth Floor, Castle House,
75–76 Wells Street, London W1T 3QH
Distributed in the USA and Canada by Publishers Group West

1 3 5 7 9 10 8 6 4 2

Designed and typeset by Jerry Goldie

Printed and bound in Great Britain

Library of Congress Cataloging-in-Publication data available

ISBN-10: 1-84293-182-2
ISBN-13: 9-781842-931820
www.watkinspublishing.com

Contents

Acknowledgements

Our thanks are due to Michael Mann, for supporting this project throughout; to Penny Stopa, for her hard work and forbearance; to Ann Napier, for her inspired editing; to Shelagh Boyd, our copy editor, for her helpful comments and suggestions; to the White Eagle Lodge, for their generosity in allowing me to quote copyright material from a selection of their titles; to David Wright, for inspiration and enlightenment; to Pete Bailey ('Wayland'), for his unfailing encouragement and faith in us and our book; to Chris Bailey for helping us out, and to Nick Bailey for his vital input; to my parents, for providing a postal service; to my sister Lindy Nahmad, for her practical help; to Claire Fitzgerald, for her kind interest and support, and for cheering us on; to Maria and Guiletta Zawadzki (the 'Princesses') for their kind interest and for helping us to clear the 'well shaft' of our intuitive perception; and last, but by no means least, to Mik Revill, our overseeing 'knight', for his unobtrusive support and protection.

This book is dedicated to my father, Ivor Nahmad, who helped me to appreciate the vision of the east.

Preface

Following a series of remarkable events in our lives, Margaret Bailey and I were led to discover all we could about the history of Mary Magdalene.

We found ourselves in a maelstrom of conflicting evidence and theory. There were the old diehards who insisted that all was as it ever had been, and that Mary was a reformed prostitute who, although desperately penitent, was spurned by Jesus when she met him after his resurrection in the Garden of Gethsemane, Jesus saying harshly to her as she reached out to him, 'Do not touch me.'

It was posited that Jesus and Mary were not actual people at all, but were instead tutelary myths arising from the philosophical concepts of a mystery tradition. The authors who introduced this idea argued in support of it that there was a Jesus for everybody, perhaps not noting that, as they themselves are philosophers, they had created their 'own' Jesus – Jesus the philosophical concept!

There were those who suggested that Mary was a wealthy pagan priestess who administered the rites of Osiris to Jesus, and who was persuaded by him to bribe the necessary authorities to crucify him, so that she herself could revive him from his near-death coma in order that he might convince his followers of his claims (claims he egotistically sought to substantiate by also murdering John the Baptist as an expedient career move). Later, regretting her part in this stage-management, she fled from Jesus and settled in France, where she proclaimed her own mystery-religion of Isis from the steps of the Temple of Diana in Paris (formerly Para Isidos, Greek for 'close to [the heart of] Isis'), winning hearts and minds to the point where many heretical Gnostic sects arose and flourished in worship of her and the Great Goddess whom she represented. Indeed, Paris itself is said originally to have been dedicated to the Magdalene.

Others suggested that Mary had very possibly been involved in a Goddess-worshipping cult, but had been converted by Jesus, who made her his wife or sexual companion. Mary bore a child or children, who initiated (or extended, as Jesus himself was said to have been 'born of David's line') a holy bloodline which exists to this day.

Another theory espouses the idea that Jesus led a radical faction of Essene priests. This Jesus was not of virgin birth, was no miracle-worker, did not die on the cross and was not resurrected. He married Mary Magdalene, who was previously a divorced woman, produced a family with her, and then divorced her himself.

A further theory, to which we feel (to a certain extent) generally more attuned, cites that Mary, although a human being as was Jesus, had mystical origins and elements within her that made her truly the royal consort of the Anointed One who was of the line of David, and whose kingly bloodline, although reaching down to us today, has been denied and obscured by certain powerful, self-interested political and religious factions.

We felt that whilst all these recent discoveries, revelations and conclusions regarding the controversial figure of Mary Magdalene told a fascinating story, somehow, overall, their tantalizing components seemed to lack an intuitive integrity, an uplifting of the veil which would set ablaze the heart and its faculty of higher vision, that organ of spiritual perception through which we see truth, so that the obscured wonder and mystery of the Magdalene might at last step into the light of day. We seemed to begin to catch sight of a complete image within the glimmering and scattered mosaic pieces that surrounded us.

They revealed a story so compelling, so miraculous, so astonishing in its revelations and so staggering in its implications, that we felt we must offer it as our contribution to the cracking of the enigma surrounding Mary Magdalene – an enigma believed to have been purposely constructed by a patriarchal culture determined to draw a veil of invisibility and misunderstanding over all that comprises the Sacred Feminine, and which, it seems, quaked in its boots when confronted with the enormity of her true significance.

The significance of Mary Magdalene is revealed within the mysteries of her story and within the profound and mystical teachings given in her gospel. Half of it is missing. It did not reach the public domain until 1955, having been discovered almost 60 years earlier by a German academic in Cairo. We believe that this lost gospel, so recently recovered, holds an important key, a magical key which can be divined only with the wisdom of the heart.

We have another source. In the summer of 2004, Mary Magdalene actually made herself known to Margaret Bailey through means of spiritual communication. A long period of spiritual training and discipline in meditation and inner seeing had preceded this event. Margaret enters 'the Silence', so beloved and revered by Mary, as her gospel reveals. This 'Silence' takes the form of a ring of inconceivably beautiful light, through which Margaret passes in order to commune with Mary and to receive her teachings for today.

It was Mary herself who had instructed us to research her story according to the new theories and revelations of our time, although when we were initially led to do so, we were following the guidance of one who, although undoubtedly an exalted being, we could never have guessed had a deep personal association with her. The fact that the two are connected at the deepest and most significant level is just one of the many astonishing discoveries we have made on this endlessly fascinating journey of what we trust is true enlightenment. The story of how Margaret and I were brought together, and the identity of the mysterious being who united us, will be told elsewhere.

These teachings, given by Mary, seem to us to be bright and clear, starlit in their economy and simplicity. They bear a lightness of touch that never veils their profundity. They are the words of Mary, coming to us today through Margaret Bailey, who has been specially prepared for this work, and, to a lesser degree, through me. I receive Mary's inspiration through a simple mediumistic technique, whereas Margaret truly enters 'the Silence' and is in direct visionary communion with her. I therefore regard Margaret as the most important source.

The human body, intellect and soul working together as a unity, is the finest instrument for receiving communion from the higher spheres. In order to do so, the body and the mind are quietened and calmed by gentle, focused breathing, the mind descends softly into the heart and waits in stillness, ready to serve. It has to remain humble, or the ego will assert itself. The heart-consciousness, which is different from the intellect, throws out the radiance which is its essence and begins to ascend to the highest sphere of which it can conceive. It recognizes that sphere because the quality of consciousness it touches resonates with its deepest inner flame. This interior recognition is monitored throughout the span during which communion with the consciousness of the higher spheres takes place. Therefore control and responsibility are not surrendered; the conscious self, receptive and silent, obedient to the light, makes of itself a vessel, whereas self-consciousness, the thrust of the lower self which is based in the ego, is kept firmly in abeyance.

This is the method I used to elicit the information given on the following pages. A short period of preparation as described above preceded my work on it, during which I would enter into communion with Mary Magdalene and after which I would enter a state of deep inner listening whilst actually writing. However, what I received was not officially sanctioned in my eyes until Margaret Bailey had entered the Silence (the Silence which incorporates the Orbit of Sharon, that sphere of incomparably beautiful light where Mary dwells and of which she is the heart) and presented my gleanings before Mary, seeking reaffirmation from her that I had heard correctly.

These reaffirmations, plus Margaret's own revelations from Mary and the insights which came to us from our lengthy discussions, throughout which disclosures and illuminations were received at a breathtakingly rapid pace (afterwards duly subjected to our usual method of scrutiny) are what comprise this book.

My own illuminations from Mary, and those of Margaret, mutually clarify and verify one another. I can give an example of mine. It was received after we had intuited a very clear feeling that Mary wished to correct some modern (and in fact ancient) assumptions about her meaning and significance. It relates to the sexual aspect of her mysteries, so open to misinterpretation from hostile repression on one hand, and a much too materialistic and hedonistic 'modern' approach on the other (with a bit of esotericism thrown in to lend it apparent authenticity):

> *There is an element in sexual desire which is the desire of*
> *matter for itself. It is destructive, harmful to relationships, and*
> *it deadens the heart. Sexual union must strive to rise above this*
> *ruinous element before it can be compatible with the will and*
> *the purpose of spirit.*

Very shortly afterwards, we watched a television documentary which showed an example of matter's 'desire for itself'. It concerned a seven-year-old boy who appeared to be 'pregnant'. Within him was a kind of foetal sac, containing his 'twin brother', who had continued to grow inside him after his birth. The 'brother' had long hair, a face, genitalia and limbs, but no brain or heart. The entity could never be human or achieve any kind of conscious existence, but nevertheless would have kept on growing inside its host until eventually the physical stress killed him. We were given the intuition that cancer also expresses this 'desire of matter for itself', a desire which, if not transmuted, quickly turns into a devourer and killer of that which it desires – itself. We were further advised that all distress and dysfunction within the psyche of humanity is linked to this untransmuted materialism, which exists on both basic and subtle levels of being. Later, we discovered this very teaching given in Mary's gospel.

I give this little example to show that we are by no means dreamily channelling Mary's teachings in an effusive and complacent manner. We always look for confir-mation that we have got the message right as far as we can, and search deep within ourselves via meditation, prayer, and clarification from the outer world in the form of the more usual methods of research that what we are hearing with our inner ears really does apply. In fact, we feel that the concept of spoon-feeding is not one that Mary will entertain! In other words, without allowing ourselves to be bound and gagged by our commonsense, we do aim to use the facility!

We are only too aware that anyone can jump on the bandwagon of the current fascination with Mary Magdalene and claim to be receiving all sorts of teachings and channellings; and we consider that there can be no doubt that Mary is indeed speaking to those with ears to hear. All we can say is that, until recently, we had no idea that such a keen interest in her existed. We had heard of *The Da Vinci Code* by Dan Brown, but as we tend to steer clear of blockbuster novels, neither of us had read it or understood that its content involved Mary Magdalene. However, as has been discussed, from the end of July of 2004, we were firmly directed from a spiritual source to learn all we could of the current Mary Magdalene debate. We perceived from this foray that some ideas are circulating which we think are unhelpful, to say the least, and that although many revelations have been made which do reveal elements of the glorious truth of the Magdalene, we feel that her 'tower' [1] has not yet been properly raised.

Our exposition of the teachings of Mary Magdalene includes some of the hidden teachings from The Gospel of John, which go hand in hand with her revelations. We hope these will help to lay to rest the negative football-team-supporter approach which seems to have overtaken some of the advocates of this mystery, who believe that there has always been some kind of power struggle between John (either John the Baptist or John the Beloved, no-one seems quite sure – but then that is part of the answer to the enigma) and Jesus!

We hope that the validity of what we have received from Mary will be self-evident, without the need for any strident claims by us. The Magdalene legacy is not that of a bloodline. It is infinitely more profound and immeasurably more significant. It is a legacy of transformative love.

NOTES

1 'Tower' is part of the translation of 'Magdalene' and is a deeply significant symbol of the Sacred Feminine. Other meanings are 'Magnificent', 'Great Queen' and ('the Magdalene') 'the All'.

PART I

The Story of Mary

CHAPTER ONE

The Woman at the Foot of the Cross

*A*lmost 2,000 years ago, three women stood by as Jesus the Nazarene slowly expired on his cross. They were part of a large group of Jesus's followers, all of them female, who had gathered at a distance to be present at his crucifixion. According to John's gospel, the three who waited before the cross were Mary, the mother of Jesus, her 'sister' Mary, wife of Cleopas, and Mary Magdalene.

Who was this mysterious woman, Mary Magdalene, portrayed through the centuries as kneeling at the foot of the cross, her hair always painted in hues of flame, red or gold? Why is she given such scant mention in the gospels, the terse references to her seeming to indicate that she was too great a luminary in the Christian story to omit altogether, yet, that the cause of plausibility must be served with the greatest possible economy, the veil of silence lifted briefly, reluctantly, cursorily. What threat did she embody?

Mary Magdalene, the repentant prostitute, is the only traditional image the Church has sanctioned of this strangely stirring and enigmatic figure, although nowhere in the canonical gospels or other records is she ever referred to as such. Luke's gospel calls her 'Magdalene', a name that is presumed to indicate her place of origin as the town of Magdala, an assumption which is again inaccurate, because evidence shows that in Mary's day, Magdala in Galilee (now called el Medjdel or Magdel) was not so named, but was known as Tarichea. It is more likely that Jesus himself gave her this evocative title, and, as we shall see, its implications are far-reaching and profound.

The re-evaluation of the significance of the Magdalene today echoes a secret tradition that spans an entire age, reaching back to the middle years of the first century, when records confirm that Mary settled in France and began her mission of healing, baptism and instruction concerning 'The Way', as the earliest Christian teachings were known. Yet the current interpretation may still not fully embrace the true depth and significance of what she expressed in her deeper being, that profundity of transforming consciousness which comprises her sacred mysteries. There is a danger that what she is seen to represent – the body, the life force expressed through the medium of blood and the act of sex – may be too narrowly understood, however liberated and esoteric our modern context may appear to be.

A gross mantle of materialism has been deliberately and systematically woven around Mary Magdalene through the centuries by powerful and despotic detractors, limiting her significance to a false scenario comprising the physical body and the exploitation of the life force through the act of prostitution, and her later repentance. Although the Catholic Church withdrew this accusation in 1969, the identity of the penitent Magdalene remains largely unchanged, except for progressive thinkers, particularly Christian feminists, who see her as a devoted and significant disciple and who have separated her from the identity of Mary of Bethany, she 'who had lived a sinful life in that town', according to Luke's gospel. Yet even this apparently positive step has obfuscated the powerful and essential role of the Magdalene, because if the act of anointing Jesus (performed by Mary of Bethany) is no longer associated with her, it is even more difficult to discern her true status under the distortions of the centuries.

Let us home in on Mary Magdalene and hold in unwavering focus those strange and magical lights which glance so fugitively over her story and her significance. Though purposely and conspiratorially concealed for so long, their radiance could never be entirely hidden, nor the truth that they so mysteriously and fleetingly illumine, forever obscured.

CHAPTER TWO

Mary of Bethany

*I*n the Synoptic gospels (Mark, Luke and Matthew) the story is told of how a woman called Mary anoints the feet of Jesus with 'perfume'. This key incident is cited in the gospels of Mark and Matthew as occurring at Bethany, in the house of Simon the leper, two days before the Passover. Luke, on the other hand, speaks of it as happening at Capernaum, at the outset of Jesus's three-year mission, in the home of Simon the Pharisee.[1] In each case, Mary is referred to as a 'sinner' by the resident Simon. The word 'sinner' is a slightly inaccurate translation of *harmartolos*, whose exact meaning we shall examine later.

We might pause briefly here to reflect that whenever a 'Simon' appears on the scene in relation to Jesus, some concealment or misrepresentation seems to be afoot. There is the 'infamous' Simon Magus and his consort Helen, disciples of John the Baptist, who so weirdly mirrored the spiritual journey of Jesus and Mary Magdalene, except that Simon used magic as a form of illusion to perform his 'miracles', proclaimed himself a god, and exhibited Helen as a dancer in chains, presumably using the idea of the Sacred Feminine Principle in bondage to arouse the prurience of his audience so that its impact might swell the ranks of his followers. Simon the Magus attempted to buy the Holy Spirit from Peter the disciple and so initiated the crime of simony, which offers materialistic instead of spiritual surrender for the bestowing of holy grace. Although he saw Helen as a personification of wisdom he also saw her as a whore. He and his consort seem to be caricatures of Jesus and Mary.

Another Simon connected with Jesus is Simon of Cyrene, who is claimed in one of the texts of the Dead Sea Scrolls to have masqueraded as Jesus just before the Crucifixion, being crucified in his stead whilst Jesus looked on from a niche, sniggering up his sleeve at the ignorance of the onlookers.

Simon called Peter initiated the Church of Rome, which as we shall see was violently opposed to the early Celtic Church that enshrined the true teachings of Christ which Mary Magdalene, Mary Jacob and Mary the Virgin were so deeply influential in establishing throughout Britain, France and Spain. Simon Peter hated the Magdalene and on more than one occasion threatened her life. Here we have a third scenario where a Simon is involved in a seeming distortion of the truth that was Christ's legacy. And the false Judas Iscariot, betrayer of Jesus, who sold him to the authorities for thirty pieces of silver, is described in John's gospel as 'Simon's son'. Moreover, Jesus calls him the 'son of perdition' (eternal death or damnation). Whilst this is obviously not a reference to Simon his father, it still might be grist to the mill of our theory, especially as Judas is cited as 'Simon's son' at a very interesting point in John's gospel story concerning Mary's anointing, as will be explained later. Those who interpret Christ's teachings at a deeper level will realize that when Jesus seemed to refer to Judas as the 'son of perdition', he was actually identifying the instinct that urged Judas to the act of betrayal and not the man himself – that urge which was born of Earth, not spirit, and therefore was doomed to carry its perpetrator to self-destruction. Nevertheless, his reference to the 'son of perdition' within this context again seems to implicate 'Simon', not as a man but as a symbol of falsehood.

Believing, as we do, that the drama of the life of Jesus contains many gradations of deeper and yet deeper meaning, we feel that the presence of a Simon is a kind of code or sign to be on the alert, signalling that a clearer truth may need to be assisted in its birth and released from the attendant recorded circumstances, which perhaps reflect a misleading image. This seems particularly to be the case when the hidden mysteries of Jesus are implicated: his secret teachings, which may be partially obscured or rendered incomplete within the context of the canonical gospels; the question of whether or not he died on the cross; the case of his miracle-working and healing, which some allege was merely magicianship, and the nature of his true relationship with Mary Magdalene.

It is almost as though two mirrors were held up to the student of the Christian mysteries, one reflecting truth, 'The Way', as the teachings of the Christ were known in their earliest and purest form, and the other reflecting falsehood, the Missed Way, or, to indulge in semantics, the Road of Mists, as it is sometimes called. Do we believe that the entire truth of Christ's teachings has been made available to our understanding, or does one mirror show, on the other hand, that certain concepts indicate gaps and contrived omissions which ensure that the circle of tolerance, inclusion and loving kindness which the teachings sought to inscribe, ultimately fails to close? Do we believe that he died on the cross or that some elaborate subterfuge was instigated? Or, we might rise above this double-headed materialistic theory and realize that of course he cannot have *died* on the cross, because the spearhead of his entire mission was to deliver us from the prince of this world, Death itself, which ensnares us in limitation and the futility of materialistic thinking, from which no breakthrough into truth can be made.

Do we believe, as has lately been suggested, that the miracles and the healing demonstrated by Jesus were simply a clever illusionist's pantomime, paraded to gain cult following, or do we believe that matter can indeed be mastered and that we ourselves (as he himself told us) contain the potential to master it as he did, that its restrictions do not contain the whole truth of existence, but that it can be made into a fitting receptacle for the impregnation of divine truth, eternal and beautiful? And was Mary Magdalene a weeping remorseful prostitute whose only relevance to Jesus was that he dispensed forgiveness to her, or was she, to him, Mary the Magnificent, the All, the Bride, as the Gnostic gospels explicitly state?

We believe that all these points are relevant to the unveiling of the obscured Magdalene, and that Simon is the hidden key that unlocks the soul-chamber wherein the two mirrors dwell, one reflecting life and one reflecting death, in the deepest, most profound meaning of each state. We are certainly not implying that 'Simon' is any kind of ill-omened name! On the contrary, the name Simon, in the case of the Magdalene mystery, is the way-shower, the catalyst for us to fathom our greater being in the search for truth, to beware of surfaces, convention and self-deception. The name means 'obedience', which is a clue in itself.

We cannot confirm our theory, and it may well prove to be spurious, but for the moment we are content to follow the promptings of a half-intuited suspicion. We think that Simon the leper and Simon the Pharisee, as they appear in relation to the anointing woman in the gospels of Mark, Matthew and Luke, announce a certain obfuscation. We would prefer to rely on the testimony of John's gospel, as his is the only one that makes no mention of Mary's 'sins', and especially as the accounts in the Synoptic gospels (each, tellingly, in the presence of a 'Simon') led directly to the association of Mary Magdalene with prostitution.

In 591CE, whilst giving his *Homily 33*, Pope Gregory I was inspired to declare:

> *She whom Luke calls the sinful woman, whom John calls Mary,*
> *we believe to be Mary from whom seven devils were ejected*
> *according to Mark. And what did these seven devils signify,*
> *if not all the vices? ... It is clear, brothers, that the woman*
> *previously used the unguent to perfume her flesh in forbidden*
> *acts.*

It is very tempting to imagine the righteously indignant (and titillated) pope bringing his fist down with a crash on the table before him (presuming there was one) to punctuate his statement, and the grunts of enthusiastic assent rising in a chorus from the assembled 'brethren'.

There are five points that it is important to consider at this juncture. The first is that all the gospels, either within the canon or outside it (those outside it being the Gnostic gospels, the Dead Sea Scrolls and The Gospel of Mary, whilst the canonical gospels are those of Mark, Matthew, Luke and John) invariably mention the disciples' dislike and suspicion of Mary Magdalene. This cannot be any reflection upon Mary's personality or integrity, as Jesus himself clearly held her in highest esteem and tender reverence, and she is spoken of as comforting and rallying the disciples when they are sunk in a lethargy of despair after his crucifixion. It is much more reminiscent of the other Beatles' resentment of Yoko Ono when she appeared on the scene as the beloved consort of John Lennon – an outsider, a woman, and a person who was given greater status in her access to the leader of their 'band of brothers'!

There was something about Mary Magdalene that singled her out from other women, and we may be reasonably certain that it was not the act of prostitution. Nevertheless, an important fact which throws light on this problem has emerged from our own sources. We will reveal it in a later chapter, but for now, in an effort to better understand Mary and her social predicament, we will concentrate on some of the other reasons why she was so shabbily treated. Despite the inroads of feminism, it is still the custom today for men (and, perhaps even more regrettably, women) to refer to a woman who angers or threatens them as a 'slag', and the habit must have been even more deeply ingrained in the sternly patriarchal country and times of first-century Judea.

Evidence concerning Mary Magdalene suggests that she was exceptionally beautiful, gifted in oratory, of an independent mind, highly intelligent, learned above the level attained by most men, passionate, fearless, unconventional, open and direct in her actions and speech, and somehow set apart from her community, possibly connected with an Isis-worshipping temple in nearby Egypt. This is not a reassuring range of qualities for the rough-and-ready tradesmen and fisherfolk that followed Jesus, who were already made to feel embarrassed and inadequate when people laughed at their accents, and when often they could not comprehend the Saviour's discourse but Mary could without fail.

Their pride would have been further diminished by the fact that they were being charitably supported by Mary, as the gospels state that Jesus and his disciples depended on her for funds. It is hardly surprising that they, and other men of the area, similarly piqued, resorted to a traditionally favourite psychological weapon of name-calling in an effort to undermine the woman who insulted their dominant manhood by not being exaggeratedly diffident, servile and passive.

The second point is that, although many people obviously found her unsettling and attacked her status and character, she was never accused by anyone of literally being a prostitute. She was defined in Luke's gospel as *harmartolos*, which labels her as one who does not in some way conform to Jewish law. It does not refer to prostitution and in fact is not a specific term for any crime. It is associated with archery and means 'missing the target', which seems to suggest that it was applied to her as a general slur on her respectability, a negative insinuation rather than a positive, out-and-out accusation. After all, if she was an operator in the business of prostitution, why not directly label her as such?

Harmartolos might possibly be described in association with Mary as 'one who is ill-thought of, one who is whispered against', as might happen to any unconventional, intelligent, forthright woman of uncommon talents in those days, who dared to step out of line. Ostracism is the weapon inevitably applied to attack the credibility of individuals who seem to threaten the status quo. And, as we explain in our fourth point below, there was a further reason, partly connected with her Egyptian link, why Mary might be disapproved of and considered *harmartolos*, one who breaks the Jewish law, and also why she might in her own right be a woman of means.

The third point concerns the fragrant oil or unguent referred to by Pope Gregory I as 'proof' that she perfumed her flesh in preparation to commit 'forbidden acts'. In fact, in John's gospel, (12:1–8) the aromatic oil which Mary used to anoint Jesus is identified as 'ointment of spikenard', a perfume so costly that it constituted more than a year's average wage. When rebuked by Judas for using it to anoint Jesus's feet rather than selling it and giving the money to the poor, Jesus defends her action, saying, 'She has done a beautiful thing to me'. The idea that Mary used the precious and exorbitantly-priced ointment of spikenard 'to perfume her flesh in forbidden acts', that is, to use it as an enhancement of the allures of a common street-walker, is obviously ridiculous and clear proof that the pope had not properly considered the implications of his lurid conclusion. It is also most unlikely that Jesus would have declared her gesture 'a beautiful thing' if the former recipients of her perfume had been Mary's clients in sin! In fact, as we shall see, Mary's choice of spikenard is deeply significant and a symbol of the profound commitment and love that she and Jesus clearly shared.

The fourth point concerns her status within the family at Bethany. This family was evidently very important to Jesus and offered him support and sanctuary throughout his mission. His love for Mary, Martha, Mary-Salome and Lazarus, and apparently their parents, is mentioned throughout the gospels (although the mother of the Bethany family is only referred to once in context). It is in and from Bethany that his closest disciples congregate after Jesus's crucifixion and, in company with the Bethany family, set out for foreign shores, seeming to suggest that their house was a familiar meeting place, a centre for those who were his greatest devotees. It is reasonable to suppose (as shall be discussed later) that the family were near relatives of Jesus – his aunt, uncle and cousins - and that they had associations with the mysterious Essenes, a secret religious brotherhood which had established a community at nearby Qumran.

The Bethany family never failed to extend him a warm welcome and, from the gospel accounts, appeared to enjoy a comfortable station in life. There is evidence that Mary and Lazarus became very close during Jesus's mission, as, indeed, they probably were before it began; and, although there was some passing friction between Mary and Martha (at least on Martha's part) in one important gospel story, the two sisters were as equally devoted to one another as they were to their brother, as is proved conclusively by historical records which speak of their later intrepid travels and mission together. All indications are that the sibling relationship between the four was normal, harmonious and happy, and the entire family unit likewise. Mary and Martha shared the household tasks, although it seems as if Mary might have been a little dreamier, rather more mystically inclined than her practical-minded sister. No poverty or financial distress is ever mentioned in connection with this family. The idea that Mary would include prostitution on her daily agenda is an extremely peculiar one, to say the least!

Our fifth and final point is that, if Mary had practised prostitution, Jesus and the disciples would have been guilty of living off immoral earnings, as the gospels clearly state that Mary supported Jesus's ministry from her own pocket.

Although Mary Magdalene has been cleared of the charge of prostitution, we cite these things to show that the accusation against Mary of Bethany (the two are unmistakeably one and the same) was only ever, at best, highly speculative, and in fact disintegrates upon examination. We believe it is important to dismiss this notion once and for all, because the idea of Mary Magdalene as a prostitute, penitent or otherwise, was purposely introduced to invalidate her shining significance.

The statues of the Black Madonna, which Mary introduced to Europe, taking the first one to be exhibited there with her to France, bear a meaning other than the obvious association with Isis and her son Horus, although that link is important and revelatory. They also signify that for almost a millennium, the glory of the Magdalene has been eclipsed by the shadowed body of contrived, age-long shame and deception created by those who profit from keeping our collective vision in darkness, producing a blindness with which humanity has struggled as if trying to wake from a charmed sleep. Yet already, the first rays of dawn are beginning to break over her obscurity, and the darkest hour is behind us.

NOTES

1 The teaching of Jesus as described in Luke (7:36–50) seems directly to concede that Mary of
 Bethany was a 'sinful woman'. Biblical scholars have stated that this unnamed sinful woman
 should not be identified as Mary Magdalene and was not necessarily even Mary of Bethany,
 but in fact their stance makes no sense. She is clearly described as weeping, anointing the feet
 of Jesus with perfumed oil, and wiping it off with her unbound hair. The idea that some
 obscure woman other than Mary Magdalene (Mary of Bethany) should also randomly have
 performed an identical rite of such intimacy is ludicrous. The teaching was given as a parable
 about the cancelling of two debts by a moneylender, one huge and one small, including the
 question as to which of the two debtors would be most grateful to their creditor. When Simon
 the Pharisee answered that the debtor who owed the larger amount would be most grateful,

Jesus is described as indicating the unnamed woman, drawing attention to her actions, and saying, *'Therefore, I tell you, her many sins have been forgiven – for she loved much. But he who has been forgiven little, loves little.'*

Many strange sects arose because of this teaching, one of its most famous adherents being the Russian priest Rasputin, who practised licentiousness in order that he might enjoy a greater measure of divine forgiveness! The Church of Rome incorporated its understanding of it into the office of confession, in which the ministering priest, on behalf of Christ, forgives all sins confessed. This seems to be an unsatisfactory interpretation of Jesus's teachings, because it implies that, as long as one always remembers to go to the confessional afterwards, one can endlessly indulge in the sin!

Our sources confirm that this teaching has been misrepresented, and that a garbled version of the circumstances in which it was given appears in Luke's gospel. As was so often the case, Jesus and Mary gave the teaching together. It reflected the guidance explained in Mary's gospel concerning opening our hearts to love, whereby we begin to ascend the seven steps up the pyramid of our being to enlightenment. As we do this, our hearts become attuned to love, which is the Spirit; and the desire to 'sin', or to abuse ourselves or others, is transmuted into the desire to express love. When we express love rather than the elemental force of wrath, our 'many sins' are forgiven, or the numerous areas in our psyche in which we failed to express love are healed, and their darkness overcome. Therefore, we must 'love much' to be 'forgiven'. When the heart refuses to open to love, and one 'loves little', very few of the areas in our being which need forgiveness or healing are reached, and so continue to starve and suffer. This teaching also incorporates the idea that when we forgive someone their debt to us (a debt of injustice), instead of obeying the urges of wrath and trying to get even, we open *their* hearts to love by our act, even if only at first upon a subliminal, hidden level. In so doing, our own heart opens to love, because that is the natural outcome of a decision to forgive – therefore we create a 'win-win' situation.

Mary offered herself as a demonstration of this important esoteric instruction, which had to be given to the followers of Christ in a way that they could understand within the strictures and confines of their perception and culture, enabling Jesus to say, *'Look at this woman…she loved much, so her many sins were forgiven'* [or made whole]. The use of the past tense gives the clue to the fact that Jesus was referring to an enacted drama performed by Mary for the edification of the onlookers.

Later obfuscation of Mary's role and significance, and the uncertainty of factual detail also displayed elsewhere in Luke's gospel (when Jesus goes to visit the Bethany household, Luke seems to be unaware of its exact location or reluctant to name it, as he refers to the town as 'a certain village' and fails to mention Lazarus as resident there as well as Martha and Mary) combined to confuse the real message of the teaching. It was certainly not intended as a divine insurance policy for those who wished to 'confess Christ' but who had no desire to change their behaviour! We can also be certain that neither was it any confirmation by Jesus that Mary, in her dramatic role as 'Everywoman' or, rather, 'Everyhuman', was actually a 'sinful woman'!

CHAPTER THREE

The Hieros Gamos

*A*ccording to John's gospel, when Mary anointed Jesus as he sat at supper with her brother Lazarus (which we consider very significant) and Judas Iscariot, the fragrance of ointment of spikenard wafted forth and filled the entire house. The gospels of Matthew and Mark confirm that Mary applied the oil, not only to the feet of Jesus, wiping off the excess moisture with her hair so that she should share in the sacrament, but also to his head.

The details of this act seem to confirm that it was a ritual of profound inner meaning, because spikenard is an oil from India used in Tantric ceremonies (sacred sexual rites) for the specific application to the hair and the feet. It is an oil for the use of deeply committed lovers whose devotion is such that it creates a wider circle of radiance than that which would simply perpetuate their own joy and blessing, a ring of conscious union of such power and beauty that its encircling extends for the upliftment and benediction of all. Spikenard has secret properties of a subtle and spiritual nature, enabling lovers to open up to one another in a very specific and highly potent way which initiates a sublime dynamic of mystical proportions. Of course, the virtues of spikenard can offer only service, not instigation. This sacred union cannot come into being without the ignition of an extraordinary and enduring love which each holds for the other in equal measure. Mary's anointing of Jesus has been spoken of as her farewell to him, and surely so it was, but it was also much more.

There is ample evidence to suggest that Mary's action was part of an Egyptian rite concerning Isis and Osiris, whereby the priest-king is anointed by the priestess-queen in preparation for their ritual union, the *hieros gamos*, or the sacred marriage. During their sexual conjoinment, the male becomes inundated with the spirit of God and the female with the spirit of Goddess, the two aspects which dwell within the Godhead. Each fecundates the other with their opposite quality so that in spirit they become a single entity, a combined channel for the glory of that unified Godhead. Afterwards, the priest-king was empowered to reign at the outer level, and the priestess-queen at the inner. His power flowed from the spiritual channel within her, and there could be no kingship without her and the initiation of the *hieros gamos*.

It is important to remember within the context of Jesus and Mary's situation that Jesus was proclaimed as Christ the King, and that the title 'Christ' or 'Christos' means 'the Anointed One'. Only six verses after Christ's impassioned defence of Mary, The Gospel of John gives the prophecy in the scriptures which foretold his 'Christing', or his ascension into kingship:

> *Fear not, daughter of Sion: behold, thy King*
> *cometh, sitting on an ass's colt.*

Mary, with her spiritual insight fostered in Egypt, would instantly have recognized the symbolism. The ass was the secret sign of Seth, the god of darkness and death who slew Osiris and whom Horus, son of Isis and Osiris, vanquished. To ride the ass is a demonstration of its submission and the rider's mastery. The ancient prophecy is therefore saying to Mary: 'Fear not, daughter of Sion! Your King shall overcome death!'[1]

With the precious oil of spikenard, Mary of Bethany 'Christed' Jesus, and he moved into the final phase of his mission and his destiny. At the same moment, she truly became Mary the Magdalene ('Magnificent', 'Great Queen', 'the Tower', 'the All'), as he became Jesus the Christ.

This explains why Mary of *Bethany* is involved so intimately in his story up until this point, and then seemingly disappears, to be supplanted by Mary *Magdalene*, who, according to John's gospel, steps out of nowhere to take her place with the other two Marys at the Crucifixion. This sudden appearance has always been a puzzle to readers of the gospels, but the simple solution is that Mary Magdalene was not truly born until this moment, and Mary of Bethany, her old and, to some extent, unawakened self, was cast off to fade away.

The other two Marys were Mary, mother of Jesus, and her cousin Mary, wife of Cleopas (Mary Jacob). Mary (and its derivatives) is the supreme name of the Goddess in cultures across the world, and of course it was the triple Goddess who must witness the king's death so that, through the Holy Spirit dwelling within her, he could be reborn. So say the rites of the sacred marriage as they were enacted through the ages, for after their act of sacramental sex, the king is sanctified and separated from the queen. He awaits his sacrificial death (sometimes only ritualis- tically enacted), certain in the knowledge that he will rise again – through the power and the blessing of the Goddess, symbolized by Mary the Bride, Mary the Mother, and Mary the Crone. All three aspects are the personification of wisdom.

It is important to remember that when Mary Magdalene is suddenly thrust upon our awareness, she is spoken of as having had 'seven devils' removed from her by Jesus. This is surely a veiled reference to the chakra system, those seven points of energy, linked to the ductless glands, which are located along the spine and exist in our subtle or etheric body. Our source has disclosed that the so-called release of 'seven devils' from Mary Magdalene actually referred to a teaching given by Jesus and Mary on the significance of the chakras, a teaching which Mary expounds in her gospel.

Psychics see the chakras as many-petalled, like flowers, spinning rapidly when opened and activated. They interface with the spiritual plane and are like valves which control and transmit the subtler energies, ushering them into our physical energy-field and our earthly consciousness, sometimes shutting down for a while when there is a danger that we might become overcharged. Wonderfully, astro-physicists are beginning to perceive that galaxies are constructed upon much the same many-petalled, spinning principle, looking like vast flower-discs and perhaps offering us an important clue as to why creation-myths across the globe almost invariably include the concept of a sacred garden. Adam and Eve first initiated their love in a holy garden, and, of course, Mary was reunited with her beloved Jesus when he arose from death and greeted her in the garden.

To clear and purify the chakras forms a part of the rites of the sacred marriage, and constitutes one of the qualities of spikenard, for although the chakras are understood to run up the spine to the crown, in esoteric lore the spine is as a sword or a rod which is actually thrust into the Earth, and the chakra system begins at, or just below, the feet. The chakra points in the feet are a reflection of the first major chakra at the base of the spine. Only when the chakras are clear, may the sexual rites of the sacred marriage be enacted.

Spikenard not only clears and purifies the chakras during the *hieros gamos*, it activates them and opens them and ushers in the Great Awakening, so that those of the male resonate with those of the female in sublime and dynamic harmony, creating symphonic beauty which contains the power of creation itself. This is called the Song of Songs, and is why the Song of Solomon is the Song of the Sacred Marriage, and is so secretly and potently associated with Jesus and Mary Magdalene.

When Mary knelt at the feet of Jesus to anoint him with spikenard, she performed a ceremony of initiation which awakened his chakra system as he awakened hers. The other gospel accounts relate that Mary sobbed unremittingly as she enacted this rite, anointing not only the head and feet of Jesus with the precious oil, but her own hair and head also. They shared a deep, intimate knowledge that his sacrificial death was almost upon him, and Mary could not restrain her heartbro-ken sorrow. None but her knew of his fate, except perhaps Lazarus, who, it seemed, looked on in respectful silence.

Judas Iscariot, on the other hand, was clearly disgusted at all this secrecy passing between the two, (or perhaps three), sensing that something crucial was underway which he could neither understand nor participate in.[2] He snaps nastily at Mary for scandalously wasting money on the spikenard when she could have sold it and given the money to the poor (in Mark's gospel (14:4), more than one of the disciples gives the same harsh rebuke). It is at this point that John, the writer of the gospel, introduces the catalytic Simon, and certainly it is poignant to consider how every time the anointing is mentioned in all four gospels, the woman who performs the anointing is accused of 'sin', in the presence, direct or indirect, of a 'Simon'.

Mary's 'sin', according to Judas, is that she lavishes expenditure, or gives unstintingly of her best, in her ministrations to the spiritual realities within. Should these not be ignored, and all giving be directed towards the pragmatic duties of life, such as administering to the needs of the poor? demands Judas. Who more than Jesus underlined the importance of always giving to the poor? We believe that he included in this directive, not only those who require help with their material needs, but the poor in spirit, those sorely in need of the mercy and succour of spiritual enlightenment. Giving to the poor in this sense does not mean preaching or condemning or forcing certain views on people, but offering love – the goodwill, friendship and kindness which is the light of the spirit radiating from within, and which throws a sustaining glow upon another's dark and difficult path.

Jesus constantly urges those who will listen to his teachings to 'love one another'. This is his message to the world. But it is also essential to honour and minister to the realities of the spirit, to turn inwards and nourish oneself from the source: the light and the beauty dwelling at the heart of our being which is the still flame of the spirit burning within. Unless we do so regularly, how can we bring forth the necessary substance to give to the 'poor'? We can only give what we receive.

In his response to Judas's objections, Jesus emphasizes this need to give our time, and of our very best, to spiritual realities, to going within, withdrawing into one's own being and seeking to touch the essence of the Godhead, in times of prayer, meditation and ritual. He explains to Judas that our practical duty to help and give of ourselves to others will always be there waiting for us when we emerge from prayer, meditation or spiritual ceremony ('the poor you always have with you') and that the light of the spirit, the Christ within, is not to be found on the outer planes of living, but only by going deep within for regular periods of communion, and so being enabled to bring it forth to illumine and transform the mundane world ('me you have not always'). With these simple words, he gives a teaching on one of the greatest spiritual (and scientific) laws which permeates all the cosmos: that energy, or spiritual consciousness, always flows from the greater to the lesser source. Therefore, Mary is right to give so generously in her ministrations to the spiritual reality within, because doing so enriches her power of giving a thousandfold ('what she has done will be told throughout the world, in memory of her').

In essence, Jesus is saying, 'We are right to attend to the needs and the promptings of our soul, so that it may be beautified and glorified by the spirit, and give of itself with ever greater capacity.' This is important in relation to Mary, because she is symbolic of the soul, the tender and beautiful inner self whose gentle sweetness and refined sensibilities it is the tendency of the coarse and trampling earthly mind to override, scorn and silence. When we are true to the soul, we find the light of the spirit, and we cannot be bought or sold in enslavement to materialism – a truth Judas had yet to realize. Here are the actual words:

> *Then took Mary a pound of ointment of spikenard, very costly,*
> *and anointed the feet of Jesus, and wiped his feet with her hair:*
> *and the house was filled with the odour of the ointment. Then*
> *saith one of his disciples, Judas Iscariot, Simon's son, which*
> *should betray him, Why was not this ointment sold for three*
> *hundred pence, and given to the poor?*

Is it more to Mary that Jesus answers and addresses his discourse, speaking words of love and comfort?

> *Let her alone. ... Why are you bothering her? She has done a*
> *beautiful thing to me. Against the day of my burying has she*
> *kept this. For the poor you always have with you, but me you*
> *have not always.*
> *Verily I say unto you, wherever my truth is preached*
> *throughout the world, what she has done will be told, in*
> *memory of her.*

'You have done a beautiful thing to me ... wherever my truth is preached throughout the world, what you have done will be told, in memory of you', Jesus is saying to Mary, comforting her grief. This is no ordinary event. The spikenard has been kept for this special day, this sacred hour, as Jesus announces.

It is a Friday, the day of the Goddess – we know that the Crucifixion happened on a Friday, as the gospels specify the day, and that the Last Supper took place the evening before it. Mary's anointing was performed six days before the Passover, so the day must also have been Friday, seven days prior to the Crucifixion itself. This supper mirrors the Last Supper. Mary has unbound her hair to 'dry' the feet of Jesus (actually to anoint her hair and head with spikenard). This in itself is significant, because Jewish custom dictates that a woman must only unbind her hair in the presence of her husband. Mary is now the Magdalene. Jesus is now the Christ.

Did the sacred marriage, the *hieros gamos*, take place that night between Jesus and Mary? Perhaps their place of consecrated union was the flat rooftop of Mary's Bethany home, a segregated place specially for sleeping outdoors. There, in the peace and the silence shining down from the Moon and the stars, a wonderful event for humanity took place, the mystical fusing of Jesus, the Light of the World, the Divine Masculine Principle, and Mary, Goddess in her soul of the rising stars and the glorious dawn, the Divine Feminine Principle. The rays of the Christ Being shone down upon them from the spiritual realms and became one with them in a zenith, a perfect noon, a union which became a ring of pure and everlasting light, complete and unfading. Perhaps in rapt silence they greeted the dawn together, anointed by the radiance of the rising Sun in the utter stillness of that morning hour which succeeds the darkest watch of the night. It must be that both drew strength, comfort, tranquillity and courage (meaning heart-steadfastness), one from the other throughout those hours, for the trial of the coming events that lay seven days, a chakra system, ahead of them.

Many think it scandalous to suggest such a thing, and yet Jesus occupied a human body and lived a human as well as a divine life. Many, too, will object to the thought that Mary could have initiated him into the cusp of his Christhood by ritually anointing him. And yet Jesus's mission had begun with a similar anointing, a baptism performed by another cousin, John the Baptist. John initiated at the start of his mission, Mary at the end of it. John and Mary, the Alpha and the Omega.

When Mary, now the Magdalene, followed him to his cross, some say she was pregnant with his child. There is much evidence to suggest that there was a child, a daughter called Tamar (a name linked with 'Sarah', as both names indicate royalty), who becomes part of the story later, in France and in Britain.

For now, we might wonder if it can really be that the Christ and the Magdalene took part in pagan rites, and embraced a pagan truth, as events seem to suggest. What was the meaning behind the *hieros gamos*, the rites of Isis and Osiris? Why did Jesus and Mary enact their roles?

NOTES

1 It has been supposed that 'daughter of Sion' refers to the city of Jerusalem because of the biblical texts found in the Second Book of Samuel, 5:6–7: *And the king [David] and his men went to Jerusalem unto the Jebusites, the inhabitants of the land: which spake unto David, saying, Except thou take away the blind and the lame, thou shalt not come in hither: thinking, David cannot come in hither. Nevertheless, David took the strong hold of Zion: the same is the city of David;* and the First Book of Kings, 8:1: *Then Solomon assembled the elders of Israel…unto King Solomon in Jerusalem, that they might bring up the ark of the covenant of the Lord out of the city of David, which is Zion.*

   Thus it seems reasonable to equate 'daughter of Sion' with Jerusalem. But other clues make the picture clearer. In the New Testament, Romans, 11:26 states: *And so all Israel shall be saved: as it is written, There shall come out of Sion the Deliverer, and shall turn away ungodliness from Jacob.* The reference is again to Jerusalem, but Zion is now spelt 'Sion', and the allusion to it is made with reference to 'the Deliverer' (the Christ). Could it be the Holy City from which the Christ Being descended – the heavenly Jerusalem – which is being cited here rather than its earthly counterpart?

The matter is settled by the text in Hebrews 12:22–23: *But ye are come unto mount Sion, and unto the city of the living God, the heavenly Jerusalem, and to an innumerable company of angels…and to the spirits of just men made perfect.* Surely 'Sion' is none other than the Sphere of John or Shar On? As the preceding text explains, this mount Sion is not within the physical realm (*For ye are not come unto the mount that might be touched*, Romans 12:18). If there remains any lingering doubt that Zion and Sion identify, respectively, the earthly Jerusalem and, in contradistinction, the heavenly one, it is dispelled by the shining confirmatory vision of John in Revelations, 14:1: *And I looked, and, lo, a Lamb stood on the mount Sion, and with him an hundred and forty and four thousand, having his Father's name written in their foreheads.* This is the 'name of Light' that Mary will help us to manifest, associated with the 'unicorn's horn', an extension of the crown chakra located in the middle and at the top of the forehead which is an expression of pure and exalted 'virgin' consciousness; and the Lamb, symbol of the Holy Balm dwelling in the heart of Goddess, the Holy Balm which is sign and signature of Mary Magdalene, the rose at the heart of Shar On, tells us the secret identity of the 'daughter of Sion'.

2 To be fair to Judas Iscariot, we believe it is true to say that he loved Jesus and did not intend that his betrayal should lead to his Saviour's death. Judas Iscariot represents that mindset in humanity which believes that only the sword wields power. It holds that talk about love and peace and brotherhood is all very well and good, but that it properly belongs to a time when freedom and victory have been won by means of the sword and such luxuries can therefore be indulged in with impunity. This attitude prevails where materialism holds sway in the perception, preventing any understanding of the spiritual reality at life's core, and the mighty and incontrovertible laws and processes at the heart of that reality. Judas believed that Jesus only had to say the word, and the great throng of his followers, and other groups sympathetic to them, would rise up in arms and free their homeland from the despised yoke of Roman rule. He thought that if he betrayed Jesus to the Roman soldiers, his act would twist his arm and force Jesus to sound a war cry against the authorities before he could be taken into custody. Then freedom could be won, and Jesus's teachings could continue unhindered once the mayhem was over. In fact, there was great conflagration and many street battles broke out when Jesus was first seized, but he refused to give the rallying cry and incite his followers to armed uprising. This astonished Judas Iscariot, who was an example of the worldliness that will not bow its knee to the greater wisdom of the heart.

CHAPTER FOUR

The Virgin Birth and Isis on Earth

*I*n considering the question of the virgin birth it is helpful to explore the circumstances surrounding the birth of the two children, Jesus and Mary.

First we need to ponder some possibilities concerning the meaning of the virgin birth. Its symbolism is important – that of virgin matter becoming impregnated with the quickening dynamic of spirit – and, knowing that the dynamic of inner truth leads it towards outward expression, it seems inconsistent to deny the literal truth of the virgin birth. But we believe it has been misunderstood because of the unfortunate tendency towards misogyny, sinisterly prevalent in both sexes, which seems to have begun in the East in the remote past and gradually become global.

It was certainly entrenched in the time of Jesus. One of the old Jewish laws horrifically states that if a man takes a wife and suspects that she is not virgin, simply because no trace of blood can be found on the bed linen the morning after their first sexual union, he has the right to dump her in front of her father's house and insist that she be stoned to death. A similar one, conveying the same even-handed and reassuring sense of justice, declares that if a woman is raped in a town or city, she should also be stoned to death (because she could have cried for help and so prevented the rape!), but if she is raped in the countryside she should be 'forgiven' (for having been raped!) because, naturally, out in the wilds no-one could have heard her pleas for help! Of course, these old laws were probably hardly ever put into practice, as common human decency would normally have prevailed and found an escape route from the terror of their application. Nevertheless, their very existence throws into sharp relief the vicious mindset of the time concerning the status of women (which still continues to this day, and certainly not only in religion and the East).

The idea of the virgin birth seems only to have perpetuated and compounded the problem. It appears to state explicitly that woman is of Earth and earthly matter, and that Divine Spirit is exclusively male. In other words, Jesus had an earthly mother, but God was his father obviously implying that God is Father – all male –

and not in any way Mother! The resonance of this concept has still not died away, and because of it, or perhaps more accurately, further bolstered by it, certain Victorian gentlemen whiled away their lives in the composition of great tomes which posited that women were without souls.

We believe that Joseph was Jesus's earthly father, as much as Mary was his earthly mother, and that the idea of the virgin birth is correct, insofar as Mary the mother was technically a virgin, directly prior to becoming impregnated with Jesus, due to some physical impediment (Joseph and Mary had been trying for a child for some time before Jesus was conceived). We also believe that the Holy Spirit (whose essence is feminine, the Mother) entered her in order to prepare the vehicles, both bodily and subtle, for the incarnation of the mighty and majestic human soul that was Jesus, so that he could express the perfect Christ essence without restriction.

Our spiritual researches also indicate that this same Holy Spirit blessed and purified Mary Magdalene's mother, Mary Jacob, at the same time and in the same way, for Mary Jacob was pregnant with Mary Magdalene as Mary the Virgin was pregnant with Jesus, at the same time and in the same vicinity. These two great souls incarnated together, the baby Mary arriving in December of that year and the baby Jesus in January. We even have the dates. Mary was born on 25 December, and the baby Jesus on 6 January of the following year. The babies were the same age (concieved at the same instant), only Mary arrived a little earlier.

This assertion will seem outrageous to most people's sense of credibility, as of course Twelfth Night, 6 January, was once 25 December. Eleven days divided the new Christmas Day from the old after the Gregorian calendar took over from the ancient Julian calendar by which our dates were formerly calculated. That is why there are 12 days of Christmas, and why the Eastern Orthodox Church still celebrates Christmas on 6 January to this day. Nevertheless, we would ask our readers to look at the magical, mystical implications of what we are asserting. Both souls expressed the perfect Christ Light, the ineffable Being within that light which has always existed, and which unites both the Masculine and Feminine Spiritual Principles.

There is a special reason why, in the East, Jesus's birthday is traditionally celebrated, and in the West, that of Mary Magdalene. Both shone forth with the glory of the Christ Being, but we might look at the East as Father and the West as Mother, according to the mystical order of things. The midwinter festival of Mother and Child celebrates, as representatives of the Goddess, Mary the Virgin, Mary Magdalene the Bride (who was also Mother), and the magical potential of the Child, the issue of Divine Father and Divine Mother.[1] Yet the child itself bears two aspects. One of the reasons why we are always so delighted with a white Christmas may be because the bright whiteness of the snowfall is symbolic of the virgin's purity, is also considered as the essence of the Christ Light, and is the traditional attire of the bride in the West. In December, Divine Mother gives birth to the Sacred Feminine, and in the New Year, to the Sacred Masculine Principle. The two are really of one essence. Nevertheless, they manifest these distinct masculine and feminine aspects. The two Christmas Days, once conjoined, are a perfect expression of a deep inner truth objectifying outwards into actuality – the feast days of the Spirit and the Bride, Christ and his consort:

> *The Spirit and the Bride say: 'Come!'*
>
> *Let all who hear say: 'Come!'*
>
> *May all who thirst drink freely of the Water of Life.*

REVELATIONS, 22:17

This leads us back to the pagan question, because of course pagan festivals have always taken place at midwinter. But if the underlying truth that they celebrate – the Return of the Light, the coming to Earth of the Son and Daughter of Light – were to appear in mundane human form, then naturally it would have to be at midwinter, when the light is 'reborn' and begins to increase, that both came into earthly incarnation. And so indeed it was.

These great souls came not to destroy, but to fulfil, that we might have life, and have it more abundantly. They did not come to invalidate other religions, whatever form they might take. They did not come to instigate a further religion, but to bring the Light to the people of the world, to quicken it within every soul, that we might embrace the truth and the beauty which our own belief-systems offer us, yet steadfastly turn away from impulses within them (arising from within ourselves) which do not express truth and beauty. How are we to know what is truth and beauty, and what is not? By the light of the Christ within our own heart. It does not matter what our religion is, or whether we have none at all. Like the Buddha, spiritual enlightenment is all that the Christ is concerned with, is all that the Christ *is*. Buddha wants to save us from suffering, the Christ wants to save us from death. When we gain a clear perspective, we find that the two are the same.

Why did all the 'trappings', so to speak, of spiritual greatness centre around Jesus? Why did he perform miracles, and not Mary? Why did a great star appear above his birthplace, and (as is erroneously believed) not Mary's? Why was he crucified, and not Mary?

Jesus represented the outer, active, positive principle of the Christ Being, whilst Mary was its still, secret, unseen, intuitive vessel. It is easy to misinterpret these words, because our culture attaches so much importance to what is 'active' and 'positive'. In fact, when the expression of these qualities is one-sided, understood only from the masculine aspect, they become self-destructive. Mary was also 'active', but her action was on the subtle, unseen planes of reality. She was also 'positive', completing the circuit of consciousness from the other side, the veiled side, of awareness.

We call this form of giving a 'negative' force, but no mistaken concepts or pre-conceived ideas of the term as it is conventionally applied should attach to our understanding of it. When a battery creates a circuit of power, we use the power rather than futilely separating its current into moralistic ideas of 'good' and 'bad', 'strong' and 'weak', 'black' and 'white'. Without the so-called 'negative' contribution, the 'positive' force is impotent, just as, in the *hieros gamos* or the Sacred Marriage, the king cannot rule or otherwise express his kingship until the queen has fused her power with his.

This simple idea of the circuit a battery produces, and the mysteries of the *hieros gamos*, might prove useful in gaining an enlightened understanding of Mary's role in Jesus's mission, and answers the question as to why the outer realities seemed to revolve solely around him. It also illuminates the true meaning of the great myth of Isis and Osiris, wherein, after Osiris's death and mutilation, Isis wanders grieving upon the face of the world, devotedly collecting together the scattered pieces of her beloved consort's body, until at last she has assembled the whole except the penis. She then constructs a penis from her own magic and conceives a child fathered by Osiris via its agency.

The child is Horus, Christ Consciousness (symbolized by the mystical Third Eye, the single eye that hones consciousness in its feminine and masculine aspects into a single point of gnosis), who is destined to triumph over death, or Seth, Osiris's brother who slew him.

The story of the missing penis is a strange one, obviously central to the meaning of the myth. We believe it signifies that male and female genitalia are not two different organs in the way that they are manifest on Earth, but in fact are one and the same organ of generation. The penis and the testicles reflect the tract of the vulva leading to the uterus and the ovaries. One is the other, inside out.

Not until Isis realizes that her own organ of generation will complete Osiris, can she conceive. She then brings forth Horus, Osiris reborn (in fact, Horus was a fusion of both his parents). Only when she frees herself from any sense of separateness or division (and, culturally speaking, from the notion of woman's weakness or impotency) can she give birth to the world, for in the creation-myths Horus appears as the supreme parent of humankind, fertilizing the Earth with his virility – a virility born from her, as in the *hieros gamos*. So closely associated was Mary Magdalene with Isis, Queen of Heaven, goddess of the dawn and the rising stars, not only by her later followers but by Jesus himself, that she was hailed by many heterodox groups in Europe as Isis on Earth.[2]

Throughout Earth's history up to this point, the divine drama of the mysteries of the Godhead could be enacted only at the soul or subtle realm of consciousness. Many great teachers and leaders had arisen heretofore to show the way and to help their pupils or peoples to gain a degree of mastery over the imprisoning faculties of the vibrations of matter into which we are born when we enter our earthly life and form. Techniques were mastered which caused the inner eye to open, the inner ear to hear. Yet these insights and realizations were still, in great measure, only for the elect. When Jesus and Mary, the sacred couple, incarnated upon the Earth, they came to bring the hallowed mysteries right through into matter, for they embodied and enacted them. Thereafter, *all* people, from the humblest to the highest in society's ranks, could be given the knowledge that would set them free. Moreover, the incarnation of Jesus and Mary liberated humanity as a whole from the need for any intermediary between a person and their communion with the Godhead and the exalted worlds, a liberation which was previously only available to certain mystic tribes, peoples and individuals and which, marvellous and priceless gift as it is, we have hardly begun to appreciate and utilize, even though it has been ours for almost 2,000 years. Wondrously, the sacred couple entered densest matter and personified sublimest truth so that matter itself could be transmuted and its sanctity and deliverance assured: Isis and Ra, the Bride of Light and the Son, Mary Magdalene and Jesus – the Christ.

NOTES

1 The crone is also present to make up the sacred trilogy. She is the winter herself, known in Celtic tradition as the *Calleach Bheur*, the Hag of Winter. Many other cosmologies include a supernatural hag as the personification of winter.

2 It is worth noting that the traditional birthday of Isis, as well as several other major goddesses, is 25 December.

CHAPTER FIVE

Jesus, Mary and the Essenes

*N*ow that we have explored the reasons why we believe that the Christ manifestation was not a myth but a genuine event which took place on Earth
almost 2,000 years ago, and why we consider that the Christ manifested simultaneously in two beings, in a sublime partnership between male *and* female –
Jesus-Maria Christ – we would like to share more of what our spiritual investigations
have revealed regarding the family and upbringing of the Christ-couple.

We are convinced that the family of Mary Magdalene was related to Jesus.
However, nowhere in the New Testament is it stated that this is so, except for one
ambiguous instance where Jesus meets his aunt, Salome, whom we believe was, more
accurately, his aunt '*Mary*-Salome' (Mary-Salome Jacob). Our information on this
point (as well as being confirmed by our sources) comes from a different quarter.

In 1992, Dolores Cannon published her book *Jesus and the Essenes*. It is an
unorthodox source of information because it details recorded transmissions from
past-life regression involving an Essene teacher (Benzahmare, nicknamed Suddi)
who lived in the time of Jesus. Suddi is said to have taught Jesus and his cousin, John
the Baptist, who were known to him in their boyhood as BenJoseph and
BenZachariah (son of Joseph and son of Zachariah). This extraordinary account
proved to be unfailingly accurate in minute detail wherever its statements could be
independently verified, many of the sources of later verification being obscure and
difficult to access. Because Dolores Cannon and her subject could not feasibly have
consulted these documents, and because of her obvious sincerity, caution and thor-
oughness, we accept Suddi as a valid testament. Others no doubt will not, but it is
worth remembering that over half of the global population believe in reincarnation
and that, the more one ponders the issue, the more logical and sensible the idea
becomes. Moreover, Suddi's testimony throws light on many questions and obscured
areas concerning the life and times of Jesus and his associates and followers. We have
also consulted our own sources before making his testament part of our story (*see*
Preface).

For instance, he confirms that Lazarus was a cousin of Jesus as well as John the Baptist, indirectly suggesting that the entire extended family of Jesus was associated with the Essene brethren. Scholarship, both archaeological and academic, concludes that the Essenes were a community of people who lived secluded lives in the towns and the villages of Judea, and in the northern desert areas around the Dead Sea and the river Jordan. According to Suddi, the communities were far more widespread, and extended to Egypt and beyond. Some groups were exoteric, others deeply esoteric, hidden and guarded. Qumran was a secret community. There were no official records of the settlement, and Herod's soldiers certainly did not suspect its existence. There was, however, a rumour abroad among the local populace that Essene brethren were located there. They were feared by the establishment (the Sanhedrin and the Pharisees), and Suddi states specifically, 'There are many who would find out about our community and see us destroyed.'

Essenes from the Qumran community ventured abroad into the surrounding areas to teach and to gather information, but they wore robes to hide their identity, discarding their usual white garments (reminiscent of the Druids, the Celtic priesthood who mirrored these keepers of wisdom in many ways) and donning more conventional attire. The esoteric communities, such as the one at Qumran, guarded mysterious items and artefacts of what might be termed spiritual technology from an age so remote that no records or history remain of it except what is secreted within the protective bosom of such societies. Some of this technology, and the information regarding it, the Essenes themselves were unable to comprehend. It seems from recent research that there were also numerous offshoots from the main body of the Essenes, and that Jesus was linked with many of these exoteric groups as well as the esoteric centre at Qumran.

Because of this, difficulties presented themselves regarding the marriage of Mary and Jesus, as some of the less enlightened members of these differing groups would have considered Mary an unsuitable wife for him, due to her status and because of her chosen religion, even though the initiated Essenes would have recognized that the mystery teachings of Egypt and those of their own were conjoined at the roots. Jesus himself had a deep understanding of this truth, as numerous instances in his ministry testify, in particular the fact that the Lord's Prayer, the beloved orison that he himself gave to his followers, was a rendition of a religious lyric to Osiris.

It seems that Mary and Jesus did conceal their marriage from public knowledge, and that this was decided upon, in particular by Jesus, to shield Mary from the condemnation and spite of her detractors. In view of the ostracizing of the Bethany townsfolk and the outright hostility of several of the disciples towards Mary, perhaps he could not bear that she should endure further misery for his sake. Yet the deeper meaning behind their decision was concerned with the fact that Jesus and Mary both knew he would be crucified. If Mary had been recognized, not only as his wife but as his equal partner in the Christ ministry, she too would have been put to death. Not only was this an agonizing prospect, especially for Jesus, but it would have greatly reduced the impact of his sacrifice and their joint mission. It was vital that Mary remained on Earth, to dispense the teachings of 'The Way' and to bear their child, conceived on the night of the anointing at Bethany. This child would not continue their bloodline, for she would die without issue; but the significance of her birth and her life was vital to the great task of calling humanity home to the light.

Essene means 'holy one' and, according to Suddi, their origins are lost in antiquity, connected with those who preceded Abraham and the first people of Ur. There is an association with Mary Magdalene and her bloodline here, as we shall see. Also, Jesus says in The Gospel of John (8:58) 'Before Abraham was, I am.' This seems to have a mystical meaning in that he was expressing the truth that the Divine Child of Light, the issue or first-born of the Father-Mother God, the Christ within him whom he sought to ignite within us all, existed before the time-space-matter continuum began; but it does also seem to link him and his lineage with the Essenes; and Suddi confirms that the Essenes were 'of the line of David', as Jesus himself was.

The Essenes studied the Torah (Jewish holy law) and the cabbala, but they also drew from a fund of recorded wisdom more ancient than these, accessible only to themselves. They were a disciplined and mystical society, ruled by Elder Brethren and a supreme Master who ensured that all lived in conformity with the 'Book of the Community Rule', but they were by no means puritanical or repressive in their day-to-day lives or their application of the law. Suddi speaks of the Essenes as embracing all branches of knowledge and philosophy, medicine, arts, crafts, gardening and copying and preserving texts. The spiritual teacher, White Eagle, describes them as living gloriously, arranging their day around rituals to the angels and to the Divine Source, and as the wonder of all those who knew of their communities because of their remarkable resistance to disease. They considered it a sin to be ill and conquered suffering with the strength of their highly trained spiritual will and mental discipline, although they were not rigid, harsh or severe in their dispensation of this philosophy. They were humanitarian, egalitarian, progressive and wide-ranging in their thinking, deeply spiritual in their approach to life and preservers of much sacred knowledge.

They recognized Jesus as the Messiah and awaited his coming. After his birth, they helped the family to escape to Egypt. John the Baptist, who was a few months older than Jesus, remained under the protection of the community with his mother Elizabeth. Suddi commented upon Elizabeth's great distress at the death of her husband, Zachariah, who had been killed by Herod's soldiers when they came in search of her baby in order to carry out the king's edict that all male children under the age of two should be slaughtered. His wife and son had already escaped to the hills, to the secret community of the Essene brethren at Qumran, but Zachariah, who himself was of the Essenes, insisted on staying behind to face the soldiers, perhaps because he believed that if he died for the sake of his son, his sacrifice would ensure John's continued existence. So Elizabeth became 'the widow', her grief made more severe because she blamed herself for not insisting that Zachariah accompanied her to Qumran.

Much esoteric significance attaches to Elizabeth, the mother of John, and it seems appropriate to explore this for a moment before returning to our main theme. Elizabeth is, for instance, the *Mona Lisa* (Madonna Elizabeth) portrayed by Leonardo Da Vinci, 'Mona' being a shortened form of 'Madonna'. She bears a certain relevance to the Magdalene, her enigmatic smile equating her with the concept of the Woman Who Knows All, as Mary Magdalene is called in some of the Gnostic gospels. She is also portrayed as pregnant, on the one hand as Elizabeth with her son John, and on the other as the Magdalene, the Tower of Truth, pregnant with the cosmos itself. The background to the painting seems to be shifting and fluidic as one observes it, and it depicts the group of mighty rocks near Leonardo's home, where he often went to meditate on the origins of life – our own origins with which the Magdalene is associated.

Elizabeth is also one representation of the 'widow' referred to by the Knights Templar, those warrior-monks so closely linked with the secrets of the Magdalene, when they spoke mysteriously of the 'Son of the Widow' whom they revered in their ceremonies. There is also a mystical link with Horus, the son of Isis (with whom Mary is identified), who was born after the death of his father Osiris and who put to flight the Lord of Darkness, Seth; so the Osirian link extended to John the Baptist as well as to Jesus.

There is a yet more deeply esoteric meaning to the 'Son of the Widow'. It refers to Mary's daughter by Jesus, who is called 'son' or 'sun' because the light of the great Christ Being, shining through Jesus and Mary, was expressed in unity through her. She was also called 'son' because she embodied the mystery of Horus, the son of Osiris, born to Isis after his father's death. Horus represented the light of the new age, and indeed many esotericists refer to the new age as 'The Age of Horus'.

These things tell us how profoundly connected the Knights Templar were with the secret mysteries of Jesus and Mary, and Tamar their daughter; and that they recognized who she truly was, and her sacred significance to the Earth. The worship of Baphomet, the goat, by the Knights Templar was related to their mystical explorations into the Realm of the Christed Beings. Jesus and Mary had been given to the Earth in the sign of Capricorn, the goat who, through rites connected with the *hieros gamos*, was transformed into the pure exalted form of the unicorn. Jesus is associated with the unicorn, and the 'Lady' in depictions of 'The Lady and the Unicorn' is Mary Magdalene.

If John the Baptist and Jesus studied under the tutelage of the Essenes, did their cousin Lazarus do likewise? Unfortunately, we can glean nothing from Suddi as he was never asked this question. Yet, there is reason to suppose that Jesus prepared himself for his life's work in the company of both cousins at Qumran, simply because they were so significant to his mission, and because Suddi clearly knew of Lazarus, having identified him to Dolores Cannon as the cousin of Jesus. Because of the age difference between Lazarus and his two cousins, they might have presided over him in a teaching capacity rather than sitting alongside him as fellow students.

Did Mary Magdalene, the sister of Lazarus and cousin to John and Jesus, also study with the Essenes? This is not impossible, as girls were educated to the same standard as boys in the Essene community at Qumran and shared fully in every aspect of life, including teaching.

It is apposite to comment at this point on the strange creed of the Essenes as revealed in the Dead Sea Scrolls, which seems to indicate that they rejected 'women, the weak, and the impure'. If this were so, of course, it would overturn any validity in Suddi's testimony, as he clearly states that within the Qumran community women enjoyed the same status as men and that the infirm were cared for with great humanity and respect. Our source has revealed to us that this creed applied to a certain esoteric group within the Essene culture that was associated with the Children of Solomon, a highly trained and mystically educated school of warriors also known as the 'Night-Protectors'. Their sacred duty was to protect forbidden knowledge, secrets of such an elevated spiritual nature that the entire global civilization would have been endangered if they had been revealed to ordinary humanity.

There were two divisions of these high-ranking warriors. One consisted of males and was attuned to the mysteries of the Sacred Masculine Principle. Any female energy, or any man who suffered from physical, mental or moral weakness could not be included amongst these mighty ones, for no weak link could be allowed to establish itself in the protective field that their essence created. More esoteric, hidden and powerful even than these protectors was the school of female warriors, also linked with the Children of Solomon and also Night-Protectors. They were attuned to the mysteries of the Sacred Feminine Principle and no male energy, nor any woman who suffered from physical, mental or moral weakness could be allowed to penetrate the ranks of these women of high degree.

These rules did not imply contempt, rejection or condemnation of anyone. They were set in place simply so that the community could be perfectly protected, and, in its secure integrity, serve the greater community of humanity until the time should come for its outer form to be dissolved and its usefulness to pass into new structures and organizations. These new structures and organizations would include the Rosicrucians, the alchemists, the Knights Templar (plus other orders of esoteric knights) and the Freemasons.

It seems likely that Mary did receive instruction from Essene teachers at some point in her early life, considering her deep and immediate understanding of Jesus's wisdom, message and purpose, all of which were filtered through an Essene essence. Yet the Essenes seemed to perceive the Godhead as the all-male Yaweh, although according to Suddi's revelations, their knowledge was so profound in some areas that they must have embraced a thorough understanding of the Sacred Feminine Principle in order to have grasped the secrets of the universe and utilized the forces that they did.

CHAPTER SIX

The Egyptian Connection

*M*ary's knowledge of ritual and her deep understanding and assumption of the role of Goddess seems emphatically to suggest that her religious background was influenced not just by the Essenes, but also by the Egyptian mysteries, and that she may even have been a priestess of high standing in a temple connected to an Egyptian mystery school.

A new version of Egypt's ancient religion was being expounded at the time, which united Isis and the bull-headed Serapis (an amalgamation of Mithras/Serapis and Osiris combining the mysteries of both religions, which arose due to Greek influence in Egypt) rather than her traditional consort, the unadulterated Osiris. Despite the sway of the influential modern cult, Mary's religious choice seems to have centred on the time-honoured rites of Isis and Osiris. For this to be true, of course, it would have been necessary for Mary to spend some time in nearby Egypt. This she might have done in her early girlhood.

It seems that when the holy family fled to Egypt, they found sanctuary there at the home of Joseph's cousin, Clopas or Cleopas (identified as such by the second-century Jewish-Christian chronicler, Hegesippus). This means that both Joseph and Cleopas (whose name is the Aramaic rendition of Cleopatrus, the male form of Cleopatra) must have had Egyptian connections, not at all unusual in those times, when two of the five districts of Alexandria were occupied by Jewish people. It also means, of course, that Jesus himself had Egyptian associations. Hegesippus states that Cleopas was Joseph's brother. Our own source, however, confirms that he was Joseph's cousin. This might explain why some chroniclers referred to him as the 'stranger' or the 'foreigner'.

Mother Mary's cousin, Mary-Salome Jacob, had accompanied the holy family to Egypt. A strikingly strange reflection of one another's circumstances had already established itself concerning the two young girls. They had become pregnant at the same time, literally the same day as far as could be calculated. Mary Jacob had been seduced by one Matthew Syro, a Jarius priest and Levi of Alphaeus. Matthew

Syro seems to have taken advantage of his position as Chief Priest, subordinate only to the office of High Priest, to have predatorially pressed his attentions on the young Mary Jacob. Why he did not marry her we have been unable to discover, but, from the impression of the story given to us, it seems that he may have been married and that his treatment of her was cynical and abusive, without honourable intention. The vulnerable young mother had been admitted into the household of Mary and her significantly older husband Joseph as an act of solicitude.

Joseph had had his own struggle with the incident of his wife's pregnancy, which no doubt increased his sensitivity to Mary Jacob's situation and his wife's eagerness to offer her a home, and, being obviously a kindly and open-hearted man, he was probably also outraged at Syro's treatment of her.[1]

Concerning the conception of Jesus, we believe that there might have been some problem on Joseph's part regarding his acceptance of it. Joseph was much older than Mary, and it could simply be that the timing of his success in siring a child caught him a little off guard, raising insecure questions as to whether the child was his. Mary could not conceive, and he must have believed it was because of his age. Then suddenly she was pregnant. Whatever his fears were (and they do seem to have arisen from some source) angelic communication came to him as well as to Mary, and his perplexities were resolved.

Joseph's reassurance from the archangel Gabriel (angel of women, birth and the Moon) might have transferred itself via Joseph's recounting of it to his cousin Cleopas, because when the holy family and Mary Jacob came to Egypt, presumably to the sanctuary of Cleopas's household, the reflection of one another's lives continued for the two Marys in that Cleopas and Mary Jacob were soon married. Cleopas stepped forward, elderly as he must have seemed in her eyes, for she was still a young girl although older than Mary the Virgin, to offer himself as her protector, husband and guardian to her baby girl. Mary accepted, perhaps free by this time of any hankering after the caddish Syro, and gave birth to Martha, Salome and John (born as Lazarus and afterwards called John by Jesus, who bestowed it as a spiritual or soul-name on his young cousin) whilst the entire extended family was living in Egypt.

This raises the interesting question as to whether the rumours of Jesus's illegitimacy and his mother's dalliance with a stranger, to which his detractors gave credence, attached themselves to her and her son because of Mary Jacob's close association with Mary and Joseph, and the fact that her pregnancy was concurrent with that of Joseph's wife. Perhaps the identity of both Marys was confused in later years, and the bigoted condemnation and scandal surrounding the misused Mary Jacob was transferred to the wrong Mary.

It seems that Mary Jacob and Mary the Virgin became devoted companions throughout life, Mary Jacob standing with her cousin (also sister-in-law), Mary the mother, and her daughter, Mary Magdalene, in silent empathy with their grief as they witnessed the Crucifixion. Her own would hardly have been less, for it is said of the three Marys, aspects of the triple Goddess:

> *Three there were who always walked with the Lord: Mary, his mother; Mary, her sister; And Mary Magdalene, who was called his companion; For Mary is his sister, his mother, and his companion.*

THE GOSPEL OF PHILIP

There could be no clearer statement of the close association of the triple Goddess with the Christ than this verse from Philip's gospel. Mary the Bride, Mary the Mother and Mary the Crone (which was once a deeply respectful title for an older woman, and did not carry the stigma it carries nowadays, so out of touch are we with women's sacred mysteries) 'walked with him always'. 'Mary', the Goddess herself, was indeed his sister (symbolizing Jesus's relationship with the entity of womankind as the spirit of wisdom), his mother, and his beloved wife or consort.

Our theory concerning Mary Jacob, later the wife of Cleopas, as the mother of Mary Magdalene and the companion of the holy family in their flight to Egypt is a new one, but it does answer the puzzle as to why two women referred to in the gospels as 'sisters' should each have been given the name Mary. When Mary, wife of Cleopas, is understood to be Mary the Virgin's sister-*in-law*, the issue is no longer confusing.[2]

It would also explain why the family at Bethany were so important to Jesus (his love for them is explicitly stated several times throughout the gospels). Mary, wife of Cleopas, would have helped to bring him up, in company with his four cousins, Mary, Martha, Mary-Salome and Lazarus, during the years spent in Egypt. And of course it explains the intimate bond that must have existed between Mary the Virgin and her cousin, as well as the close sympathy between mother and daughter, for them all to have been united in their grief at the foot of the cross. It also suggests the reason why Mary the Gypsy – as Mary, wife of Cleopas later became known – was rumoured to be not only a priestess but also a repentant prostitute, weeping endless tears in the wilderness, just as folk tradition describes Mary Magdalene as entering a secluded cave in France, and spending the rest of her days in sobbing penitence for her alleged career as a street-walker.

Now we know why Mary Magdalene was called *harmartolos*! Her otherness, her status as a priestess in an Egyptian temple, her intelligence and independence which flouted the conventions of perceived womanhood were, in themselves, bad enough, according to the narrow doctrines of the Bethany townsfolk, but for her to be illegitimate as well really put the icing on the cake for her detractors! Whilst both mother and daughter would have stood equally condemned in their eyes, Mary Jacob's social status had been rescued by Cleopas, and she was no longer *harmartolos*. Not so, Mary her daughter, for nothing could remove the stigma of her illegitimacy. Her enemies must have sensed her power and significance, and have been prepared to go to any lengths to ensure that her name was sullied and invalidated for all time. It seems that in the confusion and panic of creating the Magdalene myth, both mother and daughter, partners in 'sin', were tarred with the same myth-perpetuating brush!

Although we hope we have laid the ludicrous suggestion of prostitution finally to rest in the case of both women, it is of course possible that Mary-Salome was a priestess in her own right, passing on her function to her daughter when the rest of the family left for Bethany. This leaves the question of Cleopas, who was supposed to have been a Roman whom Jesus converted. We suggest that this report was (purposely?) distorted, and that Cleopas was indeed Jesus's second cousin, perhaps the holder of an office granted to him by the Romans, who became a devout follower of Jesus.

Moreover, there is one reference in the gospels to Jesus's aunt 'Salome', mother of 'John'.[3] We believe that this is actually Mary-Salome Jacob. If our surmise is correct, it has not been necessary, after all, to rely on Suddi's testimony, although this case, as ever, yet again demonstrates his bull's-eye accuracy in his rendering of his account.

As will be discussed, John the beloved disciple was almost certainly Lazarus, Mary's brother. If the mother of Lazarus was in fact Mary-Salome, wife of Cleopas, who gave her names to two of her daughters, Mary Magdalene and Salome, might not she be referred to in the New Testament as just Salome, rather than Mary-Salome, especially if the true identity of Mary Magdalene and Lazarus was being fudged, as indeed seems to be the case?

This would resolve the further problem of other gospel accounts, which refer to Mary-Salome being present with Mary the Virgin and Mary Magdalene at the Crucifixion. There seems to be confusion as to whether Mary, wife of Cleopas, was there with the other two Marys, or whether the third woman was actually Salome, Mary Magdalene's sister. In fact, if our theory is accurate, Mary-Salome and Mary, wife of Cleopas, are one and the same.

It seems likely that Mary Magdalene, although Jewish and the daughter of Jewish parents, did not regard her Essene heritage as being in any way incompatible with her temple training. Indeed, there would have been Essene teachers in Egypt who could easily have provided instruction for the entire extended family living under Cleopas's roof. Both Mary and Jesus seemed to embrace the philosophy of the Essenes in unison with the mysteries of the ancient Egyptian religion. Both a form of the ritual of the Eucharist and that of baptism were practised by the Essenes and by the Egyptian mystery schools. Water symbolized the purification of the soul, that first body of clothing which the individual spark of spirit assumes on its journey downwards into matter and individualization, which, according to mystics, is in itself like a form of rarefied and ethereal water. But the Eucharist symbolized the Spirit itself, the holy or spiritual essence of blood which unites all the human family. The vessel wherein this essence is found is the Holy Grail of Christian mysticism, and the ritual of the Eucharist is closely associated with Jesus and his teachings. Yet its genesis was not the Christian teachings, but those of ancient Egypt.

The knowledge guarded by the Egyptian mystery schools was instigated, according to Suddi, before the establishment of any 'little Egyptian kingdom', and it had its beginnings in 'a time before time', when the physical universe had not yet come into being. Of such mysteries, Suddi implies, we must speak in terms of secret dimensions rather than a location in human or planetary history. That Jesus embraced these ineffable mysteries cannot be doubted, and that their source reached back through the sacred rites of Isis and Osiris was a truth he clearly endorsed.

The spiritual teacher White Eagle says:

> *Do not think that the Christian religion commenced with the coming of the master Jesus. A like religion has always been presented to people in different guises and under different symbols, according to the age of humanity; and as the world advances in spiritual evolution, people will receive even finer and more beautiful truth.*

WHITE EAGLE, *DIVINE MOTHER: THE FEMININE,
AND THE MYSTERIES*, P55

Moses, anciently the great lawgiver of the Jewish people, bears the name of Osiris, because Moses is a linguistic form of that name. Suddi tells a fascinating story about him, saying that his Hebrew blood came from his father, not his mother as the traditional story states. Moses was the son of an Egyptian princess who brought him up in the royal household. The cradle of rushes story was put about to protect her from condemnation, because the father of her child was one of the Hebrew slaves from the House of Joseph.

When Moses discovered this as a young man, he embraced the Hebrews as his own people and declared himself a slave as they were. Sacrificing his status left him vulnerable in the court, and when he became Nefertiti's lover, the Pharaoh, who was to marry her, grew jealous, banishing Moses to the wilderness, where he was expected to die. Instead, he led the Children of Israel to freedom.

When he brought down the Ten Commandments on tablets of stone from Mount Sinai, he was said to shimmer with a perfect radiance. Suddi tells of 12 commandments, representing each one of the 12 tribes. As two of the tribes have been lost, so have two of the Commandments.

These basic laws for human society which Moses seems to have received directly from the Godhead were all outlined in Spell 125 in the Egyptian Book of the Dead, the 'Declaration of Innocence' or the Negative Confession. They are the laws of the universe 'written in matter in letters of light'. Apparently, 'Honour thy mother and father' meant 'Honour thy Mother-and-Father God' as well as our earthly mother and father.

According to Suddi's story, because the father of Moses was a Jewish priest of the faith and his mother was the princess of Egypt, he was given instruction not only by the Hebrew priests but also by the religious ministers of Egypt. This would have strengthened the connection between the two religions, as demonstrated by the fact that Moses defined the Jewish law in terms of the Commandments which already existed in Egyptian mystical literature. Yet, Suddi confirms that the secret knowledge of the Hebrews and the Egyptians was always shared between the esoteric wisdom keepers in the Egyptian temples and the Essenes, long before the time of Moses.

There is also a belief that Moses was actually Akhenaten, who attempted to establish a monotheistic religion in Egypt during the same period (the 18th dynasty), but was driven out of Egypt and exiled to the Sinai desert by Rameses I. The story does not conflict with the details given by Suddi and is supported by a wealth of evidence, even though he makes no mention of this particular part of it. If true, it means that the lawgiver of the Jews, the first great internationalist, was once the ruler of Egypt. The close and vital link between the two religions would have been such that, at the deepest esoteric level, there would indeed have been no disparity between belonging to an Essene community and entering an Egyptian temple.

We believe that the figure of the sphinx is in fact a statement of the interpenetration of the spirit of both mighty religions, the mysteries of Judaism represented by the body (the Lion of Judah) from which arises the great emblem of the Egyptian mysteries, the head of the Sun god, Ra. Ra, as his head appears upon the shoulders of the sphinx, is also a symbol of Christ Consciousness, the Christ which will come forth from Judaism, but will be one with the enlightenment of ancient Egypt. Isis is combined with the Sun god in this symbol, because she is the spirit of Egypt itself. The femininity of the sphinx is one of its most persistent legends.

Both Mary and Jesus certainly understood their religious convictions at the deepest esoteric level, and it is likely that, aware from the beginning of their shared destiny, Jesus helped his beloved cousin to prepare for the great adventure of her temple training, supporting and encouraging her as together they explored the dimensions of their growing enlightenment.

Mary was the Daughter of Sion written of in ancient scriptures. Prophecies of her advent exist alongside those concerning the coming of the Messiah. A passionate, beautiful and consummately lyrical poem, comprising one of the books of the Old Testament, combines prophecies of both Jesus and Mary appertaining to the remote future. It is the Song of Songs, which is Solomon's – the lyric of the Sacred Marriage. Although it seems that Solomon claimed these mystical lyrics as his own, it is almost certain that the Song of Songs originated in a time far preceding that of Solomon, possibly in ancient Sumeria, and was adjusted according to his understanding of the *hieros gamos*.

'Solomon' means 'the sun of the world' or 'the light of the world', and this mighty king of wisdom and justice, together with his opposite half, the Queen of Sheba (Solomon, who loved and revered women deeply but could be seen as something of a devourer where the feminine sex are concerned, certainly met his match in the Queen of Sheba!) might be thought of as forerunners, shadows of Jesus and Mary, breathing a rumour, whispering an intimation, of what was to come.

Mary's Egyptian childhood, of course, would in some measure explain her sagacious and natural apperception of Egyptian religious themes. However, she is so profoundly associated with the Isis mysteries that the deeper truth of the circumstances of her childhood is surely that she was preordained to have grown up in the land of the great goddess herself, rather than that an opportunity arising from random chance precipitated her into their midst. Mary's strong Egyptian connection would also compound the problem of her *harmartolos* status due to her illegitimacy, providing, as already mentioned, a further insight into why she was so much disapproved of in Bethany. Perhaps she was the only one of her family to embrace the Egyptian mystery religion (except, maybe, for her mother) and continued her observances when the family settled there in later years. It would indicate, too, why she might have been a woman of means in her own right. A high-ranking Egyptian priestess would have been provided with her own resources from temple funds.

Our source confirms that Mary did hold such a position, entering the temple at the age of thirteen. She remained in Egypt alone for some years, rejoining her family at a later date, before the mission of Jesus began. Certainly this would explain why she was so distrusted by the Bethany townsfolk, and why she was treated with such hostility as an outsider or a foreigner, whereas the rest of the family seemed to be better tolerated.

It is also interesting to consider that women were allowed much greater freedom and independence in Egypt than they were permitted in Galilee. If Mary had spent some years there alone, first as a girl and then as a young woman attached to a temple, her time in Egyptian society would have been highly formative with regard to her development as an individual, and she would have had difficulty in adapting to the new and much more repressive situation in Bethany once she returned home. Perhaps the male inhabitants of the town, as we have already considered, might take considerable exception to her less-than-cowed mien. From the beginning, Mary and the course of her momentous mission were lodged between a rock and a hard place.

NOTES

1 Although our sources confirm that Joseph did indeed show kindness and compassion to Mary Jacob, it seems that he himself had fathered a love child prior to his meeting with and marriage to Mary the mother of Jesus. This love child was a son, named Joseph after his father. Some condition or illness on the mother's part prevented the couple from marrying. The facts are obscure, but they seemed to revolve around a tribal or social taboo. Joseph's guilt made it difficult for him to accept this first son, who became a metalworker. Jesus, clearly anxious to assuage the sorrow his half-brother felt at his rejection by his father, took great pains to establish a stable fraternal relationship with him, and the two remained close throughout his life. This theme of the brotherly association of the royal heir or king with a dispossessed or mysterious metalworker is reflected throughout mythology, notably in the Arthurian cycle, where Wayland, the supernatural elvish or dwarvish metalworker, forges the noble sword Excalibur for the use of King Arthur.

2 Although our source refers to Cleopas as Joseph's cousin, it seems viable that the couple would have been regarded in the light of aunt and uncle to Jesus and his siblings, as certainly seems to have been the case. This scenario, descending into history, would explain why later chroniclers referred to Cleopas as Joseph's brother and Joseph's wife as 'sister' to Cleopas's wife.

3 The gospel account refers only to 'John'. Before the evidence concerning The Secret Gospel of Mark was uncovered, it had always been understood that the reference was to the mother of John *and* James, sons of Zebedee, and therefore that their mother must be called Salome, as that was the name given to her in the text, although in it James is not mentioned. As the men were twin brothers and often cited in the same frame of reference, it was unlikely from the start, prior to the uncovering of new evidence, that Jesus's 'Aunt Salome' (a title he would have given her rather than her full name, Mary-Salome, because no doubt he would have heard his mother, Joseph and Cleopas referring to her as 'Salome' to avoid confusion between the two Marys when they were all living together in the same household in Alexandria), should have been mentioned only in connection with John, rather than the usual 'James and John'. There is no evidence elsewhere to suggest that James and John Boanerges ('sons of thunder') or their father Zebedee were related to Jesus.

CHAPTER SEVEN

Soul-Communion

*D*id Jesus and Mary share a close relationship before attaining adulthood? The answer seems to be that they did. Our sources indicate that Mary and Jesus grew up together for some years in Egypt, Jesus at first taking a kindly brotherly interest in Mary, aware of their special bond from her birth and, in fact, establishing a close and fraternal relationship with all his cousins. He returned to Nazareth with his parents whilst still a boy or youth, and it seems that his aunt, uncle and cousins followed them some time later, emigrating to Bethany where Cleopas had perhaps been granted some office by the Roman administration.

Meanwhile, Mary stayed behind in Egypt to receive her temple training. Our source reveals that this was in part due to her illegitimacy, not because of Cleopas's unkindness or rejection of her, but because Mary Jacob and he were concerned about the taunts she might (and later did) receive in Bethany where her mother's history was known, and the effect they might have on the development of a sensitive and intelligent young girl.

Jesus was not entirely deprived of Mary's company throughout these few intervening years before she joined her family at Bethany, because he travelled extensively in the company of his merchant uncle, Joseph of Arimathea, whose immense significance to this story we will consider in Chapter Seventeen. Joseph often brought Jesus to Egypt – and to Mary – to receive further esoteric insight and wisdom from the priests and priestesses of the Egyptian mystery schools.

It is important here to note that, as Suddi testifies, Jesus did not come into the world with all his knowledge and wisdom already provided and accessible. He had to strive for it, and a learning process was necessary, for such are the dictates of the gift of freewill. Although he was a man of divine destiny, Jesus still had the right to choose whether or not he would fulfil that destiny. Whilst the expansion and rapidity of his learning compressed the educational essence of countless ordinary lifetimes into no more than a decade or so, there was still a need for its accommodation before he could begin his mission.

Suddi states that it was of urgent concern to Jesus to simplify the great esoteric traditions and the deeply secret, guarded knowledge of the spiritual wisdom keepers across the world, and to put it into uncomplicated, direct language and lucid images that everyone could understand. To this end, he further developed and refined the art form of the parable. This form has its roots in the ancient literary craft of fable, but rises above its glib restrictions to become a new verbal art, entirely Jesus's own creation.

Jesus's decision to make esoteric knowledge available to the common populace in this way scandalized many secret priesthoods, especially that of the Mandaeans, that mysterious religious group which still exists today, comprising the much persecuted Marsh Arabs in Iraq. Their keynote is still secrecy. It has taken scholars years of trust-building before the Mandaeans were prepared to divulge anything at all about their way of life or their religion. John the Baptist headed their sect from the beginning of his own mission until his death, hailed as their 'King of Light'.

To this day, the Mandaeans hate Jesus and call him 'the lying Messiah', believing him to be responsible for the death of their beloved John the Baptist. This is not because, as some suggest, they believe that he actually had John done to death, but because they believe that the esoteric truths, enshrined in their religion, have to be kept absolutely secret, and must not be shared with outsiders under any circumstances, most certainly not with the profane. That Jesus did share such secrets with tax collectors and insubordinate females such as the woman at the well shocked them deeply, and they were not able to accept his inclusive philosophy, which taught that social outcasts had the same right to justice, compassion and respect as the most devout, that they too were deserving of the inner secrets, and that all were equal in the sight of God.

This was, according to them, Jesus's great 'lie', and his revelation of sacred secrets that they saw as the domain of their leader, John the Baptist, led, in their eyes, not only to John's death but also to the death of Jesus himself. They believe that both deaths were divine retribution for 'spilling the beans' only, in their view, Jesus was the guilty party, being the instigator of the crime, whereas John, so to speak, was an innocent bystander, forced to suffer the consequences of Jesus's 'treachery'. This situation gives an added insight into the sheer force of condemnation from all sides with which Jesus had to contend, and the rigidity of the mindsets his teachings had to break through during the course of his mission.

Today's scholars are beginning to find many correlations between Jesus's precepts and philosophy, and those of the ancient Greek and Egyptian mystery schools. This has given rise to, in our view, all kinds of erroneous conclusions, such as that Jesus's own religion was really Greek or Egyptian. In fact, such correlations might be found to exist between Buddhism and Jesus's teachings, or Hinduism and Jesus's teachings, or the doctrines of Zoroastrianism, the ancient Mayans, the native Americans, the shamans of Russia, the Druids of Britain and other European lands, and even the complex and intriguing religion of the Aborigines, and Jesus's teachings.

To all lands, to all peoples, did the young Jesus go, learning, listening, sharing wisdom fires, partaking of the deep communion of meditation, ritual and worship, entering with his heart-consciousness into the hearts and souls of his brethren who taught him and revealed to him the beauty and the mystery of their ways, their window on universal truth. And then, when his inner and outer education was complete, his journeyings done, Jesus reached into the innermost heart of the fruit of his spiritual lessons and brought forth its kernel, its immaculately refined essence, and distilled it into the simplest, the most pure and perfect teachings ever to be given to humankind, heart to heart, soul to soul, in consummate humility, courage and truth, lit by the ineffable luminescence of the Christ within. This miraculous act of Jesus, perhaps his greatest miracle, was not achieved without the inspiration of the Magdalene, as will shortly be discussed.

To those who would point out that some of the lands mentioned were unknown in those times, we would say that they were not necessarily unknown. Items of flora and fauna belonging to North America, for example, appear in European carvings and imagery which predate the time of America's discovery. (An instance of this can be found at Rosslyn Chapel, near Edinburgh.) Mystics far inland knew via their own agency of Jesus's arrival on their shores, and journeyed in advance to meet him. Where this was not possible, a means of remote communication took place, somewhat akin to our idea of astral travel.

All the while, back in Egypt, Mary performed her temple rites, journeying through a deep interior process of learning in spiritual company with her beloved Jesus (actually Yeshua, with strong stress on the first syllable, which gives the positive *yes*, so fitting as a name for the Christ). As he explored at the outer level, so she helped him to internalize the spiritual substance which was gradually imparted to him. And she was not always physically absent on these voyages. On a significant number of them, she was at his side in body as well as in soul. Yet, during those times when land and sea stretched between them, no true separation could impose itself upon them. In a timeless place beyond the limitations and constraints of time and space, they came together, unifying their essence in a boundless act of spiritual love, in the Song of Songs, in the secret Bridal Chamber. So the Christ Being entered into them, and so Yeshua the Christ was prepared for his mission, blessed and accompanied always by the inner presence of Mary, his beloved, in his heart.

When Mary of Bethany enters the gospel story, the intimate understanding between them is already indicative of a profound and tender bond. Martha, Mary's sister, complains to Jesus when he and his followers are guests at the Bethany household: 'Lord, dost thou not care that my sister hath left me to serve alone? Bid her therefore that she help me.' Jesus answers her, saying, 'Martha, Martha, thou art careful and troubled about many things. But one thing is needful: and Mary hath chosen that good part, which shall not be taken away from her.' Mary sits immovably at Jesus's feet, deaf and dumb to all Martha's remonstrances. Jesus's message is clear – 'please do not disturb us!' Of course, as in every part of Jesus's ministry, there is a deeper significance here than the merely personal and pragmatic. Nevertheless, for the time being, Mary and Jesus are inseparable, and seem to be sharing some deep soul-communion beyond that of teacher and student.

The spiritual teacher White Eagle says of this event:

> *Martha, you will remember, blamed Mary because she neglected to help in the domestic work. Jesus said, 'Mary hath chosen that good part', (Lk.10:42), meaning that Martha on that occasion should have recognized what was happening within Mary. Martha did not know, but Jesus was aware, that Mary was opening her innermost being to spiritual truth. ... Mary understood the Master as none of the others did. ... We should say that Mary had been initiated into true brotherhood through what is sometimes called the feast or ceremony of love, when the spirit and soul of the initiated becomes merged with all its other brethren, which only happens when the soul is raised to consciousness and understanding of true love.*

> THE LIVING WORD OF SAINT JOHN, WHITE EAGLE

Martha seems to have better realized the profundity of her sister's role on the occasion of the supper when Mary anointed Jesus, as she is spoken of as serving at table without, this time, complaining of Mary's absorption in their guest – or maybe she had just given up on Mary whenever her sister was in the company of Jesus!

Mary's understanding of Jesus was unspoken, immediate and all-embracing. She worked quietly in partnership with him on at least two reported occasions, one being his anointing and the other the raising of Lazarus, which points to the likelihood that they received esoteric training together. We think she was present on all occasions when he performed his major miracles.

On the day that Lazarus was raised from the dead, Martha first met Jesus on the road to Bethany, bewailing the fact that he had not been there with them, for then Lazarus would not have died, but comforted by Jesus's promise of resurrection. During this time, though aware of his coming, Mary sits quietly meditating in the house. This is important, as Suddi tells us that it was through leading the recipient of his healing and his miracles into the sanctuary of mutual meditation that Jesus was able to touch the heart of the sufferer, and so bring about his wonders. Here we have Mary performing a spiritual service to help Jesus touch the heart of her brother, Lazarus, even though he has been dead for four days. John's gospel, after reporting that Martha affirmed her belief in the Christ, then tells us:

> *And when she had so said, she went her way, and called Mary*
> *her sister secretly, saying 'The Master is come, and calleth for*
> *thee.' As soon as she heard that, she arose quickly, and came*
> *unto him.*

JOHN, 11: 28–29

There is here another hint of the special relationship between Mary and Jesus. Mary remains in stillness and quietude until she is secretly called to Jesus's side by Martha. Only when Mary is present does he raise Lazarus from the dead. We believe that this further confirms the crucial role that Lazarus and Mary played in Jesus's mission, and were set to play in the future (we stand at the dawning edge of that time today).

Jesus also shares Mary's grief. Not until she is before him (having fallen at his feet in her grief for Lazarus) does he begin to express sorrow. Upon the arrival of the group of mourners in her wake, Jesus weeps with them. This cannot be because he is mourning Lazarus's death. He knows that there is no death, and he knows that Lazarus has only 'died' so that Jesus might be allowed to demonstrate to the gathering that death truly has no dominion. In a moment, Lazarus, arisen, will stand with them again. And yet he weeps. It is interesting that it is Mary who seems to unlock his grief. Jesus is expressing that true brotherhood which not only sympathizes, but actually experiences the selfsame feelings of distress that others are feeling.

A distinction needs to be drawn here between the sway of the mob, where forces of anger or hysteria become infectious, and the true empathy of the heart. The first is the excitability of psychic invasion, which infects the solar plexus and the lower mind; the second is the embrace of the spirit, whose location is the heart and the higher mind. First, Jesus links with Mary's sorrow, then that of the crowd, and finally, with that of Lazarus himself, who lies within the tomb, 'groaning' in his spirit for delivery:

> *When Jesus therefore saw her (Mary) weeping, and the Jews*
> *also weeping which came with her, he groaned in the spirit, and*
> *was troubled. ... Jesus wept.*

41

Jesus therefore again groaning in himself cometh to the grave.

JOHN, 11:33–38

It is Mary, the Sacred Feminine Principle, who stimulates the well of compassion and tenderness in Jesus's heart. We are not suggesting, of course, that without Mary, Jesus would literally have lacked such tenderness and compassion, but rather that the whole of his life was an unfolding drama of the cosmic mysteries played out before us in details clad in shining light that we might begin to understand the deeper truths of the spirit – the essence of reality. Therefore, Jesus shows us here that it is the presence of Divine Mother within him which unlocks the magic of love and compassion in the heart – Divine Mother symbolized by Mary. Only when Divine Mother and Divine Father are as one in the eternal glory of the Bridal Chamber (the enlightened heart) can we express our true humanity – the indwelling humanity which saves us from death and destruction, not only of the spirit but that chaotic darkness dwelling on the outer planes as well – the darkness of war, division and hatred.

Perhaps this is why the Catholic Church portrays Mary the Virgin as constantly imploring God the Father to be merciful to sinners, why the Shekinah – the mystic Feminine Light of the Godhead in Hebraic lore – argues with the Father in defence of humankind because of her compassionate nature, and why, in the Gnostic gospels, Mary Magdalene conducts the *argumentum ad misericordiam*, as her stand in persuading Jesus to have more pity for sinners condemned to hell.

It seems that the raising of Lazarus was not the only miracle which Mary Magdalene's presence facilitated, for she must also have played a part when Jesus demonstrated divine abundance through the loaves and fishes miracle. We suggest this because the loaf, or corn, and the fishes (denoting the mermaid-goddess, Pisces) are both symbols which belong to Isis and to the goddess-powers within the heart of the Magdalene, she who afterwards became known as 'Mistress of the Waters'.[1] The corn and the fish are also symbols of the Sun and the Moon, surely referring directly to Jesus and Mary Magdalene and seeming to indicate that they worked together on the inner spheres to rise above the limitations of matter and provide sustenance for the multitude.[2] Jesus fed them with the true bread of life, for the nourishment the crowd received was ingested on a much deeper level than merely that of the physical body, the plane of materiality. And the bread of life was given through the ministrations of the Piscean avatar, as symbolized by the two fishes. The number of barley loaves is also significant – five, the number which became the great symbol of Mary Magdalene down the centuries for the followers of her secret tradition. Throughout the ages, Goddess is eternally depicted holding a five-eared sheaf of wheat. The number five is also reflected in the five-sided star or pentacle of

Venus, who mirrors Isis and whose sign is the dove in flight. This is the dove of the Holy Spirit, which hovered over Jesus as John the Baptist baptized him in the holy waters of the river Jordan.[3] Significantly, the consort of the bride in the Song of Solomon continually refers to her as 'my dove'. The sign of the five-pointed star or pentacle is also visible in the sign of the rose. The mystic form of the rose is linked with the human form. Roses are built on a calyx of five sepals. A figure sketched around the sepals, joining their tips, creates a pentacle, the symbol of sacred proportion or the 'Golden Mean'. This is the point on a line where the smaller part is in the same proportion to the greater part as the greater part is to the whole. Also known as Divine Proportion, the Golden Mean declares itself in every single line of the pentacle. If we stand with our legs apart and arms spread wide, we ourselves make the form of the pentacle. It is also interesting to consider that the three-dimensional form of the pyramid has five planes (four sides and a base).

There is another 'five' connection, too, for we are told by David Wright, one of the great seers of our time, that Mary is active on the plane of the fifth dimension in the spiritual worlds. We would add that she is by no means limited to this supernal sphere and, in fact, is working to link the fifth and the sixth dimensions with the sphere of consciousness of earthly humanity, which comprises the fourth dimension. The numbers five and six lead us back, of course, to the rose and the lily symbolism which is so utterly that of Mary – 'I am the Rose of Sharon and the Lily of the Valley', sings her prophetic voice in the Song of Songs. So the essence of Mary is indicated by the five barley loaves, and the essence of Jesus, the Piscean saviour, by the two fishes, the zodiacal sign of the age. Additionally, perhaps the two fishes of the sign confirm that there were two conjoined saviours, the opposite directions in which the fishes are swimming being indicative of their genders.

NOTES

1 A delightful story is told in the New Testament of Jesus, Simon Peter, and a fish. A tax was demanded of Jesus by the authorities, but both he and the disciples were without funds. Jesus asked Peter to go to the shores of the Sea of Galilee, where a fish would come to him, bearing a shekel (the amount required to pay the tax) in its mouth. Peter did so, the fish duly appeared with the shekel, and the tax was paid. This enigmatic little episode is highly reminiscent of folktales from around the world which relate how animals, birds, fishes and even insects come willingly to the aid of kind-hearted and deserving humans. This need not tempt us to discount the story, because the species of fish which gave Peter the shekel has since been named in his honour 'St Peter's Fish', and it has recently been discovered that the female not only carries her eggs in her mouth, but also her young, enduring near-starvation rather than risking their welfare. When they finally leave, she carries a substitute in her mouth – any rounded, small item such as a pebble, a coke-bottle top – or, in first-century Palestine, a coin such as a shekel.

2 Ancient documents provide evidence that the early Church, before the takeover by Rome, considered that the bread of Communion symbolized Mary Magdalene, and the wine represented Jesus.

3 It might be significant that in the Northern tradition, which has a link with the East via the connection between the Essenes and the Druids, the Earth Mother is called Jord.

CHAPTER EIGHT

The Triple Goddess

*I*n considering the origins of Mary Magdalene, we can only draw on hints and echoes, secrets and dreams. Locked into our materialistic age and our mundane sphere, where our global culture seems, for the most part, specially designed to imprison us in circumscribed vision and to cap our humanity with false boundaries and barriers of worldly perception, we can only grope blindly in the material darkness of our time and stumble hesitantly after the fiery tails of myth and fable. And yet, we are assured that the time will not be long in coming when these self-imposed limitations will be swept away, and our true humanity restored to us in the fullness of its glory. Until then, we can do little more than seek to 'mount to the infinite by the ladder of the impossible', as the poet Yeats so splendidly expresses it. It seems apt here to take a little time out from the story of Mary to try to catch a fleeting glimpse of who she truly was, for although Mary Magdalene was entirely human, she was also divine.

Before detailing what we know of Mary's greater being, it is important to gain an insight into the other two Marys, for throughout their lives they worked together devotedly as a team. This mystical coming together of three women is echoed down the ages in the Three Graces, the Three Norns (sisters of wisdom and far-seeing in Scandinavian myth), the three weird sisters in Shakespeare's *Macbeth*, and numerous other examples.

As misogyny darkened the world, the feminine three became uglier and uglier and more and more sinister, especially as the symbol of the three relates to the form of the pyramid, and that symbolic 'pyramidal mound of flesh' in the female genitalia whose 'rising power' is so important and sacred to the alchemists. And so we see that the pyramid is a feminine symbol, and its power and significance relate to the inner, spiritual regions of human consciousness. That is why they were used as burial chambers – where the inner 'king' or 'queen' within us all has his/her true residence or resting place – but such a facility comprises only one very small part of their wider significance.

Through this 'pyramidal' organ, women could, in a heightened and sanctified state, give forth certain ethereally-charged secretions (the *rasa*) which, when ritually ingested, would activate the inner organ of vision in the recipient and bestow the power of prophecy, spiritual enlightenment, lucid inner seeing and divine ecstasy.

In Tantric mysticism from ancient India, the great power of the Goddess was contained within the fluids of her transcendental body. This source of primal energy is the power of the soul, for the soul is the first body to clothe the spirit when a spark of it individualizes and 'falls' into the world of matter, there to learn, first self-con-sciousness, and then God-consciousness. Without the soul, humanity could have no existence in the sense that we know it. It is because of the Goddess and her bestowing of soul-power that we are able to descend to Earth as independent entities, taking on, first the soul-body so similar to the ethereal vibration of water or liquid crystal, and then coarser and coarser bodies as we journey ever deeper into the material plane, until we emerge as a foetus with all our bodies intact, from the most subtle to the physical, and, after full development, ready for our use on Earth. It is her gift to us.

The transcendental fluids, which carry the soul-power that the Goddess gives, appear to spiritual vision as a kind of etherealized water, of a measureless beauty and purity. It is from water that all life arises, both at the level of the soul and of the physical body, for, as we know, everything that lives had its origins in the sea, and it is from the waters of the womb that all things are born. Our very blood has a com-position almost identical to that of sea water, and the Goddess name 'Mary' means 'of the sea'. This ensouling power of Divine Mother is why the Sacred Feminine is known as 'First Thought' or 'first matter', because it creates the first pure and exalted body or 'bridal gown' for the spark or seed of spirit as it incarnates. There are many overlapping bodies, but we can think of them as seven in number, each body attached to and located from one of the seven chakras.

From this esoteric truth it seems that certain misconceptions have arisen, such as, that women represent matter, the body, and the Earth, whilst the rarefied male essence is the true immanence of the spirit. This is correct only insofar as Goddess provides for us to come to Earth, provides the sphere of materiality – the cosmos – in which we may evolve. It does not mean that Goddess is of any less pure spiritual substance than God!

Nevertheless, considering the sacred truth of Goddess as our Earth Mother, and the holiness of water, it is not surprising that her mysteries of conception and birth are so celebrated in Tantra (which means 'continuity' and has echoes of the clew or thread created for us by the feminine spinning divinities from their own essence to lead us through the distracting maze of life to our true heart-centre, where sits Goddess). It is from Tantra that the idea of *rasa* arises, that Divine Feminine fluid which conducts the Goddess power, and which is associated with menstrual blood. The rose is a symbol of this Goddess power, or 'first matter', being in itself a representation of matter made perfect, fragrant and beautiful and of divine proportion. It has always been emblematic of the heart and of Goddess.

Laurence Gardner calls the *rasa* the 'designated Vehicle of Light' and, of course, that is exactly what the soul is (the first vehicle of the spark or flame of spirit). Its secret is that, eventually, even the coarsest, outermost body of the spirit, which is the physical form, will become so refined as to develop into the 'designated Vehicle of Light'. In ancient times, the womb which produced the *rasa* was known as the 'utterer' of the divine 'Word' spoken of at the beginning of John's gospel, therefore named the 'uterus'.

It seems that the rituals associated with the 'rose' of female genitalia and its pyramidal rising power were at some point infiltrated and corrupted by agencies who wished to enslave the power of the Sacred Feminine Principle. Of course, it is easy to crudify and vulgarize such ceremonies, which then conduct their power into dark and distorted channels fitting the image of weird disfigurement evident in the *Macbeth* witches. This was the whole point of harlotizing the Feminine Principle, as was done so blatantly in the case of the Magdalene herself – the process either blocked the potency of the spiritual feminine dynamic, or twisted it into hideous forms so that it took on a night-hag aspect.

This result, of course, furthered the cause of the misogynists very efficiently, because then people became afraid and reviled the powers of women from that centre within humanity which is the most dangerous, conflagrational and self-per-petuating – the domain of the lower instincts which, when cunningly manipulated, produces fear, bigotry, superstition and hysterical persecution. The outbreak of witch-burnings, as we shall see, was by no means unconnected with those intelligent and organized forces which conspired against Mary Magdalene. In fact, they have shaped our history in ways undreamt of, as we hope to reveal. And, as we stand at the edge of a new century and a new era, it is poignant to consider that the world still polarizes the Feminine Principle into the two extremes of virgin and harlot by means of the schism which exists between East and West.

As a Muslim friend said to me, 'Do you really think that women are free in the West – with all the damaging pressure on them to look a certain way, for them to be tied to their bodily image through the fascism of popular culture, and to receive public taunts if they do not conform to premeditated standards of attractiveness, and for such methods of policing to be applied with the justification and applause of the media and the spokespeople of your society?' Wise words, especially when we are so ready to deplore the 'policing' of women in Eastern societies, and yet, for the most part, even fail to perceive, leave aside object to, what is essentially the same process in our own culture.

It is appropriate here to explain that we do not intend to blame the Church for this curse of misogyny which began to wash over the world in a dread and dark tide many aeons ago. The Church was most certainly a willing and very powerful vehicle for it, but there were, and are, many other vehicles. The great danger is that if we blame this or that establishment for a human shortcoming, it tempts us to relieve ourselves complacently of any need to seek out and overcome the enemy inside our own heart. And so, whilst we energetically accuse and condemn, the worm within sinks thankfully into protective custody, ready to invade insidiously and rear its poisonous head before very long in a new time and in a new form.

We believe that the myth of Eve being smitten by a serpent in a 'garden' (the new-born cosmos, or perhaps the cosmos as it was about to be born?) is very important to our understanding of this mystery. To our vision, it is as though, when the primal human matriarch received the wound and the kiss of the serpent's 'temptation', something unutterably marvellous and exquisite beyond all bounds of mundane comprehension was bestowed upon humanity which, according to our freewill choice, could be magnificent beyond measure or, by the same token, could lead us into a monster's belly of darkness and suffering. We have largely chosen the latter course, but the day is not far off when we shall no more choose this painful and sorrowful path, but turn again to the light, for the radiant ring of truth will reveal itself as unbroken, and nothing will stop us from being gathered into the heart of its centripetal power of justice, compassion and universal love. It was this perfect unbroken ring which Jesus and Mary created by unifying their consciousness so that the Christ Light could descend and embody the mystery of its divine being through their sacred marriage.

CHAPTER NINE

The Lost Bride

*T*oday, after long years of burial, the suppressed memory of Mary Magdalene's true status as the female Christ is at last rising back to the surface of human awareness. Many people are recognizing Mary Magdalene as the 'lost bride' of the Song of Songs, or the Song of Solomon, and the 'lost bride' of the mysterious Fisher King who appears as the kingly guardian of the Holy Grail in the story of the knight Perceval's attempt to recover it. (It is interesting to consider that Perceval's quest for the Holy Grail actually began as a quest for his mother.) This Fisher King is in agony because he has a wound that cannot heal. It bleeds and gives him great anguish, so that his life is a continual supplication for healing.

A clue to this symbolism may lie in the fact that the bleeding wound is located in his genitals (strangely reminiscent of the lost penis of Osiris, whom only Isis can restore), and his only hope of being made whole is if Perceval is able to win the Holy Grail. This he is enabled to do, not by any great act of warriorship but, simply by asking questions of the ethereal maidens who carry the Grail – in other words, Perceval must incorporate its meaning into his consciousness and firmly ground it there. This he fails to do, and it is only Galahad, Lancelot's son, who is finally able to attain the Holy Grail, so ending the misery of the Fisher King's mutilation. (It is worth bearing in mind that Jesus was called the 'Fisher of Souls' or the 'Fisher of Men'.)

The triumphant culmination of this story is still an unfulfilled prophecy, because of course the Holy Grail has not yet been won. The Fisher King's other half of his true self was torn away violently from his genitals, and until we, as a planetary consciousness, retrieve her, we are doomed to limp along with only half the ring of supreme consciousness available to us, no doubt wondering why, in our ignorance, our civilization should keep short-circuiting with such resounding regularity.

It is also pertinent to remember here that the romances of the Holy Grail originated in the South of France, from the Languedoc, where the Cathars and the Knights Templar adored Mary Magdalene, and worshipped her divinity and her mysteries.

In this sense, we can almost regard the Song of Songs as, in part, a paean of the

Fisher King before he is cruelly bereft of his bride, leaving him in agony and bleeding at the heart and the genitals where she has been so brutally torn away. But more than this, the Song of Songs is a magnificent prophecy, an exquisite lyric of the time when, in the future, the perfect antiphony between the Sacred Masculine and the Sacred Feminine will manifest through heart-centred human consciousness:

My beloved spake, and said unto me,

Rise up, my love, my fair one, and come away.

For, lo, the winter is past,

the rain is over and gone;

the flowers appear on the earth;

the time of the singing of birds is come,

and the voice of the turtle-dove is heard in our land.

The fig tree putteth forth her green figs,

and the vines with the tender grape give a good smell.

Arise, my love, my fair one, and come away.

THE SONG OF SOLOMON, 2:10–13

The next verse is as the Christ calling to the Bride, hidden and veiled, or Jesus to Mary Magdalene, obscured and denied, ushering in her era as she takes her true place at his side:

O my dove, that art in the clefts of the rock,

in the secret places of the stairs;

let me see thy countenance, let me hear thy voice;

for sweet is thy voice,

and thy countenance is comely.

THE SONG OF SOLOMON, 2:14

This is followed by the mysterious exhortation, still in the voice of Jesus, or the male consort:

Take us the foxes, the little foxes,

that spoil the vines:

for our vines have tender grapes.

THE SONG OF SOLOMON, 2:15

Foxes are carnivores, not fruit-eating animals. What can this strange verse mean? Its message seems to refer directly to certain agents or forces that will 'spoil the vines'. The 'tender grapes' on these sacred vines are the new teachings, the fruit of the great light which Jesus and Mary brought forth to baptize the world. The voice of the Song is specific: these are 'our' vines, meaning the vines of the two lovers combined; what we might think of as the 'true vine'. The fox has always been a symbol of cunning, deceit and trickery in folktales across the globe, the word 'fox' itself, as a verb, being synonymous with 'confuse' and 'deceive'. If the Song of Songs is a prophecy, as we believe, then the word 'fox' was very carefully chosen to accurately describe and warn of the future despoilers of the sacred teachings, even though, within the outer context of the lyric, the image of birds or insects would have made more literal sense.

The prophecy is clear. One day the foxes, the little foxes, *will* be taken off guard, taken away, or laid siege to, in the sense that a city or country is 'taken'. The voice of the Song gives triumphal verification of this, announcing immediately after verse 15:

My beloved is mine, and I am his:

he feedeth among the lilies.

Until the day break, and the shadows flee away,

51

turn, my beloved,

and be like a roe or a young hart

upon the mountains of Bether.

THE SONG OF SOLOMON, 2:16–17

This seems to proclaim the indivisibility of the divine union, confirming that, although the foxes may spoil the tender fruit of that union for a certain span of time, the sacred marriage is ongoing, the Divine Feminine continues to feed the Divine Masculine ('he feeds among the lilies') and the rites of the *hieros gamos* will continue in secret 'until the day break and the shadows flee away' – until the obscuring darkness created by the 'little foxes' and by the wilful blindness of humanity is defeated by the dawning light. ('Turn, my beloved, and be like a roe or a young hart upon the mountains of Bether,' would seem to be a metaphor for the *hieros gamos*, the 'tender' fruits of which comprise ultimate enlightenment for the world.)

The lily and the rose symbolism which occurs in the Song of Solomon (the voice of the bride says in the opening verse of Chapter 2, 'I am the rose of Sharon and the lily of the valleys') has many meanings. It has been suggested that 'rose' is a mistranslation, as there were no roses in Palestine during biblical times. Even so, roses did exist in surrounding countries, trade routes were busy, and travellers chronicled their experiences and discoveries. Exotic imports were numerous, particularly in the time of Solomon, who may have had the text of the Song of Songs transcribed from sources which had their origin elsewhere. As the bride is speaking symbolically, it seems likely that 'rose' is the correct translation, although Laurence Gardner's rendition of it (the 'bulb') is also deeply symbolic, suggesting goodness, beauty and potency (love, wisdom and power) complete and contained within itself.

Bulbs are often in the shape of a teardrop, which Mary has revealed to us is of great esoteric importance. Nevertheless, we think that the 'bulb' reference is to the lily, as the lily grows from a bulb and is self-contained in its essence, thus perfectly expressing in form its hidden, inner significance and balancing its own symbolism with that of the rose in an immaculate double emblem of the mystery of Mary Magdalene; for if Mary Magdalene is the 'lost bride' of the Song of Songs, and we believe that she is unquestionably, then just as unquestionably the lily and the rose are emblematic of her mysteries. Certainly the rose has long been associated with her. Laurence Gardner explains in *Realm of the Ring Lords* that the lily and the rose are linked with Goddess rituals to do with the power of consciousness and spiritual evolution.

The priestesses who conducted the rites were the Fragrant Ladies or flow-ers (the 'lilies' or 'lotus flowers') that produced the sacred secretions which were used in the ceremonies to enhance and refine the organs of spiritual perception, the chakras, with which we believe the mysteries of Mary Magdalene are particularly concerned. The secretions and rituals in question were linked with blood or the spirit, as symbolized by the rose, and water or the soul, as symbolized by the lily.

The classic symbol of the lotus flower or lily opening in clear water is recognized the world over as a signature of the fragrant spirit dwelling in the still waters of the soul. When the lily is a symbol of the spirit, then the rose becomes its innermost centre, the 'jewel at the heart of the lotus'. The rose, as previously mentioned, is also a symbol of matter perfected, the perfect receptacle for spirit. The two flowers therefore are symbols for the body as sacred vessel, and for the soul and the spirit. This is a perfect description of Jesus's bride, for she combines these mysteries.

'Sharon', according to Laurence Gardner, was anciently defined as the Orbit of Light (Shar-On), an inner world of the spiritual realms associated with advanced enlightenment. The 'rose' of Sharon would therefore refer to its centre point, its innermost heart. This, we believe, is the ring of perfect consciousness that Jesus and Mary created together – Sharon, the Ring of Light – through which Margaret Bailey passes to commune with Mary. And Mary is always there, in the centre, at the very heart, of the Ring of Light – the Bridal Ring.

The words, 'I am black, but comely,' which occur in the Song of Songs, have been the subject of much recent debate. Mary Magdalene, as the daughter of Mary Jacob and the Jarius priest Syro, was a Palestinian Jewess, although her family had links with Egypt. She was not Ethiopian, as has been suggested. Nevertheless, the darkness of the depictions of Isis and the importance of the Black Madonnas do emphasize the special association of the black races with the Goddess. Psychologists have noted many correlations between the mindset of misogyny and the mindset of racism.

The hues of the robes of the Goddess are traditionally black, white, and red with gold at her heart, embracing the colours of the races across the globe. The black races in particular are said to be remnants of highly advanced civilizations whose knowl-edge and spiritual technology ranged far beyond anything our modern-day society is at present able to comprehend. By living under certain conditions which protect them from the narrow restrictions and prejudices of the intellect, various tribes have preserved areas of knowledge that would otherwise have been lost, and without which humanity would, in the future, have been rendered helpless in the face of the plethora of problems we have created for our planet.

This sacred and essential wisdom is beginning to surface through the human channel of several wisdom keepers, in particular Malidoma Patrice Somé, whose groundbreaking work, *Of Water and the Spirit*, has begun to lift the veil which

shrouds the secrets of Africa. Until the unbroken ring of Goddess-God consciousness is restored to humanity, we will not properly be able to grasp and utilize these
secrets.

Whilst fully acknowledging the subliminal emphasis on the importance of the
black races and therir link with Goddess consciousness that the words 'I am black,
but comely,' indicate, in their outer sense they refer, in part, to the bride's rejection
by her brothers and sisters, her 'mother's children'. If the bride is Mary Magdalene,
and her 'mother' is the Great Goddess herself, as the father of Jesus was God, then
it is ourselves, the children of that Divine Mother, who have rejected the bride and
'become angry' with her (what better way to describe worldwide misogyny than
irrational anger?). As with the Black Madonnas, the 'blackness' of the bride seems to
point to the obscuring shadow that we have, as a global society, thrown over her.
After all, why should a black woman of great beauty refer to herself as 'black, *but*
comely'? In this sense, the words might mean: 'My beauty (my essence) is hidden.'
('I am hidden from view, but I am beautiful.')

The bride goes on to say:

Look not upon me, because I am black,

because the sun hath looked upon me:

my mother's children were angry with me;

they made me the keeper of the vineyards;

but mine own vineyard have I not kept.

THE SONG OF SOLOMON, 1:6

The sense of the words is ambivalent, and seems to refer to sunburn, but also to a
deeper mystical meaning. They could also be understood to say: 'Look not upon me,
because I am black' (you are unable to see, or recognize the truth about me) 'because
the sun hath looked upon me' (the Divine Sun – the Christ – has shone upon me;
therefore my light has become so dazzling that, in your unillumined state, you can
no longer interpret what you see, and thus I appear *to you* to be black). This
perception of utter radiance as blackness, caused by limitation and restriction of true
vision, is referred to as 'the shining darkness'. It is noteworthy in this context that the
military salute derives from a gesture of devotion made by knights to the representation of the Goddess when they rode off in her sacred name to perform valorous

deeds designed to restore justice, mercy and peace to the community. The knight shaded his eyes, the ritual action meaning 'I am unworthy and unable to look upon the radiance of your dazzling spiritual beauty.'

The verse closes with the words: 'they made me the keeper of the vineyards; but mine own vineyard I have not kept.' This is surely a statement of what would come to be: the Sacred Feminine Principle would globally be forced to embrace a patriarchal religion that would eclipse and dispossess her. 'Mine own vineyard I have not kept.'

Four verses later, the great illumination occurs which puts paid to any doubt that this magical lyric is a prophecy concerning Jesus and Mary Magdalene:

While the king sitteth at his table,

my spikenard sendeth forth the smell thereof.

THE SONG OF SOLOMON, 1:12

As Jesus sat at table with the Bethany family, Mary took a pound of ointment of spikenard and anointed him with it. The fragrance filled the house.

The bride also speaks of her king as an apple tree:

As the apple tree among the trees of the wood,

So is my beloved among the sons.

THE SONG OF SOLOMON, 2:3

And, as we shall see, it is to Avalon, the Place of Apples, surrounded by the 'living waters', that Mary goes after the Crucifixion.

There is a reference in The Song of Songs to the military Order of the Knights Templar. This knightly Order is supposed to have arisen in France during the time of the Crusades, in order to protect pilgrims on their travels. We believe, however, that the Knights Templar were the very first knights to come into existence as the Night-Protectors, and that they did not arise from France, but landed there with Mary and the disciples as their first port of call on their way from Bethany to the shores of Britain and, some miles inland, to Avalon. Because Mary's mission was also centred in France, and because her mysteries were preserved there, the Night-Protectors remained in France, although some journeyed to Britain, with which they all maintained close links. These links culminated in the coming into being of

55

Camelot (Shar-On or the Ring of Light descended to Earth – the ring of light which still exists in the higher ethers and through which Margaret Bailey passes into the silence to commune with Mary Magdalene today) and King Arthur and the Knights of the Round Table (*see* Appendix One).

For many centuries they remained hidden, a secret Order linked with the Essenes and the Druids, guardians of sacred knowledge which had to be protected at all costs. When at last they did become an exoteric Order, they rapidly rose to prominence and became extremely wealthy and powerful from the early years of the twelfth century until 1307. Their wholesale slaughter took place on Friday 13 October by order of the French king, Philip the Fair and the pope, bestowing a sinister legacy of evil luck on the date of 'Friday the thirteenth', which still persists.

Interestingly, the betrayal and murder of the Templars can perhaps be seen as the second wave of the first act of European genocide which took place between 1208 and 1244, when the Albigensian Crusade, led by one Simon De Montfort, put to death over 100,000 Cathars, the Gnostic sects who, in their different ways, upheld the truth about Mary Magdalene and her mysteries, and who were said to embrace her secret Church.

If the uncanny appearance of a Simon in relation to Mary Magdalene signals distortion, deception and false accusation (*see* Chapter Two), then we can be certain that the justification for the Crusade, which was that the Cathars were corrupt and practised abominations, was a fabricated charge. The Cathars *were* heretical as far as the Church of Rome was concerned – because they refused to believe that priestly intermediaries were the essential link between the individual and his or her relationship with God, and particularly because they revered, and were guardians of, the mysteries of Mary Magdalene. (We believe that the act of gnosis – direct knowledge of God – comprised part of the teachings of Mary.) To keep the dark veil over her in place, the Cathars had to be eliminated, followed, as soon as an opportunity arose, by the massacre of the Knights Templar, who were Mary's knights. Both the Cathars and the Knights Templar were associated with Provence and the Languedoc, the area of France where Mary rooted her ministry.

The very first Knights Templar arose from the ranks of the Essenes (and also the Druids, because the two mysterious priesthoods were connected), and were the 'Night-Protectors' of Jesus and Mary on a sacred voyage that they undertook to bless and activate important chakras in the body of the Earth Mother, the holy planet herself. The divine couple left certain documents and artefacts at these points (caves, mountains, pyramids, etc.), which indicate our true human origins, among other mysteries. We believe that these documents and artefacts will begin to be discovered once this book has been published.

The point in the text of the Song of Songs which describes the Knights Templar in prophecy occurs at the beginning of verse 6, in Chapter 3:

Who is this that cometh out of the wilderness

like pillars of smoke,

perfumed with myrrh and frankincense,

with all the powders of the merchant? [1]

Behold his bed, which is Solomon's;

threescore valiant men are about it,

of the valiant of Israel.

They all hold swords, being expert in war;

every man hath his sword on his thigh

because of fear in the night.

'Solomon' is a reference for the great Christ Being (meaning 'the Light of the World'), and the 'bed' is the sacred marriage bed of Jesus and Mary, although of course we must not become ensnared in literalness when considering the divine principles which Jesus and Mary embodied. The 'bed' is their point of union – the sacred Bridal Chamber or the Ring of Divine Consciousness which they brought into being. Note the ring of 'Night-Protectors' around the marriage bed, the ring which mirrored the Bridal Ring or the holy dimension of Shar-On, which was to become Camelot, and the ring of Knights around the Round Table (*see* Appendix One).

We will discuss the important role of the Night-Protectors in a later chapter. For now, we will return to the subject of the three Marys, and take a closer view of the least known of the pyramidal group, Mary Jacob, the mother of Mary Magdalene.

NOTES

1 i.e. the spiritual essence of Jesus and Mary which expresses the Christ.

CHAPTER TEN

Mary Jacob

*I*gnorance of Mary Jacob's significance is widespread, but there is every indication, as we shall see, that she dwells at the heart of the Western mysteries, and that her counterpart is also central to those of the East. In the Goddess tradition, she represents the Crone and the Season of Wisdom (winter).

Mary Jacob was a priestess and a healer. As a learned woman, it is likely that she was associated with the Essenes, because education, particularly of a philosophical, scientific, medical, religious or mystical nature, was not normally dispensed to women of her culture and time. Only the progressive Essene brotherhood could have provided her with the knowledge and skills of a physician and herbalist, and with the esoteric training necessary for her to assume the role of priestess. From the female tradition within the Essene community (which reflected that of the Druidic priestesses of Western Europe) Mary Jacob emerged, and, like her daughter Mary Magdalene, she shared a link with the Egyptian mystery schools and their priestesses. This sisterhood strengthened when she, as a member of the holy family, emigrated to Egypt with Joseph, Mary and Jesus, culminating in her decision to entrust her daughter to an Egyptian temple where she would undergo eight years of training, from the age of thirteen to twenty-one.

Our sources disclose that, had Mary Magdalene been Cleopas's daughter by birth, he would never have agreed to leave her behind in the confines of the temple; but, because of her illegitimacy and the widespread knowledge of it in Galilee, he agreed to it, considering it a safer option for Mary when the rest of the family decided to return there. And so the circumstances of her birth directly contributed to the provision of her essential induction into the Egyptian mysteries.

In later years, Mary Jacob and two of her daughters, Mary Magdalene and Mary-Salome, became known in France as 'the Marys of the Sea', portrayed with fishtails as mermaids.[1] The word 'merry' proceeded from 'Mary' (originally the Egyptian word 'mery', meaning 'beloved'), particularly in association with Mary Jacob, and is linked in our own culture with Maid Marion, Robin Hood and his Merry Men, and with Morris dancers. England itself was once known as 'Merrie England', a tribute perhaps to the fact that it was to England that the three Marys sailed after the Crucifixion. And yet Mary Jacob is crucial to the spiritual mysteries of Britain, and possesses a huge significance that has been overlooked. Botticelli knew of it, and told of his secret to those who would understand, for it is said that Mary Jacob is the woman portrayed in ecstasy upon the conch shell in his painting *The Birth of Venus*.

Mary Jacob and her daughters, Mary Magdalene, Martha and Mary-Salome, formed a teaching group as part of their later mission, which taught the mysteries of the Holy Spirit. These mysteries impart the happiness and rejoicing which that ineffable feminine mystery enfolds within its wings, as a fragrant gift to those who would attune their souls to its resonance. However, we wonder if Mary Magdalene's sister, Mary-Salome, was ever truly one of the three 'Marys of the Sea'. We consider that some confusion may have arisen over the name of Mary Jacob, as she had bequeathed her full name (Mary-Salome) to her daughter. It seems strange that Martha should have been disregarded whilst her sister, Mary-Salome, was included within the group of revered women.

We think it more likely that Mary-Salome Jacob, the mother of Mary Magdalene, was the only Mary-Salome of the three, and that consequently the three 'Marys of the Sea' were more truly identified as Mary, the mother of Jesus, Mary Magdalene, and Mary Jacob. As this trinity of women were the mighty three who mirrored the three aspects of the triple Goddess, this conclusion would appear to make more sense.

Mary Jacob (her name is sometimes given as Jacobi) has reincarnated many times in service to humankind, always in a healing capacity. One of her great, yet purposely obscured, incarnations was as Miriam, the sister of Moses. As Moses was brought up in the Egyptian royal household, Miriam must also have had an Egyptian childhood, and it seems that she too enjoyed both Jewish and Egyptian ancestry. It is said of her in Exodus 15:20 that she 'took a timbrel in her hand; and all the women went out after her with timbrels and with dances'. In this life as Miriam she, as always, demonstrated the joy, the wisdom and the healing power of Goddess. Ancient sources refer to her as a prophetess and a high priestess, designating her as 'She to whom the people bowed and the afflicted came'. The Egyptian version of Miriam's name was Mery-Amon, and it was perhaps this famous incarnation that the deeper soul of her followers remembered when they revered her as Mary the Gypsy or Mary the Egyptian, as well as Mary Jacob's own association with Egypt in her lifetime.

She was the great matriarch who, in later times, became the mother of the beloved Magdalene, and the grandmother of Tamar or 'Sarah'. This daughter of Mary Magdalene continued the ancient healing tradition of her line, and was destined to play a vital role in the future establishment of holy Camelot (*see* Appendix One) and indeed in the future establishment of the New Age. Tamar's significance cannot be overestimated. Today, 'Sarah' is still worshipped as the goddess of the gypsies, their mighty queen and originator, although her name is properly Tamar, and the name she is traditionally known by is a deliberate obfuscation.

This great tradition of healing was continued by Mary Jacob in the lifetime when she walked the Earth as Jesus's aunt. Strictly speaking, she was, during this incarnation, the wife of Jesus's second cousin but, because of the age difference, it seems that Jesus referred to Cleopas and Mary Jacob as 'aunt and uncle', which no doubt gave rise to the mistaken tradition that Cleopas was Joseph's brother rather than his cousin. Mary Jacob knew many methods of healing and relieving pain with her herbs and her medical knowledge, and she accompanied Jesus in his ministrations to lepers and the victims of other cruel afflictions.

She has reincarnated in recent times. On at least two of her reappearances, she has returned bearing the same name; once as Mary Jacob (possibly born in 1730), the daughter of an eighteenth-century physician and occultist, Ralph Jacob, who was father to six children. She seems to have been some sort of wisewoman figure and alchemist who drew her inspiration from nature-mysticism and Goddess. The name 'Arimatheos' was given to us in connection with her. We consider that this is a connection to Joseph of Arimathea, and that it indicates the Sacred Marriage – *Arima* (an anagram of Maria) and *Theos* (God).

We believe that she is associated with Jacob's Ladder (*see* Part II) in that her medical and mystical arts lifted her into deep working communion with the angels of karma, birth and death, and that she is therefore linked closely with healing and ministering angels and representative of the divine pathway between Heaven and Earth. The biblical character Jacob, with whom she is associated, settled in Egypt, welcomed by Pharaoh because of the deeds of his son Joseph. Jacob spent the rest of his life in Goshen, in the delta of the Nile (Genesis, Chapters 25–49). Mary Jacob was of the tribe of Joseph, and her Egyptian link was a legacy from him.[2]

Her most recent incarnation was as Mary Jacobi, the American physician, born in London on 31 August 1842, in the sign of Virgo. She became the first female student of the New York College of Pharmacy, and, maintaining her French connection, of the École de Médecine in Paris. On her return to New York, she became a practising physician, a lecturer on therapeutics and professor of children's diseases at the Medical College for Women. She died on 10 June 1906. Her life and letters, edited by Ruth Putnam, appeared in 1925. She will come again in this century or the next, to lead a medical and philosophical revolution in the approach to the treatment of illness both of the body and the mind, and of wider societal disorders. She will work with Mary the mother of Jesus, with Tamar, her granddaughter when she was the biblical Mary Jacob, and especially with Mary Magdalene herself, to spearhead a revolution in medical care and in education, carrying a torch dedicated to enabling the power which is the Sacred Feminine to arise and set the world alight with a new inspiration. As when she was born as Mary Jacobi in the nineteenth century, her great themes will be the emancipation of the Feminine Principle and the nurture of children, the creators of the future.

NOTES

1 We received an insight into an occurrence of global significance which bears a relevance to the three 'Marys of the Sea'. On 26 December 2004, the world witnessed the terrible devastation and loss of life caused by the series of tsunamis which deluged parts of Asia. (We might think of this earth-shattering cataclysm building to a climax throughout Christmas Day, Mary Magdalene's birthday.) Although the human misery following this event can only be described as horrific, we believe that the eventual outcome for humanity will be very different.

Our sources revealed that the heart-rending sacrifice of so many lives was not a meaningless act of genocide by the elements, nor was it, as certain factions have understandably been led to suspect, man-made. We were given to understand that some artefacts or documents or some new revelations concerning our true origins as spiritual beings have been dislodged from their hidden and inaccessible resting place, and, once discovered, will help us to understand from both a scientific and a spiritual point of view that we are not a random manifestation of the laws of matter, but rather that we bear an inner essence and purpose far beyond the limitations of physicality and that our source is divine. When this knowledge is discovered, the oppressive bonds and dictates of materiality and material science will begin to fall away, and the true light of the spirit will dawn over our dark and turbulent world.

It was the eighth wave, the eighth tsunami, which brought about this momentous re-emergence. It is a gift from the sea, a gift from the three 'Marys of the Sea', to struggling and benighted humanity. It seems that the 'gift' will be discovered before 2007 (although not necessarily immediately made public) and its revelations will have global impact. As we begin the study of Mary's gospel, the number eight will be revealed as deeply sacred, the seven-and-one and the four-four rhythm which is the eternal flow of life. As will be disclosed, this number is deeply associated (as is Mary Magdalene) with the pyramids.

Before the knowledge divulged by those objects or conditions unearthed by the eighth tsunami can be given to humankind, a worldwide heart-opening had to occur. If this had not taken place, our closed heart-consciousness would again have failed to embrace the light of truth – and then what ensued would have been irredeemably catastrophic.

Those who gave their lives, either through death or ruination, have made the ultimate sacrifice so that humanity might be properly prepared to receive the priceless gift which is coming to us. When it does come, may our heart-response be a fitting memorial to them.

The Mayans spoke of three heart-opening events or sacrifices which would occur in the years preceding 2012, the date when their calendar begins and ends (it runs backwards from 2012). We believe that these three events are to be marked by their symbolical associations. We see now that the world has been thrown into united empathy three times – when Princess Diana was killed (the symbol of royalty beginning to turn to its true design and purpose and more closely embracing its people (*see* Chapter Twelve concerning the significance of the name 'Diana')); when the Twin Towers were destroyed (*see* Preface on the symbolism of the tower and Chapter Fourteen on the significance of twins), and when the tsunamis struck (the symbolism of the virgin birth (Christmas) and the three 'Marys of the Sea'). Ponderably, these three events have taken place within the span of eight years.

2 Jacob and his wives Rachel and Leah were the patriarch and the matriarchs of the bloodline which produced Jesus, Mary and their daughter Tamar. After the incident of his dream of the ladder of angels, Jacob was sent by God to build an altar at Bethel, the place of his dream. There he was told that his new name was Israel, and that '*a nation and a company of nations shall be of thee, and kings shall come out of thy loins*'. He was also promised the land that God had given to Abraham and Isaac (his grandfather and father), not only for himself, but for his 'seed', which he was told would blow over the Earth like dust, taking root everywhere.

Prior to going to Bethel, Jacob says to his household and all that are with him, '*Put away your strange gods*'. He subsequently buries the images of these 'strange gods', and the earrings of his people, under an oak tree. Are these people the earliest gypsies, with their vivid cosmology and their prominent earrings? Mary Jacob and Tamar's later association with them suggests that this is a possibility.

Three prominent Tamars come from Jacob's line. The first is the daughter-in-law of Judah, Jacob's son. Initially she was married to Er, Judah's first son. Er died, slain because he was '*wicked in the eyes of the Lord*', so Judah married her to his second son, Onan. Here the story becomes strange. Judah orders Onan to '*marry Tamar, and raise up seed to thy brother*', which presumably means that Onan himself would not inherit, but that his sons would, as if they were Er's sons. Onan, not liking this idea, withholds conception from Tamar, using the withdrawal method of contraception and '*spilling his seed on the ground, lest that he should give seed to his brother*' (Genesis, 38:9). His doing so '*displeases the Lord,*' who then slays Onan as well. Judah's third son, Shelah, is too young to marry, so Judah sends Tamar back to her father's house, promising to marry Shelah to her as soon as he is old enough, but clearly afraid that Tamar is somehow attracting death to his sons.

When, some years later, Tamar realizes that Judah has no intention of uniting her with Shelah, she disguises herself as a prostitute and sits on the roadway where she knows Judah will pass. He does so, and demands her services, promising her a kid in return for them. Tamar asks him for his staff, his ring and his bracelets as a pledge until he sends her the kid, to which Judah agrees. But when he sends his friend to her with the payment of the kid, she is nowhere to be found. Judah makes enquiries, but no-one in the vicinity has seen her or heard word of this mysterious 'harlot'.

Three months later, Judah is informed that Tamar has 'played the harlot', because she is pregnant. Judah demands that she be brought forth and burned, at which point Tamar comes to him and shows him his staff, ring and bracelets, telling him that she is with child by him. Judah agrees that he has wronged her by refusing to marry her to Shelah, and the matter is closed. When Tamar gives birth, she produces twins, one of which seems to declare itself as the first-born by stretching its arm out of her vagina, upon which the midwife binds the baby's wrist with red thread. But his twin brother then precedes him out of the womb, seeming to suggest that the child with the red thread (which is highly symbolic) is the one chosen to continue the bloodline, but that he must forego his rightful material inheritance to do so, perhaps choosing instead the spiritual inheritance of self-sacrifice and devotion to higher principles despised by the world, as did Jesus, Mary and Tamar.

The three men who became the first Tamar's sexual partners, Er, Onan and Judah, seem to be particularly unappealing types, the first two being 'men of wickedness', whilst Judah himself is the son of Jacob who sold Joseph his brother (of the coat of many colours) into slavery and who could not wait to avail himself of the services of the first prostitute he saw on the road to Timnath, afterwards wanting to burn his daughter-in-law because she herself had taken a partner outside marriage.

Tamar was clearly undeterrable in her determination to become pregnant via the line of Jacob, and we suggest that this was because she was a prophetess with knowledge of the future and her particular role in procuring that future. She saw that her namesake had to be born from this line, the sacred 'red thread', almost 2,000 years ahead of her own time, and she got on with the job of facilitating the circumstances her prophetic vision demanded, however unpleasant the undertaking.

The second Tamar appears in the Book of Samuel, Chapter 13. Absalom, son of King David, has 'a fair sister' called Tamar. Amnon, also the son of King David but by a different mother, becomes enamoured of Tamar and his passion assumes the dimensions of an obsession. He pretends to be very ill, and King David rushes to his side. Amnon tells him that if Tamar came to him with meat which she should dress and offer to him with her own hands, he might be able to eat it. King David therefore orders Tamar to his chamber, where Amnon rapes her. Having forced himself upon her, his obsessive passion then turns to repudiation, and he throws her brutally out of his room, distressing Tamar by this action as much as he did by raping her. This appalling treatment of his sister turned Absalom against King David (whom he partially blamed for the incident) and led directly to his famous uprising against his father. Again, this second Tamar has to endure distress and humiliation in order to procure, not the continuation of the bloodline but a continuity concerning that which was its inheritance and its grave responsibility; as a direct result of her rape, a complex set of circumstances arose which led to the restoration of the Ark of the Covenant to the Israelites. Suddi claimed that those in possession of this mystical artefact would be enabled to dominate the world once they had gained understanding of its secret potential. The Ark of the Covenant was returned to the guardianship of the Essenes, whose sacred task it was to prevent the abuse of its power.

The third Tamar, the daughter of Jesus and Mary Magdalene, was the culmination of the bloodline. Together with her mother and father, she was the reason it was initiated. She was the Holy Grail, and once she had touched down on Earth through her holy parents, the bloodline was no longer necessary and passed away with her. She died without issue at the age of 23, but the precious seed had been sown, and the purpose of the bloodline fulfilled. Of course, it is understood that the Holy Grail bears a divine significance far beyond that of a single human individual, just as the Christ Light, mightier by far than the cosmos, could not have been entirely compressed into Jesus and Mary Magdalene. Nevertheless, they were its perfect expression, just as Tamar and her reincarnation (for she did come again to the Earth) was the perfect expression in her soul-being of the mystery of the Holy Grail.

There is much discussion of the bloodline today. It must still exist, of course, because Jesus and Mary had many relatives. However, our position is clear-cut on this issue: the bloodline did not descend any further than Tamar via Jesus and Mary Magdalene. The significance of the bloodline today is simply a worldly issue concerning the rightful heir to the British throne and has no relevance to mystical issues, although it can sometimes be utilized in order that an advanced soul might descend or move very close to the earthly planes in order to give service to humanity.

CHAPTER ELEVEN

Mary, the Mother of Jesus

*M*ary, the mother of Jesus, like the other two Marys, shared a deep soul-kinship with Jesus (and of course with Mary Magdalene). Throughout the gospels, Jesus and his mother seem to clash on occasion, Mary offering reproach and Jesus seeming to respond with a certain measure of exasperation. In fact, nothing could be further from the truth.

Mother and son worked throughout Jesus's life to bring the divine teachings to the people, not only of their own time but also to those born throughout the next two millennia and beyond. She gave him opportunities to provide instruction on following the principle of deeper obedience – as when she went in search of her young son and found him discussing eternal verities with the rabbis in the Temple – and on the principle of universal brotherhood – as on the occasion when he declared that the whole of humanity were to him as his mother and father, brothers and sisters. Mary also facilitated his power to perform miracles, just as the presence of Mary Jacob seems to have enhanced his ability to heal the sick and the disabled, and just as Mary Magdalene was summoned secretly to be with Jesus when he raised her brother Lazarus from the dead.

The spiritual master White Eagle's words on the subject of mother Mary's assistance in the miracle at Cana make intriguing reading:

> *At the wedding feast at Cana his mother called to Jesus, saying, They have no wine, and Jesus answered, apparently rather sharply, Woman, what have I to do with thee?*
>
> *We suggest that these words are a mistranslation.*
>
> *What we think was meant was, 'Woman (my companion, my sister), let us share what we have; what is mine is thine too, therefore we share it. Bring me the jars containing the water, we will share what we have.'*

What they had in common was the spirit of Christ. And so, from the universal or cosmic consciousness this divine fire, this divine essence, the wine of life itself passed through the Master to the souls of others present. Through the Christ Spirit, the water (or the soul) is changed into the wine, it is infused with the divine fire of eternal life, the Christ life. This is what the mediaeval mystics called the mystical marriage.

WHITE EAGLE, *THE LIVING WORD OF SAINT JOHN*, P16

It seems that White Eagle's point about mistranslation must be correct, because in the text of John's gospel (2:3–5) Mary's response to her son's supposedly dismissive words seems strange:

And when they wanted wine, the mother of Jesus saith unto him, They have no wine. Jesus saith unto her, Woman, what have I to do with thee? mine hour is not yet come.

His mother saith unto the servants, Whatsoever he saith unto you, do it.

It is evident from her instruction to the servants that something very different from a rebuke is passing between mother and son.

Mary's pattern of incarnation in the physical life, as far as we have been allowed to perceive it, shows a pure and devoted soul who dedicated herself to continuous work on the inner planes of life, often dwelling apart from the hurly-burly of the common life-stream to work in the temples, or to withdraw into secret sisterhoods and mystery schools dedicated to the ideal of service to humanity. Before she gave birth to Jesus, she spent some years as a devotee in attendance at the Temple of the Virgin, the corn goddess of the constellation Virgo whose identity is Isis, thereby pledging her service to the greater soul of Mary Magdalene.

The concept of the 'virgin' is an important one. It relates to Mary Magdalene's teaching on the chakras in that when the heart is attuned to the Divine (whose link with each human being dwells within the heart), then the light of the spirit becomes our inner sun which illumines the chakras equally and simultaneously. Each chakra is balanced, activated and dedicated to the light so that the 'roses' come into bloom in consummate purity and power on their 'tree' or 'stem' – that rod of light which is our spine.

When this occurs, the soul is safe and secure, sealed within that radiant divine energy, virginal and inviolable. We might understand 'virgin' to mean a soul who cannot be penetrated by the marauding forces of adversarial darkness which constantly circulate the individual, seeking an entry point as she or he progresses through their earthly incarnation – an individual who remains inviolate in their soul, sealed off from the darkness, no matter what life does to them. Such a soul was Mary the mother of Jesus, as was Mary Magdalene and, significantly, Mary Jacob, even though she was seduced by Matthew Syro. The term 'virgin', properly used, does not relate to sexual behaviour any more than it relates to any other aspect of behaviour. It simply means that a person's choices will be made from the heart and that they will be acts of love, whatever the prevailing circumstances.

The idea of a 'virgin' is most often associated with femininity, but of course in the greater understanding of the word this bias does not apply. Jesus, in the Gnostic texts, referred to the Beloved Disciple as 'John the Virgin'. The title encompasses the recognition that a 'virgin' is a person who has so nurtured the light within themselves and others during the course of their incarnations in matter, in preference to merely selfish concerns, that their attunement to the light has become their nature or habit. This incorruptibility of soul provides a permanent residence or perfect raiment (a 'habit') for the Spirit.

Throughout her great multiplicity of lives, Mary the Virgin was always deeply in touch with our angelic brethren, the 'sons of the flame', and it was perfectly natural to her to be visited by an angelic presence, as she was by the archangel Gabriel, and for Mary to say to her (for we think Gabriel's essence is more feminine than masculine, even though angels strike a balance between the genders), 'Behold the handmaid of the Lord.'

Suddi speaks of the virgin as being no more than a child, sixteen at most, enfolded in a radiant aura of calm and beauty beyond her years when she arrived at Qumran with Joseph and her baby son prior to their flight to Egypt. During her life as the serene and radiant Mary, she pursued a simple and direct spiritual path, supported and protected by Joseph and their mutual bond of love. Its depth and beauty had developed over the course of many lives spent in devotion to one another.

In the early years of her marriage, after the birth of Jesus, Mary gathered around her a group of women of similarly exalted spirituality and began to teach what she knew. Just as Jesus's followers met with him in subterranean chambers, hidden rooms and camouflaged caves (many of them around the shores of the Lake of Galilee, on its wilder reaches, where the mountains descended to its margins), so Mary's sisterhood met in secret, speaking in hushed voices, secure from spying eyes and suspicious minds. She taught them of the Holy Spirit, and how it was breathed forth from the fathomless heart of Goddess. They learned how to summon angels, how to journey inwardly with them, and how to express the Goddess magic and power in simple, humble things: sewing their clothes, washing their laundry, baking their bread, nursing their children and telling stories to them made out of the stuff of their dreams and their spiritual adventures, sweeping their little houses and adorning them with the beauties of nature, until their small dwellings became veritable powerhouses of Goddess-consciousness, where every rustic feature was a deeply potent symbol of the immeasurable glory and presence of the beloved Goddess.

Surrounded and borne aloft on the wings of this invisible, all-encompassing and most holy dove of the Spirit, created by the interaction of angels and his mother's sisterhood, the little boy Jesus absorbed the sacred and inspired material that he would later weave into parables, using homely and natural objects as symbols of ineffable truth and spiritual realization. Mary Jacob and her daughters, particularly Mary Magdalene, were of course also part of this group, bringing to it the gifts of their own essence and measureless spiritual perspective.

CHAPTER TWELVE

Mary, the Light-Bringer

*W*hat of Mary Magdalene herself? – she who was said to mirror Isis, Venus and, later, the oldest and greatest goddess of them all, Brigid the White, Brigid the Radiant, worshipped in Europe and the isles of Britain since time immemorial, even before the raising of the pyramids and the first whisper of Isis had reached the hearts of the people who were to become the ancient Egyptians. It is indeed time to 'mount to the infinite on the ladder of the impossible', because now we must consider certain shining truths which normally do not come within the sphere of most people's perception of reality. We must consider the origins of Mary and the grand panoramic scope of her service to humanity.

Of the three Marys, we are given to believe that Mary Magdalene is by far the oldest and most advanced soul. Our understanding arises not from any claims made by her (none of those souls with whom we are in spiritual contact make any claims for themselves), but from the teaching of Tamar, the eminent spiritual being who serves Mary as a channel between Heaven and Earth, and from our own intuitions.

We appreciate that those who have considered the Virgin Mary as the most sublime of the women who were connected with Jesus in the biblical narrative will feel a sense of disorientation concerning the idea expressed above, but by no means does the intuition we have received constitute any disparagement of the virgin. She is the beautiful mirror that reflects the essence of Divine Mother, the Godhead herself, which of course cannot be circumscribed and entirely contained within the infinitesimal sphere of a human woman.

We are told by White Eagle that Jesus of Nazareth was not of this Earth. He had fully evolved as an individualized spark of Divine Spirit, clothed in a soul and all its bodies, before life began on the Earth planet. He underwent many exalted experiences in preparation for his great mission, which was to bring the light of the Christ, the first-born son-daughter of Mother-Father God – an ineffable and immeasurable Being of Light beyond the grasp of earthly understanding – to the Adâma, the peoples of the Earth. Mary was the feminine expression of the soul whose masculine expression was Jesus. Together, they were to form an unadulterated vessel for the palpitating light of the Christ to flood the soul-planes of the planet and thus to be earthed – not only in the hearts and consciousness of Earth dwellers but also in the very stones and soil of Mother Earth herself. We can safely assume that Mary was far older than the Earth, as was Jesus; and that, like Jesus, she underwent experiences of supreme spiritual elevation in her training to be of ultimate service to the peoples of Earth.

Mary, in her dedication to, and absorption into, the Sacred Feminine, was deeply aware of the mystical sisterhood between Venus, the Moon and the Earth, and her soul-resonances are an exquisite symphony uniting all three spheres. Her number is nine (it even occurs in the word 'feminine'), the ultimate expression of three, although she is also linked with the mysterious number eight. This number is an expression of how the Earth-plane is harmoniously connected to the seven great rays of creation – the one resonating in bliss with the seven; it is also the number of perfection, the sacred balance (4-4) which squares the circle (*see* Appendix One). The number eight is thus a perfect expression of Mary's role – her great undertaking. It incorporates the task of teaching and inspiring the people of the Earth-plane to find and keep the sacred point of balance between the physical and the spiritual realms of consciousness.

When we are helped to discover this fine point of balance which dwells in the heart, we will learn that light and darkness are two complementary forces, creating all goodness and perfection in 'beautiful order' (the literal translation of 'cosmos'). It is only when we are ignorant of the true relationship between the two and so fail to consciously maintain the balance via our own spiritual effort that disharmony is created. From this disharmony arises the emanation of evil, and consequently all the woes that flesh and soul are heir to.

The seer David Wright tells us that Mary Magdalene *was* the goddess Isis; that she influenced the Mesopotamian culture, becoming the goddess Ishtar; that she was the shining soul worshipped as many Moon-goddesses, and that eventually she entered the ethereal atmosphere of ancient Greece, becoming Diana, goddess of the waxing Moon and huntress of souls. She it was who inspired us to build our great temples in veneration not only of the Sun, but also of the Moon. Henges and cairns such as Stonehenge and Avebury in England and Newgrange in Ireland, were constructed to capture the light of the Moon as well as the Sun, and the rays of the setting Moon at the winter solstice were considered by the ancients to be as holy as the rays of the rising Sun at the birth of the summer solstice. The mystery of the great darkness that the solstice Moon celebrated was not associated with evil or blindness, but with that which was hidden and secret, obscured from our everyday selves by a veil of sublime sanctity. The Moon's path was the path of gnosis, knowledge of the divine. As Ishtar, as Astarte, as Diana, Mary led our souls along this starlit way, following the silver seasons of the Moon.

What can this mean? How can a human soul such as Mary Magdalene also be Isis, Ishtar, Diana?[1] Firstly, it is necessary to remember that Mary is a highly evolved soul, and one who is also unconscionably ancient. Moreover, she showed an extraordinary degree of devotion to Goddess from her earliest beginnings as an individualized spark of consciousness. Although she trod the adventurous path of human evolution, her spiritual and physical environment was that of a humanity far more advanced, beautiful and mightier than that which exists on Earth. Her journeys were many and often epic in proportion, but her deeper self never left the heart of Divine Mother.

This strength of resolution, of absolute refusal, no matter how strong the temptation and the confusion became, to be displaced from her true home within the Mother's Heart, infused Mary with an exquisite Goddess-consciousness which stood stalwart and strong like a tower of truth at the centre of her innermost being. She was fully human (her gospel lays great stress on the realization of this state), and in that perfect ring of radiance she was able to contain and reflect in fullest measure the glory of the Goddess. She descended to Earth many, many times to bring to the poor dull awareness of Earth's humanity a greater perception and a clearer understanding of the loveliness and the sanctity of the realms of Goddess, the meaning of the Sacred Feminine.

It is important to understand that she rarely incarnated into the outermost, grossest domain of flesh. Usually she would descend to the soul dimension only, the higher etheric, for there are many levels, many dimensions to our Mother Earth. From this higher dimension she would instruct, guide and inspire, and reveal to us the boundless beauty of the Goddess mysteries. There were earthly incarnations in the realm of flesh, but these, like those of Mother Mary, were conducted within the mystical inner life of a temple or a sisterhood as a high priestess of gifted and magical standing. She did not require these incarnations for her own soul's evolutionary development. She was already at a point of evolution much more exalted than any the Earth's lessons could bestow, having attained her transcendence upon worlds far loftier in spiritual stature than the Earth. She came back simply to help us, as an act of love.

It is important to realize, as well, the huge sacrifice it entailed for Mary to be born to Earth in a body of flesh. The vibrational rate of the Earth must have been almost unbearably dense and constricting to advanced, god-like souls such as Jesus and Mary Magdalene. Only their complete mastership, performed in a spirit of continuous self-sacrifice, continuous self-giving, which is both the spirit of love and a supremely conscious, cosmic act of healing, made their incarnation possible.

Legend, fairytale and mystery teachings tell us that, when the Earth was first formed and made ready as a receptacle for the human strain of divine life (for, make no mistake, humanity is divine), god-men and goddess-women came – in company with a vast assembly of angels from Venus, whose task it is to build beauty and perfection into ever-evolving form – and created a great settlement, a wondrous and beautiful civilization, around the area of the North Pole. In those early times, the climate was temperate and gentle, and the country of these god-people became what has passed into mythology as the Garden of Eden.

Newly evolving humanity was at first responsive to their example and their tutelage, and great continents arose out of the sea which were peopled with those who were yoked to the realization of the eternal mysteries of the spirit. Eventually, temptation came in the form of power and greed, and these mighty and regal civilizations fell into darkness. A global cataclysm took place, during which many landmasses rose and sank. Previously perfectly aligned with the North Star, the planet now underwent a disorientation, and the 'polar wobble' came into being. Afterwards, humanity found itself banished to the densest, outermost reaches of matter. Evolution travelled 'backwards' for a time, and then again began its forward march, although haltingly and painfully, overcoming its retardation with much difficulty and struggle.[2] Gradually, what we know of the processes of evolution of the planet and ourselves came into being, and what we perceive as pre-history and history began.

At the outset of earthly humanity's deviation from the spiritual plan, the god-people of Eden built a great wall around their country (constructed from other than physical material) to protect itself from the unbearable encroachment of humanity's brutalized and chaotic state of consciousness. But, as conditions worsened, they left the North Pole area and resettled in the Himalayas, at a level far above that of the physical and the etheric. A swathe of purest snow creates the necessary boundary between our civilization and theirs, for they cannot tolerate our current vibrational essence.

There they remain, god-men and goddess-women still, known more commonly as the masters, their purpose to be of service and to instruct those of us who will listen in the stillness of our hearts to their spiritual counsel. Their quest is to help us at last to bring ourselves and our planet out of our self-created darkness, destruction and suffering into the all-suffusing light of the Godhead.

It seems that Mary and Jesus were of these godlike people, yet entrusted with a special mission, a deeper and greater task than any before or after it, as a gift of their fathomless hearts to suffering humankind. This gift was a baptism of light from the Christ Being, which would be given in greater measure than had ever been made possible before. The impact and the magnitude of what they gave we have not yet even begun to grasp. The realization of this is for the future.

And so, having lifted our hearts time and time again to the highest pinnacle of our capacity in perceiving the glory of Goddess throughout the ages, this beloved soul came at last into incarnation as Mary Magdalene, entering into humble circumstances alongside her adored Yeshua, and enduring, like him, the taunts, indignities and humiliations imposed on them by those who did not understand. And, although Mary Magdalene was not crucified on the cross, she was indeed crucified by the imposition of a mentality, a soul dysfunction, that stretched across the centuries and made of her an outcast and an embodiment of human weakness and degradation. She, whom we should most have honoured and revered, we called a whore!

What of Mary's lineage, the whispered rumours of her coming in flesh and blood? Laurence Gardner gives us an inkling of it when he writes in his book, *Realm of the Ring Lords*, concerning the mighty Annunaki Overlords of the Sumerian civilization, citing pointers and evidence that these royal beings, who initiated the practice of electing a priest-king or priestess-queen to inspire, protect and govern communities, and introduced the concept of a 'throne', were in fact of non-earthly or extra-terrestrial origin. They were human beings, yet elevated through spiritual evolution to god-status. They were god-people.

Their teachings on royalty did not conceive of it as we understand it today. It did not breed privilege and a class system, but was instead a practice designed for those of the royal or priestly bloodline to be of ultimate service to their communities, seated in the 'holy place' (the throne), whereby they could receive a direct line of spiritual communication from higher spheres which would infuse them with the necessary discernment, discipline, compassion and courage to govern with kindly justice and to protect their people with bravery and self-abnegation at the combined levels of body, mind and soul.

Two of the priest-kings known to have succeeded in their mission were Solomon and King Arthur. From the legends surrounding them, we can glean that they did indeed protect their peoples at the soul-level as well as that of the outer sphere – hence the apparently fantastic myths concerning their years of service which were handed down to future generations. Interestingly, both of these kingly guardians fell into chaos at the end of their reign, because both entered confusion regarding the Sacred Feminine Principle. Perhaps the only priest-king and priestess-queen who conducted their mission flawlessly, achieving the highest ideals of royalty as laid down by the Overlords, or the god-people who first came to this planet, were Jesus and Mary Magdalene. Both were born of the holy bloodline, (the divine bloodline that baptized and initiated priests or wise ones into service to their people), both were born into humble circumstances, and neither claimed anything for themselves throughout their mission.

Service and sacrifice (the true meaning of royalty) were their keywords, and they created the first circle of knights – the Night-Protectors – from whom eventually emerged the Knights of the Round Table. The Night-Protectors had stood guard before, to protect ancient knowledge and persons associated with it, but their service to Jesus and Mary comprised their first mission to a king and a queen where they stood in full awareness of the profound spiritual reality of their task.

Intriguingly, another theory for which there is evidence cites that these first mighty ones of Earth (the god-people) came from the 'high places', not the skies but the upper northern regions of the planet. Again, this falls in line with the teaching that the god-people first settled in a continent surrounding the North Pole.

We believe that Mary was, indeed, of these exalted human beings (for we ought not to think that humanity exists only on the Earth), and that she has dedicated herself to the service of Earth's humanity in an extraordinary and exceptional way from the very beginning of our sojourn on Earth. Calling ever to our indwelling spirit, and coming to us, sometimes on the refined soul-planes of existence and sometimes incarnating into a physical body, she is here to help us transcend the shackles of materiality. Mary teaches us to enter into the heart of things, to learn the sacred power of adaptability, like the flowing of water, so that we may enter into heart-communion with our environment and become powerful sources of light. We learn to achieve these powers through co-operation, never through domination of others or tyranny over the natural world. She is of the soft might of water, gentle, caressing – and yet water can wear away iron and stone, and sometimes, in a great wave, it can clear all obstruction out of its path. Those who have seen Mary Magdalene in visions tell us that she is profoundly beautiful, very gentle, and yet within her there is a core of steel, an invincible strength of spirit that never fails to serve the light, however arduous the task.

We reiterate that Mary teaches us the point of balance between the physical and the spiritual consciousness. This point of balance dwells within the human heart. It is where the forces of darkness and light meet, and until we understand how to maintain this essential balance, we will struggle in darkness. It is gently to unloose our constricting bonds that she comes to us now, Mary the Magdalene, Mary the Compassionate, Mary the Light-Bringer, of a depth and sweetness of heart beyond our comprehension, bearing the pure white jar, the alabastron, the jar of light with which she will baptize us. The woman with the white jar – the perfect and mystical image of she who ushers in the new age – the Age of Aquarius.

NOTES

1 Mary Magdalene has a direct link in her deeper being with the Arabian Goddess of Eight, the supreme female deity. Her pyramidal group consists of Al-Lat, Al-'Uzza and Manat, 'the three daughters of God' in Meccan tradition. Al-'Uzza was worshipped in the form of a black stone. Black stones were also sacred objects to the Celts, seen as doorways into the goddess worlds of fairy and angelic beings, and are still considered lucky and magical in Britain and Ireland.

The Al-'Uzza black stone was taken into the care of Mohammad and enshrined in the

Ka'aba, originally a Goddess shrine, where it is profoundly revered by Muslims today. Followers of the primordial religions would have recognized the association of the black stone, the sacred site and the triple Goddess, for the theme is repeated in numerous instances throughout the pagan world. 'Allah' means 'Being and Nothingness', the union of the two concepts of God (Nothingness) and Goddess (Being). Muslim Gnostics speak of Allah (Being and Nothingness) as 'black light' or 'the luminous night', the shining darkness through which the Godhead manifests. The black stone of Al-'Uzza has a crystalline, mirror-like surface, which gives forth this shining darkness (*see* Chapter Nine).

In the Koran, Mohammad stated specifically in several verses that Goddess was to be venerated in equal measure with God. A council of clerics decided that in fact, although Mohammad was spot on in every other word he wrote, these particular verses were clearly where he had been beguiled by Satan into advocating equality between God and Goddess and men and women. They were called the 'Satanic Verses' and were removed. This denial of Mohammad's vision and truth dispossessed Al-'Uzza of her divine authority and status. Mary Magdalene *was* Al-'Uzza and the Goddess of Eight (meaning that hers was the magnificent soul who mirrored the reflection of Divine Mother from the soul-spheres as a service to the consciousness of Earth's humanity); and the dispossession of Al-'Uzza coincided historically with the dispossession of Mary Magdalene and the obliteration of her Church of the True Light in Europe.

2 Evolution being a God-force cannot really travel backwards; nevertheless, the karma the human race inflicted on itself at this time caused it to retrace its steps, so that the forces of evolution seemed to undergo a period of retardation.

CHAPTER THIRTEEN

Joseph of Arimathea

*B*efore we continue with our exploration of the story of Jesus and Mary, we would like to consider, briefly, one of its largely unsung heroes – Joseph of Arimathea. It is difficult to grasp the full scale of the importance of this truly great man and his service to the Christ-mission. Little is known of him except that he was a tin merchant, one of the richest men in the world at the time, and consequently someone whom the Romans could neither ignore nor intimidate. The Romans needed tin because it was a component of the bronze which symbolized their nationhood, and which supplied armour, chariots and other items to their vast conquering armies. Tin was always in short supply, and in the time of Jesus only one country was able to provide it in the quantities demanded by Rome. The tin mines of Britain furnished Joseph of Arimathea's merchant fleets with a plentiful cargo of tin bound for Rome, and Joseph knew of its whereabouts – the kingdom of Cornwall in the country of Britain, where he had kinsmen and a religious affiliation with the Druids.

Joseph of Arimathea shared a deep kinship of soul as well as blood with his nephew, and took him on numerous voyages around the world, where the young Jesus shared enlightenment with the chief priests and priestesses, the holy men and women, of all the great religious traditions and mystery schools upon the globe. Although he was a highly successful merchant, Joseph understood that his role as a businessman was really granted to him to facilitate the spiritual education, the quickening and development, of Jesus his nephew. It is said that Jesus visited Cornwall many times as a boy with his uncle, sometimes also accompanied by his mother and even, perhaps, on occasion, Mary Jacob and Mary Magdalene. Cornish folk-history testifies in abundance to these visits, and a multiplicity of ancient landmarks and street names bearing Hebrew titles add the weight of their testimony to this tradition.

Later, during Jesus's mission, we believe that again and again Joseph of Arimathea protected his nephew from the authorities, using his influence whenever and wherever he could, simply to keep his nephew from detention, if not death. Throughout his three-year mission, Jesus and his disciples had to, as it were, keep one step ahead of the 'police', the authorities and the establishment of both Rome and Judea that wished, as authority and establishment always do, to fiercely maintain the status quo and immediately quash any revolutionary and unsettling ideas which might threaten their survival.

Legend tells us that Joseph kept two cruets used at the Crucifixion, one to represent Jesus and one to represent Mary, for he, amongst a few others, knew that Mary was the feminine Christ, the Bride of the Spirit. As Mary caught the blood and the water that poured from the wound of the crucified Jesus in the chalice which afterwards became associated with the Holy Grail, so Joseph caught the blood in one cruet (symbolizing Jesus) and the water in the other (symbolizing Mary). He took the chalice and both cruets with him to Glastonbury (see Appendix One). The cruets were buried with his relics, and afterwards they became mystically linked with the white and the red streams of water that run from the hill today, and the white and the red dragons that were associated with the time of King Arthur, manifesting so strangely at his birth.

This collecting of the issue from Jesus's wound sounds grisly, but in fact there was a deeply magical and beautiful purpose interweaving through the enactment of the rite. Using the receptacles as they did to catch the blood and water issuing from the wound of Jesus caused by the 'blade', the spear of Longinus,[1] they put in its rightful place the crucial symbol of the Sacred Feminine. Afterwards, Joseph caused them to be borne to Britain. In doing so, this mighty soul, Joseph of Arimathea, who embraced the significance of Mary Magdalene and who was – as our sources inform us – destined to be born again as King Arthur,[2] gave us the beautiful truth of the Holy Grail in its mundane and literal form, so that we might keep it in our focus and come to understand the perfect flowering of its deeper symbolism, the fruit of which we are ready to garner today. Joseph it was who arranged Jesus's burial and who took his family and followers to safety after the Crucifixion, overseeing the work of planting those seeds that later became global Christianity, which, in spite of the misdeeds, outright atrocities, power-seeking and blindness of its own establishment and authority (which Jesus earnestly warned against – a warning sounded in Mary's gospel, as we shall see) kept the torch of the true light, the light of the Christ Consciousness within the heart, steadfastly alive.

NOTES

1 Chrétien de Troyes, a French writer of the twelfth century, first wrote an account of the Grail, naming Joseph of Arimathea as the original bearer of the Grail cup. Although the concept of the Grail precedes the time of Jesus, it has been confirmed to us that Joseph did bring such a cup to Britain (Mary Magdalene's cup), the communion cup of the Last Supper and supreme symbol of the Holy Grail (whose mystery extends beyond a physical object or a human individual). Chrétien's account has been dismissed as fiction. Nevertheless, we believe he hit upon the truth, either by virtue of the intuition pertaining to his art, or because he echoed an

earlier account stemming from the first century, which also states that Joseph brought two cruets with him to Glastonbury, one containing the water from the wound of Jesus as he died on the cross, and the other containing the blood. Many historical documents also cite the tradition of the two cruets as a reality.

2 It was further revealed to us that both Moses (whose name was the Aramaic form of Osiris) and Osiris himself, comprised the spiritual dynamic clothed in the human form of Joseph of Arimathea. After having been given this information, we discovered that an ancient term of reference to Osiris was 'the once and future king' (Graham Hancock, *Fingerprints Of The Gods*). (*See* Chapter Twenty of the present volume).

CHAPTER FOURTEEN

The John Mystery

*T*he heretical sects centred in medieval France whose inner circles kept alive the truth concerning Mary Magdalene also shared heterodox ideas concerning John – both John the Beloved, disciple of Jesus, and John the Baptist, Jesus's cousin, who prepared the way for Jesus's mission in the years before it began its brief three-year span.

The Gospel of John gives very clear and decided instruction on how we are to view John the Baptist:

> *There was a man sent from God whose name was John. The*
> *same came for a witness, to bear witness of the Light, that all*
> *men through him might believe. He was not that Light, but was*
> *sent to bear witness of that Light. That was the true Light*
> *which lighteth every man that cometh into the world.*

JOHN, 1:6–10

A definite distinction is made between John and he who was to be the bearer of the Light, Jesus the Christ, as though the writer of the gospel believed that this insistence was part of its message.

John the Baptist was a compelling figure, spoken of as attired in skins and living alone in the desert, feeding only on honey and locusts. His hair wild, his eyes ablaze with fierce intensity, this Merlinesque figure lived a ferociously disciplined life of purity and simplicity. For centuries the prophetic voice of the Hebrew culture had been absent, and in John it spoke again after 400 years of silence. He was indeed the last of the great desert prophets. Nevertheless, he was careful to allude to himself as Jesus's witness, declaring himself unfit to unlatch the sandal-straps of the one who was to come, and proclaiming that he baptized with water (the power of the soul), whilst he who followed would baptize with fire (the power of the spirit).

Considering his words, there does appear to be a certain ambiguity about them. They are the words of a prophet, and they seem to penetrate dimensions beyond the literalness of the immediate future. He refers, we think, not so much to Jesus as to the Christ Light within Jesus, which had descended to the soul-sphere of Jesus and Mary so that it might be given forth to the world as a gift of their devotion and self-sacrifice. But John also seems to speak of the future – a definite point in time within the foreseen scheme of human history.

John's words, 'The one who is to come', undoubtedly refer to the ministry of Jesus, and yet it is as if they also reach beyond the mundane limitations of one certain time and place, fixing the gaze of the prophet upon the far horizon of the distant future.

'I am a voice crying in the wilderness,' said John, indicating the sere wilderness of the material world through which the cry of the soul seeks to penetrate, commanding its chained and distracted awareness to take heed and expand into full consciousness of the indwelling spirit. John was Jesus's herald, and he proclaimed with an urgency and a solemnity, even with a heartfelt drama, which seems to indicate that he felt he and his teachings were part of the vanguard of the momentous transformation that was to come. John had his own followers, and they were many in number, for thousands were stirred by the evocative image and words of this man, and came to be baptized by him in the waters of the holy river Jordan, and in the waters of the Sea of Galilee. To some he was known as 'John of the Waters', a title which would later be extended to Mary Magdalene, and indeed to the three Marys. He, like Jesus, was a Nazorean, or a 'wisdom keeper', having studied with the 'wise ones', the Essenes (who derived from an Indo-European community, ancient of race, which originated in the regions of the North Pole when they were inhabitable, and which extended to the far East and the far West of the world) and having been sent out on his mission with their blessing.

Indeed, it seems likely that Mary Jacob was a 'Nazorean'. She too had been educated by the Essenes, and was a wisdom keeper in her own right, as in later years (and in later lives) she became a 'wisewoman'. The words 'Nazarene' and 'Nazorean' are easily confused and, in fact, we suggest that both words bear the same meaning (wisdom keeper). 'Nazarene' is considered to mean 'of Nazareth', but it is most unlikely that anyone hailing from Nazareth in Jesus's day would have been given a corresponding title, as Suddi describes it as tiny and almost 'nothing', virtually a hamlet in the middle of nowhere, without any Roman garrison nearby. In fact, it did not grow in size or appear on maps of the time until some years after the death of Jesus.

This point has led some scholars and writers to believe, understandably, that Nazareth did not yet exist when Jesus was alive, and that its presence in the New Testament as the stated dwelling place of Jesus, before he began his mission, is due to gross error on the part of its authors. We believe that Nazareth did indeed exist in the time of Jesus, not only because of Suddi's reference to it, but also because it is mentioned in The Gospel of St John, which we believe was written by John himself, the cousin of Jesus:

> *Philip findeth Nathanael, and saith unto him, We have found*
> *him, of whom Moses in the law, and the prophets, did write,*
> *Jesus of Nazareth, the son of Joseph.*
>
> *And Nathanael said unto him, Can there any good thing come*
> *out of Nazareth? Philip saith unto him, Come and see.*

JOHN, 1:45–47

White Eagle confirms that John the Beloved Disciple himself wrote all the John documents (The Gospel, Revelations, Acts and Letters). Grace Cooke spoke of receiving knowledge from the Sphere of John pertaining to the fact that John lived for over 100 years on Earth (actually in the region of 105 years) and, although there are reasons to believe that John's gospel was written later than the Synoptic gospels, the case for its being the first of the canon to be inscribed is equally convincing.

Suddi also mentions a saying, well known in the area during his lifetime: 'Nothing good can come out of Nazareth.' Obviously, this was the adage that Nathanael was referring to when Philip told him about Jesus of Nazareth. The reason for it was, it seems, that 'undesirables' had their hideouts out in Nazareth, precisely because it was tiny, nondescript and in the middle of nowhere. And it was Nazareth's inaccessibility and isolation, both social and geographical, which probably made it the perfect place for Jesus to spend his later boyhood years, and those immediately preceding his mission.

The danger to his life did not end with the death of Herod the Great. Not only did he continue to need protection from forces that sought to destroy him, with which he was furnished from certain Essene brethren who were forerunners of the 'Night-Protectors', but he also undertook many vital and deeply secret missions throughout the intervening years between his boyhood in Egypt and his ministry. It was important to ensure that no prying minds allied with hostile groups both occult and politico/religious began to work out what he was doing or where he was going. Nazareth provided him with an effective screen.

Suddi also describes teaching Jesus and John the Baptist together at Qumran (the boys were known to him then as BenJoseph and BenZachariah), and remarks on John's constitutional fieriness, and his vociferous arguments with Jesus when they disagreed upon some point of interpretation of spiritual law. According to Suddi, Jesus was always calm and meek, but John seemed to revel in heated dispute! He was certainly a force to be reckoned with, a spiritual dynamo. He represented the wise

81

and advanced soul, the initiate, who can educate, inspire and teach by example; but Jesus bore the Christ Light, alive and awake in him in full measure, which is a discovery we make within ourselves, coming to us as a revelation and a rebirth of consciousness.

When John the Baptist was imprisoned by Herod, a superficial reading of the events suggests that he became confused, as if his fate had curtailed his vision, for he sent word to Jesus, asking, 'Are you the one who is spoken of, or should we look for another?' Although his imprisonment might indeed have temporarily obscured his inner sight, we feel this question has a profound inner meaning, because the 'preparer of The Way', i.e. the student on the spiritual path must always, within the heart, question and test the mettle of the insights she or he receives. This is how divine discrimination, or the voice of the intuition, is developed. This questioning stance would have been second nature to John, as a prophet whose discerning spiritual vision had to be kept keen by the whetting of constant inner attunement to his intuition.

From another perspective, however – the one that we think particularly applies in this case – John's question includes a degree of prophecy. We do not think that he was in any way questioning or doubting the essence of Jesus's spirituality or mission. Whilst Jesus was undoubtedly the prophesied Messiah, because of the brutality, ignorance and indifference of the masses, his mission could only prepare humanity for another window of opportunity in the future. As a planetary society, humankind could have arisen and thrown off its material shackles during his lifetime. Had Jesus's mission been allowed to do so, it would have accomplished this on humanity's behalf. But the people chose that Barabbas, the worldly thief, should live and Jesus should die, and so delayed their chance of liberation. That Jesus was fully aware of this probable outcome is revealed in John's gospel when he says that his real kingdom (the Orbit of Shar-On come down to dwell on Earth) was 'not of this age'. The point to which John's query attests is that the question of whether spiritual liberation for the world might occur in John and Jesus's lifetime, or in some future age, had not yet been decided. The buoyant answer that Jesus sends to John – 'The lame walk and the blind see' – confirms this. Jesus was speaking joyfully, not only of healed limbs and eyes but of deep spiritual lameness and blindness overcome and thrown off by those who encountered him. At this point, early in his ministry, it is evident that he was hopeful of a happier outcome than the Crucifixion.

Although tiny, Palestine is situated upon a very important point in the Earth's spiritual energy-field which unites East and West and which is intimately connected with the forces of harmonization, blending, balance and radiation. The mysteries of light and darkness meet here. Palestine was the prime location on the map of Earth consciousness to at last overturn the prevailing situation as it is described in John's gospel: 'The Light shineth in the darkness, and the darkness comprehendeth it not.'

When those who peopled this part of the world chose to continue on the path of incomprehension, it indicated that the world as a whole would likewise decide to cling remorselessly to its own darkness.

John's prophetic words pointed to a distant time when another great chance would be given to us. Had the world chosen to ascend at the time of Jesus, then this future epoch would have been experienced on a higher harmonic, so to speak, than that which it is possible for us to avail ourselves of today. Nevertheless, the divine plan decreed that this time would be one of wonders and great spiritual progress.

This time is presently in its earliest beginnings. It is the Age of John – the New Age, a term which Jesus himself initiated. More accurately, it is the Age of John and Mary. But it is as the Age of John that John the Baptist perceived it, and of course he was aware that he himself belonged to the great Sphere of John in the spiritual worlds. He knew that he would return to bear witness in the coming Age of John – not as its avatar, but as its servant, once more dedicating his soul-energies to ushering in the new and most precious dispensation of all – the Second Coming. It was this veiled prophetic knowledge within him, not entirely crystallized into thought – either because of his prison environment or because the soul's knowledge, especially prophecy, often speaks in conundrums to us so that we might strive harder to attain a deeper understanding – that caused John to ask his famous question: is it you, or one who is to come after you, that we should look to?

The Sphere of St John is, of course, the Sphere of Shar-On in very slightly different linguistic form. If one softens the J and stresses the h, the two are almost one and the same word. And Mary Magdalene is the Rose of Shar-On – the Rose of John. The Sphere of John/Shar-On is the sphere of the Great Soul through which the Christ manifests – the Bridal Ring of Jesus and Mary. We can think of John and Jesus as twin souls, for each soul is twinned or mirrored with another. However, the John who was the great focus on Earth of the John Sphere was not so much John the Baptist, but John the Beloved Disciple, John the Divine, John the Apostle.

Consider this excerpt from the early Christian allegory, 'The Hymn of the Pearl', where the hero has reached the end of his quest and dons a robe of light, symbol of the purified and perfected soul:

> *The garment seems to me like a mirror of myself. In it I see all in all. I see that we are distinctly two yet one. I see Gnosis.*

As intimated by the antiphonal beauty of the inspired piece of music 'Spiegel im Spiegel' ('Mirror in the Mirror'), twin – or mirror – souls grant one another gnosis, each perfectly mirroring the light of the spirit of the other, which emerges from one source and is two, yet one. The Sufi poet Rumi saw his soul mirrored in his 'beloved',

Sham. If John is the mirror of Jesus, who is Mary's mirror? We consider it to be Tamar, that venerable being who brought together Margaret Bailey and myself (we believe that we are mirror souls), and who is Mary's clear and pure channel – her 'mirror'.

Just as there had to be two human beings on Earth – male and female manifestations of the same Spirit, to properly express the Father-Mother, Masculine-Feminine aspects of the Godhead – so there had to be two reflecting souls, divine human beings who would perfectly mirror – receive and pass on – the supernal Light radiated into the Earth-plane by Jesus-Mary. On the outer plane, the mirroring soul was John the Beloved, who continued long on the Earth after Mary's death. On the inner plane, the mirroring soul was Tamar, the daughter of Jesus and Mary, who died very early in life, long before Mary and John. These two, Tamar and John, seeded the circle, or further earthed the foundations, of the Sphere of John, the Sphere of Shar-On, of which we are all destined to become a part. Thus we see how the spiritual requirements of the Christ mission, that 'the King should be in Heaven and the Queen on Earth' (that Jesus should ascend and Mary remain behind on Earth), are perfectly reversed or mirrored in their twin souls. In this case, it is John (the King) who is required to remain on Earth, and Tamar (the Queen) who must ascend.

It might help to clarify a somewhat complex issue if we think of the simple idea that the reason why creation came into being at all was because the Divine Being needed to mirror itself in order to embrace a more complete awareness. The Divine Being is a perfect balance of both the Sacred Male Principle and the Sacred Female Principle, and both Principles required mirroring or twinning. Therefore, we might call the soul who mirrors us, but is of the same gender or Sacred Principle, the 'twin' soul; and the soul who is our 'other half', our opposite gender complement, might be thought of as our soul's 'affinity'. In the light of this understanding, we can see how John is Jesus's twin-soul and Tamar is Mary's, whilst Jesus and Mary are 'affinities', the opposite half of one another. We can disclose the secret that Joseph of Arimathea was Tamar's affinity, although of course a sexual relationship in their first-century life did not manifest as it would have been entirely inappropriate. Nevertheless, we can see how this 'mirroring' creates an infinitude of different relationships, each coming forth from the other in eternal progression, which is an aspect of the magic of the mirror.

Mary is the divine lover and consort of Jesus – but how is she related to John, the twin soul of Jesus? To answer this question, we must look at the definition of the New Age which is just coming into being. It is the Age of Aquarius, the air sign which depicts a water-bearer pouring forth the waters of the new dispensation. The jar from which the waters pour (another symbol of the Holy Grail) is represented in the heavens by three stars which are part of the constellation of Aquarius – the New Age.

These three stars hold great significance, and we think that in one sense they signify Jesus, Mary and John. Nevertheless, the three stars which configure the Aquarian jar are in themselves only representations of the three stars which (among others) actually nurture Earth's evolution. These three stars are, we believe: Sirius in Canis Major (the 'Great Dog'), Procyon in Canis Minor (the 'Little Dog'), and Betelgeux, the great bright star which is in Orion but not of it.

Together, Sirius, Procyon and Betelgeux create what is known to astronomers as the Great Triangle, a vast equilateral triangle that is one of the most striking configurations in the heavens, conspicuously bright and clear. The triangle, as the three stars mark it, is in the shape of the Chalice or the sacred V, the downward-pointing equilateral triangle which, when merged with our upward-reaching spiritual aspiration from Earth, becomes the six-pointed star, the Star of the New Age.

We have seen that the figure of the water-bearer is truly Mary Magdalene, Mistress of the Waters.[1] We see also that her jar gives us not only the waters of the new dispensation, but also the oil, symbol of the highest spiritual essence, the oil of spikenard, which anoints us all as sons and daughters of the king and the queen – royal offspring in our own right, all of one blood, all children of the royal parents – Father-Mother God. This is one aspect of the meaning of the Holy Grail, the divine cup or white jar – the Chalice of Light – with which Mary baptizes us. The keynote of the age is the meaning of Aquarius – the sign of brotherhood. And who should John be but the brother of Mary? John, symbolized so beautifully as the soaring white eagle (and for whom the teacher White Eagle is a messenger, for he is indeed of the Sphere of John) has always worked with Mary and Jesus. Prior to the Last Supper, Jesus tells his disciples to seek and follow 'the man with the water-pot' who will lead them to the 'upper room' (raised consciousness). This is not just a pragmatic directive, but an esoteric teaching for humanity as it progressed towards the age of Aquarius.

John, like Jesus and Mary, is older than Earth's humanity, and his sign appears above the entrance to the temples of ancient Egypt, the religious understanding of which these holy three inspired. For there above the temple doors, wings outstretched, gaze fixed unwaveringly upon the Sun, appears the emblem of the white eagle, the divine messenger of the Sun. Isis herself, so deeply associated with Mary, is also depicted with wings – a sign of the close soul-connection between the brother and sister, united spirit of the New Age. Let us examine the powerful evidence in the gospels which suggests that John and Mary were indeed brother and sister.

In their book, *The Templar Revelation*, Lynn Picknett and Clive Prince tell the story of how, in 1958, Dr Morton Smith, Professor of Ancient History at Columbia University, found in the library of Mar Saba some fragments of a 'secret gospel' attributed to Mark. The library belonged to a monastic community of the Eastern Orthodox Church which was situated about 12 miles outside Jerusalem. The fragments of this secret gospel were contained in a copy of a letter written by Clement of Alexandria, one of the early Church Fathers. Palaeographers have since verified that the original document must indeed have been the work of the second-century Church Father. Clement's letter is to one Theodore, who has sought guidance from him on how to handle the problem of a Gnostic sect called the Carpocratians, whose rites were based on a very colourful interpretation of Mark's secret gospel. Clement explains to Theodore that the gospel is genuine, but that the Carpocratians have misinterpreted it. He reveals that the secret gospel contains the esoteric teachings of Jesus, which were to be given to an inner circle only, and were not intended for exoteric dispensation. This is an interesting point, because all evidence points to the fact that Jesus took great pains – and great risks, for which he paid the ultimate price – to reveal the profound esoteric secrets of life to the ordinary populace. We believe that the secrets contained in this hidden gospel would have been expounded by him in their simplest form to all of his followers. Nevertheless, those same esoteric truths (for there is nothing that Jesus taught which does not resonate on ever deeper levels) have, by their very nature, a more direct, occult mode of expression; and to use these potent means of heightening consciousness as teachings for those who are unprepared would have been reckless indeed.

There is an amusing instance in the Gnostic gospels where we see Jesus dispensing just as much truth as his pupil could bear. He is careful not to push the man so far beyond his comfort zone, regarding the issue under discussion, that his psyche rebels and rejects the teaching outright. The case in question involves the disciple Peter, whose name was actually Simon. Peter was a nickname, the equivalent of 'Boulder' or 'Rocky'. He had been given this nickname, perhaps because of his muscular build and his generally exaggerated masculinity, but also because he was as unresponsive as a stone to the promptings of his soul. He was strong in intellect, but lacking in that deeper intelligence and inner knowing which is recognized as the intuitive faculty. Of all the disciples, he hated and resented Mary the most, threatening her life on more than one occasion. (Mary confessed to Jesus, 'Peter hath made me fear for my life, for he hateth all the race of women.' (Pistis Sophia, Second Book, 72:3))

We might learn from the enactment of this drama between Peter and Mary that the worldly intellect (Peter) sneers at the soul (Mary) and seeks to debase its status and significance. Peter, then, was a misogynist with fixed ideas of male supremacy. He once remarked to Jesus contemptuously, as recorded in The Gospel of Thomas, 'Let Mary leave us, for women are not worthy of life.' He did not add, 'especially Mary', but we can be certain he meant it. By 'life', Peter meant the life bestowed by the spirit, not that of the physical body.

Jesus then explained to Peter that to enter the Kingdom of Heaven, Mary would 'become male, resembling you males ... for every woman who will make herself male will enter the Kingdom of Heaven'. We feel that this is a slight mistranslation or misunderstanding, and that Jesus was really explaining to Peter that Mary would become male as well as female once she entered the Kingdom of Heaven to assume the essence of 'living spirit' – in other words, that the indwelling spirit unites both the Sacred Feminine and the Sacred Masculine into a merged emanation of divine oneness, and yet does itself consist of both these emanations. If all women are conjoined with their masculine selves when they achieve gnosis, then by the same token, all men must be united with their feminine selves. We can imagine that Jesus left Peter to draw this logical conclusion in his own time and in his own way! He also imparted to Peter at a subliminal level that he himself was Mary's male essence by speaking of her as the 'living spirit'.

Jesus taught his followers according to their capacity. To his circle of initiates, he might have explained the meaning of the *hieros gamos* and the sacredness of sex. To Peter, he gently explained that Mary had a male emanation as part of her completeness, so that the necessary teaching (that Peter himself had a female essence, and was incomplete without it, therefore making a nonsense of his expressed conclusion and stressing the perfect equality of male and female as two halves of a whole) was of such refined subtlety as to enable even the misogynistic Peter to ingest it, starting from the subliminal level outward. And Jesus parried the slight to Mary in the most powerful way possible when he told Peter – in coded terms, so that the disciple's intellect would not immediately condemn and override it – that he and Mary were one; for Peter was decidedly one of Jesus's greatest devotees.

Considering these things, it seems that the existence of a secret gospel of Jesus's esoteric teaching is not only likely, but inevitable. And what The Secret Gospel of Mark contains with respect to Lazarus is of prime significance. Two passages, omitted from the version of Mark's gospel that was incorporated into the New Testament, are of interest here. We know of them because Clement obligingly copied them in the letter he wrote to Theodore, although service to posterity was clearly not at all what he intended.

The first describes the raising of Lazarus from the dead, identifying him simply as 'a youth of Bethany'. It tells of an esoteric ceremony that was held six days after the miraculous event, in which the youth came to Jesus 'wearing a linen cloth over his naked body' and spent the night in his teacher's company, learning throughout its watches of 'the mystery of the Kingdom of God'. We have been given to understand that this ceremony involved some observance of the stars, meditation rituals, and also a merging of souls upon the higher planes while both slept, so that the deeper spiritual spheres could be visited in company with one another to serve the purpose of instruction and revelation for the young John. There is a method of rising in consciousness during sleep, rather than sinking down into oblivion, which allows the conscious memory to retain the spiritual experience of the soul whilst the body sleeps, and to retrieve it during waking hours.

During this holy night, it seems that Jesus also taught John a secret which he and Mary already shared – the true understanding and the occult rites of a profoundly spiritual ceremony. This involved the projection of the supreme power of love, the ceremony itself forming the vehicle or Earthly circuitry that transmitted the omnipotent force. The heavenly dynamic thus released could heal and renew inner and outer conditions on both a microcosmic and macrocosmic scale, and set the soul free. This mystical ceremony is a union of profound love between mirroring souls, as indeed John and Jesus were, but there is in it no element of a carnal nature. The venerable Church Father seemed to have been worried in case Jesus's faithful failed to draw the necessary distinction between the carnal and the esoteric, as it appeared the Carpocratians had done.

The second objectionable passage, in Clement's eyes, was that which confirmed who the 'youth of Bethany' actually was. Lynn Picknett and Clive Prince, who tell the story in their book, *The Templar Revelation*, state that biblical scholars had already concluded that the strangely worded passage in Mark's gospel which runs 'And they (meaning Jesus and his disciples) came to Jericho; and as he went out of Jericho with his disciples and a great number of people' etc., points to an omission. Why is nothing said about the visit to Jericho? The passage in Mark's secret gospel fills in the gap:

> *And the sister of the youth whom Jesus loved and his mother*
> *and Salome were there, and Jesus did not receive them.*

What seemed to have concerned Clement was the fact that these few words make abundantly clear that the 'youth of Bethany' was indeed the 'youth whom Jesus loved' – the Beloved Disciple, John. His aunt was waiting in Jericho with Salome and another of her daughters, but Jesus did not receive them. This is clearly the Bethany family, although it is possible that Mary was with Jesus at this time (the unnamed sister mentioned in the passage might have been Martha).

Lynn Picknett and Clive Prince point out that John's gospel, Chapter 11, describes John the Beloved Disciple in exactly the same words as those of Mark's secret gospel – 'the youth whom Jesus loved' – and that, additionally, 'Lazarus' is the Greek rendition of 'Eliezer', 'Elia' or 'Elijah', the Old Testament prophet whom Jesus himself said had reincarnated as John the Baptist; so the name 'Lazarus' is shown to be linked with the name 'John'.

It is interesting to note at which point Lazarus enters the story. It is, of course, when he is raised from the dead. 'John', the Beloved Disciple, does not appear on the scene *until after the raising of Lazarus.* This symbolic miracle was indicative of a profound spiritual truth, as were all Jesus's miracles. Lazarus had to be raised from the dead – raised into the consciousness of the Christ Being or the Christ Light – before he could receive the great initiation which revealed to him the mysteries of the Kingdom of Heaven. On that wondrous night he was reborn as an ascended soul, even though still inhabiting a physical body, just as were Jesus and Mary. Jesus himself named him John, as he was to be known from that point on, for he was of the John Sphere – the King of Light – like John the Baptist before him. Yet the John Sphere is also the Orbit or Sphere of Shar-On, the centre point of which is the Rose of Shar-On – Mary Magdalene herself (in her deepest essence) – and it is, of course, the magical domain, the Bridal Ring, of Jesus and Mary. All three souls are contained within it – Jesus, John and Mary. And all the evidence points to the fact that John and Mary were indeed brother and sister.

It seems that, as well as the problem of misunderstanding and misinterpretation, John's significance was just too closely associated with that of Mary Magdalene for the Church Fathers to allow his true identity to be disclosed. If Mary of Bethany had been revealed as Mary Magdalene, and John the Beloved Disciple had been known to be her brother, then the secret of Mary's true status as the consort of Jesus might have been more obvious, and the recognition of the coming of the age of Mary and John might have moved the concept of Christianity far beyond the rigid parameters that Peter's Church was already in the process of marking out for it.

John the Baptist was not part of this equation, but he played a vital role in the mission of the holy three, and he was of the Sphere of John. When we see the part that John the Baptist was to play in the future, we can better understand the deep significance of his role, and appreciate why, to the Mandaeans, he was the 'King of Light'.[2]

White Eagle says on this subject:

> All through his ministry the disciple most closely associated with Jesus was John – John the Beloved, whom he called to sit by his side during the Last Supper. It is significant that John was by the side of Jesus when all the disciples partook of the Last Supper before the master was crucified; and that in his last words on the cross Jesus commended John to his mother Mary. In the new age of Aquarius into which humanity is slowly moving, there is a unification or a drawing together of the two – the master Jesus and the great and beloved St John.
>
> Read carefully the Gospel of St John and the Revelation of St John, and you will find in all those teachings reference to the inner powers of every human being, and symbolism referring to each man and woman's own soul and its potentialities.

You will remember also that before the Last Supper Jesus gave instructions to his chosen disciples to go before him into the town to find the inn where there was an upper room; the disciples were to follow the man carrying the water pot. This was the symbol of the New Age of Aquarius which was to follow the Piscean Age, in which Jesus came to give his particular message to humankind, a simple message of love. Yet, if you study the teachings of Jesus of Nazareth with knowledge, you will realize the profundity as well as the simplicity of his teaching.

Jesus came to teach the people how to live the life on the physical plane within their communities. But John began to teach people the purpose of Jesus's teaching, because it is only when men and women can live the life of love and brotherhood towards each other that they can then begin to develop those soul powers of which we speak, those heavenly powers with which God the heavenly Father-Mother has endowed them. The new age then is of John – the age of Brotherhood! The Aquarian Age is the age of St John the Mystic.

We are moving onwards, upwards, until we reach the zenith of the great circle, where shines the Throne of God ... from which emanated the message of John.

Only with the dawning of a new age will men and women begin to comprehend the mystery contained in ... John's Gospel. The message of John has never been to the human mind. John spoke to the soul of the world. The teachings of the beloved John contain the mystery of the human soul; those of Jesus refer primarily to the divine Light of the spirit within the soul.

These same teachings were given in other forms in the ancient wisdom, but never as these ... never so simply, so profoundly.

St John the Divine is an ancient and great Spirit, or source of wisdom. The human vehicle or manifestation known generally as St John was brought into being by the descent of one of the great Beings about the throne of God.

This is a statement most difficult for you to comprehend; neither can the finite mind appreciate the worth, magnitude, truth and beauty of this teaching and its revelation. The revelation (in this we include all the writings attributed to John) came from a high source, or plane of spiritual power.

The Gospel of St John sets out a code of conduct which the initiated cannot help but follow. It is not a question of 'You must be good. You must love your brother or sister.' Rather it is that when illumination comes there is only one way in which it is possible to live, and that is by spontaneous love, kindness, gentleness, not only to brother man, or to the sister of your spirit, but to all creation.[3]

An earnest study of the message of John reveals that he taught concerning the power of the soul. His coming heralded the Aquarian Age, the age when all human beings will arise in spiritual light; when men and women will learn to use the full power of the soul.[4] *They will do this by reason of knowledge concerning each and all of the vehicles comprising that temple which is man-woman. The divine Revelation of St John contains an outline of universal evolution from the beginning to the end.*

St John is he who is yet to come – yes, in fuller manifestation – to the children of earth. He came then in lesser degree with his 'beloved', known to people there as Jesus of Nazareth, to help him in his work; but will return, this time in all his glory. These two brought to this earth planet the divine message of the Christ love.

When we use the term 'John', do not limit it to the one personality of which you are cognisant. Remember there is a great being who is the leader of the Aquarian Age. ... The Master, the world teacher, at the head of the Aquarian Age is the John man. We do not say the St John of your Bible; we say John, the Man of God, the man who is glorified in the Father-Mother.

The lapse of two thousand years therefore reveals not one but two souls of great purity and beauty, who brought to the world the Light of the ages. It reveals a close and deep affinity between the two.

John is so close to Jesus, so close that the two are all but inseparable, two aspects of the one truth. And following the great world teacher whom you know as Jesus of Nazareth, comes the other aspect of that one, the aspect which we understand as the Light, the Divine Light: John the Lightbearer, John who is so close to the Divine Mother because of what Jesus said at his crucifixion: Behold thy Mother.

From The Light Bringer – the Ray of John and the Age of Intuition, White Eagle

White Eagle's words cast new light on the findings of Dolores Cannon. In her book *They Walked with Jesus*, she tells the story of a client in regression who becomes Naomi, a young girl who is Jesus's niece. Naomi joins Jesus's mission and reports that John the Beloved was a great organizer, going ahead of Jesus to ensure that there was a safe place in which to hold secret meetings, that he and the disciples would have somewhere to stay, and that there was no hostile presence in the towns and villages to which he travelled that might seize him. These activities – organizing, protecting, facilitating, ministering – are so recognizably angelic in quality that they suggest that John did indeed contain an angelic essence within his soul, which White Eagle seems to corroborate when he says that 'the human vehicle or manifestation known generally as St John was brought into being by the descent of one of the great Beings about the throne of God.' And indeed we can see in the Beloved Disciple's service to Jesus's mission the great task of what White Eagle refers to as the 'John man', going before, preparing the way, 'making straight the way of the Lord', as John the Baptist did before him.

It is John the Divine (the Beloved Disciple) himself who writes the words of Jesus as he received them through inspiration – the Holy Breath – in the Revelation of St John the Divine:

> *I am the root and the offspring of David, and the bright and morning star.*
>
> *And the Spirit and the bride say, Come!*

> REVELATION, 22:16–17

And at the heart of the Sphere of St John, or the Orbit of Shar-On, is the perfect rose, the essence of Mary Magdalene the bride, of whom Jesus said in the Gnostic gospels that she would be raised up above all the other disciples and rule the New Age, the forthcoming Kingdom of Light, and whom he called 'the All' and Mary Lucifera – Mary the Light-Bringer.

As Jesus says in the Pistis Sophia (one of the Gnostic gospels):

> *Where I shall be, there shall also be my twelve ministers. But Mary Magdalene and John, the virgin (John the Beloved) will tower over all my disciples and over all men who shall receive the mysteries. ... And they will be on my right and on my left. And I am they, and they are I.*

> PISTIS SOPHIA, P231

No clearer statement than this could have been made about the true status of John and Mary, and their significance to the coming age. This pyramidal soul-group is the one that will transmit to us the truth, the beauty, the power and the consciousness of the Christ Spirit in the coming days.

NOTES

1 Jesus is also the water-bearer, symbolized by his act of pouring water from a pitcher in the upper room at the Last Supper (the ceremonial meal which reflected that which he had shared with Mary Magdalene six days earlier, when she had brought forth the alabaster jar to anoint him as divine king in their esoteric marriage ceremony at Bethany). The water was for the purpose of washing the disciples' feet, which he did as a sign that he had become bridegroom to all humanity. The exoteric marriage ceremony of the time included the ritual of the bridegroom washing the feet of the bride.

2 Our source indicates that John the Baptist reincarnated as the sage and prophet Merlin in the time of King Arthur.

3 In the books by Dolores Cannon, *Jesus and the Essenes* and *They Walked with Jesus*, which record the past-life regressions of two people who were the contemporaries of Jesus (then known as Naomi and Suddi), the principle of vegetarianism is mentioned by both clients. Naomi records that Jesus's compassion and respect and doctrine of love extended to all creation, whilst Suddi states that vegetarianism was practised by the Essene Brotherhood at Qumran.

4 We believe that this is with what Mary's gospel is primarily concerned.

CHAPTER FIFTEEN

Leonardo Da Vinci and the Secret Tradition

*C*oncerning the crucial connection between Jesus, Mary Magdalene and John the Beloved, it is helpful to study Leonardo Da Vinci's painting *The Last Supper*. Lynn Picknett, whose observations have revealed so much about this painting and its teaching, points out that the figure sitting to the right of Jesus, who is supposed to be John the Beloved Disciple, is clearly a woman. The contours of breasts and a necklace are visible, and the features are delicate and feminine. (The impression of the breasts is said to be due to a crack in the wall; if so, it is a curious strategically-occurring crack.) The spread-eagled M shape of the gathering to which Lynn Picknett refers is more doubtful – it is not very clearly discernible, although it does appear unmistakably in copies of Leonardo's painting made by his pupils. What seems to be more accurate, and which answers her question as to why the figure (which seems to be both John and Mary combined) is leaning away from Jesus, is that together, John/Mary and Jesus are creating the V shape which is the primal symbol of the Chalice or the Sacred Feminine. The Holy Grail itself is actually depicted in the painting. It is that which takes form between them. It is their child, on every level. And up through its direct centre rises a pillar, making the form of a T, to indicate the coming of Tamar, she who is the essence of the Holy Grail. Three lighted windows behind Jesus and Mary/John further emphasize the presence of the Holy Three because, of course, at this point Mary is already six days pregnant with Tamar.

This understanding of the painting (which seems to grow more and more undeniable the longer one looks at it) would also explain why there is no actual chalice. It is not present in its mundane form, but rather as a sacred and sublime symbol, created by Jesus and Mary/John.[1] In fact, in the painting, all the disciples, as well as Jesus, possess their own individual little drinking vessels. This, too, is profoundly symbolic, although it portrays another aspect of the deeper truth, and does not mean that the communal chalice did not exist in actuality. In fact, we are certain that Mary herself was present at the Last Supper, and that she brought in the chalice and filled it with wine. Supposedly, the Holy Grail is that same communal cup of wine from which Jesus and his disciples drank at the Last Supper, and which later Mary made use of to catch his blood when the spear of the Roman soldier Longinus pierced Jesus's side. If Mary did use such a cup (and we believe there is every reason to suppose that the most sublime symbolism is actually acted out in the commonplace world as a literality), then indeed she would have used the one Jesus himself drank from, the communal chalice presented to the party by Mary herself, and which obviously was kept by her as a memento of that poignant final occasion.

Yet it was not only blood that poured into the cup, but water. This blood and water symbolize the body (blood) and the soul (water). The symbol translates to a higher vibration with the mingling of the blood and the water, representing the divine fire of the spirit (blood), mingling with the fluid of the soul (water). This double symbol might mean that the chalice, or the womb of Mary, did indeed catch the holy blood in a bodily sense, for we believe that she was with child to Jesus when he was crucified. Of course, the 'holy blood' belonged to both herself and Jesus, holy because its higher, bodily essence was naturally purified by the presence of their soul-force. We believe that there is a divine bloodline which descended through Jesus and Mary, the sacred 'red thread' which has such mystical significance, but that its history is not as it has been portrayed so far.

We will discuss the bloodline fully in a later chapter, but we would stress the importance of recognizing the fact that we are *all* divine as well as human. The bloodline is most definitely not about exclusivity or genetic superiority – in fact, these concepts are the very opposite of the essence and purpose of the bloodline, which exists to unite us all, to show us that we are all of one blood – sons and daughters of the king and queen.

This was the meaning of the Sacred Chalice long before Mary and Jesus incarnated on Earth. When we pervert the true meaning of the Sacred Chalice, the result is the Nazi horror. Hitler reversed the goddess energies, as we see in his depiction of the swastika. This holy symbol of the Dance of the Goddess, belonging to both Buddhism and the Native Americans amongst other esoteric disciplines, was adopted by him, but he distorted the image, causing the spiritual energy current to dance backwards. His aim was, of course, complete domination and enslavement of the power of the Sacred Feminine. Sadly, when we view the tendency of humanity to commit such domination and enslavement down the centuries, the rise of the Third Reich begins to look almost like a deplorable inevitability, or at least a natural outcome, of such tendencies.

The second reading of the symbolism points to the meaning of the individual wine glasses. This seems to show that we each contain our own vessel, our own chalice. It is, of course, the heart chakra, which is attached to that most refined and mystical body, the higher aspect of the soul. This soul-body contains the flame, the divine fire of spirit, which is always there but which can only leap up and illumine the soul with its limitless effulgence when the heart chakra willingly opens to receive it. And so the heart becomes the sacred chalice eternally alive with the scintillating light of the spirit – the water and the blood, Mary and Jesus, creating the most holy chalice or V shape from their combined essence – the Holy Grail itself (when the symbolic M is placed on top of the V, a perfect heart shape is created). Once the little wine glasses shown on the communion table – our own individual heart-centres – are 'empty', or purified of selfish desire and open to love, the Holy Grail can pour forth its essence and fill them, baptizing them with heavenly consciousness and imbuing them with eternal life – the Light of the Christ.

The strange disembodied hand wielding a dagger which appears in the painting can now be explained as the 'blade', the sigil for the sacred Masculine. It is this 'blade' of true manhood, in the finest and truest sense and detached from any trace of dominance or ego, which is used to 'knight' the masculine soul (the essence of which all souls contain). It is also the blade which the mysterious Lady of the Lake offered to King Arthur, the blade Excalibur which gave him true kingship. We know that Mary Magdalene is deeply associated with this goddess figure and, in fact, in the painting the hand with the blade seems to emerge from Mary, although anatomically it cannot actually be her hand, just as it was not actually the hand of the Lady of the Lake herself who gave the sword into Arthur's keeping, but a disembodied hand, as is portrayed here. We believe that the blade is not pointing at the stomach of the third disciple on the left (from the observer's point of view), as has been suggested, but at his heart. It is not a threatening blade at all – the hand offers it rather than wields it. And the 'blade', the sigil of true kingship, is being offered to that disciple in the painting whom we are certain is a depiction of Joseph of Arimathea, the great unsung hero of the story of Jesus, who never asked for any recognition of his vital part in it, and yet would reincarnate as the hero whose praises all the world would sing – the legendary King Arthur. It might be argued that Joseph of Arimathea was not one of the named 12 disciples. Nevertheless, John's gospel certainly cites him as a disciple, and our source confirms that he was indeed present at the Last Supper.

How could Leonardo Da Vinci know such profound secrets as these? It seems almost impossible that Leonardo could consciously have realized or understood the deeply secret and magical messages which, to us, are scattered throughout his imagery. In *The Magdalene Legacy*, Laurence Gardner points out that *The Last Supper* has been repaired and over-painted many times throughout the centuries and, when one reads the history of the conditions to which it has been subjected, the marvel is that it has survived at all. Moreover, the hand holding the knife must have been Peter's, because a section of the painting, which was copied by a student of Leonardo's shortly after its completion, clearly depicts the disciple's arm twisting behind his back and pointing the blade at Judas Iscariot.

If there were no reality beyond the mundane actuality of life as we perceive it through the stimuli received by the five senses, it would indeed be bizarrely irrational to suggest that Leonardo's obvious intention could be interpreted to mean something else altogether. But if, as we believe, the breath of the spirit infuses life with revelation and meaning, and expresses truth through those vehicles that can contain its resonance, then the hand of Leonardo the master, sometimes consciously, sometimes unconsciously, and sometimes through pure 'coincidence', as might be the case in this instance, would furnish the purposes of that divine breath with a very fine vehicle indeed, so that even so-called coincidence might be seen to be clad in shining light.

The painting, as we look at it today, *does* show a seemingly disembodied hand, not wielding, but quietly holding a blade. And we suggest that Judas is actually the disciple on the observer's left (to the right of Jesus) who grips the table furtively and who, with his tense posture, looks as if he might be preparing to make a hurried exit, whilst the elderly disciple to whose heart-centre the blade points is indeed the venerable Joseph of Arimathea. We would agree that, in order to view things in this way, it is necessary to allow that the painting seems to have taken on a life of its own. But this is precisely what great works of art do, and, whatever the practical facts of the painting's history, when we observe it we are always in the presence of Leonardo Da Vinci.

Leonardo belonged to a secret French sect, based in Paris, known as the Priory of Our Lady of Sion (Mary Magdalene appears to be addressed as the 'Daughter of Sion' in The Gospel of John, and the 'Lady of Sion' referred to is most certainly the Magdalene).[2] Together with many famous names down the centuries from the arenas of literature, science and the arts (including Victor Hugo, Botticelli and Sir Isaac Newton), he eventually became its Grand Master. The Priory of Our Lady of Sion is reputed to know the truth about Mary Magdalene, and it is believed in some quarters that they have incontrovertible documentation, to substantiate their claims, contained in chests which are hidden in the same place as that in which her bones lie. (Our own stance on this question is that Mary's remains, as those of Jesus, do not exist.)

This, it is claimed, is what might comprise the famous Cathar treasure, which was entrusted to four Cathars just days before the rest of their company were burnt alive by the soldiers of the Albigensian Crusade. The four chosen ones escaped down the almost perpendicular sides of the mountain of Montségur, avoided the soldiers surrounding the castle on the peak who had laid siege to the Cathars, and dispersed in the direction of the four points of the compass. To this day, no-one has discovered their treasure or any information about it. We believe that it is a treasure entirely unconnected to any kind of documentation, however explosive and controversial its content might be, and that humanity will be unable to understand the nature of, or gain access to, the treasure itself, until we as a planetary society put forth a very different vibration from the inharmonious note we collectively give forth today.

It may be that Leonardo drew his knowledge from his association with the Priory of Our Lady of Sion; but it seems much more likely that his own highly sensitive intuition as an artist revealed it to him. Leonardo was, of course, a genius of the highest order, and when he used his artistic vision, he revealed to us the secrets of life itself.

We all have an earthly, commonplace self, the little frail human mind of everyday, which is slowly being absorbed into our higher, spiritual essence; but the giants of the artistic, scientific, literary and musical spheres owe their magnificent works to the fact that they have been able to find a way through to these spiritual worlds (very different from the psychic or astral planes, which are commonly penetrated), contacting them consciously and weaving their works from the treasures they find there. Consequently, great works of art and scientific achievement cannot help but express the eternal verities.

Leonardo's earthly self (that part of our consciousness which esotericists often refer to as the 'lower mind') was naturally less inspired (although undoubtedly very fun-loving!). We can never be entirely sure what his attitudes and ideas were concerning the Christian religion, because we have no idea what, if anything, he learned from the teachings of the sect to which he belonged. It has been suggested that he hated the holy family, and certainly the barely disguised phallus he placed behind Mary, the mother of Jesus, in his painting, *The Virgin of the Rocks*, seems to suggest a mark of disrespect executed almost at the level of schoolboy graffiti, with the 'rocks' setting specifically chosen as an allusion to testicles and their facilitation of the Madonna's pregnancy. But we are dealing with Leonardo here, so nothing is quite as it seems, and symbols, bawdy or otherwise, proliferate and deepen into revelation. The Roman Church of Peter was built on a 'rock', which was, of course, Peter himself. Peter of all the disciples hated Mary Magdalene and rejected her teachings and her interpretation of the early Church. It seems that the phallus of rock behind the virgin might actually be a rude sign made at Peter and the Church of Rome, rather than specifically at the virgin herself.

It is likely, also, that Leonardo believed that Jesus was a human man, not a deity (which we consider to be the true teaching of Jesus of Nazareth), and that his depiction of the phallus behind the virgin is his singular comment on the 'virgin birth' (just in case the symbolism of the rocks failed to signal its message) as well as his opinion of the 'rock' (Peter 'the rock' and his creed of masculine domination of the Feminine Principle) upon which the Church of Rome was founded. Moreover, it is very probable that, in Leonardo's opinion, the veneration accorded to the Virgin

Mary would have been more aptly offered to Mary Magdalene.

The painting depicts Mother Mary with the infant John the Baptist, and the archangel Uriel with the Christ Child. Archangel Uriel makes the 'John gesture' (a pointing forefinger and thumb which creates the sacred V of the Chalice or the Holy Grail, and which is associated with John the Baptist in Leonardo's many portrayals of him) at the baby John, who kneels in supplication whilst the Christ Child blesses him. Mother Mary also forms the 'John gesture' with her forefinger and thumb, which grasp John's shoulder, whilst her other hand is poised over Jesus's head in a Semitic blessing. The suggestion is that the identity of the Christ Child and John might be interchangeable.

I once read a beautiful story about this painting which has always remained with me, even though the book in which it appeared is long lost and I am consequently unable to credit its inspired author. The story tells of the unearthly light which falls upon the figures in the painting, a light whose quality the protagonist of the tale broods upon and is unable to equate with any terrestrial light, until he lands on the Moon as a member of a spaceship crew and takes a walk on the lunar surface to a group of rocks where the same exquisite ethereal light sheds its mysterious radiance before his wondering eyes.

This seems to be another instance of an artist attuning to eternal truth through the dynamism of the soul, because Mary Magdalene is closely associated with the Moon and her goddesses of wisdom, sharing with them a mystic fusion of identity; and so, according to this story, it could be understood that it is her unique light which imparts the strange and beautiful radiance to this mysterious painting. The outer plot of the fictional tale suggests that Leonardo had 'been to the Moon'. We think that indeed he had, in soul-flight and within a vessel of esoteric realization. The ultimate symbol for the Sacred Feminine, after all, is the Moon itself. The red-haired, red-cloaked archangel Uriel who makes the sacred V is the angel of the Earth, and almost certainly a representation of Mary Magdalene, who is also linked with the goddess of the Earth.

Both Jesus and John are in the forefront of the painting, whilst beyond Mary thunders the spraying sea. (Mary Jacob is often symbolized by sea foam or spray.) The three aspects of the great soul through which the Christ Light shone are all present (Jesus, Mary and John), as well as the three Marys, and if there is any negative connotation in the idea of all three, in both cases, being 'on the rocks', presumably because of the oppressive erect phallus that dominates the painting, symbol of the misrepresentations of Rome, it is overcome by the sheer beauty and mystical peace of the scene. It seems to say that, although the truth has to come to humanity by a circuitous route, via the rock of materialism, yet that same truth, the Sacred Light, will eventually thunder through the resistance of the domain of matter and shine in measureless blessing over the consciousness of all humankind.

It does seem that Leonardo might have believed that John the Baptist was the Christ as well as Jesus of Nazareth, the former perhaps being a 'superior' Christ to the latter, if not superseding him altogether, and this belief appears to have arisen from the teachings he was given on joining the Priory of Our Lady of Sion. If so, we suggest that this stance is a confusion of the truth, and is perhaps generated by the knowledge (no doubt corroborated by certain documentation) that the title of 'Christ' was given to many teachers and prophets throughout the ages, without bestowing on them any idea of deity.

We think the truth is that the deity of the ineffable Christ shone through Jesus, and also through Mary and John the Beloved Disciple, all of whom were human, and yet magnificent in their soul development, in a fulsomeness that the Earth had never seen before. In performing this service to humanity, Jesus, and Mary and John, became divine, but no more so than that divine potential which we all share, and which Mary described so beautifully in her gospel as 'becoming fully human'. To be fully human is to be divine.

NOTES

1 The Holy Grail, sacred chalice or V, the 'child' of Jesus and Mary, is in truth that triangle of the Star (*see* Part III) which contains the light of the Godhead and which unites with our soul on Earth in its readiness to receive union with the Godhead (signified by the upward-pointing triangle which constitutes the other half of the Star).

2 Although the existence of the society called the Priory of Sion (in contradistinction to that which is called the Priory of Our Lady of Sion) has been discredited, and undoubtedly any examination of it leads to a confused tangle of dead ends, forgeries and red herrings, we believe that behind the smokescreen there is an element of reality involving the latter organization. For the most thorough and intelligently conducted research on the matter, see *The Templar Revelation* by Lynn Picknett and Clive Prince, and *The Magdalene Legacy* by Laurence Gardner.

CHAPTER SIXTEEN

The Consolamentum and the Cathar Heritage

*T*he secret which Jesus imparted to John was that which John had learned after he had been raised from the dead, when Jesus taught him in prayer, ceremony, ritual and soul-vision, the mysteries of the Kingdom of Heaven throughout the watches of the night. It is called the *consolamentum* and we believe it formed part of the Egyptian mystery tradition at the deepest and most esoteric level.

Suddi tells us that Jesus did indeed travel to Egypt prior to his mission to learn the ancient arts that would help him to perform his numerous miracles. This has given rise in recent years to the charge that he was nothing more than a common magician, many of whom roamed the land in his day. In fact, this is a massive over-simplification of the truth. There have always been two levels on which magic is performed. The first uses trickery, deception and sleight of hand, and is based upon the development of psychological skill and co-ordinational ingenuity. It teaches both the practitioner and the observer lessons about the power of illusion. The second is the true magic, and it brings the power of the spirit through into earthly conditions so that their illusion is overcome, and the higher reality prevails. This teaches us the most profound lesson of all – that earthly conditions are in themselves an illusion, merely an insubstantial shadow cast by the real world of the spirit.

There is an intermediate level between these two, where astral conditions can be manipulated and psychic powers come into play. Nevertheless, depending on the soul-evolution of the magus, he or she must always operate in the final analysis on either the first or the second level, despite the development within him or her of psychic gifts.

Jesus, as the true Piscean avatar (Pisces is the symbol of the waters of the psyche) certainly had developed his psychic gifts to their ultimate degree, as many of the gospel stories attest. But he seems to have considered these in the light of quite ordinary attainments, and they were certainly not the sum total of his magical abilities. His miracles were of the deepest degree, true instances of calling on the spiritual forces to transform earthly illusion (the conditions of everyday) into spiritual reality.

To perfectly attune his soul to the power of such miracle-working, Jesus and Mary underwent initiations together in the Egyptian temple where she was priestess. This does not mean that Jesus was incapable of miraculous feats until he went to the Egyptian temple. His development was such that his knowledge, mastery, and soul-power already contained the potential to perform the miracles he did, and far greater than he did. Nevertheless, the initiation on Earth is a necessary activating factor in the process of such miracle-working – one that we will, in time, learn for ourselves, as indeed Jesus himself confirmed.

The *consolamentum* arose from the ancient and sacred Egyptian teachings, but we have a sense that it came far more into its own, was perfectly developed as a window onto spiritual truth, or as a well delving into its hidden waters, through Jesus's individual mastery and Mary's facilitation and blessing, than had ever been the case before in the annals of Earth's history. This surely must have been the case, because it is spoken of in truly wondrous terms as 'a power which to present-day people is quite inconceivable'.[1]

This sacred power called the *consolamentum*, and the mystery of its invocation, John and Mary took to France, and to other places on their travels, where it was bequeathed, together with the secret significance of their status as three-in-one with Jesus the Christ, to certain groups, some of whom became known as Johannite Christians. This hidden power began to rise to the surface when, early in eleventh-century France, in the regions of the Languedoc, Provence and Bordeaux, in Albi, Carcassonne and Toulouse, something mysterious began to happen. In these areas of France, to which Mary and John came in the first century, spreading the teachings of The Way – the pure and true message of the Christ – a strange revolution took place. Maurice Magre, an expert on the Cathars, states that, 'Buddhist renunciation became a moral law which spread among its followers with astonishing rapidity.'[2] He describes the roads as filling with barefoot ascetics, walking in humility and reverence for the Living Spirit and eager to tell others of the joy and revelation that had come to them. Monks in their monasteries, nuns in their convents, began to turn away from the God of the Church and to worship a holy presence within their hearts 'whose light,' Maurice Magre tells us, 'grew brighter the more they lived pure lives filled with love for their fellow men.'

Many, many people in the South of France, including great numbers of the nobility, set their feet upon this perfect and true Way. In order to live their practical, earthly lives, they took the 'middle way', recommended by Buddha for those whose lives must be lived in the sphere of worldly affairs. Others took the more challenging path of the *perfecti*, renouncing all the comforts of the flesh in order to embrace the wonder of the spirit. These sages knew how to wield the power of a lost secret, said to have been given to John by Jesus and Mary, who taught him occult rites of a deeply spiritual nature concerning the energy and consciousness of love (not carnal love). It is also said that the original founders of the Cathars (also known as the Albigenses, originally from the Balkans) and the Knights Templar were indeed these two, John and Mary, brother and sister, who stood at the right hand and the left hand of Jesus the Christ. (However, we have uncovered further information on this point outlined in Chapter Twenty-three.)

Thus, from the eleventh to the thirteenth centuries, because of the potency of the new millennium and the fresh spiritual opportunity always offered to humankind at the renewal of such cycles, the *consolamentum* became openly known and publicly used.

What was, or is, the *consolamentum*, the Comforter of the Cathars? It was a supremely elevated potency bestowed by a touch or a blessing from one of the Albigensian *perfecti* to the dying person, or the one who was being initiated into the company of the *perfecti*. During the *consolamentum*, not only the recipient, but also the gathering of ordinary people, relatives and friends of the dying who stood in attendance, would be enabled to witness the falling away of the veil of the temple (meaning the veil which separates the physical body from the vision and reality of the spiritual spheres, and which is created by our wilful blindness). There, before their wondering eyes, was revealed the grandeur and the beauty of the shining spiritual world into which their loved one stepped and was enveloped, bidding a joyful and so clearly temporary farewell, until the vision glorious was absorbed back into the hidden mysteries and the everyday scene was once more restored. This is not to be thought of merely as a glimpse of the life beyond death. It was that, but also far more, for it was a glimpse of – indeed, a connection with – life eternal, a sphere of being exalted far above the Earth-plane and those dimensions of astral existence immediately beyond it. It is easy to imagine the boundless rejoicing and hope that such experiences as these gave to the people, and how their ordinary lives were transformed into an exquisite blending and communion with the Holy Spirit, so that the common task and the daily round were blessed with a golden rapture and radiance which transported them into the realms of a quiet, self-sustaining bliss.

This sweet bliss is the influence of the Holy Spirit, that feminine emanation from Divine Mother. Is this bliss, and the *consolamentum* which inspired it, of the essence of the Holy Grail? In Arthur Conan Doyle's *Book of the Beyond*, Colum Hayward, the editor, writes that the *consolamentum* was indeed 'Precisely what the Cathar sought or believed deep in his heart to have found: in one sense the Grail; in another, "the peace that passeth all understanding"; in another, "the jewel within the lotus".'

The origins of the Cathars are obscure, but one thing is certain – from their communities arose the medieval Troubadors of Provence; and the Knights Templar, the knights who guarded Mary Magdalene and her brother John and who had settled in that same region of France, extended the hand of fellowship to them and treated them as brethren, protecting them and hiding them when the persecution of the Cathars began, 200 years after the beginning of the spiritual revolution.

The Troubadors sang the song of the magical Mary Magdalene and referred to her as the Grail of the World (we believe that she was actually the mother of the Grail), and within the varying doctrines of the Cathars, Mary and her pure and primal Church were remembered and revered with a passion and devotion that could never be destroyed, even though agents of destruction assuredly came to try to stamp out the fires that had been lit from the torch of John and Mary.

What remains of the Cathar enlightenment today is (perhaps) Protestantism, although organized religion gave it a withering breath and removed from it the fragrance of the Paraclete, that divine principle which invokes the Holy Spirit. This claim seems to be verified by the fact that, after the destruction of the Cathars, the people of the region largely turned to Protestantism, and were again cruelly persecuted by those who adhered to the Roman Church.

The destruction of the Cathars was absolutely merciless, and, as has been mentioned previously, constituted the first act of European genocide. It is interesting, considering how ominous the link with the name Simon was for the Magdalene, to note that the man who headed the Albigensian Crusade which wiped out the Cathars was one Simon de Montfort. Such was the power of the *consolamentum* that the victims of the crusade, among whom were numbered thousands of young children, went to their horrific deaths calmly and stoically, sometimes even holding hands and singing as they were put to the flames.

From what has been revealed to us, it seems clear that the Knights Templar, the Rosicrucians (who stem from the same source as the original Templars or the Essene and Druidic Night-Protectors, and who – as well as the Rosy Cross – are associated with a Rosy Crucible or Dew-Cup, which appears to be related to the Holy Grail), the Cathars, the Alchemists and other occult groups had knowledge of the secret tradition of John and Mary, and prepared for the coming of the New Age and the Church of St John and Mary Magdalene, which was to be established, not in any material or hierarchical sense, but in the mystical heart-centre of humanity through gnosis, direct knowledge of God. Inevitably, through the centuries some of these organizations lost touch with the truth and appear to have confused the identity of the Christ and John the Baptist, and ultimately of the Baptist and John the Beloved Disciple.

Grace Cooke, a woman with highly developed mediumistic qualities who founded the White Eagle Lodge, tells the enthralling story of how, in 1931, she was requested by the masters behind the French Polaire Brotherhood (a group connected with the Albigenses which had been established to pursue spiritual aims and ideals) to help the Polaires to recover the hidden treasure of the Albigenses or Cathars. This treasure, said to be priceless, was buried beneath the castle of Lordat according to the masters, and would be found within three days of the commencement of their search. It seems that the Polaires thought that they were going in search of the lost secret of the Albigenses, the *consolamentum*. Travelling to the region of the Cathars, Grace was brought into contact with an inhabitant of the John Sphere, who helped her to prepare to receive the profound teachings of the master White Eagle, named after the symbol of St John:

> During our stay we climbed each morning to the summit of the mountain [Lordat was a little village high up the mountainside, and the castle stood above it] in the hope of being led to the right spot for beginning excavations. ...
>
> From the beginning we were strongly impressed by the dual nature of the unseen powers around us. There were times when the dark forces were predominant.
>
> Then ... [there] came, like a breath of heaven, a sweet pure, gentle, loving influence like a spiritual illumination, which made us certain of the presence of immortal brothers waiting and watching. At such times as these we felt we were under the protection of great white wings, guarded by a power which must be experienced to be believed.
>
> Although we were ... amidst dangerous elemental forces and in the company of unbalanced human minds [one of those making up the Polaire party had become deranged, and had attacked another], we were constantly reminded, by the whispers of the unseen ... that Christ is all-love and his spirit has power to comfort and protect from all harm. This strengthened our will to proceed.
>
> Many times this wave of spiritual light and power caused the dark veil between matter and the inner world to become thin, to such a degree that we found ourselves in company with the gentle spirits of the Albigenses, who for centuries had walked this very plateau on which we stood. ...
>
> On the third day after our arrival, when we were idly contemplating the grand panorama of mountains under the intensely blue sky with, in the distance [the path winding away towards], the ancient castle of Montsegur, my attention was caught by the sudden appearance of a shining form. ... 'Shining' is the only word to describe the aura of the spirit who appeared, but his manner was as normal as that of any human being might be who, while out walking, had stumbled by chance on a stranger.

He appeared simple, kindly, and treated the situation as naturally as if it were customary for discarnate people to talk to men and women. He looked like an old man at first sight; that is to say, he wore a longish white beard and his hair was silver, but, apart from this his skin was youthful and clear, as though a light shone behind the flesh, and his warm blue eyes were alight with an inner fire. He was clothed in white, in the garb of some early order of Christian Brothers [it is noteworthy that both the Druids and the Essenes wore white robes], and bore himself with noble meekness. 'Could this be one of the Albigenses?' I asked mentally. Yes. It was true; by sign and symbol he proved to me that he belonged to this age-old Brotherhood. Why had he appeared in this manner?

He indicated that he had come to help in the search. However, he said that no material treasure would be found until men were ready to use it, until they had found the spiritual treasure, which was the secret of how their own lower nature could be transformed – the base metal turned into living gold.[3] He indicated that in the life and teachings of Jesus Christ would be found the key to this spiritual treasure.

He spoke of John, the disciple beloved of the Master; how he had not died 'as most men die' but had passed onwards to a higher life in a body of light as his Master had done before him. He had remained on earth for a very long time, travelling to the East and to the West, coming indeed to this very place where he had meditated and communed with his Master.

He spoke of the inner mystical teachings from the Master which he, John, had passed on to his followers and which had been handed down through secret brotherhoods through the centuries; and that this mystical gospel was in fact the source and secret of the treasure of the Albigenses. [In this connection it is interesting to note that there is some historical evidence linking the Cathars with early Christian groups.]

FROM THE PREFACE, BY YLANA HAYWARD, TO *THE LIVING WORD OF SAINT JOHN* BY WHITE EAGLE, 1979

The treasure of the Albigenses did indeed come through the agency of this brother from the Sphere of St John. Soon after her return from the Pyrenees, Grace Cooke established and headed a branch of the Polaire Brotherhood in England. This evolved into the White Eagle Lodge, whose rituals and methods were more in keeping with the ancient Albigensian methods. The beautiful teachings of the master White Eagle are given from this community today. White Eagle's Lodge had its beginnings in France, in that same area where the traditions of Mary Magdalene and John the Divine arose and are still so carefully preserved. It seems that the negative forces of the universe must have striven to engineer historical misunderstanding between France and Britain, because the two countries do indeed have a strong soul-link, and are deeply bonded in their ultimate spiritual mission.

Ten years after her encounter in the Pyrenees with Father John (we believe that this is the title by which he is known), Grace Cooke brought through the teachings of White Eagle on The Gospel of St John, which resulted in the book, *The Living Word of St John*, part of the body of wisdom of the 'John sphere' or the Sphere of Shar-On.

Grace Cooke said of her mission to Lordat, and of the treasure there given into her care:

> It was ... a spiritual outpouring of the truth of divine living; the revelation of a vision which pointed the way of aspiration, sincerity and purity of living which would, in time, re-establish on this earth many centres of the true Star Brotherhood. Surely this is the way the spirit of Christ works! Not through grand buildings and powerful organizations which tend to deny the spirit and concentrate upon the physical, but rather through the simple pure way of brotherhood and service to one another.
>
> Is not the way of true brotherhood the inner meaning of Christ's teaching which has been misinterpreted by the Church in the doctrine of the vicarious atonement?
>
> When the soul passes through the ceremony of initiation into the temple of universal brotherhood it realizes the inner meaning of 'atonement' for it finds itself irrevocably attached to its brothers and companions in spirit – to such a degree that it suffers with the suffering of its brothers and rejoices in its brothers' happiness.
>
> In this sense it is the Christ Light in the heart which takes or absorbs into its own heart the sins or the sufferings of mankind.
>
> This can only be described as vicarious suffering, but instead of the word 'atonement' being used, I believe it should be 'at-one-ment' or perfect brotherhood of the spirit. ... It is not the man, the Master Jesus, whom the Christian world worships as the saviour and vicarious redeemer of the world; it is the teaching of the Christ Spirit or the love and brotherhood, the divine light in the heart of every man, which is the saviour of mankind. It is this little spark of divine life which the Star Brotherhood endeavours to fan into a glowing flame so that it can absorb into itself and feel what its brother feels. This light, this truth is the vicarious at-one-ment – the essence of the teaching of the Star Brotherhood.

GRACE COOKE, THE SHINING PRESENCE, P35–36

NOTES

1 Maurice Magre, *The Return of the Magi*, 1931
2 ibid
3 It is interesting to note in this context how many houses in the area formerly inhabited by the Cathars or the Albigensians still bear alchemical symbols on their exteriors, indicating an inherited tradition.

CHAPTER SEVENTEEN

The Chakra Trail

*A*s well as the many visits to far-flung parts of the world with which Joseph of Arimathea's merchant fleet provided him, there was one particular journey that Jesus undertook, which was traversed for the sake of the culmination of his great gift to the world, thousands of years in the future. For this journey he needed the bodily as well as the spiritual presence of Mary Magdalene. It took place after she had completed her temple training and had risen to the rank of priestess, when she and Jesus were twenty-one years old.

This immense enterprise was known as the Chakra Trail. For those with spiritual sight, their voyage must indeed have been a glorious and dramatic spectacle, for they were attended by a vast company of angels, among them the mighty four, the archangels Michael, Raphael, Gabriel and Uriel, who are associated with the sacred directions of the traditional Medicine Wheel, or the four arms of the Cross; and the seven great planetary beings or angels who rule the seven orbs. These orbs are Saturn, Jupiter, Mars, the Sun, Venus, Mercury and the Moon. Together with the Earth, they complete an octave of the heavenly harmony of spiritual evolution laid down for our planet and its humanity. The four archangels of the Medicine Wheel are numbered amongst the mighty seven.

It was Mary's deep affinity with the consciousness of the great planetary being herself, Mother Earth, which made her physical presence so vital to the Chakra Trail. Mother Earth and Mary resonated as one. Through the mysteries of her physical being, Mary could emanate a blessing and a magic which none other on Earth could, in order to open the mystical gateways of the Earth Mother which represented her chakra system. This chakra system forms the deeply mystical shape of a six-pointed star upon the face of the Earth, with its seventh point at its centre, Palestine itself. (The immeasurable importance and significance of the six-pointed star will be discussed at length in Parts II and III.) Within this star, at its heart, the chakra system traces the form of the Maltese cross, which comprises the dimensions of an opened-out pyramid. We consider that the Earth's chakra system is reflected in both the northern and the southern hemisphere, and that each country also mirrors it, perhaps in a kind of eternal regression, so that even a small area of land might faithfully repeat it. Nevertheless, the Chakra Trail which was undertaken by

Jesus and Mary was on a truly grand scale, and comprises the original system which all the others replicate.

It is at this point that the Night-Protectors came into being. Selected according to the most stringent criteria from both the Essene and the Druid communities, these specially trained guards had striven long and hard throughout their young lives to be deemed worthy of their mission. They were not only valiant men-at-arms (there were also female Night-Protectors), but were well versed in psychic defence and spiritual knowledge. All of them were sworn to secrecy, and all were prepared to lay down their lives in fulfilment of their pledge to protect, to honour and to keep silent.

Few people had any idea that the Chakra Trail was underway. Mary and Joseph, Jesus's parents, might have known; and certainly Joseph of Arimathea, whose later incarnation as King Arthur would highlight his magical connection to the land – to the Earth herself – facilitated this mighty endeavour, supplying ships and provisions, and overseeing the Night-Protectors (although they had their own captain). Those who had reached the highest degree among the Essenes, and the adepts in the company of Druids in Cornwall who knew Joseph of Arimathea well and who collaborated with the plan of the expedition, giving of their knowledge and magical protection and supplying a number of the heroic Night-Protectors, would obviously have been among those privy to it. We believe that Mary Jacob would definitely have known of it and given it her own potent blessing, although Cleopas, Salome and Martha may not have been told. Young John, attending school at Qumran and so closely linked within his inner being with Jesus and Mary, would have received intimations of it in his daytime reveries and in his dreams.

All along the holy Chakra Trail Jesus and Mary sent their combined blessing, energy and consciousness, the circuit of their deeply potent love. This spiritual electricity sanctified and sealed the Earth's chakras with such a magnitude of holy and ineffable fire, with such a radiance of divine virginal energy whose quality was of a beauty and a power beyond imagining, that the entire chakra system and its function as sacred channels for the Christ-Power could no longer be disturbed or blocked, either by design or by accident. Although the Earth's chakras were destined to lie almost dormant for a time, the Chakra Trail ensured that they could no longer be used for any purpose other than that which was perfectly in accordance with Divine Will. That is why, despite the horrendous machinations at this time of those forces that seek to prevent the Earth's and humanity's ascension, they cannot and never will be able to succeed. The victory of the Light is already assured. All we have to do is to embrace that Light – to make a free-will choice to strive always to express the love that is its essence – to make a freewill choice to awaken to our divine heritage of the power of the star, the power of the Light, the power of the purified heart. Then the worldwide transfiguration will begin.

At certain key points upon the face of the Earth, in caves, beside pools, rivers, wells and streams, upon mountain tops, within ancient temples, inside pyramids, in lonely valleys and in the caverns beneath venerable old trees, the divine couple enacted their secret rituals and left documents and artefacts detailing important information for the far distant generation (perhaps ours?) who would be able to decode and utilize them. Sometimes they would be warmly welcomed by ageless communities dwelling in the inaccessible places of the Earth, only too pleased to add their soul power and wisdom to the ceremonies. Occasionally these communities would be Earth people, living spiritually enlightened lives in remote places. More often they would be groups of the Star Brethren who, although still occupying physical bodies, were yet living in a sphere far beyond that of earthliness. Whatever the case, these two beloved souls were honoured and homage paid to them, for none had ever known anything like the scope of their service and mission before.

When they entered such communities, or when they stood alone beneath the Moon and the stars, conducting their rites in solitude, the Night-Protectors were never far away, standing in reverential silence, every sense alert and keen as the wind, ready to step into the breach if needed. They are there still, for they have been seen in their spirit form, dressed in full regalia of the Knights Templar, standing as sentries before the entrances to these sacred places on the Chakra Trail, their swords crossed to prevent the ignorant or the ill-willed from entering. There they will remain until the world is ready to open its heart and sacrifice its lower instincts and desires, and, learning in full the ancient sacred knowledge, at last unfurl and beat the miraculous wings of the soul.

The Night-Protectors absorbed much from these experiences, and, in later years, what they had thus learned of the soul-world, and of the angelic and fairy peoples they encountered whilst in this heightened state and whom they grew to love and revere, they passed on to their band of brothers, the Orders of knights who kept and honoured the true knightly code of heart-centred worship of the Spirit and the Bride. In time these Orders of knights became the Knights of the Round Table, and the Knights Templar. In 1307, when they were massacred by the Church, one of the charges brought against the Templars was the heretical knowledge of, and communion with, spirits and the fairy peoples. Was this a tradition handed down from the first Night-Protectors, who watched the loving communion Jesus and Mary held with these peoples, and the mutually joyful, respectful relationship they shared?

As well as a spiritual service to Earth and her peoples, the Chakra Trail was a profoundly instructive experience for the divine couple, especially for Jesus, who entered into the Earth mysteries so wholly and tenderly that his soul-perspective, his inner vision, was consummated in perfection, becoming limitless and all-embracing. Its deepest potential was realized, and within him the spirit of brotherhood assumed its ultimate reality, extending to every kingdom upon every plane. Mary shared in this expansion of vision and this awakening of the purest, brightest light in the profoundest depths of the heart, and indeed nurtured and fostered its quickening.

The Chakra Trail took eight years of physical toil and travel, and yet their journeyings were a voyage of joy and wonder as they entered into communion with Mother Earth and the Christ Being, and thus with the Godhead itself. Harsh conditions, danger, weariness and exertion did not drain their souls and reduce their capacity for the zest for life, as tends to happen to lesser mortals. For the first time in their present incarnation they were together without restriction or interruption, and they delighted in one another's company.

When they returned home for the final time, they were both past their twenty-ninth birthday. They had only a matter of months to seek refreshment and recuperation after their labours before they were due to enter into the full flowering of their womanhood and manhood and begin the ministry which would change the world.

CHAPTER EIGHTEEN

Love Perfected, Truth Denied

*T*hroughout their ministry, Jesus sang the praise of Mary as she in turn extolled his virtues as master and teacher. This was of course no mutual back-patting club or descent into egoism. It was rather the supreme song of love perfected, in sublime harmony and balance between the Sacred Masculine and the Sacred Feminine – the love song we will all one day sing in the bliss of perfect fulfilment, all sorrow and affliction and heart-yearning healed at last. The Troubadours gave us distant echoes of this song, and the bliss of the mystics and adepts give us intimations of it. It is not a song fuelled by the lower passions and appetites or by an outpouring of emotionalism, but by the sacrifice of the ego, that little earthly self which, with its demands and frets and self-importance, clouds the waters of the soul so that the light of the spirit becomes difficult, if not impossible, to see. When we will no longer give in to its dictates, our soul becomes poised in radiance, and the song begins. It is the song Jesus and Mary taught us. It can truly be said, without melodrama or sentimentality, that theirs is the greatest love story ever told.

There is a Gnostic text which might be thought of as the voice of Mary Magdalene, singing of the mysteries of the Goddess and of the divine love between the Sacred Masculine and the Sacred Feminine Principles, and perhaps, even, of the rough barque into which our faulty perception of history would imprison her, causing her memory to ride on the heaving, turbulent seas of ignorance and bigotry, until at last we are inspired to receive her into the calm and clear waters of gnosis, the living waters which bear the lotus or the rose at our human heart's core. It is called The Thunder, Perfect Mind:

> *I was sent forth from the power,*
> *And I have come to those who reflect upon me,*
> *And I have been found among those who seek after me,*
> *Look upon me, you who reflect upon me,*
> *And you hearers, hear me.*

You who are waiting for me, take me to yourselves.
And do not banish me from your sight.
And do not make your voice hate me, nor your hearing.
Do not be ignorant of me anywhere or any time.
Be on your guard. Do not be ignorant of me.
For I am the first and the last,
I am the honoured one and the scorned one,
I am the whore and the holy one.
I am the wife and the virgin.
I am the mother and the daughter.
I am the members of my mother.
I am the barren one
And many are her sons.
And I have not taken a husband.
I am the midwife and she who does not bear.
I am the solace of my labour pains.
I am the bride and the bridegroom,
And it is my husband who begot me.
I am the mother of my father
And the sister of my husband,
And he is my offspring.
I am the silence that is incomprehensible
And the idea whose remembrance is frequent.
I am the voice whose sound is manifold
And the word whose appearance is multiple.
I am the utterance of my name.

GNOSTIC TEXT

Jesus called Mary Magdalene 'The All' and 'The Woman Who Knows All', bestowing on her the title 'The Apostle of the Apostles' and 'The First Apostle'. He also often referred to her as 'Mary Lucifera', 'Mary the Light-Bringer'. He spoke of her as the glorious one who would rule the Kingdom of Light in the New Age, and who, with her brother John, would tower over all his disciples and 'over all men who shall receive the mysteries', proclaiming that, 'they will be on my right and on my left. And I am they, and they are I.'

When Mary anoints him, he rebukes Judas for upbraiding her regarding the cost of the spikenard and declares, 'She has done a beautiful thing to me. ...Verily I tell you, wherever the gospel is preached throughout the world, what she has done will also be told, in memory of her.' Once, in an outpouring of love and devotion and warm commendation, he says to her, 'Mary, thou blessed one, whom I [the Christ Being speaking through Jesus] will perfect in all mysteries of those of the height, discourse in openness, thou, whose heart is raised to the kingdom of heaven more than all thy brethren.'

There are indications throughout the Gnostic texts, and particularly in the first one to be discovered, the Pistis Sophia[1] (Faith and Wisdom), which was bought by the British Museum in 1785, that Mary's role in the ministry was indeed to 'discourse in openness'. When the disciples again and again failed to understand the spiritual lesson that Jesus sought to impart, Mary would step in and, with exquisite tact, ask Jesus to clarify further, purposely, it seems, appearing as if she herself did not understand. There can be no doubt that she understood perfectly. Her task was to reflect the light of Jesus's teachings in a way that enabled Jesus's followers to understand them. It is interesting, in this context, to note that Suddi spoke of 'BenJoseph' discoursing at school in Qumran and often meeting with blank incomprehension. He is described as attempting again and again with his explanations to enlighten the listener, and when sometimes the incomprehension could not be lifted, Suddi spoke of the young Jesus as gazing at the uncomprehending one with infinite patience, respect and compassion. But with Mary by his side, the knowledge of the Spirit could shine undimmed into the Soul, and the disciples could receive it.

Peter, the Stone, intellectual but uncomprehending and symbolic in himself of the intellect, the lower mind which considers itself as supreme judge and arbitrator of reality and cognitive of all things, but which, in fact, is not equipped to understand anything beyond the narrow and severely limited plane of materiality, is shown as always trying to block Mary's reflection of the light. The intellect is a vital tool as far as organizing and utilizing the Earth-plane for the practical necessity of everyday living, of course; but it can only discern facts, not truth. Facts are not truth itself, but rather the symptoms or outcome of truth. The good intellect was given to us to serve the higher intuition, to fight its cause and facilitate its vision, and ultimately to kneel in honour of, and obedience to, the heart-mind. When it will permit itself to do this, it can become brilliantly inspired and will reflect true intelligence. And so the intellect is revealed as the handmaiden or knight of the rightful ruler, the heart-mind. When the intellect seeks to claim the throne for itself, it is as if the handmaiden or the knight overthrows the rightful queen or king, and eventual chaos is the result.

In the Age of Aquarius, where the mind is exalted and the intellect in receipt of a dynamic, expansive energy, it is essential to keep it firmly in its place as servant rather than master. When the intellect is allowed to overthrow the true vision of the mind in the heart, then the intellect – the lower mind – becomes self-destructive and endangers humanity's very existence, as well as the existence of our beloved planet and all her beautiful kingdoms and ecosystems. Yet spiritual sources and teachers tell us the news is good. We *are* beginning at last to break free of the tyranny of the unbridled intellect and to ignore its hostility and warmongering attitude towards the deep wisdom of the inner self – that still, small voice within the heart, which is how Divine Spirit, Divine Intelligence, communes with us.

Peter represented the hostile intellect, and in the Pistis Sophia (Sixth Book) he seems to resent Mary and her female companions or helpers as they answer Jesus's questions and put their own in order to further expound the truth that Jesus seeks to convey. Peter complains, 'My Lord, let the women cease to question, in order that we may also question,' and, 'My Lord, we will not endure this woman [meaning Mary], for she taketh the opportunity from us and hath let none of us speak, but she discourseth many times.' This is the tendency of the intellect. It imagines that the light of the Spirit (true understanding) is all for itself, and will not recognize the real state of things, which is that that supreme light must first be reflected through the perfect clarity of the illumined soul.

It is not to be supposed that Mary is holding the floor for her own sake in the scenario revealed by Peter, because she is actually working alongside Jesus to impart the Christ teachings; that is her duty and her service. But Peter, the intellect, mistakes her status as competitive posturing (which is actually all coming from himself). Instead of listening to Mary and thereby being enabled to understand Jesus, Peter wants to shut her up so that he can try to directly commune with Jesus for the sake of his own aggrandizement, even though he openly admits and demonstrates again and again that he cannot understand his master! He is not equipped to do so; but had he only listened to Mary instead of scorning her, he would have understood.

Peter's hostility, anger and resentment towards Mary reached a dangerous pitch. In the Pistis Sophia Mary confides to Jesus:

> *My Lord, my mind is ever understanding, at every time to come*
> *forward and set forth the solution of the words which [thou]*
> *hast uttered; but I am afraid of Peter, because he threatened me*
> *and hateth our sex.*

PISTIS SOPHIA, SECOND BOOK, 72:3

In The Gospel of Mary (Mary Magdalene's own gospel), when Mary gives an account of the teachings which had passed between Jesus and herself, Peter accuses her of lying! This is the common stance of the intellect; it claims that the soul lies. 'We want facts, not the recordings of the eye of the intuition or the imagination!' it stridently insists, even though the voice of truth has said, 'Where there is no vision, the people perish.' We cannot, of course, judge Peter, although it is evident that he made life very difficult for Mary and obstructed her mission with malice and vehemence. With the help of Paul he founded the Church of Rome, which proved itself to be extremely hostile to the early Celtic Church, the primitive establishment which taught the truth of 'The Way' and which might be seen as the Church of Mary Magdalene, or the Church of the Three Marys.

At this stage, Peter represented the prevailing misogyny which would overtake the Christian message and slam the door brutally on the true significance and status of Mary Magdalene. He sought to make himself her enemy, although Mary refused to entertain the concept of enemies. But is this unfortunate stance of Peter's his true memorial? – Peter the Stone, in whom Jesus saw so much good alongside so much almost wilful blindness and arrogance. We believe that Peter did eventually choose the light of his higher self and overcome the mutinous elements of his lower nature. He had created a difficult situation for himself, because his heart longed to be filled with the light of Christ, and yet his attitudes and philosophy partially blocked the inflow of that light. His life led him on a course which reflected the coruscating desire of his higher nature and which, coupled with unremitting and Herculean effort, freed him at last from the tyranny of his own ego.

Peter worked as a missionary in Britain and France after the Crucifixion, making prolonged stays in both countries. A weathered tablet of stone, unearthed in Whithorn in Scotland, bears testimony to his presence. Its first-century inscription reads: *Locvs Sancti Petri Apvstoli* (The Place of St Peter the Apostle). On his last visit to Britain, Peter received a vision of his forthcoming death in Rome, brought to him in spirit by Jesus, who came to impart renewed strength and fortitude to Peter before he faced his final initiation. ('Knowing that shortly I must put off this my tabernacle, even as our Lord Jesus Christ hath shewed me.' 2 Peter 1:14.)

Peter's vision was given to him on the site of the church which was later built in his honour, and which eventually evolved into Westminster Abbey (the Abbey of St Peter). Shortly after his vision, Peter returned to Rome, where Christian and Jewish persecution was ongoing. He was soon seized and tried for his evangelizing, and cast into what has been described as 'the most fearsome [prison] on the brutal agenda of mankind'. Over 3,000 years old, this torture chamber was known as the 'Mamertine'. The link with the Earth Mother is obvious from its name and location, for the Mamertine was a subterranean cell gouged from the living rock beneath Rome. There were two chambers within it, one on top of the other. A hole in the ceiling of each chamber provided the only route of entry from above. The lower chamber was little more than three metres in depth (about ten feet) and was the death cell. Apart from the faintest glimmer from the aperture above, the cell was steeped in darkness and was filled with the stench of human effluvia and excrement, for it was never cleaned.

Peter could not have been expected to survive this terrible incarceration. He was chained to a pillar in an upright position so that he could never rest or sleep properly, and was routinely starved and tortured for nine months – the human gestation period. In almost total darkness, in the depths of the Earth, surrounded by his own faeces and that of prisoners who had endured the horrors of the Mamertine before him, all of whom had perished, many descending into lunacy before their death overtook them, Peter, the Rock, somehow survived. In that dreadful womb, he faced and overcame his lower nature, whose essence was exteriorized all around him. His faith never wavered, and throughout the nine interminable months of his appalling initiation, he converted his jailers (Processus and Martinianus) and 47 other Romans. When at last he was led out into the light of day, he was dragged into the barbaric spectacle of Nero's circus, and was crucified there in AD67.

He insisted that his executioners hang him head downwards on his cross, declaring that he was unworthy to be honoured by dying in the same upright position as had his Lord, Jesus Christ. Strangely (and yet not so), this can be linked with the position the baby in the womb assumes prior to birth. And so, through death and the baptism of suffering that preceded it, Peter was born into the light. His indomitable spirit was just as valiant, but now made pure and humble, ennobled by his last great battle with the stony obstruction within his soul that caused him to persecute Mary. We see him as a great white knight emitting a blaze of light, eager now to serve, not only his master Jesus, but Mary and the cause of Mary, which is to ignite the sacred flame of Divine Mother, the consciousness of the Sacred Feminine, in every human heart. And there is a tenderness emanating from Peter, as though he would strive with every spiritual muscle to save humanity from enduring what he had to suffer in order to cast aside foolishness. He says to us that there is a kinder, better way – if only we will follow it. This is Mary's great hope and aspiration for us.

Nevertheless, at the time of the spreading of the teachings of The Way, a year or two after the Crucifixion, Peter, and later Paul, did preach an understanding of The Gospel of Christ (that gospel which rightfully included the teachings of both Jesus and Mary) which militated against the essential inclusion of the Sacred Feminine. Theirs (Paul's at least initially) have been called the outer teachings, which established a Church that constructed an accurate edifice, an exterior that faithfully reflected the scale of the original plan, but which lacked the tender inner essence that would fill the world with magic and beauty and the transcendental power of the presence of Goddess, lifting us in tender arms so that our consciousness might blend and shine with the scintillation of the stars – if only we had allowed ourselves to embrace it.

Of course, St Peter and St Paul were not solely and individually to blame for this regrettable state of affairs.[2] In one sense, they were both worldly men beset with problems of misogyny. Unfortunately, the consciousness of the majority of humankind resonated with the lower, domineering, materialistic chord within human nature, as the selection of Barabbas over Jesus at the time of the Crucifixion testified. And so, although Jesus and Mary had done all in their power (restricted due to the operation of human free will) to raise human consciousness in order to enable it to find its heart-centre, because humanity refused to co-operate, the Church *had* to be founded on the rock of materialism – Peter's untranscended Stone! What Peter and Paul with their undeniable qualities laboured to construct at the outer level should rightfully have been filled with the grace and sanctity of the Holy Spirit.

Because of humanity's wholesale refusal of the inner light which is the Christ Being, imbalance and ignorance secured a firm foothold, and the rise of the Masculine Principle at the expense of the Feminine Principle continued unabated, infecting virtually all religions and political systems. John's gospel might have steered us back on to the true path, for more than any other it holds the key to our complete understanding of the teachings of the Christ as they were reflected through Jesus and Mary. If scrutinized with an alert eye, it reveals, let us say, certain operation scars where material has been removed. This is particularly evident at the start, where John meticulously reaches back to the commencement of creation with the famous words, 'In the beginning was the Word, and the Word was with God, and the Word was God.' Three sentences concerning creation follow; and then suddenly the text leaps forward with disconcerting alacrity to the introduction of John the Baptist.

It seems likely that a description of the birth of Jesus and Mary might have followed that famous opening paragraph – 'And the light shineth in darkness; and the darkness comprehended it not.' (1:5) We consider that John had taken it upon himself to make clear to us that the light of Christ shone through two souls, and, ultimately, three, although John makes no claims for himself. He knew of the secret marriage between Jesus and Mary, and he knew that the star had shone over them both at the place of their birth (interestingly, some Gnostic texts refer to Jesus as a 'twin', although their context is not literal). We believe that agents of the early Roman Church, anxious to maintain the patriarchal status quo, took out many references to Mary and her teachings on Goddess, our Divine Mother. John related a number of stories of Jesus and Mary working together to bring enlightenment to their followers which outlined and offered clues regarding the importance of their early work (particularly the Chakra Trail) as well as their three-year mission.

Throughout these narratives, John celebrated the significance and status of Mary as the divine consort of Jesus – his feminine counterpart – definitely and directly. We believe that copies of his unexpurgated gospel still exist, and will be discovered in due course. Fortunately, humanity has the key that Grace Cooke gave us, through her recording of White Eagle's interpretation of John's gospel, to unlock its mysteries. Those who tampered with John's gospel were not entirely able to obliterate its emphasis on women's spirituality and the inclusion of the Sacred

Feminine. Not only do its contents abound with significant women and describe *eight* miracles (the ancient goddess of the region was known as the 'Goddess of Eight' and eight, as well as nine, is a number deeply associated with the teachings of Mary Magdalene), its deeper truth is contained in perfection in its Gnostic symbolism and cannot be eradicated, so intrinsic is it within the text itself.[3]

The question arises as to why spiritual teachers such as Grace Cooke, White Eagle and the spokesman from the Sphere of John (we believe that one of his titles is 'Father John') did not enlighten us as to the true status of Mary Magdalene? We consider that it was not quite the right time for humanity to be given this revelation. The realization of the wonder of her true significance had to strike us and lift us like a huge tidal wave, because there is so much obstructing debris, accumulated through the ages, which must be washed away before we can receive the mystery of her blessing. It is not a truth that could successfully have been imparted to us through others' teachings, however exalted. Her return had to pierce us at our heart's core, and her teachings had to come, not vicariously, but through herself alone. It is through aspiration to serve this sacred purpose that we humbly offer our book, not only to our readers but to Mary herself.

Although Jesus by no means made it secret to all of his followers, Mary's great role in the Christ mission was to some extent obscured and denied throughout its three-year span, mainly because the disciples were loath to accept her as the equal of Jesus, their master. Nevertheless, John the Divine (an apt name for Lazarus, her brother) did know of it, and in later years preached it openly, leaving a written record of it, as we have discussed. According to their gospels, Philip and Thomas also accepted and honoured Mary's status. However, their recognition of her came after the Crucifixion. Mary's gospel records a crucial moment, which took place following this dire event, where she gives teachings to the disciples that only the consort and equal of Jesus could have received. The men dispute among themselves, Andrew and Peter continuing to deny Mary, but Levi arguing firmly in her defence. He obviously resolves the issue, because, after being comforted and encouraged by Mary, they all take up the challenge to go forth and preach the Gospel of Christ.

Mary's gospel, as well as giving a pure and beautiful teaching on the nature of the soul and its adversaries, and particularly on the chakra system – those seven points within the soul which are reflected in the body as nerve centres or ductless glands and which are called so evocatively the Seven Eyes of God and the Seven Virgins of Light – was also about this crucial moment. It recorded the point where the disciples accepted her exalted relationship with Jesus, and followed her teachings (she always delivered them as proceeding from the Christ, which Jesus himself had done, creating a channel through which the Christ could speak directly to those 'with ears to hear'). The significance of this moment is enormous, because it marked the beginning of the Church of Mary Magdalene, which was the true Church of the

Christ. Had this pure demonstration of The Way constituted the direction in which Christianity eventually flourished, our world today might have been very different, healed of its warmongering and divisiveness.

But there was a dissenter in the camp; although the other disciples allowed Mary and her teachings to inspire them and lead the way, Peter simply could not bring himself to accord the Magdalene her rightful status. He was silenced, but he was not converted. Did he make a decision on that fateful day, recorded by The Gospel of Mary, to set up his own Church, to preach the gospel in the way he saw fit, and to ensure that Mary was silenced in her turn, her rendition of The Way and the Church overthrown? Peter still boiled with resentment and rage against Mary (it was not long since he had, directly or indirectly, threatened to kill her), and no doubt he was still smarting from the pain and shame of denying Jesus three times before cockcrow immediately prior to the Crucifixion, as Jesus had predicted. Perhaps, in the traditional male way, he blamed Mary for his misdemeanours, as Eve and Pandora were blamed before her for all the ills of humankind.

And there seems to be a special significance in the three denials; was it Jesus, Mary and John he denied? one after the other, although at the outer level he was asked by his enquirers only about Jesus and would not have realized the significance of the three denials. We believe that Peter preached a very different version of The Gospel of Christ from that of not only Mary, but also John, and it was by the agency of Peter's Church that John, through omissions from his gospel, was silenced as well as his sister. Moreover, the cockerel itself is a bird linked with Mary Magdalene and associated with the Sphere of John, as we shall see.

So Mary's gospel reveals that the disciples did not afford her true recognition and acceptance until that important day which the gospel itself records. This huge turning point and its relevance for the future of humanity cannot be overestimated. Although Peter was able to impose the legacy of his own blind spot on the establishment of the Church of Rome, his blindness cannot persist forever, because Mary's vision was honoured and cherished in the early days of Christianity, and her Church, the bridal chamber of the Bride and the Bridegroom, was born to the Earth and was not denied.

Throughout the three-year mission, Mary had to endure humiliation and friendlessness from the disciples. She bore all with a sweet humility, but also with an unshakeable dignity that gave intimations of the mighty strength at her core. This strength, and the status Jesus conferred on her, was what thoroughly rattled the male disciples. The Gospel of Thomas records:

... the companion of the Saviour is Mary Magdalene. But
Christ loved her more than all the disciples, and used to kiss her
often on the [mouth[4]]. The rest of the disciples were offended ...

They said to him, 'Why do you love her more than all of us?'
The Saviour answered and said to them, 'Why do I not love you
as I love her?'

The response of Jesus to the fretting of his disciples over this matter is to reassure them that they are by no means excluded from the ring of perfect love which Jesus and Mary create together. Relationships that spring from the supreme balance of the Sacred Marriage in its most exalted form do not exclude others, but hold them in the warm embrace of the central sun which the two lovers ignite with their union. There is absolute fidelity (unadulterated consummation or perfect conjoinment) which, resonating at a higher level, forms completion or the unbroken circle; and then from this circle or ring of light there radiates forth a great wave or expanse of love which surrounds others and is self-sustained in its selfless giving.

The love between Jesus and Mary was the ineffable dynamic that would have nourished and blessed the disciples unstintingly, shining a light of the sublimest pulchritude into the darkest corners of their ignorance and blindness and delivering them healed and whole into the fullness of their divine humanity – if only they had accepted it! But their jealousy of Mary closed their hearts to the gift of this unique ray of love – part of the ultimate mystery of the Christ Being – because they could not see the shining truth of its nonexclusiveness, its essential all-embracing quality. Only after the Crucifixion did most of them at last accept it, and then begrudgingly, and in small measure.

Yet, from the first, Jesus sought to show them the reality that their jealousy obscured – 'Why do I not love you as I love her?' he asks, seeking to teach them enlightenment through the process of self-questioning their doubts. 'Why does the light that proceeds from our love enfold you in any less measure?' is his question, offering them the realization that divine love such as he and Mary shared did not fade, dim or lessen, as is the nature of earthly light. And although the undeniable truth shone fully in their faces, they would not be convinced, so caught up were they in the lower-mind concept of egotistical preference.

In this instance, Mary could not offer them elucidation, for in their ignorance they would have considered it insult added to injury. Even though the most sacred and profound truths were constantly revealed to them through her agency, as she worked with Jesus to give birth to the seeds of truth that they received from the heart-light of the great Christ Being, she always had to work as if obscured by a veil, as if the gift of the great teachings were really nothing to do with her, when in fact they were everything to do with her. This stance of humility and self-abnegation (very necessary, because without it the disciples would have shut themselves off from her enlightenment completely) gave rise to their misreading of the situation concerning the 'casting out of the seven devils' from Mary. This was actually a teaching given by Jesus and Mary to the disciples to show them the significance and potency of the chakra system and its true identity as the arterial system of the soul.

Their teaching showed how the soul should be considered as consisting of not only the soul that is the higher essence of the everyday personality belonging to a single incarnation, but that greater being in which our true Self resides, the Soul Temple, which is built from the accumulated effort of many, many lives that the individual experiences on Earth. From the lessons of these lives, garnered by the higher essence of the Self present in us throughout their span, which comprises what we call the soul – and the spirit within it – of any one incarnation, that Self or spirit which is the spark of true individuality within each one of us, builds for itself the glorious Soul Temple. This is the ultimate and supreme body, imbued with divine life and consciousness, which – when it is complete – will finally enable that same spark of Spirit or Self permanently to dwell within it and assume every aspect of Beingness, so becoming a co-creator with God-Goddess. It (we) will no longer be a 'little spark', but a perfected Being in our own right, scintillating with light.

And so Jesus and Mary reveal to us, as they revealed to the disciples, that what we call our soul in our present incarnation is more truly a single strand of our great Soul which resides in the spiritual spheres and which contains that ineffable spark or seed of light, the point of God-life within us all. Throughout our lives we are each connected to that unutterable mystery – the point of our spirit contained within our greater Soul – via the strand of it that we call the soul of our present incarnation, whose true dwelling place is the bridal chamber of the heart. The seven chakras are the blossoms of the rose tree blooming within the structure of the soul whose energies must remain clear and beautiful if they are to quicken the development of the soul so that it may conduct the consciousness of the indwelling spirit through into earthly life, which is the whole point of incarnation.

It is a point worth remembering that the angels hold the human race in great admiration for their brave expeditions into deepest matter, for it is from these farthest reaches of creation that the dynamic of the divine may penetrate into unknown dimensions of the uncreated darkness and bring back marvels, wonders and treasures of the spirit that reveal new vistas of creative possibility. The initiation of matter is the hardest of all, and the chakra teaching is vital to our understanding of our own potential and our remembrance of our mission. Without it we forget how to fully embrace soul-awareness, how to become fully human, and the darkness of matter blinds our inner eye and shuts down true vision.

In order to help the disciples understand how it is that our chakras become blocked, and what arises from our lower nature to congest them which must be healed and transformed, Jesus and Mary taught of the 'seven devils' which can waylay and hold hostage the high vibrational energy of the seven chakras. These are allied to the 'Seven Deadly Sins' and can loosely be designated as pride in the crown, lust at the brow, envy in the throat, anger in the heart, covetousness in the solar plexus, gluttony in the sacral or spleen area, and sloth at the base of the spine. This is no rigid formula, of course, but it provides a working model. Together, Jesus and Mary clearly demonstrated the expulsion of negative energy from these seven centres, the arteries of the soul, and the consequent inrush of pure, clear energy which resonates with the consciousness of the spirit, and can therefore reflect it.

The idea that Mary actually *needed* her chakras to be cleared is indeed absurd. She was, in the highest and the deepest sense, the most royal and divine woman on Earth, and had mastered such lessons countless aeons before Earth life even came into existence. Nevertheless, the disciples, or more probably those later editors who distorted and omitted some of the material of the gospels, referred to Mary as 'she who had had seven devils cast out of her'. This is particularly ironic when one considers the fact that she left us such a beautiful and mystical teaching on the chakras, the soul, and their adversaries in her own gospel. It is possible, however, that Jesus did attune and awaken her chakras so that they reflected the full glory of her Divine Womanhood prior to her anointing him with spikenard a week before the Crucifixion, when she in turn made him the Christ, the Divine Son.

NOTES

1 There is strong evidence to support the idea that the Pistis Sophia is actually a highly edited third- or fourth-century rendition of an earlier text called Questions of Mary, which, if true, would further support our conclusion.

2 St Paul later became influenced via a very interesting source and eventually incorporated the true inner essence of the teachings of 'The Way' into his doctrines, albeit in a veiled and disguised form. There exists convincing evidence that hostile forces within the Church forged documents in his name to throw the faithful off the scent.

3 See *The Gospel of John*, 1899, the Reverend W R Inge

4 This word was inserted by scholars, as it has been lost from the original text. However, our source confirms that 'mouth' is the missing word.

CHAPTER NINETEEN

The Crucifixion and Resurrection

*J*esus and Mary had decided together that, because of the level of resistance to and denial of their mission, no more could be accomplished by his remaining on Earth. They saw that their ministry could be made more powerful, however, if Jesus were to ascend to the heavenly spheres, and Mary were to remain on Earth to establish the teachings of The Way – the King in Heaven and the Queen on Earth. And so it was decided, in order to enact a drama that humanity would one day understand, that the worldliness in human nature should be allowed to scourge Jesus and put him to 'death', as it clamoured to do. This outcome had been predicted, of course, and was the fulfilment of a prophecy that extended beyond the Earth-planes.

Jesus and Mary knew before their coming that the Crucifixion would be the almost inevitable culmination of their joint mission, and that the divine truth they embodied would, by the volition of the Godhead, assume the verity of the ultimate sacrifice. Nevertheless, nothing is set in stone, and humanity could have made a huge evolutionary leap and chosen the Christ Light instead of the thief and murderer, Barabbas (Mary's gospel gives further enlightenment on the choked soul-state which gives rise to the choice of wholesale impoverishment, suffering, annihilation and death over the flourishing abundance and healing fulfilment of eternal life). If this had happened, Jesus's great sacrifice would have been one of transcendental joy in his self-giving, and the light he emitted, conjoined with Mary, would have subsumed the unredeemed darkness of the Earth. Instead, humanity's choice sealed his fate. His anointing was Mary's goodbye to him, and the culmination of their Sacred Marriage. Her tears were an expression of her divine compassion and love, her sacred wisdom which bade her to release him of all earthly ties, and her human heart, which could not help but grieve over this separation and the sorrow of the Crucifixion.

On that terrible day the three Marys stood before the cross, the three who were emblems of the three aspects of the Goddess, Mary the Bride, Mary the Mother, and Mary the Crone – Mary Magdalene, Mary the mother of Jesus, and Mary Jacob. John the Divine, the twin soul of Jesus, stood alongside them. Through the mystery of the Great Mother, expressed in the composite vehicle of the three Marys, Jesus would rise again – not only via the ascension of his spirit and the higher aspect of his soul, as is normally the case – but (and yet in a perfect outworking of divine law) also through a miracle involving the spiritualization of his physical atoms, in the body which he occupied on Earth.

Suddi tells us that Jesus controlled the impact of his mortal sufferings, and quickly left his body. First, he spoke to the thief on his right, who had suddenly, right at the end of his life, understood the meaning of the Christ Light. The murderer on his left kept his heart closed, thus ensuring that his own vibratory rate would prevent him from reaching any but the lower astral levels after death; but to the thief, Jesus promised Paradise, knowing that because of the man's open-heartedness, Christ could ensure that he rose to a much higher plane than would have been the case had the thief died alone.

From the cross, he gave his mother into the care of John; Joseph his father, being so much older than his wife, had now died, and Jesus knew it was his mother's destiny to journey with John and the other disciples to new shores, where the roots of the Christ teachings would be established and nurtured. At the mystical level, this act emphasizes the closeness of John to Divine Mother and her angels. Jesus encouraged one of the Roman soldiers to express the compassion the man felt in his heart by asking for his thirst to be alleviated, and was duly given the sponge of vinegar to drink from. He spoke a prayer to the glory of the Father-Mother God, asking for forgiveness for his tormentors and himself. He seemed to wish he could have done more for humanity, and he gave forth from the cross a great outpouring of love and blessing to those representatives of it around him, both friends and foes, although it is certain that he could not have done more than he did, and that the stupendous gift he and Mary gave to us has not yet been realized in all its cosmic dimensions. And then came the signal to the Magdalene that he was about to leave his body – 'It is finished.' All that he could accomplish on Earth in a physical state had been done, and it was time for him to go.

It was late February and the Moon was full, already shining down upon the scene from a blue daylight sky.[1] Although it was early in the evening, approaching five o'clock, the sky darkened and great Earth tremors began. The darkness became inpenetrable and absolute – without starlight or moonlight to lessen its intensity. This period of eery and unnatural darkness fell across the entire globe, and was noted by many astronomers of the time. Suddi relates that Earth herself, the exalted being who is the Earth goddess and with whom Mary Magdalene was as one, shuddered and cried out against this reprehensible act of human barbarity.

Countless souls, either through neglect or wanton cruelty, die hideous deaths. Jesus, whose qualities as a man and as a divine being (we are all a combination of both states) have stimulated profound love and devotion in human hearts, willingly underwent his crucifixion as a means, among many other lessons, of teaching us to empathize deeply with suffering, and to strive to prevent or alleviate it. The horror his greatest devotees felt at witnessing his terrible death should properly be the horror felt by any human being who witnesses savagery committed against any other living being. This spiritual law he sought, through his own suffering, to convey to his followers and to coming generations.

If such was the expression of the anguish of the Earth Mother herself, in squalls and tremors and sudden darkness, how must Mary his mother and Mary his lover have felt, along with John the Divine, his twin soul, and Mary Jacob, his devoted aunt? The faithful Joseph of Arimathea, standing by in readiness to bear him to the prepared tomb in the nearby garden he owned, must also have felt the weight of the unspeakable agony that bore down upon them. They all knew the secrets of the spirit, that he would rise again; and yet their baptism of suffering and grief had to be undergone.

Because the Sabbath starts at dusk on Friday evening, and it was not permitted that crucifixions or criminal punishments be carried out during the Sabbath period, the soldiers reacted to the gathering darkness by running a sword through the three crucifixion victims to make sure that they were dead, so that they could be released from their suspension (the usual method of ensuring death was to break the legs of the crucified after they had hung on their crosses for one or two days). Despite the modern idea that hundreds were crucified at the same time that Jesus died on his cross, this is a misconception. Only three were brought to Golgotha to die on that evening, Jesus being the central figure between the thief and the murderer.[2] Because of the elevated site, all the city could view the event.

It was at this point that Joseph of Arimathea stepped forward to catch in two cruets the blood and the water that gushed forth from the wound of Jesus, which he kept as sacred vessels that bore the symbolic essence of the Christ to the land where the first Church of the True Light would be established. Mary also caught the blood and the water in a cup, where it mingled and became one. This chalice would afterwards be associated with the Holy Grail – not the mystery itself, but its emblem, as the contents of the cruets were sign and symbol of the Christ essence. The blood and water were magical because they constituted the rush of energy, the giving forth, that was the physical symbol of Jesus's supreme sacrifice, his life laid down and his whole self given as an act of love for humankind and devotion to the Godhead.

The body was taken down from the cross and laid in the nearby tomb which Joseph of Arimathea had prepared for its reception. To the tomb came the three Marys, accompanied by Joseph of Arimathea and Nicodemus the disciple, who brought spices and oils so that the women might anoint Jesus and cleanse his body. Nicodemus, as well as Joseph and John, was the only male disciple to attend the

Crucifixion. Jesus's female disciples (other than the three Marys) watched in mourning from a respectful distance.

He was wrapped in linen with the spices and aloes, the great sealing stone was heaved into place to close the tomb, and the three Marys and their companions departed to their homes to pray and to meditate. From this point on, Mary the mother of Jesus lived with John and the Bethany family. Mary Magdalene retired into solitude, for she had work to do. Her spiritual presence was required whilst Jesus entered the underworld for a period of three days, there to rescue as many souls trapped on the lower astral planes as would permit him to do so.

This three-day rescue mission to the underworld (a shadowy astral region attached to the Earth where souls remain trapped, usually because they have been unable to detach themselves from the emotional preoccupations of their physical lives) was Jesus's last great gift to struggling humanity whilst he was attached to the Earth. He set free countless confused and unhappy souls, and a great clearing of the astral levels took place which was reflected in a purer, brighter etheric and psychic atmosphere on Earth, one which allowed his followers to receive and understand his guidance from spirit much more clearly, and to use this beautiful translucency to shine an unalloyed light onto the paths of those who wished to receive the Christ illumination. As before, Jesus and Mary worked together, soul within soul, to bring about this great healing mission.

On the first day of the week after the Crucifixion, Mary Magdalene came to his tomb. It was very early, at that hour of deepest darkness just before dawn, and all was quiet. Mary had come to say her last goodbye. With her she carried the unguent spikenard, not in the large alabastron which she had used to anoint Jesus into his Christhood, but in a small green vial which she had kept carefully since the anointing a week earlier. The remainder of the spikenard was secreted within. Mary had used it when she, in company with Jesus's mother, her own mother Mary Jacob, Nicodemus and Joseph of Arimathea, had attended the poor broken body of Jesus after it had been brought from the cross to the tomb. Now she came to the tomb again so that she might be with her lover's physical body for the final time, in privacy and in silence, in deep communion and devotion, the spikenard intended this time also for her own use, so that she might more easily cross the threshold between mortal life and the gateway to the higher worlds.

What might Mary's thoughts and feelings have been at this moment, what were her expectations? She knew, of course, that Jesus was not 'dead' and could not die, and she knew that now, three days after the death of his physical body, he had entirely left behind his earthly shell. He was gone. We believe that she had accompanied his spiritual being, herself in spirit, as together they had descended to the lower astral regions and delivered the people incarcerated there from their imprisonment. When she returned to her body, it was before first light on what we know today as Easter morning, although the goddess Eostre, mistress of renewal and the spring tide of rebirth, had long been venerated at this season, and we think that Mary was not without connection to this deity.

Weary from the ordeal of her farewell to Jesus at his anointing, the merciless horror of the Crucifixion and her ministrations in the underworld, Mary had kneeled and prayed to the supreme Godhead in the silence of the early hours. This, we believe, was for her the most difficult time of all. Bearing up stoically under the empathetic agony of the Crucifixion for the sake of her lover, his mother and her brother John, the sheer weight of the trauma now fell across her shoulders. Mighty in soul beyond our comprehension though she undoubtedly was, she was yet on Earth, constrained in a vulnerable physical and emotional vehicle, and her heart was human as well as divine. She pondered as she knelt in the darkness of her room that Jesus's last service to humanity whilst he was on Earth had been given, and he was even now leaving behind the Earth spheres – leaving her. Although she and her lover could never truly be separated, yet a separation of a kind was already underway, and she knew that her years on Earth would be long. She was pregnant and alone, and upon her success or failure in the Christ mission the fate of humanity hung. She had not as yet even managed to convince the disciples that they should accept her as their leader. As she knelt in the hour before first light, the moment must have seemed grievously solemn, grave and weighty almost beyond endurance.

Bearing her vial of spikenard, she had set out for the tomb, and as she approached it she saw that the stone had been rolled away from the entrance. What follows, as related in The Gospel of St John, imparts important information concerning the nature of the resurrection of Jesus. On seeing that the stone has been moved from the tomb's entrance, Mary is obviously thrown into terrible distress. She runs to find John, who is with Simon Peter, and tells her brother in anguished tones, 'They have taken away the Lord out of the sepulchre, and we know not where they have laid him.' Mary at this point was at her lowest ebb. The body of her beloved Yeshua, so dear to her, and the precious temple in which they had shared the *hieros gamos*, was gone, taken, perhaps to be further mocked and vilely desecrated. After seeing him die on the cross, the despair at being unable even to protect his mortal remains must have been overwhelming.

John was as horrified as his sister, and outran Peter as they both raced towards the tomb. He stooped and saw the pile of linen clothes, discarded; and the napkin that had been wound around Jesus's head neatly folded in a separate place by itself (indicative of the separation of the consciousness of Jesus from his earthly incarnation). He was too shocked and distressed to enter, but Simon Peter went in and confirmed that the sepulchre was empty. The two men left, perhaps to try to find out who was responsible for stealing the body, perhaps to nurse a grief that had now become even more wretched. (John simply says that they returned home.)

Mary needed the silence and the solitude which surrounded her at the empty sepulchre. She remained at its entrance, quietly weeping. Sensing the presence of angels (her devoted brethren, with whom she had always been familiar and intimate), she knelt and looked into the tomb. She saw sitting there two angels in white, one at the head and one at the feet of where the body of Jesus had lain. These angels were Saturnian angels, angels of the Law of the Godhead. They presided over the birth of Jesus and Mary, for Capricorn, their astrological sign, is ruled by Saturn. (The Capricornian goat, for this very reason, was sacred to the Knights Templar, who celebrated its mystery in their homage to Baphomet, the Goat, whom the Roman Church leaders denounced as the 'devil' at the time of their persecution of the Templars.) It makes sense, therefore, that these angels would also preside over the physical 'death' or passing of both Jesus and Mary. That was indeed what they had been called to do, and why they asked, with profound compassion, 'Woman, why weepest thou?' They shared her grief, and yet sought to gently remind her of the shining truth that, although temporarily shrouded from her, she surely comprehended even more deeply than they, for in her greater self, the full glory of her soul and her spirit, was she not goddess of the rising of the stars, goddess of the dawn, Eostre/Isis herself? Had she truly forgotten what the daily rising of the light meant?

'Because they have taken away my Lord, and I know not where they have laid his body,' Mary answers them, still benighted and steeped in grief and loss. The angels give no reply, but instead, in true angelic mode, combine their power in order to minister to the manifestation of another presence which will utterly comfort her. Mary feels the manifestation and turns her head to look back, but she is still unable to see in the obscurity which prevails both within and without. She thinks the gardener is standing there.

In the paling darkness, the question is spoken again, this time by the human figure. 'Woman, why weepest thou? Who seekest thou?'

Mary says to him, 'Sir, if it is you who has removed him, tell me where you have laid him, and I will take him away.'

Then comes the infinitely tender, 'Mary.'

It is at this point that the light breaks in upon Mary, and that the first rays of the dawn illumine the form of Jesus. Mary and Jesus are present as light-filled beings in the Holy Garden. Easter morning is born.

There follows what the Church interpreted as the ultimate rejection of the impure harlot. Mary, awake at last, responds with the intimate 'Rabboni', which means 'my Teacher' or 'my Master', but in the sense of one devoted lover to another. She clearly moves towards him to embrace him, but Jesus says, 'Touch me not; for I am not yet ascended to my Father.' Such was the orthodox interpretation. It has also been suggested that Jesus forbade Mary to touch him because she was pregnant.

Physical contact between a husband and a pregnant wife was forbidden by Jewish law because the impregnated woman was supposed to be contaminated until she had performed certain rites after giving birth. The idea that Jesus, who spent and ultimately sacrificed his life in order to free human consciousness from unkind and superstitious nonsense of this kind, would forbid Mary to touch him because he considered her 'impure' (for the latter explanation designates her as 'impure' as the first) seems to be wildly off course.

What we believe really happened (and an accurate linguistic interpretation of the sentence seems to bear this out) is that Jesus asked her not to embrace him because the atoms of his body were still in the process of becoming spiritualized; he was still 'ascending'. If he had entered her physical embrace, he would have experienced a strong pull back towards Earth, towards his beloved Mary who of course still occupied a corporeal body, and he would have found it difficult to avoid the desire to remain with her at the earthly level. This would have been distressing for both of them. Mary understood immediately, and advanced to a deeper level of communion where they could bathe in one another's light without the obstruction of the body. In this state of raised consciousness, Jesus asked her to go to his brethren, and to tell them that he was not dead, but that, 'I ascend unto my Father, and your Father; and to my God, and your God.' We believe that the correct interpretation of these words is, 'I go to God the Father and the Mother, for my God the Father is your God, and your God the Mother is my God, and the Father-Mother God is God of us all.' This exhortation to Mary not only bids her to reassure the disciples of Jesus's continued existence and that there is no death, it also places upon her the vital task of confirming to his followers that God is both Mother and Father, the perfect balance of the Divine Masculine and Feminine Principles.

What is further revealed is that Jesus did not return to Mary and the disciples in a physical body. There can be no doubt that Mary knew that his earthly shell had been cast off. There was no expectation on her part to find an arisen Jesus in a body formed from the elements of Earth when she visited the sepulchre. After all, it is not too uncommon for people to experience a return to their physical vehicle after they have actually 'died', as numerous reports of near-death experiences attest. This must have been the case in the time of Jesus as it is in our own. And Jesus had amply demonstrated, via Lazarus and the daughter of Jarius, and perhaps through many others, that a return to the physical body after the soul has crossed the threshold of death is possible as long as the earthly vehicle has not begun to deteriorate beyond restitution. The arisen Jesus demonstrates a different, deeper truth to us.

Jesus had spiritualized his physical atoms until his physical body became his true body – the body of light, which receives a baptism of divine fire from the heart of the Godhead that makes it eternal. Thus does the little spark of spirit that has descended into matter many, many times in impermanent, incomplete and limited bodies finally attain full man- or woman-hood in a permanent, complete and limitless body of light – the Soul and the Spirit made one – the Mystical Marriage. When the spiritual vibration of the ascending light body is as high as was that of Jesus (and, when her time came, this would have applied to Mary also) the elements which are not required for the light body, those which belong to the Earth, return to the Earth in such perfect vibrational reunion that there is no decay or corruption and nothing at all remains of the structure of the physical vehicle. This process requires the work of harmonization. It is a spiritual procedure or force which directs, harmonizes and reunites the physical atoms with their own element, a kind of vaporization which does not involve destruction, only returning and reuniting. The process is fulfilled by exalted human and angelic intelligences working together from the spiritual side of life to energize or spiritualize the light body and reintegrate the elements of the Earth body with Earth herself. At some point in the future, when we have learned The Way of Light, the process we call death will involve no corruption or destruction of the physical vehicle. There will only be ascension and harmonization, and no decay or disintegration.

John's gospel reports that when Jesus came again amongst his disciples after the Crucifixion, Thomas could not believe he was actually present until he touched Jesus's wounds. This does not mean that Jesus's body was physical. The ascended body holds the pattern of what was impressed upon the physical body for a brief time, until the body of light is ready to erase it. And so we learn from Mary that Jesus demonstrated ascension and harmonization for us, and arose in his true body, not the mundane vehicle composed of material or earthly elements which he had used during his incarnation. Nevertheless, there were elements or higher patterns of his physical body that were absorbed into the rarefied spiritual vibration of ascension, transforming them into his body of light. The process Jesus underwent after the Crucifixion was a beautiful and perfect manifestation of divine law, and was very different from the usual passing, where the physical body is left behind and enters a state of corruption.

Another most significant point Mary reveals to us is that, until the ultimate sacrifice of the Crucifixion had been made, it seems that the *consolamentum* as a teaching dispensed by Jesus did not come into existence.[3] The spiritual power necessary to generate this immeasurable gift of vision could not be released until the supreme act of self-giving, represented by the Crucifixion, had been fulfilled. From then on, those who had been initiated into the secret teachings of 'The Way' could give it forth. It certainly was not something of which the disciples could avail themselves at the Crucifixion. This is why Jesus said to his disciples, before the final farewell (after the Crucifixion); 'If we do not go, the Comforter will unable to come to you.' His words also reveal that this 'Comforter' (the *consolamentum*) was Mary's gift too, because the special connection between the material plane and the highest spititual realms, which enabled it to be given, was created via the agency of the King (Jesus) being in Heaven and the Queen (Mary) remaining on earth.

For a short period of time following the meeting of Jesus and Mary in the garden, the disciples underwent deep, transforming experiences which could be given to them because the King of Light had ascended, and the Queen remained on Earth. Their learning was heightened and quickened by the balance between the two lovers as Jesus taught them in his light body, and Mary 'earthed' or grounded the energy of the spiritual consciousness flowing into herself and Jesus and out to them from the Christ Being.

This was a very necessary scenario. The essential training and initiation of the disciples needed to be speeded up because hostile forces were on the move. Both Jewish and Roman contingencies wanted to see the disciples silenced, and the teachings of 'The Way' stamped out forever.

NOTES

1 February is the month sacred to Brigid, the great Celtic goddess into whose mysteries Mary was initiated and with whose sacred mantle she was invested when she set foot on British shores. Our source has given us the date of 28 February as the day on which the Crucifixion took place. This is according to the current calendar. In the Old Testament, the Book of Leviticus tells us that the Passover (the Jewish New Year feast, commemorating the 'passing over' – sparing – of the dwellings of the Israelites whose doorposts were marked with the blood of the lamb when the vengeful angels were summoned to smite the Egyptians with the death of their first-born; see Exodus 12) takes place in the evening during the 'first month'. This month was known to the Jewish people as Nisan, beginning in March and extending into April. The first full Moon that occurred in Nisan was the day upon which the evening Passover feast was held. Although the Crucifixion took place at full Moon (within the same 24-hour period as the evening Passover) on 28 February according to the method by which we calculate our dates today, it is important to remember that the Gregorian calendar supplanted the old Julian calendar in 1582, and was adopted in Britain in 1752. The modification of dates caused by this change of calendar meant that 11 days were eliminated from the old Julian year. Therefore, for all dates prior to the installing of the Gregorian calendar, we have to count forward by 11 days to equate our modern dates with the old Julian dates. This means that, according to the old calendar, the first full Moon of Nisan must have fallen on 10 March in 33AD, giving rise to the celebration of the Passover on that evening, which was followed by the Crucifixion on 11 March. This loss of 11 days from the old calendar makes sound astronomical sense, but it does cause some strange shifting-sand sensations when one considers how it has affected the calculation of the dates of the birth of the two Christ children, who were in any case born 11 days apart (actually 12, with the 12th day inclusive, to indicate the zodiacal round, Jesus being born on the 12th day after Mary's birth). If we move the dates on 11 days so that they equate with the 'New Style' of the Gregorian calendar, we find

THE SECRET TEACHINGS OF MARY MAGDALENE – PART I

that Mary was born on the 6 January, and Jesus was born on 17 January. Prior to our consideration of this, there had been much mystification as to exactly why 17 Janauary was such an important date to the Priory of our Lady of Sion and to the Knights Templar. Now we know! Moreover, 6 January, our own 'Twelfth Night', the important 'Three King's Night' for much of Europe, and held especially dear to the Greek and Russian Orthodox Church which celebrates Christmas Day itself on that date, could be seen as Mary's birthday according to the old calendar, and that of Jesus according to the new. We feel that there is more to this change of calendar than mere practicality, however pressing the latter was in order to ensure that the summer and winter months were not displaced; and that Pope Gregory acted on the advice of those who were party to secret knowledge concerning Mary Magdalene when he constructed his new calendar (there were other methods open to him by which the displacement could have been rectified). Pope Gregory XIII (note the significant 13!), by astronomical sleight of hand, ensured that the entry into the world of both the Christ children would thereon be celebrated. (For a further discussion of this mystery, *see* Notes for Chapter Twenty-eight, Part II, footnote 1.)

2 Those familiar with the works of Rudolf Steiner will recognize the esoteric meaning of this symbol, where the central Christ holds in check the necessary but unspiritualized forces of the psyche named Ahriman to the left, and Lucifer to the right – the murderer and the thief.

3 We believe that a certain magical power similar to the *consolamentum* was practised by ancient Egyptian adepts, although it was less vivid in its revelations and accessible only after lengthy ritual and spell-casting.

CHAPTER TWENTY

The Journey West

*T*he Romans and the Sanhedrin (the overseers of the Jewish religious law) believed that, after the ignominious death of the 'King of the Jews', the threat posed by his teachings would gradually defuse. This was not the case. The conversions continued, headed by the disciple Stephen who had courageously and spectacularly led the defence of Jesus during his midnight trial in the Court of the Sanhedrin and whose evidence and argument had eventually been overthrown by the force of sheer illegality. He converted between three and five thousand daily, for despite the Sanhedrin and the circus of the Crucifixion, many of the Jewish people were very receptive to the light which shone from the teachings of 'The Way'. The authorities were no doubt also aware that strange happenings were afoot concerning Jesus's family and closest followers (they were holding secret meetings with Jesus, who appeared to them in his light-body), and the disciples and the Bethany family, charged with spreading the teachings of Jesus, were in danger. Only the famous and commanding presence of Joseph, the Nobilis Decurio, saved them from being seized outright. (Nobilis Decurio was an honorary title given to Joseph by the Romans in recognition of his high position as Minister of Metal Mining.) Joseph was the head of the Christian underground in Judea and the chief organizer of their swelling numbers. He had been imprisoned for a brief time on the authority of other Jewish Elders in the Sanhedrin shortly after the Crucifixion because of his association with Jesus, but was soon pardoned and released, not as an act of clemency but because of his connections and status. The persecution of the Christians, led by Saul, got underway at this time, and Stephen was stoned to death at his command and in his presence by the gate that still bears the disciple's name, uttering the prayer, 'Lord, forgive them, for they know not what they do,' as he met his fate. He became the first martyr for Christ and the teachings of 'The Way'.

To give birth in safety, Mary returned to her temple in Egypt, where her daughter Tamar was born. Sarah, a devoted attendant of Mary who also served in the temple, became the little girl's nurse. This young Ethiopian woman understood who Mary truly was and, like the Queen of Sheba before her, was a member of her soul-group.

The fact that Tamar occasionally needed a nurse suggests that Mary herself was travelling and teaching at this time, journeying into Egypt and the surrounding lands, even though Saul's secret police were active everywhere, penetrating far beyond Judea. Romans, Greeks, Jews and Egyptians, all fell foul of Saul's secret police (a Gestapo-like organization within the greater body of the Sanhedrin) if they were found to be devotees, or consorting with devotees, of 'The Way'. Records of the time state that the prisons were filled to overflowing with Christian converts, awaiting almost certain death. The Roman authorities, who were surreptitiously in league with Saul, turned a blind eye to his activities. Long afterwards, when the Roman persecution of both Jews and Christians began, Saul (renamed Paul and now a devoted Christian) met a cruel death at their hands.

Within three years of Jesus's crucifixion, the situation was such that it seemed unlikely that even the illustrious Joseph of Arimathea could hold back the dark, blood-filled tide of extermination as far as Jesus's immediate followers were concerned. He began to plan their escape. Before anything was decided upon, Joseph was given word by the Romans that he would have to leave the country. He was advised that he must take with him all of Jesus's closest followers if they were to be spared their lives. They were seen as a hardcore group and would have been eliminated long before had it not been for the protection of Joseph, who was known in many lands other than those occupied by Rome, and whose death at the hands of the Romans would have caused political disquiet. Rome was by this time deeply perturbed by the presence of the ever-growing ranks of the Christian converts, afraid that they might begin to represent a threat to its empire. The officials who sought out Joseph told him that he must dock on shores that were outside the Roman dominions.

Joseph immediately sent word to the disciples and to the family at Bethany. They were all to assemble there and settle their worldly affairs in order to undertake a voyage with him which would take them away from their homeland forever. We believe that a number of the Night-Protectors also gathered at Bethany with the disciples, ready to join up with others of their company who were guarding Mary Magdalene.

First, the party travelled to Egypt, for of course it was essential that Mary Magdalene and her little daughter should accompany them. Sarah joined the party, as did Marcella, the handmaid of the Bethany sisters. They all eventually set sail from Alexandria, escorted by the Romans. One of Joseph's great merchant boats awaited them some miles offshore, stocked with provisions. They were told that the Romans would put them aboard and leave them free to sail where they chose, as long as they did not dock in Roman territory. When they reached the boat, they found to their horror that no sails were hoisted – because there were no sails. They had been removed, together with all sets of oars and any material that might be used to improvise them. The rudder of the boat had also been extracted. Their escorts forced them on board and set off back to Alexandria, leaving them abandoned in the middle of the ocean.

Joseph and the three Marys went among the men, assuring them that all would be well. The Romans had deserted them, certain that they would meet their deaths, but they would not die. The Father-Mother God would steer them on their course and they would be saved. Jesus appeared again among his disciples at this time. Some witnessed a ceremony wherein Jesus and Mary met with the ethereal beings of the air and the sea. These beautiful spirits, eager to do the bidding of the divine couple, were commanded to take the vessel in a certain direction, and served their master as faithfully as they had borne him up when he walked on the water to save Peter from drowning. Driven by the wind and the waves, with Jesus and the noble beauty and radiance of his spirit as its figurehead both encouraging his followers on board and directing the subtle intelligences in the elements, the vessel swept around the coast of Africa until it came to the Straits of Gibraltar. There the ship paused, to be met by many small boats which made their way from Morocco and Spain, filled with faithful supporters of Jesus and Mary and their teachings.

Friends of Joseph of Arimathea were also out in force, ready to provide aid for his sake and, because of their great respect and trust in him, sympathetic to the doctrines of 'The Way'. All had been given messages in dreams, visions or the direct voice of intuition that a ship bearing Joseph, the holy family and the disciples would soon appear in the Gibraltar Straits, and that they required help.[1] A watch was set, and as soon as the vessel appeared on the horizon, a cargo of further provisions (the first ample stock had been ransacked by the Romans) and a supply of oars were despatched to the merchant ship. There was great joy and relief as the boat parties and those on board came together, and many discussions concerning the laying of future plans. Communications were entrusted to the helpers, and word went out from them to the followers of Jesus, informing them of what had taken place and that Joseph and his companions were bound for France and Britain, where the teachings would be established.

Although the pause in their journey which occurred in the Gibraltar Straits took place because of a vital practical necessity, it was also indicative of a deeper truth. The famous Gibraltar rock juts into the sea on mainland Spain at a point where the coast of Africa seems to step out to meet it. It is a place where, from an aerial view, the two continents almost meet across the sea. Although the gulf of water between them today is deep and impassable except by boat, it was not always so, which is why the rock is inhabited by African monkeys. The meeting at Gibraltar on this holy journey paid homage to the point, historically and geographically, where the Spirit of Africa, the Goddess, Isis herself, passed from Africa to Europe, bringing her blessing, her wisdom, and her promise of ultimate healing for the world. The soul of Africa is destined to rise again in its full glory, a glory which will make the world wonder, for we have never even begun to understand the secrets she holds at her heart.

Farewells were said and the party set off again, a new sense of wellbeing and adventure pervading their ranks. Now speeded by oars and steering a course well known to Joseph, they came at last to the wild coast of Provence in Gaul (ancient France). They dropped anchor in the harbour of the town now known as Saintes-Maries-de-la-Mer, in the Carmargue, landing on 25 May in the last year of Tiberias, 36AD. Here Mary Magdalene, her colleague Sarah, her little daughter Tamar, her mother, her sisters and her brother John rested in the homes of some Druid friends of Joseph of Arimathea. The Night-Protectors also remained in Provence with this group.

Little Tamar needed care and stability after her long and arduous voyage, and could travel no more until she had recovered. Joseph, in particular, ensured that she was comfortable and secure, for already a deep familial affection had sprung up between the child and the venerable and kindly patriarch.

Joseph himself, with mother Mary and the rest of the disciples, continued on to Marseilles, where Philip and a number of converts to 'The Way' had preceded him. There was much rejoicing at their reunion, for Philip (the disciple whose gospel, above all others, revered Mary Magdalene and shows conclusively that Jesus did not regard sexual union as either shameful or repugnant but rather as an act of sanctity) was Joseph's dearly loved friend. On meeting again, both men realized the full extent of the miracle which had steered Joseph and his party safely across the vast sea straits to Marseilles. But they could not linger there for long. There were large areas of Roman occupation in Gaul, and although news travelled relatively slowly compared to today, Joseph could not establish his base there with any security.

NOTES

1 In the British Museum in London stands the famous Welsh Llywel Stone. For 140 years it was displayed so that the carved scenes depicted on it were turned to the wall and hidden from view. Public protest has ensured that the scenes are now visible. They are three in number, consisting of; i) a pyramid and a sphinx; ii) a man bearing a crook crossing waters; iii) the man carrying the shepherd's crook turning north. As Alan Wilson (*see* Appendix in *The Drama of the Lost Disciples*, George F Jowett) points out, maps from ancient Roman times were compiled with north turned 90° to the left. Allowing for this orientation, the figure with the crozier (Joseph of Arimathea) is seen to be travelling west from Egypt, through the Mediterranean to the Gibraltar Straits and then bearing north towards Gaul and Britain. In Wales, seven chapels are arranged around the site of the Llywel Stone, the 'chakra system' of Joseph's settlement, built on the principles of the Church of Mary Magdalene, the true Church of Christ.

The crozier that Joseph carries bears a most interesting symbolism. It is directly related to

Osiris, the Heavenly Shepherd who leads the enlightened back to their true home in the starry heavens, because human souls in the ancient Egyptian esoteric tradition were considered to be imperishable stars, of which the constellations were but dim reflections. Every Pharaoh of Egypt bore the crozier or the shepherd's crook to signify that she or he was the representative of Osiris on Earth, guiding souls back to the Star-fields of the Righteous. It is noteworthy in this connection that Joseph starts out on his voyage to Britain from Egypt.

Joseph of Arimathea's future rebirth as King Arthur also links him via this symbolism with Osiris. We believe that the soul of Joseph was concerned with the very inception of the ancient Egyptian civilization and its mystical systems. As Jesus's uncle, he facilitated Christ's (Jesus and Mary's) entire mission on Earth from birth onwards, and, like Osiris, the 'Shepherd of brilliant stars', led their enlightened followers to Glastonbury (the Heavenly Looking Glass or Mirror). (See Appendix One.) Here in the Vale of Avalon a great Temple of Stars has been discovered, connected directly to Mary, her Sisters in Light and the disciples, and also to King Arthur and his Knights of the Round Table who sit in state as the constellations of the zodiac headed by the 'Dayspring Star', the Sun, King Arthur himself. Intriguingly, King Arthur is also associated with the starry heavens, in particular the constellation commonly known as the Plough or the Great Bear which is linked with the Pole Star via its own 'pointer' star, and with Archangel Michael, the angel guardian of the Sun.

CHAPTER TWENTY-ONE

To Britain

*D*eep within his heart Joseph knew that the Christ mission could not remain based only in Gaul. The country of Gaul, although it was sacred and would always be profoundly associated with the mission of 'The Way', bore spiritual links with Britain where he had an ancestral root and a vast number of friends and associates, many of them very highly placed, to which historical records bear witness. (Joseph had connections with all the ruling families of Britain and his daughter Anna was married to the king's youngest brother. Eventually, all of Joseph's children married into British royal households.) It was Britain that was calling him, for whose land and peoples he had a natural affinity and love.

To encourage him further, a British druidic delegation of bishops (bishopry was originally a druidic concept) travelled to Marseilles to greet him and to offer a formal invitation to bring the new teachings to Britain. They promised him the gift of land, a safe haven and long-standing protection from the antagonism of the Romans who, although they had twice been ousted from British shores, continued to covet the mysterious isle and would renew their attentions for a third time under the command of Aulus Plautius only seven years after the arrival at Glastonbury of Joseph and his companions. These pledges were made to Joseph on behalf of his good friend King Gweirydd (the original St George), Prince of the Royal Silurian dynasty whose dominions extended over Cornwall and South Wales. After some months, and after procuring another boat more seaworthy than the first vessel which had taken something of a beating on the high seas, Joseph and the disciples set sail for the English coast, this time accompanied by the druidic delegation which had aided them since they had landed in Gaul.

Mary and her group at Provence joined him, although her brother John would shortly return to Gaul to set up a mystery school whose beautiful and mystical teachings, together with those of Mary, were to be so hideously repressed by the Albigensian Crusade and the Church of Rome. The party landed on the coast some miles from Glastonbury, which was an important cultural centre of the Druids and well known to Joseph. This land had been venerated by them as deeply sacred for hundreds of years, and was holy ground long before the Druids had organized themselves in Britain.

Glastonbury[1] at that time was an island called the Isle of Avalon – The Place of Apples, a fruit deeply sacred to the Goddess, as its association with Eve, the Lady of Life, attests. Two thousand years ago it was surrounded by freshwater wetlands, land which was covered in expansive tranquil lakes from the tor to the sea, 25 miles away. The area exuded a magical calm and beauty, and was surrounded by ancient forest (the tor itself was wooded in Neolithic times).

Avalon was an island created and blessed by the sea, so potently associated with Mary Magdalene and indeed with all the three Marys, for the wetlands had once been salt marshes, and their rich blend of minerals and nutrients deposited by the seawater (akin to human blood) had eventually transformed them into orchards, crop-yielding land and freshwater lakes teeming with fish and fragrant lake flowers. The beauty and bounty of Avalon was famous throughout the land. In these serene and enchanted waters surrounding the holy Isle of Avalon, Mary Magdalene with her Sisters in Light, Mary Jacob and Mary the mother of Jesus, baptized the hordes of converts who flocked to Glastonbury.

In those early years of the Church, there was no conflict whatsoever with the Druids. This happened later, when the arid breath of Rome, first with its empiric blast, and then with the equally scorching doctrines of the Church of Rome, the Church of Peter who so despised Mary Magdalene, hissed forth its devastating ruination. It culminated in the 'Pelagian Heresy', the forbidden philosophy of a monk of the early Church (the Church of Mary Magdalene) named Pelagius who summarized its teaching by proclaiming that the Earth was good and sweet, that humanity was not intrinsically evil, and that the joy and the beauty of nature, emanating from a fatherly and a motherly God, were what blessed and sustained human life. This was the true teaching of 'The Way' as it first issued from Jesus and Mary Magdalene, and then from Tamar, their daughter. Tamar taught St Paul this beautiful doctrine, and he came to Britain from Rome to teach (and to further absorb) the truth he had learned from her, establishing the famous Abbey of Bangor in Wales. The doctrine and administration of the abbey was known as Pauli Regula – the 'Rule of Paul'. Its twentieth abbot was Pelagius. The Church of Rome denounced his thinking as severely heterodox, insisting instead that humankind was naturally wicked, the body vile and sinful and nature and the Earth likewise (especially the act of procreation) and that all deserved nothing more than mortification and contempt. The result is the pitiful state of the planet today.

St Augustine was despatched from Rome to crush the early Church, which had flourished first in Britain and France and then in Spain. He arrived towards the end of the sixth century, after the death of Arthur and the madness of Merlin. He and his retinue met with the British bishops, who would have none of him and his withering philosophies. But Augustine relied on conspirators within the Celtic Church and the governing powers in Britain, monkish collaborators who had established themselves during the 40-year reign of the Peace of Arthur (500–540AD) and who had made inroads into the conscience and philosophy of Arthur, resulting in his overthrow by Mordred in 541AD.

Combining their forces, these monks, together with Augustine and his following from Rome, gradually undermined and finally demonized the true Church of Christ, eliminating the last stronghold of druidic power, the wisdom-source of Britain, throughout her islands. The culmination of this process was to deify Mary, the mother of Jesus, in Rome in 600AD, for the express purpose of destroying the following of Mary Magdalene and directing the veneration of the people to a woman whom they could uphold as engendering the statement: 'Behold the handmaiden of the Lord', twisting the sense of her words so that they appeared to mean, not the perfect soul-response to the Father-Mother God that Mary the mother had intended, but that the 'Lord' was solely representative of the Masculine Principle, and that Mary, the Universal Woman, was bowing down in self-confessed servile submission to it. Significantly, the Cathars, with their secret tradition of the status of Mary Magdalene, refused to worship the Virgin. Mary the mother was, of course, Mary Magdalene's Sister in Light, and there was certainly no unworthy and petty jostling for position between the two. This would have been impossible in souls so perfectly attuned to the light. The scenario was created entirely as a political strategy by Rome, an augmentation of the method now revealed in the madness of Pope Gregory when, only seven years prior to the deification of Mary the mother, he had declared that Mary Magdalene was a prostitute.

The relevance here is not a choice between personalities, but that Mary the mother was seen purely as a symbol of virgin matter waiting to be impregnated by Divine Light, which was considered exclusively masculine. This concept of it casts the Feminine Principle in the role of passive object, whereas Mary Magdalene demonstrates that the Divine Light is both masculine and feminine in essence, and expresses in the potency of her being a perfect equity and unity with Jesus.

The Druids had understood for many years that a new teaching was coming to the Mystic Isle of Britain, a teaching which would fulfil and universalize their own (the doctrines of the Druids were noble and beautiful, and did not involve human sacrifice as the Romans professed). They knew long before Jesus was born that one called Yesu and his divine companion would bring the new light to Britain, having supernatural foreknowledge of the name and proclaiming it to the world in the Celtic Triads ('Who is the King of Glory? The Lord Yesu;/He is the King of Glory.') They had taught the boy Jesus on his protracted visits to Britain, and although a span of 20 or 30 years was normally necessary to pass through their grades, Jesus was able to graduate in a fraction of the time, as was the case concerning his lessons at Qumran.

The Druids also knew, although they did all they could to prevent it from occurring, that the new teaching would be so revolutionary, so direct a route from earthliness to spiritual freedom and exaltation, that the dark adversarial powers would rear and strike with the full weight of their ingress into humanity's inner soul-citadel (an ingress permitted by humanity itself), bringing down a dense curtain of obscurity and confusion for a time. Nevertheless, they, who were of the Sphere of John and whose wisdom was universal, would stand by as silent watchers through the centuries of darkness, ready to step forward and bring the ineffable Orb of Light to illumine the heart and the path of every true seeker, whatever their clan or creed. Thus would the great gift to the world of Jesus, Mary and Tamar, the great vision and prophecy of John, and the great travail and task of Joseph of Arimathea and those who established the teachings of 'The Way', at last be fulfilled.

When Joseph of Arimathea's party arrived at the Isle of Avalon, they were welcomed by King Gweirydd (named by the Romans as Arviragus) and his nobles and Druids. At the same time as the Magi of Persia, the Druids, too, had marked in the heavens the great Star of Prophecy known as the Star of Bethlehem. They knew it heralded the 'Day Spring', the light of the world which would usher in the new dispensation of the coming age – the glory of 'The Star' that was prophesied to rise out of Jacob and his tribe and line, the Line of David – Jesus and Mary Magdalene. For it seems to us certain that the Druids knew also of Mary Magdalene, she who came forth from Mary Jacob and who preceded the birth of Yesu by 12 days, the zodiacal round. It was with deep reverence that these wise ones of the Mystic Isle greeted the three Marys, the child Tamar and Joseph and his companions. The moment transcended history, becoming immortal and sacred. It still resonates in the subtler atmospheres today.

None were more aware of this than the Druids, the 'people of the oak'; and between the Druids, the sacred women and child of Jacob, and Joseph of Arimathea, there passed a breath, a tremor, a suspiration from the Great Spirit which contained the promise of things to come, things that would be born on and spring from the very soil of Britain. A rumour was heard of a glorious spiritual resurgence for all the world, breathed forth from an ancient ancestress linked with Rebecca, the mother of the patriarch Jacob, who had raised the first cairn of stones heavenwards as an altar in the first pyramidal form, as Jacob had done at the place where he had watched the angels come and go on the ladder between Earth and Paradise. The Druids at that moment had sensed a great call rising from the heart of Britain, the winding of a sacred horn from a sacred beast. Mary Magdalene, Mary Jacob, Tamar and Joseph of Arimathea entered the spirit of Britain, became one with the land, and would forever more be bound up inextricably with Britain's ultimate destiny as the Grail of the World. The depictions of Mary Magdalene seated upon a white horse are symbolical of this moment. Her name means Beloved Great Queen, incorporating the idea of a 'great tower' or 'magnificent female one' (literal translations of

'Magdalene'), the title which Jesus bestowed upon her and yet which was irrevocably hers.

The great Mother Goddess was known in Britain as Morig-Ana, the same name in translation as 'The Magdalene', and her symbol was the white horse. The Celtic white horse is associated with the dragon, representing the spirit of the dragon in its most rarefied, ascended form. In Celtic cosmology, the horse is an emblem of the creative fire of the supreme Godhead, and is a symbol of the primal energy streaming forth from the first dawn of creation. One of the Mother Goddess's most beautiful and beloved manifestations was as Brigid, goddess of spiritual fire and the Divine Forges (the process of forming a soul-temple fit for the divine flame of spirit, a spark of which is the individuality in each of us). We derive the English word 'bright' from our former worship of Brigid, because the Gaelic pronunciation of the word is, phonetically, 'Breet'.

Just as Isis-Osiris had reflected the light of the great Christ Being in the past, out of which had arisen the golden glory of the Egyptian dynasties, so now did Mary Magdalene and Jesus reflect it again in even greater measure – their light was the light of the Spirit and the Bride, or Christ-Brigid, the ineffable Being of Immeasurable Light, both male and female. Mary and Jesus took their reflection of the light to the highest octave that can be achieved on this Earth.

We believe that in spirit, Mary Magdalene mounted the white horse and became one with Brigid, as she always truly was in essence, entering the British mysteries as their queen and goddess (in the sense of a god-woman rather than in any departure from her humanity). In association with this inner ceremony, Joseph of Arimathea gave King Gweirydd the white flag with the red cross emblazoned upon it, signifying the red cross of manifestation – the Earth, humanity, physical matter – with the white light of the Christ shining behind it, supporting it, upholding it and inseparable from it. The flag is emblematic of Jesus and Mary Magdalene, of God and Creation. But again, we should be careful of falling into the trap of seeing Mary as symbolizing Creation, and Jesus as God; for although in one sense we might think of the red cross as the sign of Mary, and the white light or background as that of Jesus, the feminine essence is there in the white light, and the masculine essence pervades Creation.

King Gweirydd celebrated the momentous occasion by making his promised gift to Joseph of 12 hides of land, perpetual and tax-free, one for each of the disciples. Although there were many more than 12 in his company, King Gweirydd and the Druids knew that in a mystical sense the Holy Twelve would always exist in sacred perpetuation, prototypes of the human or Adâma creation, and that a 13th ruler, representative of the Christ Being and manifesting through both a male and a female vessel, would Light their Way.

The Druidic calendar and their zodiac had always been calculated on these principles, and indeed the mystery of the Glastonbury Zodiac, which is said to lie on the land itself and has many secrets to reveal to us, reflects this divine precept of the Holy Twelve gathered around the ineffable 13th point.

With the royal and chartered gift of land to the Josephian Mission came a pledge of protection. The patronage of Gweirydd, 'George', was the mighty shield of Joseph and his companions, and of all the first Christians, who were still threatened by Rome. When the Roman persecution began, this fearless Prince of the Silurians routed it. Gweirydd/George was the great British enemy feared by the Roman Emperor Nero, and the first 'George' to bear the flag of Jesus and Mary Magdalene, the red cross of the manifestation of creation coming forth from the white light. The later St George, who was Roman, was a reflection of, not the original, St George. The English patron saint was from Wales, not from Rome, which is why the dragon emblazons the flag of that country, and why a much deeper understanding of the meaning of the dragon is necessary than that which usually obtains in considering the interpretation of the story of St George and the Dragon.

Although the lower mind, the baser instincts of humankind, are represented by the dragon in the traditional tale, this is only one manifestation of the limitless potency of the ancient and mighty race which we call and dimly conceive of through myth as dragons. The cockerel, the announcer of the coming of the light and earthly representation of the mystical firebird, is closely associated with the divine dragon, and the Gnostics, those who generally embraced the teachings of the Sphere of John, have the cockatrice, the magical cockerel born from a serpent's egg, as the symbol of their doctrines.

All the universal life force, all the mysterious creative dynamic which we receive through the agency of light itself, is brought to us through these fire-bearing beings. The wisdom which is their core showed us the entity of our lower mind in dragon form as an act of mercy, giving us thereby a soul-teaching which would enable us to better understand the nature of our lower mind and how to master it. The energies within it do partake of the dragon nature, yet in its most basic and unevolved form.

Mary Magdalene/Brigid herself, symbol of Divine Fire, can be traced back by bloodline to that most mysterious ancestress and progenitor of the human race, Tiamat the Dragon Queen, the great Mother called 'She who bore them all' in the original account of Creation.[2] The mystery of Mary Magdalene with her flame-red hair is rooted in, and embraces the concept of, creation being made manifest, the principle of genesis. It is rooted in the concept of the creative fires of divine nature, bringing forth creation in a burst of ecstasy and implanting their own essence within that creation so that its conscious components would strive to achieve again that ecstasy, and in so doing, by an act of alchemical transformation, lift creation itself back into the arms of its glorious parent as an integrated being in its own right. The passion, the brilliance, the transformative vigour of these transcendental fires that pour from the heart of the Godhead in an eternal song of love comprise the dragon essence, the essential vehicle which informs creation with the pulsing dynamic of life. It gives the holy fire-breath to inert matter, inert ether, inert thought. It is both male and female, and yet when it gives life, when it hovers over the face of the waters, it becomes female, the Dragon Queen, She who bore them all.

We find the mysteries of Mary Magdalene dwelling like a jewel in the heart of these mysteries of the beginning of life on Earth, and we cannot properly conceive of the full embrace of the great sphere of her humanity if we limit ourselves to mundane concepts of her existence. Thinking mystically, imagining mythically, will afford us glimpses of a joy and a wonder which extend beyond the parameters of first-century Palestine and will bring us home to a place in our hearts, no matter whether we are male or female, from which we have been largely excluded and of whose existence we have been denied even the most begrudging acknowledgement. We do not believe anymore that the beautiful presence which belongs there is sobbing, sinful, rejected, unworthy, contaminating, desperate, pitiful, shameful, sullied, on its knees and cast out. We believe that it is Mary, most beloved and honoured one, She who Knows All and will call the exquisite unicorn of the soul down from the high places so that we might know it again and follow its ascending path without blindness; Mary, Shepherdess of the lost and lonely aspects of our being which will all be gathered again in the fold of the heart, where Mary truly resides and is and will be forever.

The story of the establishment of the Church of Mary Magdalene, dedicated to the One True Light and demonstrating the teachings of 'The Way', is a noble one indeed. It involved the great labour and striving of Joseph of Arimathea, who was the first to light the torch of this vital new philosophy across the world, and of all the devoted followers of Christ. It was facilitated and blessed by the Druids, the Essenes and the kings, queens and nobles, first of Britain, and then of France and Spain. It was inspired, guided and lit up from within by the combined soul-essence of John and Mary Magdalene led by the light of Jesus from the inner spheres, and also by the other two Marys, by Mary Magdalene's sisters and, eventually, her daughter Tamar. It was embraced and given soul-expression by the Celtic bards, notably Taliesin and, later, Merlin and all at Arthur's court.

It sounded a note, a song of such beautiful refrain that, even though many destroyers and deniers and silencers came to stamp it out forever, they never could succeed, for it echoes on today and haunts our hearts still, sweet and soul-piercing as ever it was, waiting for a suffering world to take it up again and, finally, to swell its strains with such a united voice that the inner wastelands which devastate our collective consciousness will break into blossom and proclaim the springtide of the new era, as the Song of Songs predicts:

Lo, the winter is past, the rain is over and gone;
The flowers appear on the earth; the time of the singing of birds
is come, and the voice of the turtle dove is heard in our land.

THE SONG OF SOLOMON, 2:11–12

When Joseph of Arimathea and his companions disembarked, he thrust his staff of thorn into the turf of the hill they began to climb in order that they might view the surrounding countryside, needing to rest and use the staff as a support. Henceforward the tor became known as Weary All Hill, and legend says that his staff burst into bloom, from then on blossoming twice a year, once in May and once in December/January, to mark both the arrival of the teachings of 'The Way' in Europe and the birthday(s) of the Christ.

The thorn is a tree sacred to the Mother Goddess, and, together with the rowan, was Brigid's tree. With co-operation from the angels of form and the secret fairy peoples of the hidden ethers, such a miracle as Joseph's blooming staff is possible. Yet its nature points indubitably to the presence of Mary Magdalene, for the spirit beings who obeyed the command of Brigid rejoiced in Mary Magdalene – Brigid being that feminine essence of the Christ Light anchored in Britain but until this moment without the use of a human vehicle perfected to the point where such a sublime goddess-consciousness could become one with and shine unhindered through a single human soul.

When Joseph's staff burst into bloom on Weary All Hill, the heart of the mystic forces in Britain opened to receive the new baptism of light, and Mary became on Earth what she had always been in Heaven: one with Brigid and one with the divine rose, the fire-flower of love, which dwells at the heart of Britain, the Mystic Isle, the Grail of the world. The co-operation of the beings of the inner spheres, the angelic and fairy spirits who wrought the flowering staff miracle at the command of the Christ Consciousness expressed through Brigid and earthed through Mary, demonstrated thereby the love and honour in which they held Mary Magdalene and Joseph, for may blossom is a homage to the Goddess, and the Staff or the Rod is sacred to the Father-God. Not only were their ancient and mighty human souls beautiful to the angel and fairy peoples, but their presence on the Chakra Trail (for Joseph had been with Jesus and Mary on much of it) profoundly endeared them to these ethereal beings.

With their help, Mary, Jesus, John, Joseph and his companions would in the future build Camelot (*see* Appendix One), the New Jerusalem, the perfect Soul-Temple which would receive the imponderable flame of Divine Spirit. When Camelot came to Earth, the British peoples (and those of other nations) were not the only denizens who recognized Arthur and his consort as their rightful leaders. The fairy and angelic beings present upon the Earth also gave their allegiance, thereby making the era of Camelot one of the most magical in human history.

George F Jowett's remarkable book, *The Drama of the Lost Disciples*, tells the story of how Joseph and his companions arrived in Britain and built the first Christian church in the world at Glastonbury, then called the Isle of Avalon, using the ancient building technique of wattle and daub. On the Rose Line[3] which extends from Palestine, through to France, the Channel Islands, Britain and eventually to the North Pole where once, aeons ago, the very first Edenic civilization was created upon the Earth, Glastonbury forms a sacred heart, containing the Rose of the Ages which became the Rose of Jesus and Mary Magdalene. Upon the maps of the ancient world this Mystic Rose would always appear, indicating that it showed the way and gave sacred direction to the soul (as does the Medicine Wheel of the Celts and the Native Americans, for the Medicine Wheel is another sigil for the Rose). It is this Rose we must use, in a deeply spiritual yet also very practical and simple way, to heal the nations and to heal our own confused, dismembered hearts.

The history of the Josephian Mission is supported by numerous historical documents from a great variety of sources, even by that most pragmatic of compilations, the Domesday Book, where the granting of the 12 hides of land is recorded in detail. It is a matter of wonder to us that the landing at Glastonbury of Joseph and his companions, including John and the three Marys, is still referred to in recent publications as a 'legend'. If this is a legend, then any historical event not in living memory must be so called, for there could hardly exist more documentary evidence attesting to the actuality of the incident. It also confirms what we have been told by our source: that Mary Magdalene came to Britain, bringing with her 'the Sacred Child to the Mystic Isle that it might evolve'. Her mission and her Church were centred equally in France and in Britain, later establishing themselves in Spain. There is more folk memory of her in France and in Spain than in Britain, because Camelot was destroyed and her memory was forced into hiding, where she became 'the Queen of the South', like Sheba before her. With the deification of Mary the mother in 600AD, 40 years after the fall of Camelot, the references to 'Mary' throughout the early Arthurian tales were considered to have concerned the Virgin. This in fact is not so, although the identity of Mary Magdalene was veiled for the sake of orthodoxy. A clue lies in the many depictions of the Lady and the Unicorn, which was a motif of the period. Mary Magdalene is the lady, and she is intimately associated with the mystical unicorn, who in one respect is her eternal lover, Jesus.

After dwelling for some years in Britain where she befriended, amongst many others, the dynamic, learned and beautiful British princesses Eurgain and Gladys, her aunt, Mary Magdalene set sail for Gaul with her daughter, her mother and her sisters and several of the disciples. Although she often visited Britain, and maintained particularly close links with Glastonbury which was quickly becoming renowned as a great centre of learning and initiation, Mary spent much of the rest of her life in Gaul.

Eurgain, the daughter of King Caradoc I and who later became the esteemed friend and guide of St Paul, was baptized by Mary as the first female convert to 'The Way', and the two became close friends. Eurgain went on to become St Eurgain, founding her famous college monastery on the coast of southeast Wales. She was Mary's pupil, the two learned women discussing and enacting together the rituals of the British mysteries, for these beautiful rites of nature and the Earth were by no means incongruous with the teachings of 'The Way'.

Another saint strongly associated with Mary Magdalene is St Dwynwen, who was born in the fourth century and whose veneration was centred in Anglesey. This compassionate holy woman, 'beautiful as tears of frost', was the Celtic Venus. Her wisdom and understanding were such that her blessing encompassed even those relationships which were forbidden by the Church, as long as the lovers were in every way true and devoted to one another and to the principles of the Light. St Dwynwen's open heart and broad understanding seem to suggest an early tolerance of and respect for homosexuality, afterwards overridden by Roman orthodoxy.

In the Magdalen College Library at Oxford University there exists a manuscript written by Maurus Rabanus, Archbishop of Mayence, 776–856AD. It is entitled 'Life of Mary Magdalene' and, in the words of the archbishop, was compiled 'according to the accounts that our fathers have left us in their writings'. It tells of the classic beauty of Mary and of the clear musical voice in which she proclaimed her truth, and of how she was adored as a holy woman by all who encountered her. George F Jowett says: 'The ancient texts resound with her glory.' The archbishop's account was written several centuries after the devotion afforded to Mary Magdalene was suppressed by the Church of Rome, although it has recourse to the earliest records; but it nevertheless confirms the extraordinary impact that Mary had upon those who listened to her teachings. All of the early Christian influence in Europe concerning 'The Way' came straight from Glastonbury, where Mary performed countless baptisms, and the ancient documents confirm that she introduced 'multitudes into the faith'. Clearly, those who encountered Mary recognized who she truly was.

Accounts of Mary's significance and status survived to some extent in France, and certainly the Languedoc is saturated in legend concerning her, although the full truth had to be hidden and camouflaged. Even so, as late as 1209, the whole township of Beziers in the Languedoc, almost 20,000 people, willingly went to their deaths rather than publicly deny that Mary Magdalene was the consort of Jesus. They could easily have avoided the slaughter. The pope's men had come for 200 Cathars who were living in their midst, and asked only that the townspeople deliver them into their hands to be tried as heretics – their heretical belief being the assertion that Jesus and Mary Magdalene were lovers. Instead, the people of Beziers sided with the Cathars, refused to give them up and declared that they shared the same belief, which was holy truth, not heresy. As punishment, the entire populace of the town was massacred on 22 July, Mary Magdalene's feast day. We believe that these people knew that Mary Magdalene was the feminine Christ, as they knew that St John the Beloved Disciple was yet another aspect of the Christ, and that to them, denying her absolute union with Jesus would be equivalent to denying that he himself was the Christed One. They would rather die than commit such heresy.

In Britain, where the most rapacious attacks on the original teachings were launched from Rome, the truth about Mary had to be deeply encrypted in codes so secure that only the elect in spirit could discern the poignant verity which had been so deeply buried by force of arms and, we venture to say, by sophisticated techniques of both psychic and psychological warfare, in denial and suppression.[4] The work was carried out so efficiently that the concept of Druidism terrified the people and passed into their folklore bearing associations of human sacrifice, cannibalism and vampirism, wisewomen became evil witches and nature a hostile force full of spirits who would hurt, attack, corrupt and blight if the forces of the Church were not constantly arrayed against them. The true teachings of 'The Way', which fully embraced the knowledge of the Druids, the mysteries of the Sacred Feminine, the wisdom of women, the sanctity of nature and the domain of her fairy and angelic peoples were utterly overthrown. Its chief culprit, in the eyes of the Church of Rome, was Mary Magdalene herself, who had to be entirely denigrated and denied and forced into the guise of the defiled and outcast one.

It is said that Mary Magdalene brought the first Black Madonna to Britain, later carrying it with her to Gaul. The symbolism of the Black Madonna can be understood on many levels. The most obvious is that it represents Mary herself, nursing the child of her beloved Yeshua who had died on the cross. Jesus rose again, but the Christ Light he bore to the world, and which the world at first rejected, was destined to be resurrected not only through the spiritual emanation of himself and his twin soul, John, but through his true consort Mary and their daughter Tamar. Thus the family trio embodies the myth of Isis, the slain Osiris and Horus, the Child of Light, born after the death of his father.

The Madonna is black because of the shadow of denial with which our culture has enshrouded Mary and the Sacred Feminine, as a symbol of the 'Shining Darkness' (that which is utterly bright but whose radiance we refuse to admit into our consciousness, which our vision then renders as dazzling blackness) and as an emblem of the soul of Africa, which is exalted in the heart of the Goddess and will eventually emerge empowered and unburdened, ready to grant the rest of the world access to its life-giving mysteries as soon as we have learned the soul-wisdom which will safeguard us from our tendency to despoil and exploit. Mary's own message, which is that the Holy Child was brought to the mystic Isle of Britain so that it might evolve, concerns not only Tamar but the birth of the Light in Britain, which will one day flood the Earth.

The Black Madonna nurses Horus, the Child of Light, who is Tamar and the coming age of freedom and brotherhood. What will be born in Britain is destined to be a gift of freedom and spiritual realization for the whole world. The Holy Child was the Holy Grail – in one sense, most certainly Tamar, for she would be the channel through which ultimate liberation could take place – the Woman of Knowing, or the source of wisdom that needs to be connected to the masculine-orientated outlook which is ours today.

NOTES

1 What we know as Glastonbury today also consisted of another smaller island known as Wytren, or Glass Island ('Glastenic'), which was so called because of the 'glassy wave' or the glassy purity of the waters surrounding it, and which also makes reference to the glass industry of the ancient Britons which flourished there. Interestingly, there is an area in Glastonbury called Galilee. It suggests an important link with the biblical Galilee, which means a 'ring', a 'circuit' or 'a wheel, rolling', as the Sun moving through the 12 signs of the zodiac. Twelve hides of land were given to Joseph and his companions, which surrounded the first Church of Christ as if it were the Sun and the twelve hides were the zodiacal signs. It was also where Camelot ('ring of light') was established. When we think of the lakes surrounding Avalon, and the inland sea or lake of Galilee, the connection between the two places becomes so distinct as to formulate itself into a mirror image, and in fact the idea of Glastonbury as the 'Heavenly Looking Glass' or the 'Heavenly Mirror' is one which is gaining ground today (*see* Appendix One). The mysteries of the great Glastonbury Zodiac, actually laid out on the sacred land itself, are being uncovered, and Katherine Maltwood, who discovered this Temple of Stars in the Vale of Avalon in 1925, posits that it is the original Round Table, with King Arthur and his 12 chief knights still seated upon it as signs of the zodiac. We believe that this is indeed true, but that the Temple of Stars was created or its energies renewed by Jesus and Mary Magdalene, when 'the Queen was on Earth and the King was in Heaven'. The Temple of Stars also bears within it a representation of the chakras as the magical soul-stairway to Heaven. These ideas connect with the hidden truth in Mary's gospel.

2 See *Realm of the Ring Lords*, by Laurence Gardner, p52.

3 In his novel, *The Da Vinci Code*, Dan Brown explains that the Rose Line was any meridian line or line of longitude drawn on world maps from the North Pole to the South Pole. One particular Rose Line was chosen by early navigators as the one from which all other possible longitudes would be calculated. Nowadays, that special point on the globe whose longitude connects the North and South Poles is in Greenwich (England). Prior to this choice, the prime meridian of the world had passed through Paris. Both the French and English locations are extensions of a ley line (ley lines comprise a grid of subtle energy which embraces the Earth) that moves through Palestine and Rome to France and Britain, where it conjoins with the

Arctic Circle. The fact that this was the chosen Rose Line arises from mystical knowledge, because this particular ley line passes through the Earth's heart chakra and conducts sacred energy around the planet. The association of this 'showing of the way' with the rose derives from the Compass Rose which anciently appeared on almost every map. It was a depiction of the Wind Rose, denoting the Sacred Breath which suspires or blows from eight major directions, creating eight major winds. From these eight supreme winds derive a further eight half-winds and sixteen quarter-winds. In total, the directions of the winds create 32 points of the compass which, when configured within a circle, give a perfect representation of a traditional 32-petalled rose. The northernmost direction of the Compass Rose is traditionally marked by the fleur-de-lis – the lily. Numerologically, the number 32 (3+2) equates to 5, a potent symbol of the Sacred Feminine. The secret of the Rose Line thus blooms into a marvellous unfolding of symbolism associated with Mary Magdalene and the teachings of her gospel (*see* Part II). The rose in the heart linked to the Sacred Breath, the eight levels of ascension of the pyramid of our being through which we must travel (northwards or upwards) in order to reach the supernal Silence which opens into the heavenly realms, symbolised by the lily, are all whispered secrets of the Rose Line. The Wind Rose itself is a perfect depiction of a chakra – the chakra which must balance all the other chakras of our being if we are to become 'fully human' – the Rose which is a symbol of the heart and the magical chakra at its centre. 'I am the Lily of the Valley and the Rose of Sharon,' sang the mysterious woman – a feminine deity – in The Song of Solomon. No wonder that the response of the orthodox, offended by the theme of Dan Brown's book, is to hotly deny that the Rose Line exists! One may as well deny the existence of the winds, or the four points of the compass. The rose is a symbol of Harpocrates, the God of Silence; and Eros, the God of Love, bears as his name an anagram of 'rose'. Behind these two male gods of the relatively modern classical world shines a single and much more ancient feminine divinity, showing us that when we love, the Rose blooms in the heart, and that then the heavenly realm, the mystical Silence, may be attained.

4 Although the study of psychology was not yet part of any educational curriculum as a formal discipline, there were certain groups, both occult and exoteric, who knew how to effectively apply the measures cited above.

CHAPTER TWENTY-TWO

The Return to Gaul and Mary's Passing

*M*ary's mission in Gaul was intimately connected with that of her brother John (formerly Lazarus). They were the supreme teachers of 'The Way' and were in soul communion with Jesus and with one another, a communion whose fruits had to be given practical application because the teachings continued to evolve, not in their principles, which are timeless and unassailable, but in the perfect expression of their deployment, which is limitless in scope. The full story and meaning of Mary's presence in Britain and in France, that magical time when the King was in Heaven and the Queen was on Earth, cannot be told here as it would tend to deflect from the essential simplicity of Mary's message, but it will be revealed elsewhere.

The day the three Marys landed on the coast of Gaul with Joseph and the companions was 25 May, a significant date because it falls in the tenancy of that strange, magical, 13th sign of the zodiac, Arachne the Spider, the Eight-Rayed Being, Queen of magic, the soul, and women's mysteries. Arachne occupies that part of the zodiacal circle which is otherwise tenanted by Taurus and Gemini – the last two weeks of Taurus and the first two weeks of Gemini, making 25 May its central point.

Eventually Mary settled with Tamar, her mother Mary Jacob and her sisters Martha and Salome in a complex of limestone caves which extend for more than 200 miles into the area of southern France. In this network of sacred caves, Mary and her companions performed mystical rites connected with the Earth Spirit or Earth Mother in order to release a wellspring of strength, spiritual renewal, healing and vision to nourish the collective soul of the peoples of the Earth. Mary was sometimes seen in one of the caves at Sainte Baume ('holy balm', a name which was bestowed on the town in honour of the Magdalene and which makes reference, not only to her jar of spikenard, but also to the apperception that she herself was in essence the 'holy balm' – healing, comforting, lifting the soul into the higher worlds which are its birthright and ultimately transforming consciousness itself). Legend has it that when seen in the cave at Sainte Baume, she was naked, protected from prying eyes only by her luxuriant red hair which snaked almost to her feet. There may be some truth in these strange reports, as the performance of some of the sacred rites within the caves might have required that the electromagnetic currents which connect us to the Earth were not interrupted or diluted by clothing. It is also true that our hair is a very efficient conductor of these forces, as is born out by the story of Samson and the depletion of his strength via his shorn locks.

There are many stories from folklore, regarding this period, of Mary and her family's life. It is said that they developed the power to emit a mystical light which allowed them to move around the caverns and passageways without difficulty, and that many miraculous healings took place within the caves as inhabitants of the local towns and villages came to these holy women for help. It is further said that each morning a gathering of angels carried Mary Magdalene above the cliffs into the higher ethers, where she could commune with her beloved Yeshua and become at one with the great song of creation, from Earth below to highest Heaven above.

Mary and her companions continued for many years, travelling and proclaiming the message of 'The Way'. She never aged, nor did any dilapidation overtake her physical frame, but a quiet dignity of ancientness eventually cloaked her being, beautiful and noble in its bearing. As the time drew near for her ascension, she put out a call to all the disciples, to all her friends and followers with whom she had walked her path. Many were scattered across the globe, but all heard the call of Mary, and all turned pilgrim's feet towards Glastonbury, for it was to Glastonbury that Mary returned from her home in Gaul to experience her final rites of passage. They all assembled in a chamber adjoining the first Church of the True Light, the Church of Mary Magdalene (see Appendix One), raised to the glory of the Christ Light in Glastonbury, then known as the sacred Isle of Avalon, the first ground to receive the tabernacle of the new teachings.

Here Mary came amongst them in her body of light, offering her blessing to them all and urging them to continue in the path of the light, to continue to show 'The Way' to all those members of struggling and suffering humanity who were ready to accept its teachings. In reverence and wonder those assembled watched as Jesus appeared at the side of Mary, and she and he slowly fused into one, becoming a single being of radiance, inexpressibly brilliant and beautiful, giving forth a power of love mighty enough to spread supportive arms beneath the Earth and wings of healing above it. The 'Jesus-Maria' stone that stands before the entrance to the Lady Chapel in Glastonbury Abbey marks the very spot where this wondrous conjoinment took place. In the perfect stillness of that sublime moment, all were bathed in the light of the star, the perfect 'dayspring' which had shone over all the Earth as Mary and Jesus had been born.

Watching that scene through the same hallowed light of the star almost 2,000 years later, it seems to us that many more were gathered in Mary's presence than the human assemblage of the time. The call to our hearts is eternal, and concerns not religion, but our highest, spiritual selves. All of those whose hearts have been touched by Mary stand there and are ever present, in the here and now, listening to that divine call to our higher nature and receiving from her hands and her heart the holy healing balm which is her signature and her deepest essence.

CHAPTER TWENTY-THREE

Tamar's Story

*T*amar, the daughter of Mary and Jesus, spent much of her childhood with her mother in the limestone caves of Sainte Baume. Here she received her training in the profound Earth mysteries which she would one day need to wield in order to enable the outer manifestation of Camelot, the holy city, to appear on the face of the Earth itself. She was indeed the Holy Grail, that point in consciousness where the Earth and the spirit become one – an externalization of the *nous*, as described in Mary's gospel, and another manifestation of the Spirit and the Bride, spoken of so enigmatically at the end of the Revelations of John ('The Spirit and the Bride say, Come!'). She was to be the embodiment of the Great Invocation, combining the spiritual qualities of her mother Mary, the 'Woman Who Knows All' (so named in the Gnostic texts, and said therein to have been given the title by Jesus) and those of the man called the Christ, her father, the Light of the World.

Tamar forged a deep connection with the gypsies, the wandering people said to comprise the lost tribes of Israel, and was vociferous in their defence in both England and France, for there were many prolonged visits to Britain by both her and her mother during her lifetime. She restored their soul to them, which had been diminished by centuries of persecution, and reminded them of their heritage – that they were a mystical people, beloved of the Goddess, and that they preserved many secrets of the feminine Wise Ones who had once been venerated on the Earth. She was qualified to say so – her own grandmother and mother were of the tribe of these Wise Ones, healers and mystics whose ancestress was the great Dragon Queen herself. Between the gypsies and Tamar there occurred a conjoining of traditions, a commingling of skills and secrets. She became their adored queen and protectress.

In the town of Saintes-Maries-de-la-Mer, where the three Marys first docked, there is a church in whose crypt stands an altar dedicated to Sarah the Egyptian, supposedly Mary Magdalene's black servant girl, who was made the patron saint of the gypsies. Every year on her feast day, 25 May, thousands of devotees parade her statue through the town to the sea, where it is ritually baptized, echoing, perhaps, a far distant memory of baptisms administered by Mary Magdalene, her mother and sisters and, eventually, her daughter Tamar. Sarah was actually Mary Magdalene's dedicated friend, a colleague of her temple, who became Tamar's nurse. It is Tamar, of course, whom the gypsies salute, her identity carefully overlain with that of Sarah. Interestingly, both names denote royalty, 'Sarah' meaning 'Princess of the Royal House', whilst 'Tamar' means 'Palm Tree' as well as an amalgamation of 'Royal One' and 'Holy One' (the palm tree signifies royalty and blessedness). Tamar was indeed 'Tamar the Egyptian', for that was her birthplace. Mary had sought sanctuary in her temple in Egypt to give birth to Tamar after the horror of the Crucifixion.

Eventually, it was considered unsafe for Tamar to remain in Gaul. She shared a deep soul-kinship with her great-uncle, Joseph of Arimathea, and he and the Night-Protectors took Tamar to Ireland, where she was protected in an underground dwelling and taught by the mystic people of the ethers – those who express the inner consciousness of the Earth – whom today we call the fairy peoples. Stories of Deirdre in her dún echo the life of Tamar, the fiery-eyed mystical princess who was one with the Earth mysteries and the scintillating illumination of the spirit, and who, separated from her family and intimate friends, might have known sorrow sometimes, particularly as the establishment of the true teachings was being threatened by the doctrine of Peter, now allied with that of Paul who had joined forces with Mary's detractor of old (although later Paul regularly resisted Peter's dogmatic approach to apostleship and the two often quarrelled vehemently).

During her sojourn in Ireland, her family were unable to visit her except in spirit, because there were those, members of dark occult brotherhoods, who sought to kill her and were therefore eager to know where she was domiciled. There were powers in ancient Ireland connected with the fairy peoples which were able to blind the sight of the distant-viewing eye that these occult groups used to try to pinpoint Tamar's whereabouts. It was essential that, within this incarnation, she should attain womanhood so that she might bear the light within her in full measure and give it out to the world in order for a crucial seed to be sown. The angelic and the advanced or noble fairy hierarchies were as deeply aware of this urgent requirement for the sake of the Earth and her peoples (including themselves) as were the priests and the brotherhoods of the white light.

For the same reason, Mary Magdalene, her sisters and their mother remained in safety in the natural city of the limestone caves wherein they could retreat indiscoverably if the need arose, although the choice of the caves as their dwelling place was made to fulfil a purpose more profound and spiritually significant than the pragmatic one of protection, vital though that was. The caves lay on the meridian towards the heart chakra of the Earth, and represented 'the earth beneath our feet', the sacred ground below that will come into prominence in the future due to the secrets it enfolds, harbouring them until the time is right for their revelation.

Tamar was particularly at risk, however, and could not be certain of safety without day and night protection. Occasionally, keenly aware of her loneliness, Joseph of Arimathea would dress as one of the Irish peasantry and visit her in secret. The rapport between them was so tender and harmonious that these visits comprised the happiest times of Tamar's life, and served as compensation for the enormity of the sacrifices demanded of her by her destiny.

At about the age of 21, Tamar set sail for Rome, where she strove with all her being to change the direction in which Peter and Paul were establishing the orthodox Church. She was welcomed and given residence in the Palace of the British, the home of the royal Silurian family (who were actually being held hostage there, although they were courteously treated by the Roman government).The famous Princess Eurgain, a devoted friend to both Mary and Tamar, was there to greet her, and they rejoiced in their reunion. Tamar met Paul on his visits to the Palace, which considerably increased in number and duration whilst Tamar was a guest of the Silurians. The New Testament places Paul on his third missionary journey at this time. We believe that during the years of this third mission, Paul came to Rome for a little over a year to deal with business relating to his apostleship, but in particular to visit Tamar, the daughter of the 'being of light' (Jesus) who had appeared to him on the road to Damascus. The fact that he was drawn to Rome to meet her indicates how alive he was to the intuition in his heart, even though his mind could not at first understand or accept her esoteric revelations.

The Church which she and the Three Marys had formed in Britain and other parts of Europe was the early Celtic Church, the Church of the True Light, which gave forth very different teachings from those of Peter and (apparently) Paul. The latter constructed (by and large) the correct edifice, but it was founded on the rock of materialism and did not contain the sacred innermost teachings which transform the soul, so that it no longer wants to slay, dominate, condemn or set itself apart from its brother or sister. Her quest could not be entirely fulfilled because, as was the situation at the time of the Crucifixion, the majority of humanity was too inclined to embrace those teachings which endorsed domination and earthly powers.

Paul was at first unable to assimilate her understanding of the Christ teachings into his own, although he did not, like Peter, regard her as one of Jesus's womenfolk who had grown too big for their boots and scandalously thought they knew what they were talking about. Paul fell in love with Tamar, but his passion was not returned.[1] She had been brought up by Mary in the druidic, Celtic culture of Britain and France, and she fully expected to be accepted as an equal by men and to have her wisdom, perception and ideas taken seriously. Paul's initially entrenched and unprogressive ideas about the status of women, and particularly his unresponsiveness concerning the recognition of the Sacred Feminine enshrined in the vision of 'The Way', ensured that he would be dismissed by Tamar as a suitor and thereby lose the love of his life.

It might be worth adding that both Peter (and, at first, Paul) were absolutely terrified of her, which was one reason why Paul dared not immediately and outrightly embrace her doctrines. Tamar wielded many powers, and she had not entirely inherited her parents' vast reservoirs of patience! Nevertheless, she was a highly exalted soul and would never have harmed another. It seemed that she forbore Peter and Paul, as far as it was possible for her to endure with patience the foolishness that would lead to the apparent obliteration of the true teachings of Jesus and Mary.

It is true to say that Tamar profoundly influenced Paul. Her transforming impact, mighty and dynamic as it was, took time to filter through the skins of orthodoxy and prejudice with which his true self had become obscured during his years as chief of the secret police within the Sanhedrin priesthood. Although his form of orthodoxy was initially constricting, he did not remain literal concerning the Christian precepts as Peter did, and indeed absorbed much of the mystery teachings of 'The Way' directly from Tamar. Ultimately, he was unable to process these teachings so that they became new doctrine or direction for the Church he was founding, but he did impart them secretly to those who had the soul-capacity to understand them. A Gnostic teaching explains that Paul's letters have a deeper meaning, which can be read symbolically only by those who have been initiated into the esoteric teachings of the Inner Mysteries, dispensed in the oral tradition. Paul's teacher in this oral tradition was Tamar.

We are assured by the seer David Wright that Paul's soul was conjoined with the consciousness of one of the great masters of wisdom who serve humanity from a transcendental plane located in the Himalayas, and that Paul's energies today constitute the flagship for the renewal of mysticism and the vision of the soul in the discovery of the road to enlightenment through the Christ.

Biblical scholars now think it likely that the famous misogynistic letters attributed to Paul were not actually written by him, and our source confirms this. It is certain that Peter and Paul's vigorous disagreements, culminating sometimes in downright rows, started after Tamar's life-giving philosophies began at last to prevail within his heart.

Although Tamar remained in Rome for many months, valiantly struggling to help Paul to see the light, he continued in his (apparently) helpless incomprehension and his exasperating tendency to dwell on their personal relationship rather than Tamar's polemics.[2] Paul's initial attitude to some of the Christian teachings represented Tamar's and her parents' greatest scourge – the interpretation of spiritual truth by the mind of materialism, even though eventually, because of the heart-piercing caused by his love for Tamar, her refusal of him as a suitor and her martyr's death, he was able magnificently to overcome this stance. When she was eventually seized by the Romans, Paul was heartbroken but, for the time being, unconverted.

Tamar was imprisoned in Rome and left to die of starvation – a fate poignantly symbolic, for Peter and Paul's Church of Rome (through the deliberate falsification of Paul's teachings) would thrust the same fate on the status of the Sacred Feminine. She did not 'die' in the usual sense, but ascended, as her father had done before her. The event attracted no wonder, for Tamar's was an underground communal cell where many Christians died, and their remains were often left to the scavenges of the rats. The absence of a body would not have been noted under such conditions.

Paul's grief for Tamar was intense, and we believe he may have been imprisoned by the Romans for a time, or at least held under house arrest as he was during his future imprisonment in Rome, because of his valiant attempts to secure her release. The heart-piercing to Paul caused by her death, and her ability to draw close to him in the depths of his spirit once she was released from her earthly incarnation, finally opened Paul's consciousness to the deeper truths of 'The Way'.

In the New Testament and other historical documents, more than six years in total are missing from his recorded life as a missionary. There is monumental evidence to support the idea that Paul spent these years in Britain. What he had learned from Tamar convinced him that Britain was indeed a 'mystic isle' and that the British were the 'chosen Gentile people'. Paul also had a longing to meet Tamar's mother and to spend time with her family as well as to extend his mission. He landed in Portsmouth at a place which was named 'Paul's Grove' in his honour, a name by which it is still known today. From there he made his way into Cambria (now Wales), where he founded the Abbey of Bangor according to the principles of 'The Way' as he had learned them from Tamar. It later became a monastery and was called by St Hilary and St Benedict the 'Mother of Monasteries'. Its educational curriculum was famed throughout the world and attracted many thousands of scholars. In one sense, the Abbey of Bangor was Paul's tribute to the holy woman who had admitted to his heart the full glory of the teachings of 'The Way'. We believe that Mary was in Wales during Paul's years there, although he also visited her several times in Gaul.

Princess Eurgain was Paul's remaining link with Tamar, and she eventually became the leading light in the Paulian Mission. A brilliant scholar, a prodigy in the arts and an inspired musician, she founded 12 colleges of Christian Druids for Culdee initiates at Caer Urgan (Cor Eurgain), endowing them generously with lands and wealth. All of them excelled to the highest degree in learning and philosophical innovation. Princess Eurgain set a lofty feminine standard whose original inspiration was associated with Mary Magdalene and Tamar. She also founded the first *cor*, or choir, in Wales, which became famous as the finest in the world. The lyricism and musicality of the bardic tradition was expressed anew in these globally-renowned choirs. The Eisteddfod, known the world over, is held every year by the Druidical Order of Wales, its choirs representing an unbroken tradition which stretches back to the Paulian Mission. Although Wales was 'the Land of Song' before the coming of Mary Magdalene and Tamar to Britain, it is inspiring to think that the famous Welsh choirs, in their spirit and tradition, still express today the soaring and eternal song of Mary Magdalene and her daughter Tamar, she who is the Holy Grail and whose true glory has not yet been revealed to the world.

For Mary, the death of Tamar was another deep sorrow to a heart so often crucified throughout the course of her life. Nevertheless, it could not be considered in the same terms as those in which we view death today, because the beautiful miracle of the *consolamentum* was on hand to bring shining reassurance to those struggling in the darkness and the circumscribed vision of the earthly planes, and Mary was, in any case, able to be with Tamar in full consciousness as she put aside her material body and ascended into the light.

NOTES

1 The fourth-century Bishop of Salamis in Greece, a Judaean Christian who dedicated himself to the denunciation of 'heresies', told of a story from The Ascension of James which claimed that Paul was originally from Greece but had converted to Judaism because he had fallen in love with 'the High Priest's daughter' and wanted to marry her.

When she spurned him he turned against the Jews and did everything in his power to undermine Judaism (i.e., became a Christian!). We believe that this story is a garbled account of Paul's love and courtship of Tamar, which happened *after* his dramatic conversion on the road to Damascus, and which, following her death, finally led him to embrace the true heart of the Christian mysteries as they were taught by Jesus and Mary. The Jewish 'High Priest' was Jesus himself, although of course an entirely different construction is applied to the story to suit the agenda of its narrator, who wished to assassinate the credibility of Paul the Apostle. Although Paul disguised these inner teachings that he had received from Tamar, the hostile element in the Roman Church was quick to detect them, he was named as 'the enemy' by certain factions and denounced as heretical. The high esteem in which he was held and his position as Chief Apostle proved impossible to erase, however, and so another tack was tried. Some of Paul's letters and other documents which appear in the New Testament were forged to make it appear as if he refuted these mystical teachings in his own name, and, in particular, as if he was contemptuous of women and sexual union. This effectively veiled any true understanding of Paul and ensured that Tamar's teachings, revealed through him, could not penetrate to the heart of Christian doctrine, which would have been unrecognizable in many instances had it done so.

However, there is more to Paul and Tamar's fascinating story. After Tamar's death, Paul's continuing mission as the 'Apostle to the Gentiles' took him into Asia Minor. He sailed north from Byzantium along the coast of the Black Sea to the maritime provinces of Bulgaria. This country enjoyed close cultural links with Byzantium, and significant amounts of Byzantine pottery and art have been discovered in several of its cities. Paul met a wandering tribe from its borders linked to an esoteric school operating within Bucharest. The meeting did not occur by chance; rather, Paul had long been expected. The wandering tribe, and the mystic brotherhood within it, received all of Tamar's secret teachings from Paul as a sacred trust. The knowledge they received was part of a legacy that they had guarded throughout the ages. These people were allied to the gypsies, whom Tamar loved and who we believe were of the original tribe headed by Jacob (later Israel).

It is from this sect of Paulicians that the Bogomils arose, the community in the Balkans from whom the Cathars originated. (Certain historians, among them A Toynbee, *A Study of History*, 1939, have been convinced by the accumulation of evidence that the Bogomil, Paulician and Cathar faith was indeed a single religion.) How fitting that they should have set their focus in France at the start of the new millennium, bringing 'The Way' to the land where John the Beloved Disciple and Mary Magdalene had lived and taught for so long, and where Tamar had spent so many formative years of her young life – in a sense, bringing it home! Now it becomes clear why the stories of the Holy Grail arose from the region in France where the Cathar enlightenment took hold, and why the mysteries of the Cathars, including the *consolamentum*, were so strongly linked with the mysteries of the Holy Grail. Tamar was the human expression of the Grail. Her teachings embodied those of her uncle, John the Beloved, her mother Mary Magdalene, and were also instinct with those of her arisen father. Paul was her messenger, who enshrined her teachings in his heart and who strove to impart them secretly, so that orthodoxy and worldliness would not obliterate them forever (as a measure of what Paul was up against, the dire warnings of the outraged thirteenth-century patriarch Germanus who preached against the 'dark mysteries' of the 'satanic Bogomil heresy' provide an insight). Of course, all this means that the origins of the Bogomils are not so obscure as has been considered, and that much more of their story needs to be revealed. We are confident that further revelations will be given. Meanwhile, it is interesting to reflect upon the fact that Paul established seven churches during his mission. We believe that the number is significant and is an expression of Mary's chakra teachings.

2 According to contemporary descriptions, Paul was short, stocky and suffered from baldness. It is both poignant and amusing that, apparently because he was convinced that his personal appearance was what stood between himself and Tamar's affections, he took against men with plentiful hair and declared that flowing locks were unholy!

CHAPTER TWENTY-FOUR

Secretum Domini

*T*he Lady Chapel in the ruins of Glastonbury Abbey marks the site where the first church, the Church of Mary Magdalene, stood until it was eventually replaced by the Abbey itself. The church was completed in 39AD, and was later encased in lead to prevent its disintegration. In 630AD, St Paulinus erected the Chapel of St Mary's above its remains, which was destroyed in 1184AD when the original abbey was burned to the ground.

A very strange story is told of this first wattle church and the Jesus-Maria stone. The words are said to have been carved on it by Jesus himself during one of his early stays in Britain. The legend explains that as a youth, Jesus saw that his beloved Mary Magdalene and the Apostles would come to Glastonbury after his death. The young Jesus erected a temple at the spot where the wattle church was later built by Joseph and his companions, who constructed it around Jesus's original temple. Jesus prepared the Jesus-Maria stone to stand at the altar of this temple, as an expression of honour and reverence to Mary, and to proclaim that the Christ Church should be the Church of Mary, not of his mother but, as we believe, of Mary Magdalene. He used the non-Hebraic form of 'Jesus-Maria' because of his apperception of the initial European future of 'The Way', understanding with perfect psychic as well as spiritual vision that Mary's truth would at first be obscured, and then at last re-emerge in a resurgence consisting of heart-opening joy.

In 540AD (the last year of King Arthur's reign), St David arrived at Glastonbury to rededicate the new church, which was an extension and reparation of the old one; but that first night as St David slept, Jesus came to him in a dream and urged him not to rededicate the church, as he himself had long before dedicated the church in honour of Mary, and the sacrament ought not to be given again by someone other than himself. St David was honoured to comply and the original consecration remained unchanged.

Before the Isle of Avalon was renamed Glastonbury by the Saxons, two frequently occurring names were found inscribed in the manuscripts of the old record-keepers which clearly referred to something so important and renowned that generally no explanation of them was added as it was considered unnecessary. The names were Domus Dei and Secretum Domini. Domus Dei means 'The Home of God' or 'The House of God', echoing Bethel and Bethlehem, which all subsequent churches, grand or humble, were named, and which actually refers to the original temple that afterwards became the first little wattle church built at Glastonbury amidst the 12 hides of land. Secretum Domini means 'The Secret of Our Lord', and refers to 'Our Lady's Dowry', registered by the Jesus-Maria stone that marks the record and site of this 'Dowry', and which was the gift, of Jesus to Mary, of the church and the sacred Isle of Avalon, therefore honouring her as the Holy Queen of Avalon.

The two names, Domus Dei and Secretum Domini are always cited together, naming the same place, because they express the idea that the wattle church is the home of Jesus and Mary conjoined as one, God and Our Lady, or God-Goddess uniting their light in their son-daughter the Christ Being, who is reflected again in the human/divine Jesus and Mary Magdalene. It is universally considered that the 'Mary' of the Dowry was Mary the mother. It was, of course, Mary Magdalene. Why else should this Dowry be spoken of in hushed and reverential tones as 'The Secret of Our Lord'?

There is one other clue. Although Joseph of Arimathea (Joseph of Mary and Jesus) took Mary the mother into his care after he and his companions had sailed from Alexandria, she was originally given by Jesus into the care of John at the time of the Crucifixion. Prior to the Crucifixion, Jesus had arranged that Joseph would look after Mary Magdalene's welfare. Joseph was ever afterwards known as Paranymphos, which means both 'Guardian' and 'Bridesman'. In other words, Joseph was made the Guardian of the Bride. It is strange to think that people still insist this title refers to Joseph in relation to Jesus's mother!

These beautiful old testimonies to the truth of the Jesus and Mary Magdalene story are not fabrications or unsupported tradition. As well as many other respected sources and documents which authenticate their historical actuality, the great Domesday Book itself gives the names and links them as one (without realizing what it was doing, or there would have been a number of incensed pontiffs knocking on the door in the night as its scribes slept in their beds!). It states:

> *The Domus Dei, in the great monastery of Glastonbury, called*
> *The Secret of Our Lord. This Glastonbury Church possesses in*
> *its own ville XII hides of land which have never paid tax.*

DOMESDAY SURVEY FOLIO, P249B

St Augustine, not a friend of the teachings of 'The Way' but unable to resist the allure of Glastonbury, waxes lyrical concerning these legends, although like everyone else after Mary Magdalene's Church was stamped out, he does not discern the true identity of 'Mary':

> *In the Western confines of Britain there is a certain royal island of large*
> *extent, surrounded by water, abounding in all the beauties of nature*
> *and necessaries of life. In it the first Neophites of Catholic (meaning*
> *'universal') Law, God beforehand acquainting them, found a church*
> *constructed by no human art, but divinely constructed, or by the Hands*
> *of Christ Himself, for the Salvation of His people.*
>
> *The Almighty has made it manifest by many miracles and mysterious*
> *visitations that He continues to watch over it as sacred to Himself and*
> *to Mary, the Mother of God.*

FROM *EPISTOLAE AD GREGORIUM PAPAM*

Indeed, Mary Magdalene and Jesus continued to appear in visions and dreams to those who visited the 'royal isle' (whose spiritual queen was Mary), as William of Malmesbury, the twelfth-century Saxon historian, relates in his last work, *De Antiquitate Glastoniae,* when he attests to the vision of Christ appearing to St David in a dream and firmly instructing him not to interfere with his original dedication of that first holy temple to Mary. The Church of Mary Magdalene could not truly be stamped out, because down the ages Christ himself has taken care to preserve it.

We believe that in his youth as he carved the Jesus-Maria stone, Jesus, with his perfect psychic senses, saw far into the future and perceived that miraculous moment when he and Mary would fuse into one and radiate a mighty blessing to the souls of all who would stand within their light. He prepared the stone and set it as an altar in the exact location where the magical event would take place, in honour of his fathomless and eternal love for Mary Magdalene, a love that would one day embrace all the world through her beloved and divine presence.

PART II

The Gospel of
Mary Magdalene

CHAPTER TWENTY-FIVE

The Discovery of Mary's Gospel

*M*ary's beautiful and enigmatic gospel is part of a collection of texts, three in number, referred to by scholars as Papyrus Berolinensis 8502. They were acquired by the German academic Dr Carl Reinhardt in Cairo in 1896, 18 years before the outbreak of the Great War. It is understood that Dr Reinhardt found them on sale in an antique shop containing many Egyptian relics.

Since the suppression of all other gospel texts besides the canonical four by the decree of Emperor Constantine in the fourth century, nothing had been known of The Gospel of Mary Magdalene until Dr Reinhardt's discovery. A rumour of it had always existed among heretical groups, particularly in France, where the Magdalene was so deeply revered. A persistent belief can be traced back to the areas where the teachings of Mary held the greatest sway, telling of a book of esoteric teachings written by Mary which she translated into code and placed in hiding, as if she knew of the desecrations that would follow. This book is known among her followers as 'The Book of Love'. It was not 'The Gospel of Mary' as such, but Margaret Bailey and I believe there is a connection between the two books, for Mary's gospel does indeed contain clues as to the esoteric teachings of the Christ (the great Christ Being reflecting itself through Jesus and Mary). However, by its own choice, humanity was ill-prepared for these teachings until now.

Today, there is evidence that humanity is choosing differently, and in this context it is interesting to note the timing of the discovery of the Berlin Codex – just a single generation before the outbreak of the First World War. And, unspeakably terrible though they were, with the perspective of hindsight we can see that the two World Wars were destined to begin the process of the release of the Sacred Feminine from invisibility and bondage. The publication of the Berlin Codex was delayed until 1955, a few years after the end of the Second World War, a time when humanity could at last begin to leave the past behind and look to the future with renewed hope.

The three texts included in the Berlin Codex are of direct and complete relevance to the New Age which Christ prophesied. They are:

The Apocryphon of John, which gives further teachings and secret insights into the soul-state of humanity as it prepares itself for the Church of John and Mary, as well as instruction on how to overcome our destructive tendencies;

The Sophia of Jesus Christ, which gives the combined teachings of Jesus and Mary (Sophia is the Goddess of Wisdom or Divine Mother, the Holy Spirit of the Trinity of God, recognized as the Tree of Life by the Kabbalah, the mystic branch of Judaism) and of course;

The Gospel of Mary, with which we are concerned.

The Gospel of Mary is tiny, running only to just over eight pages. Ten pages have been lost, so less than half of the original text is extant. Nevertheless, it contains a unique poetry and grace, a mystical beauty, and a timeless – indeed, strangely modern – tone. Appropriately enough, ancient records speak of these qualities as those belonging to Mary herself (except, of course, that they do not mention her timelessness, which is something we can appreciate better from the perspective of today).

The famous Nag Hammadi Gnostic gospels were recovered in 1945 (again, shortly after the cease of hostilities) and perfectly complement the Berlin Codex, putting the message of Jesus, and Mary's hugely significant part in the story and contribution to the teachings, into their proper perspective.

CHAPTER TWENTY-SIX

The Sacred Bloodline and the 'Supplanter'

*T*o understand the teaching given in Mary's gospel, it is helpful to have an awareness of the stories connected with the sacred bloodline that culminated in Jesus the Christ, Mary the Magdalene and their daughter Tamar. This sacred bloodline can be traced back to the biblical matriarch Rebecca, who was Jacob's mother. She belonged to the soul-group of a primal ancestress who was one of the first god-people to pledge their allegiance to the planet Earth. We might understand this primal ancestress to have been a less 'restricted' incarnation of the soul who would, countless aeons later, be born as Mary Magdalene.

Being part of a soul-group means that certain souls form a 'team' around a great master (male or female) in the inner spheres, and incarnate on Earth in order to further the master's work for the benefit and progress of humankind.[1] After the primal ancestress cited above had withdrawn into the higher worlds, as the god-people did after the destruction of Eden (the once fertile and temperate area around the North Pole), those souls following the path of birth, death and reincarnation on the physical earth who had attuned themselves to her refined vibration gathered around her to serve her altruistic purpose.

To understand Mary's gospel, it is important to be aware that this primal god-woman and her soul-group are profoundly connected with the symbol of the sacred pyramid. As a symbol, the pyramid is much older than our solar system, but she was the first to create it on Earth in its three-dimensional form and to raise it as an altar to the Godhead – as an offering to the Divine, as an expression of the essence of holy Truth or 'The All', and as a mystical statement or teaching. The powers within the sacred pyramid reflect the powers of resurgence and renewal of the soul itself when it is married to the ineffable dynamic of the spirit.[2]

So we might think of Rebecca, then, as a member of the soul-group of this primal ancestress in the spiritual spheres. Rebecca was the niece of Abraham, the patriarch who was born in Ur, in Sumerian Mesopotamia from which originates the myth of Tiamat the Dragon Queen (*see* Part III, Chapter Thirty). Abraham conceived an enlightened notion of the 'One God' or the 'oneness' of the Godhead, and became the father of a nation who would proclaim this truth to the world. His wife Sarah (his half-sister) remained childless until, in her old age, she gave birth to Isaac. It is significant that Abraham's bloodline was also directly united with Egypt through Hagar, Sarah's maid, whom Sarah had previously persuaded him to marry so that she and Abraham could have children.

When Isaac was ready to take a wife, Abraham sent his servant back to Mesopotamia (the family had settled in Canaan) to find a spouse for him from Abraham's own kindred. The servant was guided by an angel, who led him to a well outside the city of Nahor, where he waited at eventide with his camels. Rebecca came to the well, and, seeing that he and his animals were thirsty, she offered him water from her pitcher, and filled up a trough so that the camels could also drink.

Here we have the woman with the jar, dispensing water from the well. The symbol gives intimations of Mary Magdalene, her descendant of the far future, and is archetypical of the Sacred Feminine. The well is the well of living waters, the well of life, and also the well of wisdom. Drawing on these waters, Rebecca gives them to the man who waits (the soul, or consciousness) and to his camels (the body). She thus demonstrates to the accompanying angel that she is the great matriarch who will bring forth the line of Jacob, leading to David and Solomon and eventually, of course, to Jesus, Mary Magdalene and Tamar.

Rebecca does indeed marry Isaac, and we read that 'God blessed ... Isaac' and they 'dwelt by the well' (Genesis, 25:11). (We believe this means, at a deeper level, that they dwelt in recognition and honour of the Sacred Feminine.) Rebecca conceived twins, the Lord advising her that, 'Two nations are in thy womb, and two manner of people shall be separated from thy bowels; and the one people shall be stronger than the other people; and the elder shall serve the younger.' The twins were called Esau and Jacob, Esau appearing first out of the womb and therefore being the son who would inherit. Esau was a keen hunter, a man of the field, whilst Jacob 'was a plain man, dwelling in tents' who sold pottage. Isaac loved Esau, whilst Rebecca loved Jacob.

There comes a point in the story of the brothers where nature spirits seem to intervene in their fate, and hence in the development of the sacred bloodline. There is no mention of them as such in the scriptures, except for the fact that, coming home one day from the field, Esau is clearly struck with what is known as 'the hungry grass'. This is actually a fairy curse, more of a prank than a punishment, although, while it lasts the experience is frightening and uncontrollable ('the luckless foot may pass .../Into the terror of the hungry grass.' Donagh McDonagh). Reports of the descent of the curse of 'the hungry grass' are not only found in folktales; occurrences have been documented in modern times throughout Britain and Ireland, and, as they are numerous there, they are presumably so elsewhere.[3] The experience of it consists of crossing open country on foot and being possessed by a mischievous elemental lurking in the grass which causes its unfortunate human victims to fall prey to a hunger so desperate that they will surrender anything – dignity, honour, possessions – in exchange for food, however humble or meagre. Thus it is, presumably, with Esau, for on coming home from the field he rushes to Jacob and begs for pottage.

It seems unlikely that the plain, tent-dwelling Jacob was ferociously materialistic. On the contrary, it appears that suddenly he was visited by a sense of his destiny. He refuses to give food to his brother unless, in exchange, Esau sells him his birthright. Esau, craven to the point where he believes he will expire with hunger, agrees. He sells his birthright for a mess of pottage. Having once obtained the promise of Esau's birthright, Jacob is helped by his mother Rebecca to deceive Isaac, who has become blind and is near death, into bestowing his final blessing intended for his first-born on Jacob instead.

Again, the force of destiny is apparent, because Rebecca dearly loved and respected her husband and would no doubt never have planned to mislead him under normal circumstances. Her very name means 'faithful wife'. Other interpretations of her name are, intriguingly, 'noosed cord' or 'ring' and the sacred matriarchal symbol of the cow. But her mission called to her through her love for Jacob, and she stalwartly shouldered her unpleasant burden of deceiving and distressing her husband in his last days.

When Esau realized that Jacob had received his father's blessing instead of himself, he vowed to kill Jacob. Rebecca, learning of his intention, advised Jacob to leave home for a while until Esau had calmed down. Rebecca arranged for Isaac to give Jacob a further blessing and to send him on a mission to seek for a wife, so that he might depart from home honourably. Like Isaac himself, Jacob's father bids his son not to take a wife from the 'daughters of Canaan', but to return to his kinsfolk and to choose a spouse from the 'daughters of Laban', his maternal uncle. It is during this crucial journey, on the run from his brother Esau after appropriating his birthright and on his way, with his parents' blessing, to find and marry his wife Rachel (although he is also tricked into marrying her sister Leah), that Jacob dreams his famous dream. When he reaches Padanaram, the place where his uncle lives, he meets Rachel the shepherdess, and rolls away a great stone from the mouth of the well outside the town, whereupon the waters flow forth and water the sheep.

The symbolism could hardly be more powerful. The shepherdess and her consort meet and marry at both the physical and the spiritual level, and the 'sheep' (those who follow after them) are given the life-giving waters. From the 'living waters' of Rachel comes forth Joseph, whose sojourn in the land of Egypt has so much spiritual and esoteric relevance, although a 'stone' has to be rolled away first (Rachel's initial years of barrenness). The 'living waters' also issue from Rachel's sister Leah in continuance of the bloodline. The true, life-giving waters are those that eventually spring from the mission and the sacred marriage of Jesus and Mary.

Jacob's dream is a vision of the bloodline and a teaching on the great plan of Goddess-God in creating the Earth and its humanity. It is a treatise on the structure of the soul and of creation itself. This momentous night is the night when Jacob is told by Goddess-God that he, and those who bear his children, have been chosen to swell the population of the entire globe, for 'thy seed shall be as the dust of the earth, and thou shalt spread abroad to the west, and to the east, and to the north, and to the south: and in thee and in thy seed shall all the families of the earth be blessed.' (Genesis, 28:14) The Godhead also told Jacob later, in the same sacred place upon the mountainside, that henceforth his name should be Israel, and that 'a nation and a company of nations shall be of thee, and kings shall come out of thy loins'. (Genesis, 35:10–11)

The strength that Jacob gained in overcoming Esau, the symbol of wrath, is tested upon the mountain of Bethel, for there an angel comes to him and wrestles with him all night. Jacob has overcome the natural law of wrath at the earthly level of life; now he must prove that he can overcome it at the subtle spiritual level. Jacob's spirit and soul persist in the struggle, and as the day breaks the angel releases him, commends him and tells him his name is now Israel. In the morning after his first night at Bethel, awakening from his dream, Jacob feels the full force of what he has witnessed in his soul-state. His little earthly self is overcome with fear, and he utters the well-known words: 'This is a terrible place!' or 'How dreadful is this place! This is none other than the house of God, and this is the gate of heaven.'

We believe that the name and the destiny of Jacob equate with Goddess-God's plan for the world. The meaning of his name gives us a clue – 'the supplanter'. Esau, we are told, was born red and hairy. His message from God is that he shall 'live by the sword'. God declares in Malachi, 1:2–3: 'I loved Jacob, and I hated Esau, and laid his mountains and his heritage waste for the dragons of the wilderness.' This text intimates that the man of peace was beloved by God, but the man of strife, the blood letter, the man of wrath, was not acceptable to the Godhead and that the elements of destruction which dwell in the spiritual wilderness, created by the rule of wrath he himself has instigated, would lay waste to his inheritance (eternal life).

Esau shares many similarities with his kinsman Ishmael, who was full of wrath and initiated conflict wherever he went. He is the physical man, the predator, the man of Earth, who in one sense is the rightful heir to the Earth, being utterly of it. But if Esau inherits (for one or the other, Esau or Jacob, is destined to be the founding father of all the future races), the fate of humanity can only be death, because he is unredeemed. If, however, Jacob, the elected man of God, can struggle triumphantly against his red, angry brother, the elemental rule of Earth which is wrath itself can be overcome, can be supplanted. The Christ may descend, using the vessel of the bloodline, because it is of the bloodline that Jesus and Mary will be born. Abraham, in the beginning, is promised 'the Christ'. Jacob sees the promise in his dream. He has already taken the first steps towards supplanting Esau by depriving him of his birthright when he lays himself down to rest with a stone for a pillow on that fateful night.

When Jacob awakes, overwhelmed by what he has seen, he takes the stone which supported his dreaming head and anoints it with oil, declaring that 'it shall be God's house'. He builds an altar there and calls the place (a mountain) Bethel, the same place where his grandfather Abraham raised the first altar to the God he had conceived of in his heart. This concept of the elemental rule of wrath being supplanted or overcome is essential to a proper understanding of Mary's gospel and is worth bearing in mind.

We would like to draw attention to the crucial role played by women in the development of the sacred bloodline, for Rebecca's dedication to its continuation, regardless of personal cost, was not without precedent. In just the same way, Lot's daughters gave their father wine to dupe him into committing incest with them (Genesis, 19:32–38) so that the Moabites might come into being. From the Moabites would arise Ruth, the matriarch from whose issue the royal line of Israel would descend. Ruth's son, Obed, was grandfather to King David, and from this line, important Essenes would be born who would teach Jesus, John the Baptist, John the Beloved and Mary Magdalene in Alexandria and Qumran.

The first Tamar, too, placed the development of the bloodline above her own safety, adorning herself as a harlot and sitting by the roadside to deceive her father-in-law Judah (Jacob's son) into impregnating her so that the bloodline would not cease. Similarly, the second Tamar endured rape and humiliation from Amnon her brother, King David's son, which led to the return of the Ark of the Covenant to Jerusalem and, through the deaths of Amnon and Absalom which were both linked with her rape, to the eventual reign of King Solomon. Following in this tradition, the third Tamar – she who was the culmination of a destiny older than the cosmos, the human vessel of the Holy Grail – suffered isolation and an early death in order to seal the bloodline from continuation once it had fulfilled its mystical purpose. It is women who, again and again, demonstrate in this long history that they have sacred knowledge of how vital the bloodline is, and where it is leading.

The men involved, on the other hand, seem often to be in some kind of resistant stupor. Lot offers his two daughters like lambs to a pack of wolves when his house is surrounded by hostile men who are suspicious of the two angels he is entertaining (angels that will on the morrow destroy them and their homes in the smiting of Sodom and Gomorrah), saying, 'These virgins have not been near any man; take them and do with them what you will, but do not attack my guests.' They are the daughters who eventually give his seed continuance through incest when they realize that the bloodline cannot progress by any other means (fortunately, the mob were not interested in the girls, but were intent only on ousting the angels).

The two sons of Judah who married the first Tamar died suddenly, without issue, and, after she had waited for years to be married to his third son, she at last discovered that Judah had no intention of giving her to him and finally had to trick Judah himself into impregnating her by disguising herself as a prostitute.

Boaz, the kinsman of the husband of the widowed Ruth, had to arrange his marriage to her by first gaining the consent of the nearer relative whose legal right it was, above that of Boaz, to offer himself to her as a husband in place of his deceased kinsman (a law which came into effect on the sale of a parcel of her husband's land by Naomi). Only the joint schemes of Ruth and her mother-in-law Naomi, who aids Ruth by using what is clearly a gift of second sight, prompted him to initiate the set of circumstances which eventually led to their union and the birth of Obed. Here again, it is the wisdom of women which works behind the scenes, utilizing prophetic vision and risk-taking in order to correctly channel the sacred bloodline (Ruth's decision, to lie at the feet of Boaz on the threshing-floor as he slept, was a dangerous one that might have resulted in severe repercussions for her reputation and wellbeing). Although Boaz treats her with great courtesy and kindness, it is to Naomi and her monotheistic belief that Ruth offers her deepest devotion, declaring in immortal words, 'Where you go, I will go, and where you stay, I will stay. Your people shall be my people, and your God shall be my God.'

When her son Obed is born, it is into Naomi's care that he is given. Prior to his birth, Naomi refuses to be called by her given name, assuming the name 'Mara' instead. Although its meaning is 'bitterness', it is also the name by which the great Mother Goddess has been known since the beginning of time – Ma, Mara, Mari or Mary – the 'salt of the sea' or the 'bitterness' dispensed by the Mother to all things born into the physical realm so that they might begin to remember their spiritual birthright. The message is clear – it is the matriarchal line that is of foremost importance, despite the culture and the mores of the times.[4]

Down the ages, the women of the line procured its continuance through great personal cost and self-sacrifice. Their sheer determination, their wombs and their schemes ensured its survival against all odds. It comprised a stairway down to earth, down into physical matter, which the prophesied two – Jesus and Mary – would descend at the appointed time to teach us how to redeem matter itself and supplant suffering with joy. Thus, those of us who perceive something of the inestimable blessing that Jesus and Mary brought to the world (Tamar's has yet to be given) might consider it fitting to ponder sometimes on the gift of the bloodline passed down to us from the matriarchs of the Old Testament by means of their resolute and warrior-like intrepidation.

It was foretold that the coming of Jesus and Mary would 'arise out of the Star of Jacob', the great star which burned with the spiritual fires of what we know as the Pole Star, the star to which once the Earth was aligned and to which it will one day be aligned again. Our Moon also has a special connection to this star. The Star of Jacob was the Star of Bethlehem, the name which contains the sacred name of Bethel – Beth-El, House of God, Beth meaning 'house' and 'El' meaning the 'Highest of the High' or the Supreme Godhead – where Jacob, echoing his great ancestress, raised his pyramidal altar after his famous dream and declared, 'This is a terrible place; this is the House of God on earth and this is the Gate of Heaven,' afterwards giving it the name of Bethel. 'Bethlehem' also means 'The House of Bread', emphasizing the presence of Mary at the side of Jesus, for Mary was always associated with the Bread of Life and with the Corn Maiden in the constellation of Virgo who is a representation of Isis, she whose domain was the House of Bread. In the earliest ceremonies of the Eucharist, the blessed bread given to participants was always given in the name of Mary as the wine was given in the name of Jesus, the Holy Two who brought the Christ to Earth.

The Star of Jacob afterwards became the Star of David and the Seal of Solomon, the six-pointed star which became the symbol of the Jewish people. The difference between the two is this: the Star of David contains inner divisions, whilst the Star of Jacob does not. The latter is a symbol of perfect unity, a unity which will one day conjoin all the nations of the world in indissoluble brotherhood.

NOTES

1 There is another sense of the term in that 'soul-group' refers to the fact that a single soul bears many aspects, and that each human being on Earth represents only a part of that greater being which is their soul in the higher worlds.

2 See *Supernature* by Lyall Watson.

3 See *The Middle Kingdom*, Chapter VIII, by D A MacManus, for an entertaining account of an instance of the 'fairy hunger'.

4 When, in the Book of Ruth, Boaz declares to the elders that he is to make Ruth his wife, the elders declare: *We are witnesses. May the Lord make this woman, who has come to your home, like Rachel and Leah, the two who built up the house of Israel. May you do great things in Ephrathah and keep a name alive in Bethlehem. May your house be like the house of Perez, whom Tamar bore to Judah, through the offspring the Lord will give you by this girl.* It is notable that the blessing of the elders paid greater tribute to the matriarchs than to the patriarchs, although at the end of the Book of Ruth, the genealogy of Perez is given: Perez was the father of Hezron, Hezron of Ram, Ram of Amminadab, Amminadab of Nahshon, Nahshon of Salman, Salman of Boaz, Boaz of Obed, Obed of Jesse, and Jesse of David. This shows that Ruth, mother of Obed, was King David's great-grandmother.

CHAPTER TWENTY-SEVEN

Jacob's Ladder
and the Pyramid

*J*acob's dream relates directly to The Gospel of Mary. The symbolism of both is poetically simple and esoterically profound. Jacob dreamt of a ladder 'betwixt earth and heaven'. Upon this ladder, angels came and went, some ascending to Heaven, others descending to Earth. We think that one important understanding of this dream is that the angels are actually carrying human souls down into incarnation to be born and bearing those that have 'died' away into the heavenly spheres. This is what Jacob sees, and why it shakes the foundations of his perception. He beholds the ladder of mortality, creation itself. He sees how all who are born come into being, and how all who die return to the spiritual worlds.

In connection with this, the Mithraic teaching of the ancient mystery schools is most interesting. Its precept was that souls descended into incarnation and re-ascended at their death, climbing a ladder of seven steps which consisted of the stars and the planets. Origen, a third-century Egyptian philosopher, describes it as 'a ladder with seven gates, and at its top an eighth gate'. The eighth gate opens out into the starry heavens; not the world of the physical cosmos but the spiritual region where the Goddess presides, the true soul-sphere. The ancients called it 'the field of imperishable stars', the wisest amongst them who coined the phrase well aware that physical stars do actually perish, although they live for unconscionable periods of time.

This is the sphere of the Bridal Chamber, where the soul and the spirit become one. Goddess has led her children – the little sparks of Divine Spirit, sent down into a stucture of seven bodies in order to learn self-consciousness, the densest of those bodies being physical matter – up again through the seven levels until in the soul-sphere they attain gnosis, or reunion with the Godhead. When this happens the little sparks, which are eternal, can invest their purest and most refined body, the beautiful soul-body which is like a wedding garment, with the gift of eternality, a gift earned by their sojourn on Earth and given to them by their conscious reunion with the Godhead. Thereafter they become self-realized god-people, one with the source but also fully individuated.

Fairy tales, which are teachings from the masters in the spiritual spheres, can help us to understand this mystery. Cinderella (literally, 'little spark') must lose her inheritance and work as a servant in the kitchen (a soul labouring on Earth in a physical body) until she is united with her prince (her Christ-self). Here we are shown that the magic and the beauty of the soul, which creates a beautiful carriage and a beautiful dress for the little spark of Eternal Spirit, cannot step over the threshold into immortality – into True Being – until the union of soul and spirit takes place. At midnight, when the powers of darkness or matter hold their greatest sway, they disappear, and Little Spark's perception is that she is cut off from them, left without the garments of her soul. On her third visit to the palace (the Third Degree), Eternal Spirit, her true self in the Heaven world who is at one with the Godhead and has never departed from it, manages to retain a tiny part of the soul-body before it succumbs to the powers of matter – a small *glass* (symbolic of the soul) shoe, appropriate because the feet carry the soul forward, steering the vessel and partaking in the cosmic dance of life. It is to the dance that Little Spark goes to seek union with her prince, her Eternal Spirit. Now that the Spirit has this clue, it can discover whose foot fits the shoe, who it is that will provide the soul-body fit for 'him' to reside in and conjoin with and grant 'him' gnosis. When he does so, the Sacred Marriage takes place, and Cinderella and her prince are one.

The story of Sleeping Beauty is another fairytale showing us how the little spark has to fight its way through a terrifying wilderness (taking on the rigours of the descent into matter and all that life within it entails) before it reaches the intact memory of itself, its perfect soul-state, which has fallen asleep in materiality. On kissing this sleeping beauty, the tender inner self which she represents awakens, and soul and spirit are as one in the Bridal Chamber.

When Snow White has to retreat to the mountain (the world of matter), she encounters the Seven Dwarves which represent her seven bodies or chakras. They have to dig and delve each day, mining for gold and jewels (the gifts of experience which release the light of the spirit) in the hard stone of the mountain. Snow White perfects the dwarves by enfolding them in her love; they learn their lessons and her tutelage releases them into joy. When she falls asleep under enchantment and is placed in her glass coffin (note how, once again, the archetypal symbol for the soul is always water, glass or crystal) their untiring devotion to her memory attracts the prince to Snow White, and the Sacred Marriage takes place.

The mystery schools taught that the cosmos has seven levels, through which the soul, lit within by its little spark of spirit, must proceed in order to attain union and freedom. For each of these seven levels, the soul has a body. We contact these bodies through our chakras. Within each level is a demonic force, a teacher and tester, who will not allow the soul to continue until it has mastered the lesson of each 'climate' and each body. Some doctrines further revealed that the 'demon' of each level would contend with the soul as it sought to pass on to the next plane, and that the soul needed to know how to answer these challenges before it could safely ascend to the following realm or climate. So it was not just a case of lackadaisically learning the lessons of the soul – they had to be fully and triumphantly mastered.

In connection with Jacob's dream, it is interesting that the ascent of the soul is seen in many ancient religious disciplines as mounting a ladder of seven steps to the eighth region, the starry skies or the ogdoad, the 'eighth', and it is instructive to note that the seven steps are equated with the seven planets of traditional astrology. These include the Sun and the Moon, but not the Earth. Therefore, the soul in earthly incarnation is also in itself a representation of the 'eighth' in that together, the seven planes of creation and the soul create the one and the seven – eight. And the ogdoad, the starry heaven, is also 'the eight'. Therefore the ogdoad is the perfectly realized form of its mirror reflection, the little soul on Earth (really just a strand of the complete soul) setting forth on its matter-journey through the seven levels of trials and testing. This organization makes a perfect octave, whereby in the structure of music, the seven tones unite in an octave when the first tone of one harmonic (seven notes) is in harmony with the first tone of the next harmonic. They are the same note, only the higher obviously vibrates at a faster rate than the lower. They are the one and the seven, the eighth, the octave, a unit of harmony in the symphony of creation. Now it is easy to see why, although the number seven permeates the structure of the cosmos, the number eight is so sacred. It is intriguing to consider, too, that 8 has a conjoined serpentine or dragon shape, and that Mary Magdalene is associated with creation, the Dragon Queen and the number eight. The Song of Solomon, which seems to tell of her coming, is composed of eight chapters.

To return to Jacob's dream of a ladder upon which angels ascended and descended, carrying human souls into and out of incarnation (as we believe), a fascinating piece of information has come to light in our researches. The ladder depicting the coming and going of souls to and from the Earth which is the symbolic image of so many of the ancient mystery religions was actually set into a pyramid. Its earliest form seems to be the Sumerian ziggurat, a pyramid composed of seven steps, at the top of which lay the 'Eighth Gate' or the 'Bridal Chamber'. In this instance, it was symbolized by a magnificent bed. Once a year, a Sumerian priestess would wait there for the visitation of the Godhead.

And so Jacob's dream is revealed as taking the form of a pyramid, the mysterious symbol of the Sacred Feminine. The Bible does not explicitly say that his dream of a ladder was a dream of a pyramid, but the ladder connecting Earth and Heaven did take the form of a pyramid in the mystery teachings that were circulating in Jacob's day. There is a further clue in that Jacob raised a 'cairn of stones' in honour of his dreaming there of the 'house of God'. We believe that the cairn of stones was actually a replica of a pyramid. Jacob also called the place of his dream the 'Gate of Heaven'.

That is exactly what the pyramidal 'ladder' portrays – seven steps leading up to the Gate of Heaven – the 'Eighth'.

The pyramid expresses the sacred number three, the Holy Trinity or the three emanations of the Godhead, which are a unity, a central point, but which issue forth as Mother, Father and Divine Child. They are three principles of one vast being, Consciousness itself, in which we live and move and have our being. But is there a hidden principle of four contained within the trinity, the elemental square upon which creation is based?

CHAPTER TWENTY-EIGHT

The Square of Construction

*T*here are four pointers which may help us to conceive of this four-square or cuboid principle on which the pyramid is constructed, and what it might mean. The first is the appearance of the Star of Bethlehem over the stable (actually a cave, which is where animals were often housed). We believe that both Jesus and Mary were born here, in this humble stable. It is inspiring to think of the perfect brotherhood of all the elements of life that were present within the stable: the man and the women, the boy and girl child, the animals, the wood of the manger, the grasses within it, the stone of the walls and ceiling, the earthen floor, the small fire burning in its ring of stones, the pitcher of water standing nearby, the air that moved through the cave, warm with the tang of the fire and fragrant with animal musk and fresh hay – a perfect moment in the great cosmic drama as it hung suspended in sweetness and peace before the toil and tribulation began.

The four elements in harmony with humans and animals, and of which we are composed, were represented by the star. Suddi tells us that the star prophesied to 'rise out of Jacob' comprised four great stars or luminous phenomena, each of them slowly moving together to form one great central light, speaking of them as the 'coming together of the four'. He explained the Essene prophecy which said that, from the four corners of the Earth, four stars would rise together, and when they met and became as one, the Messiah would take his first breath. Suddi spoke of them as four permanent named stars whose paths crossed in the heavens that night, and whose light was strong enough to cast shadows. When they merged, the light focused into a great point and the phenomenon they created was like a very large, exceptionally bright full moon that gave a soft light almost as vivid as daylight. The Star of Bethlehem looked like a pearl or an orb of light (associated with the Orb of Shar-On or the Sphere of John), and from it descended a beam like a serpent's tail which hung above the precise point in Bethlehem (Bethel-hem – 'House of God') where the births took place.

We feel we need to make it very clear that, according to our source, it was Mary who was born on that night in Bethlehem. She and Jesus were one, but she was born first, on 25 December, as the sacred serpent of light formed a pointer over the cave-stable where the Christ (Jesus and Mary) would be born to the Earth. Jesus and Mary represented the collective soul and spirit of humanity. They showed us the vast drama of the plan of creation, Goddess-God's plan to send us forth and call us back upon the great wheel of experience which is the sphere of physicality. This wheel is divided into 12 segments, 12 ages or zodiacal spans, the voyage through which will teach us all we need to know in order to attain gnosis and become a self-realized being. Mary is the alpha (the start or beginning) of this mighty soul-voyage, and Jesus is the omega (the end or the triumphant culmination). This is symbolized by their birth in 'Galilee' (a ring or rolling wheel, the zodiac itself) and Mary's voyage to Glastonbury (Heaven's Looking Glass, the mirror of the zodiac, and also, just as importantly, the throne of the Soul of the World, for the soul is always rep-resented by water, crystal or glass). It is why the alpha had to remain on Earth, and the omega ascended. And it is why there were 12 days between the birth of the alpha and the omega – 12 zodiacal 'days' or ages lay between them, the 12 zodiacal spans which constituted the great circle in its completeness, the perfect ring that was in its one half, Mary, and its other half, Jesus. They were born in the sign of Capricorn, the sign of the mountain gazelle or more properly the unicorn, the con-stellation which the ancients believed represented the Gate of Ascension for the soul. It is the point on the sacred circle which marks the beginning and the end.

The star hung in the sky like a great lantern for the span of a month (the duration of the Capricorn tenancy in the zodiac). By the end of that time, it had faded away. The four stars which were to merge were marked by the Wise Men, for esoteric communities had been watching and waiting for many years for this astro-nomical event. The Wise Men had associations with Ur, a city of Babylon (Sumerian Mesopotamia) and the place of origin of Abraham, although the Wise Men of Ur were not, in fact, from Babylon. Ur was actually a great ancestor, a being of spiritual magnitude beyond the comprehension of ordinary earthly consciousness, rather than a city. The city was built in his-her name and memory, and was a gathering place for all those of Ur. It was pronounced 'yore' and has since passed into our language as indicative of all things wise, ancient and distant.

So the Wise Men of Ur gathered together in spirit, in preparation for their travels as the time approached for the four stars to become prominent, but they did not set off on their travels from Babylon. Suddi tells us that they came from four different points of origin – from the four corners of the world. Their call came before the astral phenomenon began, sounded by prophecy, calculation and mystical prompting.

One of those who set out on the journey to greet the Messiah did not arrive. We believe that this member of the group of four represented the hidden fourth principle contained within the trinity discussed above. All four travelled towards a gathering point just outside Bethlehem, following the star throughout each stage of their journey; but only three of the sages survived. The fourth was from the east[1] and died of natural causes – heart failure – which of course from a spiritual perspective was symbolic of the cause of humanity's initial denial of Jesus and its wholesale denial of Mary – the failure of the collective human heart to perceive who she truly was.

The fourth Wise Man acted out the symbolic drama for us, so that in time we should come to understand. He bore, as his gift, a collection of pearls of remarkable size and purity, retrieved from the Persian Gulf, as well as a number of precious sapphires and rubies. The sapphires were of the finest, almost black variety, and the jewels symbolized the colours both traditionally associated with the Goddess and the Dragon Queen. The pearls were reminiscent of both the full Moon and the clear white radiance of the Christ Light, and symbolic of the Sphere of John-Shar-On, which is located within the spiritual dimensions of the Pole Star. The Pole Star is linked with the Moon, and there is evidence that the most eminent members of the great spiritual brotherhood dwelling there, whose humbler members on earth were known as the Druids and the Essenes, influenced the development and evolution of the Moon so that it might form a sisterhood with the Earth, helping Earth life to organize itself, so that physical vessels appeared which were suitable for the embodiment of the human strain.

The second pointer is the moon herself. The idea of the triple Goddess is linked with the Moon and three of her phases: waxing, waning and full. But there is a fourth, hidden phase – that which is called the dark of the Moon, when for a couple of days she becomes invisible, as though a veil had been drawn over her face in the skies. The Moon is linked with the destiny of the Earth. Human beings could not have evolved without the life-giving grace of her silver seasons. But her fourth, dark phase is just as important, not only to the physical rhythms of Earth life but to its secret, mystical aspects which ultimately steer its course. The significance of the number four also seems to be reflected in the fact that the Moon is precisely 400 times smaller than the Sun and 400 times closer to the Earth than the Sun. The time from one new Moon to another is 28 days – four weeks. Despite her three visible phases, the Moon seems also to emphasize the number four.

Mary Magdalene is associated with many Moon goddesses. Where the understanding of Goddess via the mystery of the Moon was pure, and sought after for the sincere purpose of spiritual development, it was always inspired and illuminated by the hallowed being who incarnated as Mary Magdalene. Ministering on the higher astral planes to the souls of humankind, she was called: Ishtar, Diana, Isis, Astarte (an aspect of Isis) and many other deified names, according to the age and the culture of the people. And the Star of Bethlehem – the Star of Jacob – assumed the form of a large full Moon once the four stars had come together. It was also under a full Moon that Jesus Christ made his supreme sacrifice on the evening of the Crucifixion.

The third clue is given to us by a secret teaching of Plato: that reality itself is underpinned by the subliminal structure of a trinity, within which exists a veiled fourth principle. The trinity can be understood as mind, body, and spirit or consciousness, with the fourth invisible principle being the Mystery from which all arise and which encompasses them all, or, conversely, the trinity might be seen as mind, spirit, and Mystery, with the fourth principle as physicality, the final testing-ground into which all descend. This idea reflects the concept of the individual physical life on Earth adding one to the seven planes of the cosmos, making eight, and so reflecting the ultimate Mystery, the imperishable stars of the Eighth or 'ogdoad', the octave which sounds from Earth to Heaven and from Heaven to Earth, conjoining the two. This 'ogdoad' is the *nous* of which Mary's gospel speaks, a state to which, with aspiration, we can attain. We will find it in our deepest heart.

Perhaps we can understand Mary Magdalene from this perspective, seeing her as symbolic of both the physicality – the coming into bodily being – of Creation (ignorantly, erroneously and chauvinistically portrayed as a kind of 'prostitution'), and of the holy Mystery which encompasses all its grades, from the lowest to the highest.

The fourth pointer concerning the expression of four-in-three is the pyramid itself. When we think of the three-dimensional image, we see that the pyramid is set on a square base and has four sides. When we put together the trinity that it embodies and the number four, whose principle it also contains, the total is the mystical number seven, the underlying structure of creation itself. The mysterious ladder of ascension within the pyramid is explained and confirmed. The trinity of the Godhead is the ineffable Mystery of Being, and the sevenfold ladder of Manifested Creation is an integral part of this Divine Being, up which the Soul of the All (Creation) climbs to attain union, the sacred marriage, with the Source, the Godhead. This great macrocosm is the plan and the pattern which is the crowning destiny of every microcosmic soul ever breathed forth from the heart of the Great Spirit.

The square base of the pyramid represents our earthly selves, the Earth realm to which we have descended in order to attain self-realization or gnosis. The four elements of physical life – earth, water, air and fire – have their counterparts in Darkness (earth), Desire (water), Ignorance (air) and Wrath (fire).

White Eagle, who teaches from the Sphere of John, explains that the finer essence within the four elements does indeed compose our psyche. The element earth weaves into us Darkness, which we can use to blinker our consciousness or to help us to see the light of the stars (the imperishable stars of the spiritual realms). The element water gives us Desire, which can torment us with lusts or which we can transmute into a radiant centrifugal power rather than a craven, devouring centripetal force (the power of passion being used to give forth rather than to draw unto ourselves). The element air gives us perception or mind, which we can confine in the narrow, oppressively guarded prison of the intellect or the lower mind (Ignorance) or expand into all-embracing apperception. The element fire gives us Wrath (properly translated as 'an impassioned movement of Spirit'), which we can keep and feed as the roaring fires of our lower nature, full of ego, judgement and the anger of condemnation, or channel as a consummate dynamic into our heart-centre, the transformer, and transmute into the alchemy of Love.

It is this decision, this upreaching into the arms of our higher self and the simultaneous denying of the indulgence of our lower self (denying it satisfaction, so that its fires cannot run riot but instead begin to be lifted into transcendence) that is so crucial. When we make a conscious effort to transmute the anger, indignation and condemnation that is an expression of the lower energy of the fire element into tolerance and love, we cannot help but begin the process of purification of the other three elements of our nature as well. That is why the fourth element, fire, holds the key. It is when we raise the sword of our higher self and slay the dragon of Wrath that we may begin true soul ascension. Then the elemental power of the four backs off, loses authority, kneels in honour of a higher command. The soul steps forward in all her glory, no more thrashed and bound in the coils of the dragon of Wrath but free, ready to ascend to her rightful throne. And within the mysteries of her being rises at last the true dragon, the dragon of Love-Wisdom, her wrathful energy transformed into the dynamic of creativity and inspiration, bearing the Pearl of Wisdom, the Orb of Light, the transforming light of the Sphere of John-Shar-On in her claws, at her heart. All her passion now is for light, for self-giving. We see that in actual fact there has been no slaying, only liberation and transfiguration.

This is the great sacrifice required of us – the sacrifice of the lower self, which expresses itself in wrath. Down the ages, many, many teachers have come to impart to us this supreme truth, that to feed the vital dynamic within the very essence of creation – which demands sacrifice in order that the fires of life may continue to burn – we must not sacrifice others, but ourselves, our own lower nature. In times gone by (and still today, in various communities, some of them dwelling among us in the West, particularly where the death sentence continues to hold sway) we offered forth sacrificial victims. In our own time it is more common to sacrifice others to the prevailing climate of our lower desire nature, to greed and material supremacy. But the greatest teachers of all, Jesus and Mary, are still showing us that this will not do, that we must be ready to sacrifice ourselves instead. And when we do, the Godhead answers by giving us the ultimate gift in return for our sacrifice – our liberated soul.

We consider that a mistake has been made in viewing the significance of the

Crucifixion. It is not that Jesus bought us deliverance by the shedding of his own blood. Such a notion properly belongs to the doctrines of Mithraism, where the blood-sacrifice of the bull, the male god, is believed to deliver the populace from the demand of the life forces for sacrifice. This kind of sacrifice, however, is ineffective, except in a most unsatisfactory and temporary way, like feeding the fires of craving. It continues the old superstition that Jesus and Mary came specifically to correct, and at heart it is an ignoble and savage rendition of an underlying truth. The time is long overdue to lay this phantom of misguidance from the past, which has hounded us down the centuries. It is an ancient Roman, barbarian idea (of course far older than their civilization), that the shedding of another's blood lets us off the hook. It propitiates the dark gods, which scream louder and louder for more and more horrific sacrifice, until the civilization which feeds them ends in conflict, disease and calamity. It is the way of death.

The God of Light demands only our self-sacrifice, and when we have made it, gives us life in greater and greater abundance in a starburst of love and generosity, the true nature of the Godhead. This is what Jesus and Mary demonstrated. It is true to say that their perfect act of love for us, one on the physical cross, the other on the cross of a subtler persecution, did summon a mighty gift for us, one that we have yet to understand. But this came about because their sacrifice was made in the full consciousness of their free will. It would not have occurred if they had been sacrificed by the will and domination of others.

The four elements in their untransmuted state proclaim an elemental rule and chain the soul to the material realm. They act as its enemies (they are really its teachers), each one rising boldly before it and reading it a bill of rights as to why the soul should not dare to challenge their rule and should stay locked in their domain. The soul has to refute the claims of the elements and declare the authority of a higher law. In this way it summons the power of God. Thus may it pass on, ascending from plane to plane along the seven rungs of the ladder; but it is the mastery of the fourth element (the mysterious fourth?) which gives us the power to attain to the starry heavens. Bearing these things clearly in mind, we may now pass on to a complete reading of The Gospel of Mary, its missing pages supplied by Mary herself, speaking through Margaret Bailey.

NOTES

1 The fourth wise man is said to have borne the name Artaban, and rumours of him persist in Russian legend. Although he travelled towards Bethlehem from Persia, we believe that he had strong familial and religious links with an esoteric school based in an area of Russia or Siberia, which lies northeast of Palestine, and that he is linked with the wandering tribe to whom Paul vouchsafed secret knowledge given to him by Tamar (the human personification of the Holy Grail; see Chapter Twenty-three, Part I). The Bogomils of the Balkans are associated with this

tribe, the former bringing the mysterious wisdom of the Cathars to France at the turn of the first millennium. We believe that there is much important information regarding the more advanced esoteric teachings of Jesus, Mary and Tamar yet to be revealed, and that a significant amount of it may be preserved in the area of the Balkans. This fourth wise man was the only one of the three who knew that he was to visit and revere a girl-child, and his gift of pearls, as will be discussed, was profoundly symbolic. A present of a marvellous crown was made to Stephen, King of Hungary (977–1038), who became a Christian prior to ascending the throne around the time of the first millennium. This famous crown (known as the 'iron crown') was a treasure belonging to Rome, and was a gift from Pope Silvester II. Its iconography is deeply evocative of the mysteries of Mary Magdalene. Within its design appear the elemental square, the pyramid, the circle and the Soltaire cross (see Appendix Two). The entire crown is studded with an abundance of lustrous pearls. It is symbolic of the secrets of the fourth wise man, who kept in his heart the knowledge of the feminine Christ, but who was not destined to reach his journey's end. The fact that this highly significant gift was given to the King of Hungary at precisely the time that the Balkan-originating Cathars came to prominence seems to us to be no coincidence. We think that there were those in Rome (a secret faction in existence from the time of the birth of the Christ children, and indeed from long before it, linked to the Essenes) who knew the truth about Mary Magdalene and who were ready at the time of the new millennium to bring the Church into a truer alignment with the teachings of 'The Way', but that they were yet again overwhelmed and defeated, as the terrible decimation of the Cathars would appear to bear witness.

The pearl, symbolic of the Moon, of the Sacred Feminine as the reflective vessel of wisdom, and of the qualities of the soul, is also a symbol of the egg as the source of life. It depicts the Moon, pregnant with the solar system, and especially with the speck of cosmic dust or stony matter deep within its core which would be born as our Earth (see Part III). The pearl, of course, is created by the oyster, a creature of the ocean depths which overlays its own beautiful essence over a tiny piece of stone or grit until eventually the wondrous little globe which is a pearl is formed, with the grit secreted in its heart. From this great cosmic and spiritual truth came forth into the beginnings of material existence the egg, the container of life as we know it today. Therefore, in one sense, Artaban was actually presenting the very essence of royalty, Mary Magdalene, with the sacred gift of eggs. Mary herself was to follow suit when she presented the Roman Emperor Tiberius with an egg, which, in addition to all its esoteric meaning, might be considered in the same light as the act of Jesus (the King) when he knelt before his disciples and washed their feet with his own hands. This ceremony of presenting royalty with a symbolic egg, as demonstrated by Artaban and endorsed by Mary Magdalene, was continued by the Russian goldsmith and jeweller Fabergé, who at Eastertide presented beautifully decorated eggs, often set with pearls, to various monarchs, particularly to the Russian Tsar and Tsarina. This custom of Fabergé's seems to speak of a secret tradition held sacred in the area of the Balkans which hints at knowledge of a deeper significance attaching to the usual ritual of exchanging eggs during the spring festival. It is interesting, considering the links between France, Mary Magdalene, Tamar, the Cathars, and the Balkan-originating Bogomils, that Fabergé, although Russian, was of French descent.

CHAPTER TWENTY-NINE

The Gospel of Mary

*B*efore beginning to reveal her mystical gospel, Mary has asked us to impart this message. In The Gospel of Mary, Jesus and Mary together give the great teaching of soul ascension, as they did to the disciples when they explained to them the vital significance of the chakra system and its seven bodies. They were then, quite plainly, human beings lovingly and kindly (and, it might be said, humorously, without in any way detracting from the seriousness of their mission) teaching other human beings. Mary and Jesus request that we might always think of them in these terms – as an elder brother and an elder sister doing all they can to help their younger brothers and sisters on their journey through the physical realm. To deify them is to miss the point. To use a term of our times, it's a cop-out.

In deifying Jesus, we immediately removed him to a plane where we could not really be expected to become like him. The resultant mindset told us: he is a god, we are only human. The best we ever thought we could do was to stumble hesitantly after him, trying to follow his example but realizing all the time that we were ultimately doomed to failure, being faulty, weak, mortal and burdened with sin. This is not at all what Jesus and Mary seek to show us. Such a self-defeating attitude will not get us very far. In fact it will actively hamper us. Jesus and Mary reveal to us the beauty and the glory within, attainable by us just as they themselves attained it. On the other hand, there is boundless compassion and understanding for our mistakes and difficulties. It is recommended that we fully recognize these and forgive ourselves for our shortcomings. Then healing and liberation will follow.

Jesus and Mary come to unlock our hearts, and thus there will be a natural outpouring of worship, of bliss. When we begin to discover – or, more truly, dare at last to acknowledge – the Mary within our own hearts, this will be especially intense for some. It will feel as if floodgates have been thrown open. Jesus and Mary advise that we direct this worship to Goddess-God, particularly to the Mother aspect of God, for only Goddess-God is the true source of goodness. This will greatly help our soul ascension.

Soul ascension is, for every human being who will accept it, right here, right now. If we wait until our death for this process to take place, we certainly achieve it, but we leave the Earth behind. Our greater and nobler task is to take the Earth with us! That is the destiny and the joy of humankind, to spiritualize the Earth. This process begins when we accept the discipline, the happiness and the beauty of soul ascension whilst still on Earth in our physical bodies. When we understand and apply the principles of soul ascension to ourselves and our lives, we will be ready to unfold our soul-powers. These are utterly beyond anything we can ordinarily comprehend today, but, depending on our willingness to do the groundwork necessary, and to remain poised in the enlightenment and humility of our higher nature, masters and angelic beings directed by the Godhead will come to humanity to help us to begin to develop them. The method of soul ascension which Mary gives us in Parts II and III of this book comprises an opportunity to prepare ourselves for, and in some measure to unfold, these soul powers.

The references concerning the impurity of matter and the elements which occur throughout The Gospel of Mary are not made in any absolute sense. Matter is the perfect receptacle for spirit, and the four elements are primordial and ineffable forces which emanate from a mysterious source within the Godhead. Mother Earth is an exalted being of deep spiritual beauty, wisdom and cosmic love. The impurity and corruptibility of the elements occur when their lower or mortal essence interacts with or within human consciousness to produce a downward pull or loss of balance. Although there is a testing, or teaching, constituent within the physical expression of the elements, which we have to overcome, they are, as Jesus tells us, 'without sin'. A saying attributed to him makes this clear: 'I tell you that there is nothing evil upon the earth, except that ye make it so.' The exhortations of the Christ (speaking through Jesus and Mary) that we should go out into nature to seek clarity and renewed harmony of soul and spiritual vision make evident the distinction between our mistakes and stumblings upon the path of matter and its elements, and the purity and pulchritude of their inner or higher essence.

Mary's gospel is written after the Crucifixion, when Jesus comes among the disciples to teach for the last time before withdrawing into the inner worlds, although they would all see him again in his light body whilst they were still on Earth. Mary herself wrote it, and it expresses the radiant clarity and grace, simplicity and perfect understanding, mystical beauty and strength of mind, soul and spirit which is her essence and which she distilled into her gospel. Throughout it, Jesus and Mary teach together, forming in their union the perfect receptacle for the Christ, the deity or the Master of Masters in the supernal realms who instructs through them. That is why Mary called Jesus 'Rabboni' or 'Master', and he called her 'the Magdalene', a feminine rendition of 'Master'.

Here is the teaching:

THE GOSPEL OF MARY

PAGE 1

---

1 *And the Lord said:*

2 *'The eye of the vision*

3 *is within the soul.*

4 *Let those who have the vision see.*

5 *Those that would listen,*

6 *let them hear.*

7 *For those that listen*

8 *will hear the breath of Silence.'*

9 *And then the Lord said:*

10 *'Let us return*

11 *to our true nature.'*

PAGE 2

---

1   *'And I say unto you:*

2   *You can open your heart to Love.*

3   *Love has no bounds.*

4   *Love must be unfettered on all levels.*

5   *Love does not cry: murder,*

6   *as this darkens our very soul.*

7   *How can we kill that which we love?*

8   *Love does not cry: hate,*

9   *for how can we hate,*

10   *when to do so we would hate ourselves*

11   *in the same process?'*

PAGE 3

1   *'Love does not cry: greed;*

2   *how can we take more*

3   *than that which is the measure of our capacity?*

4   *Love does not fear.*

5   *How can we fear?*

6   *For we know what we fear*

7   *is not real.*

8   *Love does not lust.*

9   *How can we grasp after*

10   *what we have already?'*

PAGE 4

1   *'Love does not envy;*

2   *Love knows we have all.*

3   *Love does not steal,*

4   *as this would take away*

5   *the very heart of our giving, which is Love.*

6   *Love does not cry: judgement;*

7   *Love is not bound*

8   *to scales of more or less.*

9   *It is the self-sustainer of its own balance.*

10   *How can we judge,*

11   *lest we be judged?'*

PAGE 5

---

1   *'Love does not blame.*

2   *To be blameless*

3   *is the true gift.*

4   *Love does not discriminate*

5   *as discrimination is not the truth.*

6   *Love does not lie.*

7   *This is just fear*

8   *to hide behind.*

9   *Love transcends 'All'.*

10 *The Breath of life*

11 *is Love.'*

PAGE 6

1   *'All that is composed*

2   *is of the elements,*

3   *and it is your attachment to this structure*

4   *that has no permanence.*

5   *Attachment to your corrupt nature*

6   *is that which binds you to matter*

7   *and to illusion and suffering.*

8   *Attachment to matter*

9   *is a force to be reckoned with!*

10   *Those who have ears, let them hear.'*

PAGE 7

1 *Mary then questioned her Master, saying:*

2 *'Describe to us the nature of matter.*

3 *What is matter? Is it eternal?*

4 *Or, at the end of an aeon, will it be destroyed?'*

5 *And the Lord replied:*

6 *'That which is born and that which is created*

7 *within the elements of nature*

8 *are woven within and related to one another.*

9 *All that is composed shall be decomposed*

10 *and will return to its origins.*

11 *Matter returns to the principle that sent it forth,*

12 *as everything returns to its roots.*

13 *Those who have ears, let them hear.'*

14 *Peter said, 'You have taught us of the elements of life*

15 *and matter, and of how all the world is woven from them.*

16 *Tell us, what is the sin of the world, that it should die?'*

17 *The Lord answered, 'Matter has no sin.*

18 *Sin has no real existence; it is you yourselves*

19 *who create it when, as in the nature of adultery,*

20 *you are unfaithful to your true nature*

21 *and act within the habit of your corrupt nature.*

22 *That is why the gift of the Christ Light was put into your heart,*

23 *and why I came into your midst,*

24 *to restore every soul to its Source.'*

25 *The Lord continued, 'That is why you become sick,*

26 *and why you die; it is the result of your actions,*

27 *which takes you away from your Source.*

28 *Those that would listen, let them hear!'*

PAGE 8

1   'Matter gave birth to a passion that has no equal,

2   a passion for itself, which is contrary to Divine nature.

3   Matter caused powerful passions to enter into you,

4   forces which arise from the attraction of opposites.

5   Thus are you pulled apart, and a disharmony arises

6   to disturb unity throughout its whole body.

7   This is why I tell you,

8   be at one; be in harmony, one with another.

9   If your courage fails you and you feel out of sorts,

10   go out into nature, and take heart from its manifestations

11   of beauty and harmony with the Divine nature.

12   Those who have ears, let them hear!'

13   When the Blessed One had said these things,

14   He greeted them all, saying,

15 *'Peace be unto you, receive my peace into yourselves.*

16 *Allow no one to lead you astray by saying,*

17 *Lo, he is here! or, Lo, he is there!*

18 *For my truth is within you;*

19 *It is within your heart that the Son of God dwells.*

20 *And I tell you, I live within all.*

21 *If you seek the Son of God, follow after Him*

22 *to your innermost wherein He dwells.*

23 *Go within; those who seek Him will find Him.*

24 *Walk forth,*

25 *and teach the truth - the Gospel of the Kingdom.'*

PAGE 9

1 'Do not impose any rules

2 beyond what I appointed you,

3 and take care not to lay down a law

4 like the lawgiver, lest you be ensnared in its constraints

5 and lose your freedom.'

6 When the Lord had said these words, He departed.

7 The disciples grieved, they sorrowed and shed tears,

8 saying, 'How can we go amongst the Gentiles

9 and announce the Gospel of the Kingdom of the Son of God?

10 If they would not spare our Lord,

11 they will assuredly not spare us!'

12 Then Mary arose;

13 embraced each one, and began to speak words of comfort

14 to her brethren, saying gently,

15   *'Take heart! He will be with you always.*

16   *Do not remain in sorrow or in doubt,*

17   *for our Lord will guide and protect you.*

18   *Instead, let us praise his magnitude;*

19   *he has prepared us for what lies ahead*

20   *and is calling upon us to become fully human.'*

21   *In saying this, Mary lifted their hearts towards the good,*

22   *and they began to discuss the teachings of Jesus.*

PAGE 10

---

1   *Peter said to Mary,*

2   *'Sister, we know that the Lord loved you*

3   *differently from anyone else. Tell us*

4   *if there were words he spoke to you,*

5   *which we have not yet heard.'*

6   *And Mary answered Peter, saying,*

7   *'I will now reveal to you*

8   *that which has not yet been made known to you.*

9   *I had a vision of our Lord,*

10   *and I said unto him:*

11   *"Lord, I see you now in a vision."*

12   *And he said unto me:*

13   *"Mary, you are blessed,*

14   *for my appearance does not make you afraid.*

15   *Where the nous is, there lies the treasure."*

16 *I replied to him:*

17 *"Lord, when someone meets you in a vision,*

18 *is it through our soul that we are able to see you,*

19 *or is it through our spirit?"*

20 *And the Lord answered,*

21 *"Mary, it is neither.*

22 *But it is the* nous *between the two which sees the vision,*

23 *and it is this which makes us fully human."*

PAGE 11

---

1   *"When we become fully human,*

2   *we become one whole body*

3   *of light.*

4   *The 'One' breath.*

5   *When we join that 'One' breath*

6   *we become whole;*

7   *we become 'at-one'.*

8   *The breath conjoins*

9   *life-death-life*

10   *at the midpoint*

11   *which is the heart,*

12   *called the noon of our being.*

13   *This is where the* nous *lies.*

14   *We are all aspects of life,*

15   *of 'One' being,*

16   *of 'One' whole.*

17   *All aspects of life*

18   *have to be overcome.*

19   *It is true that everything*

20   *in our physical structure*

21   *is composed, and will decompose.*

22   *But we can overcome this process."*

PAGE 12

---

1   *"All that is composed*

2   *is of the elements,*

3   *and our attachment*

4   *is to this structure.*

5   *Dissociate your soul*

6   *from matter.*

7   *Once the two are apart*

8   *the ascent can begin.*

9   *The breath sustains the soul*

10   *and gives it life,*

11   *and it is this which*

12   *detaches you from matter.*

13   *It is through the* nous *that we see,*

14   *for it is the eye of the vision*

15   *within the soul.*

16   *and it is with the vision*

17   *of the* nous *that we overcome*

18   *the without, within."*

PAGE 13

1   *"We can overcome the four*

2   *elements of our attachment*

3   *to matter, illusion and suffering,*

4   *and all the oppressions of the soul."*

5   *And I listened to my Master,*

6   *and I saw my soul ascending.*

7   *And as the soul ascended*

8   *to the first element (climate),*

9   *the soul asked,*

10   *"Why are we afraid of death?*

11   *For death itself is not fearful.*

12   *It is the attachment of our*

13   *matter (body)*

14   *that causes fear to arise."*

PAGE 14

1   *And Fear replied,*

2   *"Why are you afraid of the darkness?"*

3   *And the soul answered,*

5   *"Fear, why do you hide*

6   *in the darkness?*

7   *I have known you,*

8   *and your power,*

9   *but it is you who are afraid."*

10   *And the soul left with grace*

11   *and continued to the second element (climate).*

12   *On reaching the second element,*

13   *Desire was taken aback*

14   *at the soul's arrival,*

15   *having neither seen it nor expected it.*

PAGE 15

1 *And Desire said,*

2 *"I did not see you descend,*

3 *but I see you now, 'ascending'.*

4 *Why do you pretend to ascend?*

5 *Why do you lie, when you know you are mine?"*

6 *And the soul replied,*

7 *"I saw you, but you did not recognize me.*

8 *Nor did you see me,*

9 *because your power urged me*

10 *to give you a body*

11 *which you thought was yours.*

12 *I served you as a garment*

13 *and you never knew it was me.*

14 *You never felt me,*

15 *and now that I have reclaimed myself,*

16   *you are without the body I gave you,*

17   *and you cannot recognize me."*

18   *When this was said,*

19   *the soul left, rejoicing greatly.*

20   *When the soul entered the third element,*

21   *which was Ignorance,*

22   *Ignorance questioned the soul:*

PAGE 16

1   *"Where do you think you are going,*

2   *you who are dominated by wicked inclinations?*

3   *What are you thinking?*

4   *How can you possibly want to leave me?*

5   *Indeed, you have no discrimination at all,*

6   *and you are clearly out of your mind."*

7   *The soul answered:*

8   *"Why do you judge me,*

9   *as I have not passed judgement on you?*

10 *I have been oppressed,*

11 *but I myself do not oppress.*

12 *I have not been recognized,*

13 *but I myself recognize that all things*

14 *which are composed shall be decomposed,*

15 *on earth and in heaven;*

16   *not only earthly structures,*

17   *but also the things of the psyche.*

18   *You may think you are eternal,*

19   *but you are not."*

20   *On hearing this, Ignorance was slain.*

PAGE 17

1   *Freed from the third element,*

2   *the soul ascended to the fourth element,*

3   *which has seven manifestations.*

4   *The first is Darkness;*

5   *the second is Desire;*

6   *the third is Ignorance;*

7   *the fourth is Fear of Death;*

8   *the fifth is the Power of the Flesh;*

9   *the sixth is Foolish (impure or guileful) Wisdom;*

10 *the seventh is Self-righteous Materialism.*

11 *These are the seven powers of wrath,*

12 *And they tried to overcome the soul with questions*

13 *so that it might lose its footing.*

14 *"Where have you come from, Murderer?"*

15 *and "Where are you going, Slayer of Space?"*

16 *But the soul, poised in radiance,*

17 *answered joyfully,*

18 *"That which bound me has been slain.*

19 *That which enveloped me has vanished.*

20 *My desires are no more,*

21 *and I have overcome*

22 *the fetters of my ignorance."*

PAGE 18

1   *"In an age of Darkness I escaped the world*

2   *with the aid of the supernal world.*

3   *My emotional attachment to matter,*

4   *which determined my limitations,*

5   *was erased by virtue of a higher design.*

6   *I was released from the fetter of Oblivion (Ignorance)*

7   *which seems eternal, but is only transient.*

8   *Henceforth I am centred in Repose,*

9   *and until matter has run its course*

10   *my sanctuary will be encompassed*

11   *in unassailable peace.*

12   *I go now into Silence."'*

13   *Having said this, Mary fell silent,*

14   *for she had given the secret teaching of her Lord.*

15   *Andrew then began to speak, saying,*

16   'You can say what you like about what she has said;

17   I, for one, do not believe a word of it.

18   I cannot believe that the Saviour would speak

19   of such strange notions!'

20   Peter joined in his refutation, saying in anger,

21   'It is not possible

22   that the Lord spoke of these things

23   in this manner with a woman,

24   saying nothing of them to us!

25   Are we then to humble ourselves before a woman,

26   to turn about and all listen to her?

27   Are we asked to believe

28   that he really preferred her to us?'

PAGE 19

1   *At this, Mary wept and said to Peter,*

2   *'My brother Peter, what can you be thinking?*

3   *Why do you not believe the words of our Lord?*

4   *Do you really think that this is all my own fancy,*

5   *or that I would lie about the Saviour?'*

6   *At this point, Levi rebuked Peter, saying,*

7   *'Peter, you have always been hot-headed.*

8   *And now we see you doubting a woman*

9   *as worthy as Mary,*

10   *just as our adversaries would do.*

11   *If our Lord held Mary in high esteem,*

12   *who are you to question her integrity*

13   *and reject her words?*

14   *We all know our Lord loved Mary*

15   *in a way that he loved no other.*

16   *Therefore let us make amends.*

17   *Let us do as our Lord has taught.*

18   *Let us express brotherhood*

19   *one to another, and to all,*

20   *and become fully human*

21   *so that the Saviour can flourish in us.*

22   *Let us grow according to his teachings,*

23   *and walk abroad to spread the gospel,*

24   *without laying down any rules and laws*

25   *other than the Law of Christ.*

26   *Let us separate as he commanded us,*

27   *and preach his truth.'*

28   *And when they heard his words,*

29   *they began to go forth to proclaim and to preach.*

The Gospel according to Mary

Commentary on
The Gospel of Mary

*T*he first six pages of the Gospel of Mary are missing. The extant manuscript runs from Page 7 to Page 10, is missing Pages 11 to 14, and runs on again to Page 19, where the gospels ends. To clarify which text is extant and which text was revealed to Margaret Bailey by Mary Magdalene, the missing parts of the gospel given to Margaret are indicated by italics as they appear in the Commentary. They are not indicated in the earlier presentation of the gospel in order to avoid distracting the reader. The 'transcreation' of the extant gospel that follows the text revealed to Margaret Bailey remains faithful to the Coptic edition contained in Papyrus Berolinensis 8502. It includes some points of emphasis which were made in response to Mary's guidance concerning the accessibility of the text to readers of today.

PAGE 1

1	*And the Lord said:*	7	*For those that listen*
2	*'The eye of the vision*	8	*will hear the breath of Silence.'*
3	*is within the soul.*	9	*And then the Lord said:*
4	*Let those who have the vision see.*	10	*'Let us return*
5	*Those that would listen,*	11	*to our true nature.'*
6	*let them hear.*		

Here, Jesus seems to be leading the disciples into meditation. He is drawing them within and opening their subtler senses to his words. He helps them to find that inner point of peace which we must all seek in order to meditate. He directs them to an awareness of their breath and leads them into the silence of the soul. When they have gone within, he affirms, 'Let us return to our true nature' – our spiritual source.

PAGE 2

1	*'And I say unto you:*	7	*How can we kill that which we love?*
2	*You can open your heart to Love.*	8	*Love does not cry: hate,*
3	*Love has no bounds.*	9	*for how can we hate,*
4	*Love must be unfettered on all levels.*	10	*when to do so we would hate ourselves*
5	*Love does not cry: murder,*	11	*in the same process?'*
6	*as this darkens our very soul.*		

With the minds and hearts of the disciples thus centred in Stillness, it is possible for Jesus to reveal a teaching on Love, the great transformer. All the disquiets of our earthly nature will be resolved in Love. It is the higher aspect of the fourth element, fire, which will overcome wrath and allow us to transcend all that which holds us back from becoming fully human. Jesus reminds us that we have the right to choose Love, and nothing can rescind that right. He begins to explain how Love overcomes the lower nature.

PAGE 3

1 'Love does not cry: greed;

2 how can we take more

3 than that which is the measure of our capacity?

4 Love does not fear.

5 How can we fear?

6 For we know what we fear

7 is not real.

8 Love does not lust.

9 How can we grasp after

10 what we have already?'

The ascended master Emmanuel, who teaches from the spiritual spheres, has said that the only choice we ever have to make is between love and fear. Fear is the challenge of the earth element and lies at the root of all the untransmuted passions (envy, greed, desire, wrath, etc.). It can only be overcome by choosing to centre ourselves in love, which means embracing the realization that we ourselves are infinitely loved, as well as expressing love towards all people and situations we encounter in our daily lives, and towards the Earth and the human family as a whole. Emmanuel also says that the choice between love and fear has to be made continuously, with every single breath that we take.

PAGE 4

1 'Love does not envy;

2 Love knows we have all.

3 Love does not steal,

4 as this would take away

5 the very heart of our giving, which is Love.

6 Love does not cry: judgement;

7 Love is not bound

8 to scales of more or less.

9 It is the self-sustainer of its own balance.

10 How can we judge,

11 lest we be judged?'

When Jesus uses the words 'Love does not cry ...', he means 'Love does not incite us to ...' (murder, hate, greed, envy, judgement, etc., etc.), or 'It is not within the nature of Love to ...'. As his words progress, we begin to see that he is also speaking of the Commandments. These, in their orthodox form, are almost identical to the Negative Confession of the Egyptian mystery schools, where adherents would declare in the form of a prayer at the end of each day: 'I have not slain, I have not born false witness', etc., finally proclaiming, 'I am pure! I am pure! I am pure!' The Catholic Church eventually incorporated the idea of the Negative Confession into their own rituals.

The Judaic 'Thou shalt not' pervades the Commandments, together with the accompanying concept of God as dictator, which is oppressive. But in Mary's gospel, Jesus is not saying 'Thou shalt not', nor is he commanding us in dictatorial mode. Instead, he says 'Love does not', reminding us that it is not in the nature of Love to commit harmful acts (including thoughts and attitudes). It is in this very arena – the arena of wrath – that our great sacrifice has to be made. Wrath can assault us on many levels, using many different guises or subtleties. Impatience is wrath. The desire to gain ascendancy over another, even if it is just a momentary feeling of superiority, is wrath. Whatever tempts us to hurt or to belittle another can be traced back to a seed of wrath. Wrath often arises from our own pain, confusion and weariness. As it begins to surface from within us, there always exists a moment before it erupts, sometimes just a split second, when we can turn it aside and choose instead to *supplant* it (*see* Chapter Twenty-six, Part II) with love. We sacrifice our wrath to love, the Love to which we can open our hearts (it is our unassailable right) once we have agreed to let go of, and so transmute, wrath (*see* page 2, line 2). This shift of emphasis from 'Thou shalt not' to 'Love does not' is simple and gentle, yet profoundly revolutionary. It changes everything. The 'Commandments' are not a rigid set of orders barked at us by God; once Jesus begins to explain them to us in Mary's gospel, they become the shining 'Way', the 'beauty path' which leads us to open our hearts to Love and so overcome the elemental wrath and rule of our lower nature, which causes all the turmoil and suffering of the world.

Suddi tells us that there were originally 12 Commandments, as there were 12 tribes of Israel, 12 disciples and, of course, 12 signs of the zodiac. The other two were 'Do unto others as you would have them do unto you' and 'Do not follow the laws of Baal'. The last is actually a special law for the prevailing astrological age (then the Age of Aries), applied to help to prevent human consciousness from slipping back into the thought-habits of the preceding age (the Taurean Age). Thus it is a mutable Commandment, changing from age to age, although it always warns against materialism and the lower mind.

PAGE 5

1 'Love does not blame.

2 To be blameless

3 is the true gift.

4 Love does not discriminate

5 as discrimination is not the truth.

6 Love does not lie.

7 This is just fear

8 to hide behind.

9 Love transcends 'All'.

10 The Breath of life

11 is Love.'

When Jesus says 'To be blameless is the true gift', we think he means that blameless-ness is a bilateral quality. If we refuse to lay blame (a form of wrath which wants a victim or a focal point for its expression, so that that expression might be uninhibited by the claims of conscience or compassion) and, instead, offer the impulse up to Love itself for healing and resolution, then we become 'blameless' (without the fault of according blame). In overcoming the desire to lay blame, we open our hearts to Love, which will lead us to a state of grace, therefore becoming blameless in the conventional sense of the word. Thus 'to be blameless is the true gift'.

Jesus again brings the breath to our attention, telling us that 'the Breath of life is Love', and that Love transcends 'All'. The 'All' is the many combined into one body, but Love transcends the sphere of outer manifestation and takes us straight to the heart of the Source, the spiritual integrity from which the 'All' is given forth. Not only can we find the Source by focusing on our breathing, but the breath itself links us to the very essence of Goddess-God, the Source. With every breath we take, we demonstrate that we are yoked to the ineffable mystery that is the Source, the Divine Being that constantly breathes breath into us that we might live, and literally 'inspires' our higher intelligence or heart-mind.

It was this Divine Breath that Jesus and Mary shared together when they kissed. The disciples were offended when they saw Jesus kiss Mary so often on the mouth. 'Why is she so special?' they grumbled ungraciously. Mary was unutterably special because it was only with her – the other half of himself – that Jesus could share the holy breath and complete the circle of his spirit so that the Christ Being could use it as a perfect channel or receptacle.

PAGE 6

1 'All that is composed

2 is of the elements,

3 and it is your attachment to this
  structure

4 that has no permanence.

5 Attachment to your corrupt nature

6 is that which binds you to
  matter

7 and to illusion and suffering.

8 Attachment to matter

9 is a force to be reckoned with!

10 Those who have ears, let them
  hear.'

Jesus further explains to the disciples how physical composition, physical creation, is of the elements, that four-square base of the pyramid of being which holds us in thrall, binding us to the material realm until we assert the authority of the soul and begin our ascent into the higher worlds. Of course, we cannot blame the elements for this. It is their job to hold us firmly in matter whilst ever we remain unconscious of our deeper reality, otherwise we would, psychically speaking, float off the face of the planet and enter a kind of subconscious limbo. Unfortunately, this does actually happen to some people. From our perspective here on Earth we see it as the state of insanity, but in fact it may be defined as 'floating off' in an unconscious state – the very antithesis of true soul ascension. This stability that the elements give us is also overridden by drugs, but sadly, the resultant temporary and largely illusory soul ascent only makes genuine soul ascension even harder. There exist no methods of soul ascension which bypass the need to actually use the sinews, limbs, faculties and vision of the soul itself!

So that the elements might give us this stability, there has to be a strong elemental rule, an intelligent overlordship, in their organization. It is this strong elemental rule which is our great teacher and liberator, because when we seek to challenge it and overcome it, we unfetter ourselves and witness the dissolution of our ball and chain. We have to realize that, not only are the elements all around us and inside us in a physical capacity, but they are also within us, within our very soul. Our psyche is composed of their finer essence.

We have to bring to bear the alchemy of our higher self, our greater soul which dwells in the heavenly regions, upon the little soul of the single earthly life that we are living at the moment. The lone strand of the greater soul, which comprises this little soul, has to shine with its light and become its channel. Then the elemental substance within our own nature becomes transmuted, and is ready to ascend. It can be very difficult to see this situation for what it is, and for a long time we carry on believing that our lower elemental nature – full of desires (the element of water), darkness (the impenetrability of the element of earth), ignorance (the arrogance, and obstruction of true vision, which is the dominating intellect or the lower mind composed of the element of air), and wrath or unharmonized energy (the element of fire) – is our one and only true nature. But this is actually our corrupt nature, the nature composed of the elements of the Earth which are subject to corruptibility, disintegration and decay, not our higher and true nature, which we must open our hearts to find.

'Attachment to your corrupt nature is what binds you to matter and to illusion and suffering,' explains Jesus. He does not mean, of course, that the disciples or any others are 'wicked' because they have this 'corrupt' nature. He is just making the distinction between the higher and the lower nature – the higher, which is of the greater soul in the exalted realms, and the lower, which is made of the corruptible stuff of the elements. Subjection to the rule of the elemental overlords will always bring illusion and suffering to humanity, because it tosses us on a rampant sea of darkness, craving, ignorance and wrath. When we are bound to our lower nature, we are bound to the wheel of life, helpless, tormented and gathering destructive pace.

We then witness the joking aspect of Jesus when he remarks, 'Attachment to matter is a force to be reckoned with!' He wants to include in his teaching, the fact that we cannot master matter if we get sucked into its dull and heavy gravitational force and become gloomy and serious about everything. We need to laugh and keep a lively sense of humour!

PAGE 7

1 *Mary then questioned her Master, saying:*

2 *'Describe to us the nature of matter.*

3 What is matter? Is it eternal?

4 Or, at the end of an aeon, will it be destroyed?'

5 And the Lord replied:

6 'That which is born and that which is created

7 within the elements of nature

8 are woven within and related to one another.

9 All that is composed shall be decomposed

10 and will return to its origins.

11 Matter returns to the principle that sent it forth,

12 as everything returns to its roots.

13 Those who have ears, let them hear.'

226

14 Peter said, 'You have taught us of the elements of life

15 and matter, and of how all the world is woven from them.

16 Tell us, what is the sin of the world, that it should die?'

17 The Lord answered, 'Matter has no sin.

18 Sin has no real existence; it is you yourselves

19 who create it when, as in the nature of adultery,

20 you are unfaithful to your true nature

21 and act within the habit of your corrupt nature.

22 That is why the gift of the Christ Light was put into your heart,

23 and why I came into your midst,

24 to restore every soul to its Source.'

25 The Lord continued, 'That is why you become sick,

26 and why you die; it is the result of your actions,

27 which takes you away from your Source.

28 Those that would listen, let them hear!'

When Mary puts questions to Jesus, it is helpful to remember that, with her intuition, she is teasing out those aspects of the teaching of the Christ Being (expressed through Jesus and Mary) on which the disciples need clarification. She herself, the 'Woman who Knows All', does not require the answer!

Going deeper into the nature of matter, Jesus explains that it is not eternal; it is subject to death and decay. Having been taught that sin equals death, Peter asks what is the sin of the world, as its destiny is death.

Jesus confirms that matter is not sinful, but that it does depend on us to transmute and spiritualize it. When we are without sin, the matter of our bodies and the world of matter around us will no longer be subject to sickness, decay and death. We cause these things to arise by being untrue to our higher nature. Jesus further clarifies that sin is essentially an illusion. We create it, it is not part of the scheme of creation of Goddess-God. Nevertheless, until we overcome our tendencies, we have to live with the consequences – mortal bodies and a mortal Earth.

1 'Matter gave birth to a passion that has no equal,

2 a passion for itself, which is contrary to Divine nature.

3 Matter caused powerful passions to enter into you,

4 forces which arise from the attraction of opposites.

5 Thus are you pulled apart, and a disharmony arises

6 to disturb unity throughout its whole body.

7 This is why I tell you,

8 be at one; be in harmony, one with another.

9 If your courage fails you and you feel out of sorts,

10 go out into nature, and take heart from its manifestations

11 of beauty and harmony with the Divine nature.

12 Those who have ears, let them hear!'

13 When the Blessed One had said these things,

14 He greeted them all, saying,

15 'Peace be unto you, receive my peace into yourselves.

16 Allow no one to lead you astray by saying,

17 Lo, he is here! or, Lo, he is there!

18 For my truth is within you;

19 It is within your heart that the Son of God dwells.

20 And I tell you, I live within all.

21 If you seek the Son of God, follow after Him

22 to your innermost wherein He dwells.

23 Go within; those who seek Him will find Him.

24 Walk forth,

25 and teach the truth – the Gospel of the Kingdom.'

Jesus explains that when matter was created, it mirrored Goddess-God in reverse form, i.e., matter produced a passion for itself, a centripetal (drawing to itself) force, which is contrary to the centrifugal (giving) nature of the Godhead. As souls descending into matter to awaken our God-powers, we have to run the gauntlet of matter's destructive passions. Jesus teaches that to do so without being pulled apart (psychically) in matter's fierce play of forces, we need to maintain a state of harmony, of brotherhood with one another. The spiritual teacher White Eagle describes a triangle of brotherhood beyond whose bounds we should not step when interrelating with one another. We see the two lower corners of the triangle as representing ourselves and the person or persons with whom we are interacting, and the apex of the triangle as the inner Christ. The two lower corners create a line or track which may be seen to be running off eternally in different directions (different ways of thinking, living and being), but all diversity, though freely expressed, is united and overcome by the unifying apex, the shining light of the Christ, the sun of our innermost being. We hold this mystic shape within our hearts, and anything which might disrupt brotherhood is not allowed into the sacred demarcation of the triangle. This spiritual exercise helps us to focus on the aspiration of unity, rather than the boundless temptations to enter into disharmony that lie outside the triangle.

When our reserves of aspiration are running low, Jesus advises us to go into nature and rediscover there the countless manifestations of Divine harmony that it embodies. Then our soul will be restored. The courtship of Jesus and Mary took place in nature. When Jesus sought solitude, Mary came to him after he had communed alone with Goddess-God. Many times throughout the gospels, Jesus is spoken of as going off alone into the wilderness, usually to climb to a mountain top. Mary came to him on these excursions, and their soul-communion took place at daybreak, at sunset, beside still and running waters, within woodland groves, among the flowers of the field and within the embrace of the majestic spirit of beauty pervading the mountains. In deep meditation, each restored to the other their completeness of soul.

What dark entity was it that arose within the doctrines of orthodoxy, teaching us to despise nature? What did it want to withhold from us? That which Jesus and Mary long to give us, and bid us to find and succour within the exquisite peace of nature's manifestations.

PAGE 9

1 'Do not impose any rules

2 beyond what I appointed you,

3 and take care not to lay down a law

4 like the lawgiver, lest you be ensnared in its constraints

5 and lose your freedom.'

6 When the Lord had said these words, He departed.

7 The disciples grieved, they sorrowed and shed tears,

8 saying, 'How can we go amongst the Gentiles

9 and announce the Gospel of the Kingdom of the Son of God?

10 If they would not spare our Lord,

11 they will assuredly not spare us!'

12   Then Mary arose;

13   embraced each one, and began to speak words of comfort

14   to her brethren, saying gently,

15   'Take heart! He will be with you always.

16   Do not remain in sorrow or in doubt,

17   for our Lord will guide and protect you.

18   Instead, let us praise his magnitude;

19   he has prepared us for what lies ahead

20   and is calling upon us to become fully human.'

21   In saying this, Mary lifted their hearts towards the good,

22   and they began to discuss the teachings of Jesus.

Here, Jesus introduces a theme which is repeated at the end of the gospel: the teaching that the proliferation of laws laid down in the name of spirituality is not 'The Way'. Mary's gospel above all others emphasizes this important point.

Jesus and Mary are the Piscean avatars. They came to dissolve the binding ties which constrain humanity and constrict the spiritual blood supply to its heart. They came to show us how to be fully human, how to let go of our fears of true manhood and womanhood and be willing to step into a spiritual altitude where we do not need a child's security blanket of endless rules and regulations. They offer us true freedom, where nothing dominates our true nature and no-one can overthrow our link to the Source. Jesus's admonition, not to lay down laws, comprised his final teaching to his disciples. This in itself is deeply significant. They are his last words.

If we look at the structure of the mystical pyramid, which is a representation of our true being, we see that the base of it symbolizes the Earth, the world of matter. It equates with our base chakra, situated at the bottom of the spine. It is ruled by Saturn (later called Satan). In his 'Old Man of Earth' aspect, Saturn is the lawgiver. We can understand from this that a preoccupation with making up and laying down laws is a temptation of earth, of the lower nature, just as much as are the temptations of the flesh and the desire-nature. The 'temptation' is to make us act against Love.

There is only one law, the Law of Love, which is the law of the Christ. Jesus gives a teaching on this in the opening pages of the gospel. Nowhere is Love the focus of spiritual teaching as it is with the Christ.

The pyramid, as previously mentioned, also harmonizes opposites. Each line of the base orientates in a different direction, from north to south or west to east; but all disparity is unified in the pyramid's peak – the Spirit, the Divine Source – which makes a single point of all the diversity. It is a model for the harmonizing of opposing forces in matter.

Mary, the 'point', takes the initiative to comfort and rally the disciples. The King has ascended to Heaven; the Queen remains on Earth. The polarity between the two will greatly aid their mission. If only the disciples could have seen beyond their prejudices, they would have understood that the Christ was still with them in person as well as in spirit.

PAGE 10

1   Peter said to Mary:

2   'Sister, we know that the Lord loved you

3   differently from anyone else. Tell us

4   if there were words he spoke to you,

5   which we have not yet heard.'

6   And Mary answered Peter, saying,

7   'I will now reveal to you

8   that which has not yet been made known to you.

9   I had a vision of our Lord,

10   and I said unto him,

11   "Lord, I see you now in a vision."

12   And he said unto me:

13   "Mary, you are blessed,

14   for my appearance does not make you afraid.

15   Where the *nous* is, there lies the treasure."

16   I replied to him,

17   "Lord, when someone meets you in a vision,

18   is it through our soul that we are able to see you,

19   or is it through our spirit?"

20   And the Lord answered,

21   "Mary, it is neither.

22   But it is the *nous* between the two which sees the vision,

23   and it is *this which makes us fully human.*"

Here, the *nous* is brought into full focus. The *nous* is the mind in the heart, that centre of intelligence which includes intuition and sensibility within its compass. Jesus speaks of it as the point between the soul and the spirit. It connects our head and our heart centres via the antahkaranah, the rainbow bridge which links Heaven and Earth, but it is centred in the heart. If we remember that the soul is the first, pristine body of the indwelling spirit (it has to be kept pristine) – the spirit that is the 'little spark' which has come down to Earth to learn to grow into a fully-fledged spiritual being (an apt description, because we do develop wings) – we can understand that they seem to be virtually one. But they are not one until the mystical marriage has taken place, which can only happen after soul ascension has been accomplished.

The spark of spirit, our true self, is wrapped in many bodies, many dense layers or skins, and we have to penetrate each one before we can find it and release it. The question arises as to who is the 'I' that strives to find the spirit, if the spirit is our true self. The answer, in simplistic form, is that the 'I' which is our consciousness is a mirror image of the little spark, fed down to the everyday level of awareness through a strand of the soul, the mirror image which must reverse if it is to become 'fully human'. The 'little spark' constantly calls the mirror image back home. We find our way home to our spirit through our soul. This is why it is so vital to nurture our soul, according it high honour and ministering to it so that we might find our way to the Source, the spirit.

Therefore the *nous* does lie in the soul ('The eye of the vision is in the soul', lines 2–3, page 1), but it is also the connecting point between the soul and the spirit, the magical doorway. That is why Jesus tells us, 'Where the *nous* is, there lies the treasure.' (line 15, page 10). Nevertheless, we ourselves have to make the connection; we have to marry the soul and the spirit via our own aspiration and free will. It is a procedure we must initiate – it is not done for us. Of course, when at last the soul opens the magical doorway and fully admits the light of the spirit, then we become 'fully human'. We become a God-man or God-woman, the perfect being Goddess-God envisaged when we were first created or breathed forth from the Godhead, rather than the reverse or mirror image, the 'beast-man' or beast-woman' which we are until our soul ascends to meet and marry our spirit. Therefore, the soul (Beauty) leads forth the 'beast' (our unrealized self) through the magic door or mirror (the *nous*) so that it becomes the glorious God-being.

PAGE 11

1	"When we become fully human,	6	we become whole;
2	we become one whole body	7	we become 'at-one'.
3	of light.	8	The breath conjoins
4	The 'One' breath.	9	life-death-life
5	When we join that 'One' breath	10	at the midpoint

11 *which is the heart,*

12 *called the noon of our being.*

13 *This is where the* nous *lies.*

14 *We are all aspects of life,*

15 *of 'One' being,*

16 *of 'One' whole.*

17 *All aspects of life*

18 *have to be overcome.*

19 *It is true that everything*

20 *in our physical structure*

21 *is composed, and will decompose.*

22 *But we can overcome this process."*

The teaching on the *nous* is further expounded. This magical doorway (the *nous*) between the soul and the spirit is the mind-in-the-heart, the point of peace within. Most importantly, we discover its location through our breath. Our breath is indeed magical and deeply sacred, 'celestial fire' or *prana*. Our breath is the key.

This 'vision within the soul' which is the *nous* or the heart-mind not only can see and be seen (it sees the vision and the vision is seen), it can hear and be heard. First, we start to listen to it by listening to, and gently focusing on, our own breath. The gentle rhythmic sound of our breathing, if listened to in reverence as in an act of prayer, will take us into the Silence, becoming 'the breath of Silence' (line 8, Page 1). Once this has happened, we will be able to hear in the highest and truest sense. Our inner faculties will spring into life.

This is the teaching of the first page of Mary's gospel. It explains why Jesus repeats: 'Those who have ears (those who will allow themselves to open the ears of the heart-mind), let them hear.' Jesus encourages us to take his teaching into our heart, not just to listen to it and remember it with our intellect. We have to learn it 'by heart'.

Jesus calls the *nous*, or the heart-consciousness, 'the noon of our being'. We ascend from this point, whether it is at death or whether we embrace the great adventure of soul ascension whilst still living in our physical bodies.

Interestingly, the ancients said that souls descending into matter always came down at midnight, the mirror image or reverse of the point of noon, just as matter is the reverse of the essence of Goddess-God and our earthly personalities are the reverse image of the 'little spark' of our spirit. This midnight descent took place shortly before the soul was born as a baby onto the Earth. The full Moon or noon was seen as the saving grace of midnight, the feminine Christ Being in the sky (Mary) who shines down on us from the heavens to remind us that we need never be afraid of the powers of night or darkness. The Moon is the mystic sign of her grace.

Jesus confirms that the powers of darkness (decay and decomposition) can be overcome by the spirit, and that death on all levels is an illusion that can be transcended.

PAGE 12

1   *"All that is composed*

2   *is of the elements,*

3   *and our attachment*

4   *is to this structure.*

5   *Dissociate your soul*

6   *from matter.*

7   *Once the two are apart*

8   *the ascent can begin.*

9   *The breath sustains the soul*

10   *and gives it life,*

11   *and it is this which*

12   *detaches you from matter.*

13   *It is through the* nous *that we see,*

14   *for it is the eye of the vision*

15   *within the soul.*

16   *and it is with the vision*

17   *of the* nous *that we overcome*

18   *the without, within."*

Jesus explains the necessity for us to realize that we are not matter, nor are we driven by the exigencies of matter, before we can begin the process of soul ascension. When he teaches that the soul must dissociate itself from matter and that 'Once the two are apart, the ascent can begin', he does not mean that the soul has to detach itself from matter as in death. The sway of matter involves many realms other than just the outermost physical level. It is at these subtle planes of being that the soul must rise above the confusion and downward pull of matter, forbidding the encroachment of its identity. Then the soul can begin its flight to freedom. It is the breath which conjoins the soul and the spirit and which leads us to the *nous* between the two, and the breath, lighter than a feather, which can help us to realize our true nature, our otherness from matter. Then the vision of the *nous* is unveiled, and the power of illusion emanating from matter is overcome.

PAGE 13

1   *"We can overcome the four*

2   *elements of our attachment*

3   *to matter, illusion and suffering,*

4   *and all the oppressions of the soul."*

5   *And I listened to my Master,*

6   *and I saw my soul ascending.*

7   *And as the soul ascended*

8   *to the first element (climate),*

9   *the soul asked,*

10   *"Why are we afraid of death?*

11   *For death itself is not fearful.*

12   *It is the attachment of our*

13   *matter (body)*

14   *that causes fear to arise."*

Jesus explains how the four elements at the base of our pyramid of being (earth/Darkness, water/Desire, air/Ignorance and fire/Wrath) must first be transcended before the soul can mount to the stars. Then Mary begins to give the secret lesson of soul ascent. She meets the first great ogre dwelling in darkness and arising from its essence – Fear, one of the mightiest adversaries of humankind. She destroys its cover, reduces it to the insubstantial shadow that it is, and continues.

PAGE 14

1   *And Fear replied,*

2   *"Why are you afraid of the darkness?"*

3   *And the soul answered,*

5   *"Fear, why do you hide*

6   *in the darkness?*

7   *I have known you,*

8   *and your power,*

9   *but it is you who are afraid."*

10   *And the soul left with grace*

11   *and continued to the second element (climate).*

12   *On reaching the second element,*

13   *Desire was taken aback*

14   *at the soul's arrival,*

15   *having neither seen it nor expected it.*

Mary, speaking as the soul, encounters another mighty tyrant – Desire, or the desire-nature or body within us. Desire, engrossed in its own concerns, is shocked to see the soul arrive. It cannot recognize either the identity or the authority of anyone other than itself or its own phantasmagoria.

PAGE 15

1 And Desire said,

2 "I did not see you descend,

3 but I see you now, 'ascending'.

4 Why do you pretend to ascend?

5 Why do you lie, when you know you are mine?"

6 And the soul replied,

7 "I saw you, but you did not recognize me.

8 Nor did you see me,

9   because your power urged me

10 to give you a body

11 which you thought was yours.

12 I served you as a garment

13 and you never knew it was me.

14 You never felt me,

15 and now that I have reclaimed myself,

16 you are without the body I gave you,

17 and you cannot recognize me."

18 When this was said,

19 the soul left, rejoicing greatly.

20 When the soul entered the third element,

21 which was Ignorance,

22 Ignorance questioned the soul:

Desire tries to insist that the powers of the soul are part of its domicile over which it has complete domination. It cannot recognize the soul's independence of being, and tries to insist that she is just another aspect of its phantasmagoria.

The soul corrects the mistake of Desire, letting it know that it has no dominion, and that it is in itself just a fleeting phantasm. Desire loses its authority, and the soul is free to journey on.

PAGE 16

1 "Where do you think *you* are going,

2 you who are dominated by wicked inclinations?

3 What are you thinking?

4 How can you possibly want to leave *me*?

5 Indeed, you have no discrimination at all,

6 and you are clearly out of your mind."

7 The soul answered,

8 "Why do you judge me,

9   as I have not passed judgement
    on you?

10   I have been oppressed,

11   but I myself do not oppress.

12   I have not been recognized,

13   but I myself recognize that all
     things

14   which are composed shall be
     decomposed,

15   on earth and in heaven;

16   not only earthly structures,

17   but also the things of the
     psyche.

18   You may think you are eternal,

19   but you are not."

20   On hearing this, Ignorance was
     slain.

The soul meets Ignorance, the mind of the world, and the gospel shows us this force (which the disciple Simon Peter in part represented) judging Mary in her guise as the soul, calling her wicked or sinful, invalidating her wisdom and denouncing her insights or her soul-path as insane. Simon Peter could not bear that Mary should think independently or understand concepts which were not limited to his sphere.

The soul contends with Ignorance, and her words might almost be those of Mary today as she looks back on the way she has been treated over the past 2,000 years, oppressed and ignored, but rising above all humiliation, well aware that Peter's influence on spirituality, although it has for a long time dominated and obscured her true light, cannot last forever, because it is in part composed of materialism, the lower substance which, although not flesh and belonging to the subtler dimensions, is yet subject to disintegration. The soul snatches away the sham robe of eternality that Ignorance wears, and her brilliant light kills it, or, more truly, absorbs it.

The soul's response is the direct answer of the Sacred Feminine to the oppressions of the domineering intellect, which seeks to disempower her. It puts her foot on the first rung of the ladder to freedom.

PAGE 17

1   Freed from the third element,

2   the soul ascended to the fourth
    element,

3   which has seven manifestations.

4   The first is Darkness;

5   the second is Desire;

6   the third is Ignorance;

7   the fourth is Fear of Death;

8   the fifth is the Power of the
    Flesh;

9 the sixth is Foolish (impure or guileful) Wisdom;

10 the seventh is Self-righteous Materialism.

11 These are the seven powers of wrath,

12 And they tried to overcome the soul with questions

13 so that it might lose its footing.

14 "Where have you come from, Murderer?"

15 and "Where are you going,

16 Slayer of Space?"

16 But the soul, poised in radiance,

17 answered joyfully,

18 "That which bound me has been slain.

19 That which enveloped me has vanished.

20 My desires are no more,

21 and I have overcome

22 the fetters of my ignorance."

In order to grasp readily the esoteric meaning of this part of the gospel, it will be helpful to envisage a pyramid with a staircase spiralling up the centre. Here we can see that the soul marks out the square base of the pyramid in her earthly incarnations, moving around it in order to overcome the challenges of the four elements. The soul meets the challenge of earth/Darkness (corners 1–2), 'turns the corner' and progresses through water/Desire (corners 2–3), turns the corner again to encounter air/Ignorance (corners 3–4) and finally comes to fire/Wrath (corners 4–1). This is the last 'corner', or challenge, to the soul concerning the base of the pyramid. Here we reach the first and last corners of the base; our progression around the base in a clockwise or sunwise direction guides us to the point where the journey began. However, because this is the life force itself (fire), Wrath has to be overcome on seven ascending levels (the seven chakras leading up the spine to the crown), because of course the fire of the life force informs every level of our consciousness. This creates the ladder or the stairway up the pyramid.

Therefore, having overcome the first three challenges, the next thing the soul has to do is to encounter and overcome those elemental challenges again, this time on increasingly subtle levels. They have already been met at the ordinary plane of consciousness, ensuring that the soul manifests through an ordinarily adjusted human being. Now they must be mastered on increasingly deeper and correspondingly more powerful inner frequencies. These equate to the first four chakras: the base of the spine (earth/Darkness), the sacral centre (water/ Desire), the solar plexus (air/Ignorance), and, of course, the fourth chakra (fire/Wrath – the one which also contains the spark of divine fire – the heart).

This chakra, focal point and balancer of all the others, is the altar of our being, within which shines the holy and eternal flame. It is here that the alchemical process will take place that transforms the gross fire of Wrath – the undifferentiated life force which manifests as self-preservation or the force of the ego – into Love. This happens by offering up Wrath itself (all the desires of, and worries for, self) as a sacrifice into the divine, purifying flame of Love, the Christ, which dwells deep in the heart.

When we do this at the base of the pyramid (between the corners 1 and 4) as Mary teaches us to do, which means that we overcome Wrath and supplant it with Love by means of continual sacrifice of our lower selves on a daily basis in our everyday lives, then the divine flame in the heart, fanned and fostered by this continual sacrifice, allows us to climb the seven stairs with winged feet, making a song of celebration of our ascent. ('That which bound me has been slain. That which enveloped me has vanished. My desires are no more ... Henceforth I am centred in Repose', etc.). The fourth and central Power of Wrath has at last been overcome. The fourth Power is the fear of death, a terrible power indeed, because whilst the soul remains in ignorance of its true destiny and its true inheritance – eternal life – the fear of death holds great sway, active on many levels and sometimes manifesting as an insane terror which compromises all the true and beautiful values that the soul, in its innermost striving, holds dear. The fear of death prevents us from expressing our uniqueness, the beauty of our heart-secreted light, because we are also afraid of being slain at emotional, psychological and psychic levels. Until we can overcome the ignorance of the illusion of death, we are not free.

When we reach the Bridal Chamber – the summit of the pyramid equating to the level above the seven chakras located in the body called the 'Soul Star' or just 'The Star' – the heart has balanced and enlightened all the chakras. In their triumphant state of purification they are able to make an immaculate channel for the kundalini to rise, that perfect light of the Godhead locked into the base of our spine (representing the earth) prior to our birth which is the inestimable gift of Divine Mother to us. The kundalini, summoned by the heart to the Bridal Chamber, rises as a serpent of Light (see the references to Tiamat the Dragon Queen in Part III) and unites with the heavenly light of the Godhead (the two are of the same essence) to make us 'fully human' – Earth and Heaven united.

This is the secret underlying the pyramidal mound of rising flesh in the female genitalia, and the secret of the rising power of Goddess – the buried light rising to unite with the heavenly light, as Jesus showed us via the Crucifixion and the Resurrection. The Mystical Marriage takes place and we become one of the imperishable stars of the starry heavens (symbol of the bright heavenly hosts), centred in Repose, girded in Silence and thus immeasurably beyond the noise, strife and confusion of the lower planes, even though we are present on Earth in a body of flesh. Death will never again disturb us, because when the time comes for us to leave behind our mortal body, we will enter into the higher worlds as if we simply stepped onshore from a boat. Our life, there as here, will be a boundless expression of love and the joy which that state generates.

When we acknowledge that the zodiacal ring is what fosters human consciousness, we can easily understand that the seven steps up the front of the pyramid equate to the seven astrological planets (the other planets in the solar system are higher octaves of the same seven tones or levels of consciousness that the seven astrological planets represent) and also to the stars of the zodiacal constellations in their representation of the seven rays of creation expressing themselves through the zodiacal ring. All these configurations of seven, of course, lead us back to the seven chakras and their bodies (each chakra has a body attached to it), and the special relationship between seven and twelve (which is examined in Appendix Two). An interesting aspect of these seven steps (plus the eighth level at the top of the pyramid) is that the level that each one embodies stretches right around the pyramid. Therefore, the whole pyramid except the apex consists of the seven steps. When we reach the eighth level and enter into the Bridal Chamber, the entire pyramid turns gold, a surpassingly beautiful translucent gold expressing the alchemy of transmuted Wrath becoming pure spiritual fire.

The idea of the seven steps rising up the pyramid from its four-square elemental base at the point of fire/Wrath also gives us the fifth element, ether. The ancients called this the 'quintessence', literally, 'the fifth essence'. It was considered to be the ethereal counterpart of the mundane elements. The soul in the act of climbing the seven steps up the pyramid from its base at the point of Wrath/fire (corners 4–1) expresses the nature of this element, because it is in our ethereal or inner essence that the fires of Wrath must be refined or transmuted to Love. That is why ether rises with the life force or fire right up the pyramid from its base – because the fifth element pervades, and extends beyond, the others. When it is purified by the divine flame in the heart, then the ether becomes a vessel for that divine flame, cloaking the soul and carrying her with it to the lower elements so that they might be transmuted. It is the stuff that the soul commands, wonderfully sensitive to her bidding, consisting of the matter from which her dreams of beauty may be wrought – the soul's own element, the white ether, another aspect of the Wedding Garment.

As the soul mounts the stairway, the 'demons' of each plane or step gather to hurl insults at the soul, trying to make it feel insecure, guilty, vulnerable and intimidated so that it will decide to return to the security of what it knows, i.e. descend again. They shout 'Murderer!' at the soul because it has slain the phantoms of Darkness, Desire and Ignorance, and address it as 'vagabond' and 'slayer of space' because it has freed itself from the vacuum or emptiness of imprisonment in the lower planes and, no longer having roots in its corrupt nature, has no home there anymore. In other words, they proclaim its victories, but in a way that is designed to cause the soul to feel culpable for having achieved victory.

Their ruse does not work, however, because the soul has learned the lesson of spiritual poise. Poise is the essential quality, because when we overcome the first three elements of our 'base' nature (the base of the pyramid), thereby gaining awareness of our higher nature and control of our animal nature, we find we are still by no means off the hook. Wrath can flood in and inflame us into expressions of darkness, untransmuted desire and ignorance against our better judgement. The poise that the soul expresses is learned from applying the Law of Love. It begins to proclaim its freedom.

PAGE 18

1 "In an age of Darkness I escaped the world

2 with the aid of the supernal world.

3 My emotional attachment to matter,

4 which determined my limitations,

5 was erased by virtue of a higher design.

6 I was released from the fetter of Oblivion (Ignorance)

7 which seems eternal, but is only transient.

8 Henceforth I am centred in Repose,

9 and until matter has run its course

10 my sanctuary will be encompassed

11 in unassailable peace.

12 I go now into Silence."

13 Having said this, Mary fell silent,

14 for she had given the secret teaching of her Lord.

15 Andrew then began to speak, saying,

16 'You can say what you like about what she has said;

17 I, for one, do not believe a word of it.

18 I cannot believe that the Saviour would speak

19 of such strange notions!'

20 Peter joined in his refutation, saying in anger,

21 'It is not possible

22 that the Lord spoke of these things

23 in this manner with a woman,

24 saying nothing of them to us!

25 Are we then to humble ourselves before a woman,

26 to turn about and all listen to her?

27 Are we asked to believe

28 that he really preferred her to us?'

The soul continues its song of freedom. It now enters the eighth climate, the region of the starry heavens, called 'The Veil of Isis'. When it penetrates the Veil, it enters the Silence, the essence of Goddess. In esoteric terms, Silence herself is a goddess, existing as an exalted dimension of the Sacred Feminine. From the Silence, all things manifest. Within the Silence, matter has no presence or power. When the soul is in the Silence, it is encircled by the creative peace of the Godhead.

Listening to these deep and vast mysteries, some of the disciples grow uneasy. They are in the presence of a soul of such magnitude that she is at one with the cosmos. Some of them decide to repudiate her wisdom and try to turn her into a liar or a mad woman.

PAGE 19

1 At this, Mary wept and said to Peter,

2 'My brother Peter, what can you be thinking?

3 Why do you not believe the words of our Lord?

4 Do you really think that this is all my own fancy,

5 or that I would lie about the Saviour?'

6 At this point, Levi rebuked Peter, saying,

7 'Peter, you have always been hot-headed.

8 And now we see you doubting a woman

9 as worthy as Mary,

10 just as our adversaries would do.

11 If our Lord held Mary in high esteem,

12 who are you to question her integrity

13 and reject her words?

14 We all know our Lord loved Mary

15 in a way that he loved no other.

16 Therefore let us make amends.

17 Let us do as our Lord has taught.

18 Let us express brotherhood

19 one to another, and to all,

20 and become fully human

21 so that the Saviour can flourish in us.

22 Let us grow according to his teachings,

23 and walk abroad to spread the gospel,

24 without laying down any rules and laws

25 other than the Law of Christ.

26 Let us separate as he commanded us,

COMMENTARY ON THE GOSPEL OF MARY

27 and preach his truth.'

28 And when they heard his words,

29 they began to go forth to proclaim and to preach.

Andrew and Simon Peter take advantage of what seems her passive silence (having no understanding), but Mary speaks with firmness, although she expresses vulnerability. The secret teaching she has given them was from the Christ. There can be no doubt about that. Then Levi champions Mary and rebukes Peter, who is obviously growing angry and violent and attempting to rouse a rabble mentality against her amongst the disciples. Levi quickly sets things back on track, and the disciples disperse to begin to teach The Gospel of the Kingdom.

Here we can see the teachings of Mary's gospel expressed in action. The two disciples who speak after Mary has given the secret teaching are symbolic of the first three elements of our earthly nature: Darkness-Fear, Desire (the blind and possessive rule of the passions) and Ignorance (the lower mind or the intellect). Andrew represents Darkness and its counterpart, Fear. He, as Darkness, cannot see how Jesus would have given such teachings to Mary and calls them 'strange notions' (he is fearful of them). Peter expresses the Desire nature and the uncomprehending intellect driven by it, two of the elements of the base of the pyramid (Desire and Ignorance) which also comprise two of the manifestations of Wrath – and Peter is certainly angry! His possessive jealousy (Desire) cannot bear that Mary might have received something from the Saviour that he had not, which makes him repudiate the gift once it is given to him! He is not interested in feeding his capacity for wisdom, but only his ego. He tries to rouse the disciples against Mary by pointing out that her teaching does not arise from the sphere of the intellect, therefore it must be untrue and Mary must be a usurper!

Then Levi speaks and quashes the claims of Darkness, Fear, Desire and Ignorance, using the pure reason of Love which the spirit of Christ, emanating from Jesus and Mary, had set alight in his heart, to put down the rule of the lower elements and take the disciples forward. Levi has not been honoured in biblical tradition for this vital and valiant act, but he certainly should be.

This is a crucial moment for Mary and for history. Had the disciples not rallied behind her, she could never have established the true Church of Christ, and she knew that Simon Peter's rendition of it would be unable to turn back the tide of human wrath that lashes the world today, in our own time, when we so much need the inspiration of the Sacred Feminine and of Mary Magdalene. Although the strength of her soul was beyond imagination, it was against spiritual law to impose her authority. The disciples had to accept her as their leader of their own free will.

Once this was accomplished, Mary's great voyage, both spiritual and physical, could begin.

PART III

The Secret Teachings of Mary Magdalene

CHAPTER THIRTY

The Dragon Queen

*M*ary has given to us, via her gospel, the beautiful teachings which explain soul ascension. When, as spirits clothed in the essence of soul we descend to the womb, we enter the world of matter composed of the elements. We are locked into the base of the pyramid which is the mystical structure of our being. Although we have to overcome all aspects of matter, it is the fourth element of fire, the life force itself whose divine aspect dwells within the heart chakra, which is the greatest challenge. Mary describes it as having seven manifestations, three of which consist of the limitations of the first three elements of earth, water and air, corresponding to Darkness, Desire and Ignorance, and the remainder of which comprise the Fear of Death, the Power of the Flesh, Foolish Reason and Self-righteous Materialism. The masterly translation and commentary on the Gospel of Mary by Jean-Yves Leloup present these last four as (the fourth) Fear of Death, (the fifth) Enslavement to the Body, (the sixth) Intoxicated Wisdom, and (the seventh) Guileful Wisdom, which provide further insight into the nature of these manifestations of Wrath, the lower fires of our consciousness.

In the East, this power of fire or life force is called the kundalini, the serpentine fire of life which is locked in the base chakra. It must rise up the spine (the sides of the pyramid) to the crown (the pinnacle of the pyramid), but not until the chakras have been purified by the divine flame in the heart, and the soul resonates with that divine flame rather than its gross and wrathful counterpart which is the power of the self-serving ego. If the latter state prevails, the rising kundalini breathes its cosmic fire-breath into the impure energies which are lurking in the chakras, causing mayhem and even insanity or death. When it rises under the conscious direction and control of the higher mind or the higher aspect of the soul, it ascends in complete harmony with the higher chakras, which are the heart, the throat, the brow and the crown centres; and thus do we become fully human.

Without this kiss of the serpent or the Dragon Queen, we remain subhuman, however technologically advanced or intellectually developed we may consider ourselves and our society. Without the kiss of the Dragon Queen, our societies will always become self-destructive and eventually end in annihilation. The mythology of religion generally teaches us to believe that the serpent is the great tempter. But this serpent represents the uncontrolled rise of the kundalini which is untransmuted Wrath manifesting in its seven coils – the seven chakras – and it does indeed tempt us to 'sin' (to stray away from the Law of Love) and leads us to actions which result in the 'death' of the soul. The soul becomes smurred and full of darkness, no longer able to transmit and reflect the perfect light of the spirit.

This serpent is the lower nature, the imposter. The true serpent or dragon is winged, for it is the embodiment of divine life forces untainted by any identification with matter. It is our higher nature, the Breath of Fire, the ineffable fire of the Godhead, borne to us by She who is known as the Dragon Queen. She is the Life and the Breath, the Soul and the Spirit, the 'All'. She is not Goddess herself, but she is the Created One who of all created beings is closest to the heart of Goddess.

This magnificent soul, Tiamat the Dragon Queen, 'she who bore them all', is profoundly associated with Mary Magdalene. Mary is, in fact, utterly of her essence, and her appearance on Earth was the direct manifestation of the Dragon Queen in human form, a tiny distilled drop of the Great One, she who loved Goddess and whose heart was given in service to Goddess more than any other. When 'the dewdrop slips into the ocean' and Mary Magdalene returns to her greater soul, she is the Dragon Queen. But she is also and always human, a woman of unimaginably high degree, yet a loving elder sister who holds healing, encouragement and inspiration in her heart as gifts for us all.

The rising power of the kundalini, the undifferentiated life force which rises and becomes transmuted into the Dragon Queen, is the reason why the alchemists so treasure the rising power of the pyramidal mound of flesh which is female genitalia. It is a perfect representation in matter of divine truth. It has absolutely nothing to do with Mary Magdalene as a symbol of sexual licentiousness! She is a symbol of the sexual forces, of course, but in the sense that these powers of life (which, untransmuted, manifest as Wrath, the ungoverned fires of life) become transformed by the baptism of the spirit, shining through the perfect, undimmed soul, into the nature of the light of the spirit itself – into the rising light which is the Dragon Queen. This power of the rising light is why, in the ancient mysteries, the god had to die in the presence of the goddess – so that he could rise again and take on the nature of the Sun, the combined essence of Goddess-God. It is why those goddesses throughout the ages who were in essence Mary Magdalene have been associated with the dawn and the rising stars as well as the rising Moon. These majesties of nature exist because of the rising power of the Feminine Principle, of Goddess, whose divinity shines through Mary.

We have made her story into the story of the prostitute (the basic life force in the lowest chakra) transforming into the saint (the spiritually transmuted fire turning into divine light and rising to the crown (the highest chakra). Yes, the story holds good in its basic teaching of a profound esoteric truth. But it is so desperately chauvinistic, so ludicrously misrepresentative of Mary, and so exasperatingly patronizing in its depiction of the unworthy female being made worthy by the holy male, that we need to let it go forever and supplant it with a wiser understanding. Mary Magdalene is the feminine Christ, she is the soul and the spirit, she is the holy fire, she is the Dragon Queen. She is not the basic, untransmuted fire. That symbol properly belongs in its application to ourselves.

Mary would urge each one of us who feels ready to accept the adventure, to walk the path of soul ascension. Love and self-sacrifice comprise the key – not self-sacrifice of a dramatic and obvious nature (we are not asked to become martyrs!), but the small, quiet sacrifices of everyday which free us from our lower nature and from the forces of Wrath. Without giving away our power or deserting wisdom, we can make such sacrifices in the name of love. They will free us.

We believe that within all of us lie DNA strands, dormant or hidden, which will be activated by divine agency as a result of our dedicated individual striving to reach a higher plane of consciousness, using the *nous* upon which Mary is so insistent in her gospel ('Where the *nous* is, there lies the treasure.'). These pioneers (ourselves in the here and now, if we will accept the challenge) will facilitate this momentous awakening so that it may be bestowed, perhaps not on every single human individual (although this assuredly will happen in time), but on all those of goodwill, all those whose hearts are open and who do not feel the need to sneer at the concept that a deeper and more beautiful reality exists beyond the realm of materialism.

Nevertheless, soul ascension is no easy matter, and there are certain tools which will help us along the way. These are magical implements that can always be relied upon and which, through our correct approach to them, become conduits for the power of the spirit. The following chapter describes these tools and how we can make use of them.

CHAPTER THIRTY-ONE

Seven Secrets of the Inner Life

MEDITATION

*T*he first tool is meditation. We cannot properly advance into higher consciousness without it. When we seek the higher realms, we need to remember that
their essence, their keynote, their vibration, is that of love. Therefore, we prepare
ourselves for meditation by quietly opening our being to universal love. A helpful
exercise for people new to meditation might be to engage in the short and simple
Moon ceremonies described at the end of Chapter Thirty-six, Part III (not the main
'Ascending to the Moon' ritual, as it is advisable to take the first few steps in learning
to meditate before attempting this longer ceremony).

There is a life deep within our consciousness that is far more vital, significant
and beautiful than the mundane level at which we normally operate. It is this point
of peace we need to find. It is enshrined in our heart-centre and will lead us through
into the inner worlds. It is the door which Mary calls the *nous*, the place between the
soul and the spirit which we must nevertheless penetrate the soul to discover,
because the soul embodies the spirit. It takes time, patience and discipline to find
this door, but it is assuredly there within, waiting for us to find it; and each
meditation session takes us inexorably closer to its discovery.

We find the *nous*, the doorway into true meditation, by focusing gently on the
breath. Sitting in a quiet place, spine erect and supported if necessary, place your
right ankle lightly over your left (this seals your energy field) and cup your left
hand in your right. Centre your awareness on your breathing, imagining that you are
drawing in and giving out each cycle of breath through the heart-centre. Think of
the highest plane you can conceive of, and give this sphere an image. It might be the
Christ, the Goddess, Buddha, Krishna, Brigid, Mary herself, or one of the archangels.
It might be a bright candle flame, or a golden point in the centre of a circle of light,
or one of the images described in the following chapters. Whatever brings you into

the beauty and the peace of the Divine Presence will lead you to and through the *nous*.

Rest your awareness in your heart-centre, gazing upon the image in your mind's eye, and open your heart to love. If you feel resistance or anger, see a single pink rose in your heart opening to the golden sunlight and giving forth its heavenly fragrance. Inhale the perfume and, if you choose, softly begin to chant the word 'Ham' as you breathe in, and 'Sah' as you exhale. In ancient Sanskrit, Ham means 'I Am' and Sah means 'Divine Spirit' or 'Divine Spark'.

When intruding thoughts assault your meditation, just return all your attention as an act of conscious will, yet with great respect and gentleness, to focus once more on the sanctuary of your heart, the steady rhythm of your breathing and chanting, and your chosen image. If your intrusive thoughts become very disturbing and clamorous, offer them to the Being upon whom you are meditating, or, if your chosen image is other than a personification, give the distracting thoughts into the care of the Lord or Mistress of your Temple (your higher self). If your mind starts to drift into cogitation and you have difficulty controlling it, it can be helpful to say very firmly out loud, 'I choose to meditate. I choose Silence.' Then return to the elements of your meditation as described above.

Gradually you will come to a place of utter peace and calm, beyond and beneath the busy traffic of your thought processes. When this occurs you have found the *nous*, and will pass through into the worlds within.

If even a split second of vision or breakthrough is beyond your reach at first, refuse the temptation to abandon meditation in disgust or despair! Your break-through will indeed come, the door will open before too long. This is incontrovertible cosmic law. It is just a matter of persistence in your practice of meditation.

Many places can be visited during meditation for the purpose of cleansing and renewing the soul and becoming at one with our spiritual essence. Some classic locations are the Temple of the Rose, the Spiritual Mountaintop, the Tree of Life, the Sacred Cave within which burns the eternal flame of divinity, the Lake of Peace, the Paradise Garden, the Isle of Unicorns, the Starlit Canyon and the Sun Temple. All of these exquisite places have given gifts of spiritual succour, repose and awakening to those who have visited them in meditation.

There are many other places, of course. Sometimes it is a good idea to question yourself as to which quality you feel the need to attune to on any given day, and select a location accordingly. For instance, if you need stability and recuperation, choose an earthy location such as the Sacred Cave or the Starlit Canyon. If your emotions are jangled and oppressed, choose a watery destination such as the Lake of Peace or the beautiful Rose Temple with its spangling of purest dew. If you feel mentally dull and uninspired, or are actively seeking inspiration, choose an airy location such as the Spiritual Mountaintop or the Paradise Garden through which move the Winds of Inspiration. If you feel you need a baptism of light, go to the great Sun Temple or enter the presence of the Christ or Archangel Michael.

It is a strange and pleasing experience to visit these places and then to rediscover the woodland in which you wandered previously, or to find a new path winding away into the mysterious depths of the Paradise Garden, or to come across a swan-prowed boat moored upon the Lake of Peace, set there by some benign agency for your use. The notion steals upon you that these places are real, as real as any earthly location, but without the harsh material vibration of Earth. The feeling of freedom, adventure and delight in life will remain with you when you emerge from meditation.

When meditating as part of the process of soul ascension, it is vital to use the experience as a means of gently opening our being to love. We need to make a conscious effort to rise to the higher spiritual worlds.

On finishing a meditation, it is essential to protect your finer vehicles, your non-physical bodies, by sealing your chakras which are the point of entry to each one. The seven main 'star-gates' or chakras are located at the crown, mid-brow between the eyes, the hollow of the throat, the heart (the chakra point is located more to the centre of the chest than is the physical heart), the solar plexus, just below the navel, and the base of the spine, situated above the anus. Imagine a ring of light surrounding an equal-sided cross of bright silver, and seal each of your centres with this powerful protective symbol (just place it in imagination upon each chakra).

If you still feel vulnerable or dreamy, imagine a spiral of light emerging from under your left foot and making seven golden clockwise spiralling rings around you from your feet to above your crown. Then see the head of the spiral run straight down the line of your chakras like a rod of light from your crown to the ground below your feet. Never forget to complete at least the sealing exercise, or you will lose the benefit of your meditation.

If you ever find it difficult to commence meditation (sometimes the pressures of the outer world are all too present), imagine a golden pyramid before you. Seven wide stairs lead to its pinnacle. Climb these stairs to the top of the golden pyramid, and begin your meditation from there. If your imagination – your power of imagery – feels out of order, call on the angel Samandiriel for help. Mary herself can also give us wonderful assistance in this area, as in so many others.

THE ROSE

Roses are built on a calyx of five sepals. If you sketch a figure around the sepals, joining their tips, a pentagram appears, the sacred pentagram upon which the structure of the human form is created, with its four limbs and head. If we stand with legs apart and arms outstretched, we make evident our pentagrammatical form, in which every single line declares the Golden Mean, or Divine Proportion, the infusion of the balance, peace and perfect justice of the essence of the Godhead.

From ancient times, the rose has often been depicted at the heart of a cross. This signifies that from the garnerings of lives lived upon the sacrificial cross of time and matter, there blooms in every human soul divine consciousness – the true spiritual essence of the rose. A profound mystery dwells in the image of the rose that blooms at the very heart of the cross; it is matter's innermost secret. The rose is a symbol of the heart and of human and divine love. When it blooms upon the cross of matter in an individual's life, the spiritual essence pervades the earthly being. In esoteric understanding, such a man or woman is seen to be 'Christed', or expressing the divine life. The rose is an emblem of matter, and life lived through matter, brought to perfection. When this point is reached, matter is no longer an emanation of spirit, imperfect because it exists such a long way off from the divine centre; it becomes spirit itself. It has returned to the centre, to the heart, it is once again heart. It has come home and is no longer perishable and corruptible. That is matter's secret, and the measure of our task here on Earth as spiritual beings clothing ourselves in matter in order to extend the frontiers, create new dimensions, of perfected creation.

The rose is fathomless in its beauty, its meaning and its promise. The use of the rose as a meditation symbol plays a vital part in our reclamation of our divine essence, our becoming fully human. When resentment, anger, apathy or unresponsiveness, arising from any source, cloud our ability to meditate, the rose will unlock our resistance.

Imagine a dew-touched rose, pink as the first flush of sunrise, as though placed by a divine hand in your heart-centre. Breathe in its healing fragrance. No matter what the outer conditions of life, this gentle focus on the rose in the heart will bring peace, a fount of purity and wellbeing and the realization that we are eternally linked to the source of Love. It will bring to you a realization of its essence beyond the stumblings and limitations of mere words and thoughts. It will lead you to that point of peace 'which passeth all understanding'.

When you have become truly aware of the rose in your heart, you will realize that it is much, much more than just a beautiful meditation symbol. It is a power in your life, part of the potency of your being. You can literally breathe forth its fragrance at the subtle spiritual level to bring healing, calm, and a pure breath of magic to any situation in which you find yourself; but it must be borne in mind that the essence of the rose is the essence of giving. Giving forth the sunlight of our being from the heart ignites the power of the rose. Then we walk in a world of repose, beauty and meaning, and put on our true selfhood, our true humanity.

This true self is depicted at the heart of every rose by its circle of golden stamens. It is a sigil, written in matter itself, of the 'mind in the heart', the intuitive mind which is linked to the 'pure reason' of divine love, found in the heart-centre.

There is a power and an essence distilled by the rose that is beyond all earthly understanding. It is there for us to draw upon, to enter into and to receive as a gift from heaven.

THE STAR

The Christ star within our heart is the most vital part of ourselves. Tuning in to the star summons the Christ Light in our being. We are protected, we can give forth healing and blessing, and our consciousness is transformed.

To attune to the star, go to the heart-centre (just touching it lightly can help our mind to rest there) and begin to focus gently on the breath. Imagine that you are drawing into your being the golden-white light of Goddess-God, and exhaling all the anxiety and distractions of the earthly life. After a little while you will find that you are both inhaling and exhaling this perfect Christ Light.

Imagine a six-pointed star shining in your heart. It is composed of two equilateral triangles, one pointing upwards and one pointing downwards. The two triangles merge and the star blazes forth, without any inner divisions.

See yourself as standing in the heart of the star, and see the star shining from your own heart. It also shines above your head, down onto your crown. These three realities all occur simultaneously.

The Christ star is connected to the Pole Star, to the Star of Bethlehem, and to the Sphere of John-Shar-On. It is the point of our being where magic resides, the full glory of the spirit. It is used in conjunction with the breath to breathe in and breathe out blessing, healing, protection, divine inspiration. The thought, the breath, the loving intention within, directs the light to its chosen destination. It is the power of Goddess-God, it is the power of the divine Son-Daughter, it is the power of pure love. Used correctly, without selfishness, the star is all-powerful. It is a symbol of the human being made perfect – the fully human being.

The teacher White Eagle says of the star:

> *Where the star shines by the will and*
> *through the love of earthly men and women,*
> *the effect over chaos and disorder, war,*
> *and all the evils in the world can be truly magical.*

Use the star! We bypass our divine heritage if we ignore it and receive its light only unconsciously. The star burns with pure spiritual fire, and it cannot be put to evil or selfish use. We can use it to beautify and inspire our lives, to protect and heal ourselves, and bring joy and vision to our daily tasks. But, most of all, we can use it to give those gifts of the spirit to others, to all humanity. And when there are sufficient numbers of us who will daily ignite that mystical light, despite the blunderings of politicians and the spectres of hatred and carnage, the world will change beyond all recognition.

THE BREATH

Mystical traditions throughout the ages have taught that our breath is magical. The angels infuse us with their essence and commune with us through the medium of air – our breath. Jesus and Mary shared the Holy Breath and were guided through it by the Christ Being, who spoke through them. Via Mary's gospel, the Christ Being tells us that 'those who listen will hear the Breath of Silence' (page 1, lines 7–8), that 'The breath of life is Love' (page 5, lines 10–11) and that the 'One breath' unites us in 'one whole body of light', leading to the *nous* at the centre of our being (page 11, lines 4–13). We are told directly and specifically that 'The breath sustains the soul and gives it life, and it is this which detaches you from matter' (page 12, lines 9–12).

The breath, then, plays a crucial part in opening the door to the spiritual worlds. We cannot attune to our soul without the aid of the breath and we cannot release ourselves from the grip of matter without attuning to the soul. Our soul ascends on our breath.

The act of magical breathing and attunement to the soul must be carried out via the heart-centre. We have to breathe 'through the heart', inhaling and exhaling through the heart chakra, because the breath is our yoke to Goddess-God. It will feel very natural to draw in the breath and release it in this way. When we breathe 'through the heart', we are breathing in the radiant light of the Godhead which fills our being, and then directing this ineffable light to the world, to humanity, to the troubled heart of another, to any negative condition which needs healing. As long as it is given as a free gift from the heart, the breath will sustain this pure light which shines from the spirit through the soul. Judgement and opinions must not be allowed to intrude, for they carry the contamination of the ego, which disconnects us from the source.

Here are some of the teachings which Mary gave us concerning the breath:

> *Open your heart, and let the heart-centre*
> *open the chakras.*
> *Within the heart is the* nous.
> *Through the* nous, *listen to the Breath.*
> *The Breath of life is All.*

Attune to the heart through the breath.
Be at one with oneself and the universe,
and your body (matter) will become blessed
as nothingness (no longer a 'thing'),
a pulsating life force
resonant with the message of Breath.

The great wind of life (Breath)
scatters us to the four corners.
This is the structure that will teach us
how to return to the centre.
When we are born as an out-breath
of the Great Spirit,
all our desire must be
to find the in-breath in ourselves
which will carry us back home.
When we find it,
the in-breath and the out-breath
become as one.
Both proceed from the heart of giving
which is the centre,
and the centre is everywhere,
even where the great wind of life scatters us
to the four corners.

Where the nous *is,*
there lies the treasure.
When you find the treasure,
therein lies the breath of infinite vision.

There is a method of breathing called 'the Mother's Breath', which is based on the seven and one or the octave rhythm, the Law of Eight. This is an excellent meditational focus for the breath, and its mystical rhythm will help us in our great task of soul ascension and in our attunement to the Moon (*see* Part III, Chapter Thirty-three). It signifies the seven rays or principles of creation held within the mystery of the All – the seven and the one.

You may not necessarily wish to use this breathing method in your meditation and periods of spiritual attunement. Quietly focusing on your breath will always gently attune you to your own rhythm. Nevertheless, practising the method of 'the Mother's Breath' until you feel comfortable with it will yield wonderful results.

It is very simple to follow. Just breathe in to a count of seven, pause and hold the breath for one count, breathe out to the count of seven, then pause again for one count before once more breathing in to the count of seven and resuming the cycle.

Do not force the rhythm or allow yourself to become breathless or uncomfortable in any way. Be as brief or as long as you wish concerning the length of time you take to count out the seven beats for the in-breath, the seven for the out-breath and the length of time you take for the pauses in between. Let comfort and ease be your guiding factors, and be careful not to jerk the breath as you count to seven. Let your breathing be smooth and relaxed in its rise and fall, and let the prompt of your counting come as if from a distance, hardly noticed except to unobtrusively measure out the rhythm.

When you feel accustomed to this breath cycle and your system has adapted happily to it, you can combine it with the techniques of breathing out the fragrance and the presence of the Rose to heal and to inspire, together with breathing in and breathing out the spiritual light to bless humanity.

THE RAINBOW CHALICE

The rainbow chalice is the heart. Use the breath and the magical shape of the six-pointed star to find it. It is the point of peace within. The chalice is, in one sense, the *nous*. See this beautiful chalice of light in the centre of the heart chakra.

When we need to send out healing, or when we need to heal ourselves by silently bathing in the light of the heart, we can draw near to the angels and ask them to reflect the heavenly colours of the rays of creation within the white-golden star of the heart.

Let the star rise from your heart to above your head, revealing the pearly chalice. It is overflowing with light. Call on the angels to shine a colour or colours into the fountain of light spilling from the chalice. Ask them out loud and outright. These colours might be:

> rose, the colour of heavenly love and reassurance;
>
> angelic gold, the colour of happiness, which dispels negativity and eases harsh mindsets;
>
> soft apple green, the colour of deep sympathy and understanding;
>
> summer sky-blue, the colour of peace and relief from pain;
>
> sunset red-orange, which gives vitality and stimulation;
>
> amethyst, which gives endurance, inner strength, and freedom from the enslavement of addictions;
>
> indigo, which enhances spiritual devotion and soothes relationships;

pearl, which brings the balm of motherly love;

gold, which brings the protection of fatherly love;

magenta, which stabilizes and steadies, comforts and balances.

Let each colour wash over you in a flood, encircling you gently in a clockwise direction. Never see the colours as deep and strong, but rather as pure, radiant and delicate, like jewel colours, flashing with a subtle vividness. It is not a good idea to bathe the whole aura in deep, strong, earthy colours. Put the colour emanation into the hands of the angels; they will know the brightness or the softness of the hue you require.

SILENCE

Silence was anciently considered to be a goddess, and from what we have learnt in our communion with Mary it would certainly seem to be a quality endowed with goddess-force. It might therefore serve us well to intone a prayer to Silence herself, asking her to enfold us in her presence. All goddesses, of course, reflect Divine Mother, and it is an aspect of Divine Mother to which we pray when we supplicate Silence.

Having prayed to absorb Silence, and to be absorbed into the Silence, see the orb of the full Moon sailing in silver peace in a midnight-blue sky. It is Silence herself, hanging in hushed calm above you.

See a flight of seven crystal stairs spiralling upwards from the Earth to the gates of the Moon, which shine like pearl. Mount the steps and walk through the pearly arch of the open gates.

Feel the Silence take you into itself, utterly enclosing you in another world – the world of Silence.

The Silence is the higher aspect of your soul. Seek it every day, if only for a few moments. Your breath leads you into silence as you practise the imagery, and sustains you there. Listen, and you will hear the Breath of the Silence.

THE RAINBOW BRIDGE

This mystic bridge is the bridge between the spirit and the soul. It is where the *nous* is located and its point of entry is within the heart chakra.

The soul is the very first body in which spirit clothes itself in order to make a stairway down to the realms of matter, the physical body being the outermost body. The little individualized spark of the Divine Spirit is clothed in the soul, but it also has to build the greater soul through its experiences in matter. It comes down into incarnation wearing the soul body, but the spirit and the soul together have to set to work to build the great Soul Temple in the higher worlds. Over many, many lives this structure is gradually constructed and perfected, until it becomes worthy to house the spirit, now expanded to a great light through self-awareness, which eventually becomes God-consciousness. When the temple is ready, the soul becomes utterly translucent and the spirit shines through her, the sacred marriage takes place and the soul and the spirit become as one.

But for the soul and the spirit to be unobstructed in their communion, the antahkaranah, the beautiful rainbow bridge, has to be realized. Then it can connect our little everyday self with the glorious seven-rayed light of the Divine. It is then that the personality no longer stands in the way of our becoming a radiant being, a being who emits light, instead of imprisoning us in selfhood (or isolation) with issues of its own.

The act of prayer, of invocation of the highest consciousness of which we can conceive, is hugely important to the process of building the rainbow bridge, because the great rule of creation is that its mode of being is reciprocal. The lesser and the greater, the lower and the higher, the younger and the elder brethren must consciously work together, the lesser and the lower ever invoking, by its own conscious free will, the grace and blessing, the infusion of the higher and greater.

This is the fundamental way in which creation works, its elementary design. (Of course, 'fundamental' and 'elementary' are words which are only appropriate for us to use at our particular earthly stage of development; they cannot really apply to a design so stupendous as the cosmos.) It embodies the principle that energy always flows from the stronger source to the weaker source. It is the principle of endless, unstinting giving upon which creation rests. It is Christ saying 'Sell all you have, and give to the poor', meaning the poor in spirit.

This scientific fact, energy flowing from the stronger to the weaker source, is a reflection of the great cosmic law which is worked out in the act of prayer or invocation. So prayers, the act of prayer, the act of invocation, contain this great cosmic secret, that they work with Divine Spirit, via the angels and other higher beings, to construct the exquisitely beautiful antahkaranah, the rainbow bridge of the soul. This is why, of course, the promised pot of gold is found where the rainbow meets the Earth. This is the solar gold from the spirit that the soul brings back to the little earthly personality, the solar gold that must indeed be rooted in the earth, in matter itself, by the soul, and breathed upon and fostered by her, until the earthly personality grows into a being of gold, a gold which is surrendered up, in its turn, to release greater light, more of the light of Goddess-God, in the little individualized spark of the spirit. And so the rainbow bridge faithfully fulfils the potential of its bilateral nature.

To find the rainbow bridge, gently rest your awareness in your heart. See the star blazing there in white light. Breathe three cycles of the Mother's Breath, and begin to see a line of white light ascending from your heart to your throat chakra, which spins and glows now with a globe of light, shining white and throwing out brilliant whirling glints of a sweet, vivid lilac colour.

Now see the line of white light extend to your brow chakra, where the globe of white light again begins to spin, throwing off rose-hued sparks of brilliance.

Continue your cycles of breathing, and see the line of white light rising to your first crown chakra, at the top of your forehead in the middle. This also begins to spin, becoming a globe of pure white light.

Now see the brilliant white light form a line across your scalp to the centre, where your second crown chakra is located in the middle of the brain. The globe of light begins to spin, a second sphere of bright white light.

Become aware that the line of light from your heart to your throat, from your throat to your brow, from your brow to the top of your forehead, from there to your crown, is forming a great bridge of light. The first end starts in the heart and runs through the higher chakras until it reaches the point in the middle of the brain. From there it extends into eternity, into infinite expansion, forming the arch of the traditional rainbow.

As you watch and realize its presence, the two crown chakras begin to rain an exquisite light-show of rainbow colours onto the bridge, and the bridge itself is transformed into a bow of brilliant crystalline rainbow colours, seven-hued and yet many times more than seven-hued.

This is the rainbow bridge, the antahkaranah, stretching between the soul and the spirit. It is yours to summon whenever you will, in the knowledge that the rainbow is truly a circle, and within that circle your spirit and your soul will find absolute union, and rejoice together in the wedding ring.

CHAPTER THIRTY-TWO

The Staircase up the Pyramid

PREPARATION – OPENING THE DOORWAY OF THE HEART

*U*ntil the soul has overcome the challenges of matter and its untransmuted energy (Wrath), the Divine Spark of light located in the heart (the spark that is our spirit) remains insufficiently developed to call and command its divine inheritance to become one with it. Nevertheless, illumination can come in a moment. Mary advises that we should never think of ourselves as far distant from achieving gnosis (direct knowledge of Goddess-God) as if it were many years or many lifetimes away, because, with aspiration, a profound heart-opening can occur at any time. The means by which the little spark expands and develops its light is by working with and through the soul, via the Earth life. Therefore our consciousness must be heart-centred, because the spirit cannot illumine the soul, thus working with and through her, unless she centres herself within the shrine of the heart. That is why the way we live our lives on Earth is so crucial. In every choice we make, every action we take – even those which seem tiny and insignificant – we can choose to make the spirit our first priority and thus enable the light of our soul and our 'little spark' to grow. The soul in her turn builds the great soul or solar temple in the higher worlds through which the light of the spirit is able to shine without restriction and thereby gather the soul and its bodies into its *orbis*.

The soul garners material for its temple by distilling the earthly experiences of the seven bodies of our being (the physical body is the coarsest and outermost body of the seven). When they have been refined to their quintessence, or when our individual consciousness, via its seven bodies, has managed to use Earth experience correctly and, throughout its pressures and permutations, has expressed the Law of Love, then the Soul Temple expands, having been provided with further spiritual essence to allow it to do so.

As the Soul Temple grows, so does the light of the little spark, until eventually it has developed to the point of summoning the divine light locked into the base chakra – the kundalini – which lies curled and sleeping there, like a dragon guarding treasure. This is why we must allow the heart chakra to balance and facilitate the other chakras. When we do this, we can be certain that our awakening is safely centred in the light, secure from all the dangers that beset the spiritual path. When the light in the heart calls to the light in the base chakra or the 'earth' (for which the base chakra is a symbol), the pathway to the Mystical Marriage comes into being, and the buried light and the heart light can conjoin with the unconscionable radiance of the Godhead. When this happens, the individuated Little Spark becomes limitless, and we as individuals become fully human. We are one with the Infinite, but we never lose our individuality. The dewdrop has slipped into the ocean, but it remains consciously aware.

So this is the function and the destiny of the base chakra, ruled by Saturn: to preserve the treasured light, and eventually to release it from imprisonment. What life lessons may we learn, then, to facilitate the opening of this chakra? How may we ascend the first step of the staircase up the pyramid?

STEP ONE – THE BASE CHAKRA

From reading Mary's gospel, we have seen how the base of the pyramid, which is the mystical structure of our greater being, equates to the world of matter into which we descend at birth. We might think of this four-square base as representative of our first main chakra, located at the base of the spine. It is symbolic of the physical life and the four elements which compose it.

This chakra is linked with the planet Saturn, the constrainer and lawgiver. The mystery of the base chakra is contained in the stars of the constellation Capricorn and reflected in Aquarius. Its colour is fiery, volcano-red. It is connected with the sense of smell, its element is earth, it is associated with Merlin and the Crone (the wise old man and the wise old woman), and its challenges are Fear and Darkness. Saturn locks the Divine Light into this base chakra, holding it securely for us until the soul is ready, from the *nous* in the heart, to summon it up the spine and through the heart. From here it rises on three levels with the grace and beauty of a fountain, springing from the throat, the brow and the crown chakras. As it rises, it awakens and vivifies the chakras in turn until each one becomes a brilliant gyroscope of light, colour and sound, permeated by the exquisite energies of the spiritual worlds.

When we have learned the lessons of the base chakra, we find ourselves on the first step of the seven leading to the summit of the pyramid. We have overcome the dark sleep of unawareness and our journey has begun. Nevertheless, we are still at the level of the base chakra; it is just that now we are aware of it! The fire of consciousness has opened an eye, and we ascend from the sleep of the elements (the physical body only aware of its animal nature) to the first step of the awareness of our spiritual nature. Again, we must overcome darkness and fear, but this time at a more subtle level.

There is a sense in which the first step is also the last, and contains all the other steps within it. This echoes T S Elliot's idea that to arrive at the end of a journey is to come back to its starting point and to know the place for the first time. Because when we actually ascend the seven steps the process emanates from our centre (or heart) outwards (we cannot truly begin the ascent until our consciousness is centred in our heart chakra), it therefore unfolds in what could be described as a 'spherical' or spiral way, rather than a linear way from the bottom to the top. Thus we can come to understand how all the seven steps are contained in the first as well as the last.

The strength, wisdom, endurance and longevity of the elephant are associated with the base chakra, and with the lessons we must learn upon this first level. The idea that the elephant 'never forgets' is an essential principle of the school of the base chakra. We must never allow ourselves to fall back into the sleep of unawareness which is induced by the lull of the Earth-plane, or we will find ourselves faced with the repetition of all its rigorous lessons. Its ultimate lesson is that of service, teaching us to override the basic earthly and animalistic instinct to look after 'number one' and pursue self-serving aims, and, with the help of the soul, to transmute survival into the ideal of service. This choice, then, to replace purely self-serving aims with service to what is Higher – in ourselves and in all beings – is fundamental to the spiritual path. Without this first step, no others can be taken. It is the very doorway to the Divine.

STEP TWO – THE SACRAL CHAKRA

The second step of the pyramid is the sacral chakra, a little below the navel. This chakra is associated with the planet Jupiter. Its mystery is contained in the stars of the constellation Pisces and is reflected in Sagittarius. Its colour is glorious orange shot through with crimson. It is connected with the sense of taste, its element is water, and it is associated with the gods and goddesses of humour, expansion, benevolence and exploration. The lesson of the second chakra is that of overcoming desire and addiction, those hooks of the lower self, and attaining the resultant gifts of peace and wisdom.

As Mary's gospel explains, the force of desire uses the soul as a garment, making a body out of her so that it can express its unappeasable nature. It harries, drives and exhausts the soul, never recognizing her presence but concerned exclusively with its own power to dominate this 'body' that it unconsciously assumes. When the soul will collude no more with this unconsciousness of herself, she arises and withdraws authority from the urgent claims of desire, asserting her own power of command. Desire is first outraged and unbelieving, then silenced into submission. Henceforth, the soul will summon, modify or dismiss desire as her wisdom, working through the Law of Love, deems appropriate.

This chakra is associated with the generative organs and with the expression of creative energy at the etheric level of life emanating from thought-power and imagination. All forms of procreative power must express the Law of Love, otherwise they become predatory and destructive.

The animal of this chakra is the alligator, which can manifest as the powerful and dangerous predator of the waters, or as the sacred dragon (which the alligator or crocodile represents in some pantheons, especially that of ancient Egypt). And the dragon, of course, is sign and symbol of the Dragon Queen, who brings the great currents of life to humanity and the physical realm and who is merciful, wise and all-encompassing in her love.

STEP THREE – THE SOLAR PLEXUS CHAKRA

The third stair of the pyramid is mounted via the solar plexus chakra. This is linked with the planet Mars, the warrior and the achiever. Its mystery is contained in the stars of the constellation Aries, and is reflected in Scorpio. Its colour ranges from green to golden green to warm, rich gold. It is connected with the sense of sight, its element is air, and it is associated with gods and goddesses of courage, victory and willpower, those divinities who bless the questing soul and the pioneer. The great lesson of the third chakra is love, in both its human and divine aspects. Its challenge is ignorance.

There is a strong link between the solar plexus chakra and the sacral or second chakra. A large network of nerves connects the two centres, and both are associated with the desire nature. The desire nature of the Sacred Feminine is emphasized in the second chakra, which is connected to the Moon by its element – water; but it reflects itself in fire – the reflected fire which is that of the lower nature. The desire nature of the Sacred Masculine is emphasized in the solar plexus centre, which is linked to the air element. In this instance, the air of the solar plexus chakra, manifesting as Ignorance, can tend to oxygenate the reflected fire of the desire nature emanating from the sacral chakra. (Here again we find Simon Peter, full of fiery impulses and hotheaded ego emanating from the reflected fire of the sacral chakra and fed by the airs of the solar plexus centre. He represents the intellect (the lower mind) driven by the desire nature of the solar plexus.) Thus the second and third chakras contain the lunar and solar energies of the desire-body which, when overcome (as Jesus says in Mary's gospel, 'All aspects have to be overcome'), metamorphose into peace, wisdom and love. Joan Hodgson, in her book *The Stars and the Chakras*, confirms this when she teaches that 'There is a close connection between the [fire-feeding] solar plexus centre and the frontal mind, both being associated with Mars.'

The animal traditionally belonging to the solar plexus chakra is the ram, the beast of sacrifice, for the lower fires must be sacrificed to the divine flame in the heart. The desire nature has to willingly offer itself in sacrifice and shut down the misuse of the air element, manifesting as Ignorance, feeding the fires of Wrath. When this damper is applied to Ignorance and the mystery of air is used correctly, which is to connect us to the higher mind (the *nous*) that feeds the holy flame of the Spirit, then those dangerous reflected or astral fires are transfigured into the blessing of the divine light of the Godhead, and the ram, baptized in its radiance, attains its golden fleece.

THE FOURTH STEP – THE HEART CHAKRA

The fourth stair up the pyramid of our greater self is the heart chakra. It is, of course, the centre of our being, our sun-self around which our being revolves. This chakra is linked with the Sun, the golden, perfected being, the Son-Daughter of Goddess-God, and its element is fire. The mystery of the heart chakra is contained in the stars of the constellation Leo and reflected in Cancer (representing the King and Queen respectively). Its colour is a calm, radiant clear gold merging into brilliant wine-red. It is connected with the sense of feeling and touch, its lesson is the ultimate expression of Love – universal brotherhood – and its challenge, according to Mary's gospel, is Lethal Jealousy or Fear of Death.

It is in the heart that the point of balance between darkness and light is found – the *nous* which connects the soul and the spirit and which lies between the two. It is the solvent of conflict. There is a rainbow bridge which connects the heart and the head centres and which extends beyond the crown chakra, a bridge which leads from Earth to Heaven and from Heaven to Earth. At both ends of the rainbow (the Earth end being our human heart and the Heaven end being our connection to the Divine) there lies buried a cup, the Rainbow Chalice. One of the cups (the heart) receives and the other (our Divine self) gives forth. When we pass through the *nous*, the chalice that we bear in our heart becomes magically endowed and gives forth as well as receiving. The rainbow bridge is the *nous*, and it is there that the chalice or the Holy Grail dwells. 'Where the *nous* is, there lies the treasure.'

The guardians of the temple of the heart are Venus, Mercury and Saturn. Saturn is the Alpha of the spine, Mercury is the Omega. At its midpoint, reflecting the heart-sun, is Venus, planet of love and harmony. Saturn, the lawgiver, ensures that the heart obeys the Law of Love. Mercury, at the top of the spine, is linked with the archangel Raphael (Merlin or Saturn in another guise). Mercury is also Robin

Hood, not lawless but an outlaw (outside the law), the golden consciousness that has transcended the constricting chains of Saturn because his lessons have been learnt and the law is within his heart. It can no longer imprison him. Venus is the point of balance between the two, the ascended soul who remains alive in a physical body on Earth. This is the ultimate goal of the heart – to spiritualize the Earth itself, and exalt brotherhood to the point of celestial harmony.

When the heart is unaware of its royal lineage (the connection it has to the Godhead) the vision of the soul fails, and it believes that the life beating in its heart is purely physical and will pass away. The soul clings to the fear of death and cannot find its unity, its at-one-ment with others. It equates ego with life and needs to feel that others are less than itself. This creates lethal jealousy, the antithesis of brotherhood. The heart that bears true knowledge of the *nous* will never make this fatal mistake.

Now we can see why the animal associated with the heart is the sphinx. This creature represents supreme consciousness rising from an animal body set four-square on the Eearth, as is the base of the mystical pyramid whose qualities, through the chakras, we are exploring; and in its most mystical aspect it signifies the fused being of the Spirit and the Bride, of Jesus and Mary – the heart-centre itself.

THE FIFTH STEP – THE THROAT CHAKRA

The fifth stair upon the pyramid represents the throat chakra. This centre is linked with the planet Venus, the planet of love, harmony and beautiful creation. Its mystery is contained in the stars of the constellation Taurus and is reflected in Libra. Its colour is fiery gold transforming into vivid lilac or ultraviolet. It is connected with the sense of hearing and listening, its element is the white ether from which all form is brought into being and is also the space in which it is contained, and it is associated with Brigid or Bride (the Daughter) and Divine Mother, the Great Goddess herself. Its lesson is that of harmonious union, and its challenge is the power of the flesh, or enslavement to the body.

Venus and Mercury work together to vivify the higher centres (the heart, the throat, the brow and crown chakras) and Mercury's influence is certainly strong in the fifth centre. But we may think of Venus as bringing us the Silence, that sphere of clarifying peace which actually opens our ears that we might hear. ('Those who have ears, let them hear,' is used as a refrain by Jesus many times throughout Mary's gospel.) Until we enter the Silence, we cannot really hear or listen.

On entering the Silence to commune with Mary, Margaret Bailey was initially given a sheaf of wheat from the hands of this exalted and loving presence. On contemplating this, we thought that the wheat was a sign of Mary Magdalene as the Bread of Life, and that it linked her with the star sign of the Virgin, meaning that the greater soul of Mary Magdalene who is the Dragon Queen actually holds dominion over virgin matter, the white ether which is the Thread of Life and from which all material form is spun and woven.

Upon the sheaf of wheat which the Virgin holds, and upon that given to Margaret, hang five ears. These five ears of wheat also link Virgo with the five-pointed star of Venus or the pentagram, associated with the secret elixir or quintessence of the alchemists. Whereas the ancient Greeks declared that there were four elements in which matter could exist, the Pythagoreans added a fifth; the element of ether, purer and more subtle than fire and endowed with an orbicular motion. Ether was said to have flown upwards at creation (note the connection of the rising powers of the goddess) and to have formed the stars as the fifth essence (the quintessence), the most subtle and refined extract of a body that can be procured.

Such a magical notion inspired the alchemists whose task it was to discover the spirituality in nature and matter; so they created essences 'five times distilled' as an esoteric principle. The ancient Roman poet Horace links Venus with the Earth Goddess, Divine Mother and the Virgin (in Virgo) when he speaks of 'kisses which Venus has imbued with the quintessence of her own nectar'.

The genesis of Virgo, the stellar goddess studded with stars, is found in ancient Egypt where the Corn Maiden (Virgo) is none other than Isis herself, her dress flowing with stars, holding either a wand of office (interchangeable with the distaff, symbol of the Spinning Woman, as her office is to weave creation) or her child, Horus, who represents the Eye of God. This eye is always portrayed singly and is a symbol of the Third Eye, that centre of consciousness which is said to lead from earthly understanding to divine apperception of the cosmos. It is worth noting that when Margaret is led into the sphere of Silence, her outlook is always that of the starry heavens.

So Venus, Isis and the Corn Maiden of Virgo are one; they are all associated with spinning and weaving, they are all associated with the fifth element of ether and the stars, and they are all associated with Mary Magdalene. This insight helped us to understand how closely linked is Mary, in her vaster being as the Dragon Queen, with the very beginnings of matter, with Earth life itself, and with the origins of the human race. These things will be revealed for our era to understand, but until full revelation comes we can, even now, grasp some important truths.

The throat chakra is linked with the element ether and with formulating the Word that began all creation ('In the beginning was the Word,' John's gospel tells us – John, who was the actual and mystical brother of Mary). It is connected with the achievement of harmonious union, a union that cannot come about until our ability to communicate with one another is harmonized in the heart. This idea of harmonious communication is symbolized by the spider's web, a network of 'etheric lines of communication' often created in an octagonal shape, at the heart of which sits the eight-rayed being, the Spinner and Weaver. The idea of harmony is contained in the number eight, which represents the octave.

Could it be that enslavement to the flesh, meaning the inability to free our consciousness from the mundane plane and its limited conceptions and so realize the wonder of our origins and the glory of our destiny, can really only be overcome by going into the Silence? By truly learning to hear and to listen through the heart, which integrates all lines of communication between one another, between ourselves and the natural world, between ourselves and our higher spiritual contacts, between ourselves and the stars and ultimately with Goddess-God. The five ears of wheat upon the sheaf of corn seem to indicate that this is so, as does the ancient Egyptian mystical teaching that the ears can open a secret doorway to the higher worlds – a secret doorway that we believe leads first to the *nous*, and thence to the apex of the pyramid, from where we can reach for the stars.

Wheat intolerance is endemic nowadays, especially in the West. Its consumption causes exhaustion and varying allergic reactions. This is a strange situation to arise concerning the ingestion of the Bread of Life, which is intended to bestow vitality and inner harmony. The Corn Maiden herself was transformed into the chalice of the Holy Grail in medieval art, signifying the life-giving and all-nourishing properties of the Grail. Could it be that our bodies and the natural world, which know about Mary Magdalene in the secret life of their cells and their primal consciousness relating to the origins of the Earth and matter, are trying to wake us up to the truth, telling us that we are failing to digest it, or digesting it in the wrong way?

When the cords of communication which link us all are harmonized and integrated in the heart, the throat chakra expands and helps us to translate the love arising from the heart into compassion, tolerance, understanding and respect for the individual needs of others, which in turn inspires true union and steadfast brotherhood unassailed by the claims of the lower nature. The centre holds, and harmony, like the element ether, assumes a constant orbicular motion. That is why we might designate the spider as the animal connected with the throat chakra, for it is the creator and spinner of the etheric thread, its handiwork is designed always upon the principles of the mandala, and its home is the centre of the web.

THE SIXTH STEP – THE BROW CHAKRA

The sixth step of the pyramid is represented by the third eye, the brow chakra. It is linked with the planet Mercury, the messenger, and with the sixth sense. It also receives the influences of the planet Uranus. Its mystery is contained in the stars of the constellation Virgo and reflected in Gemini. Its colour is a perfect rose hue, as the first blush of sunrise. It is known as 'the abode of joy' and it is a centre of command, stimulating the divine light in every cell of the body in preparation for the ascension at the crown centre. As discussed above, it is associated with the single eye of Horus, and it is towards the Age of Horus (the New Age) that we are advancing. Mercury is connected with Horus because the mother of Horus, Isis, is synonymous with the Corn Maiden of Virgo, the zodiacal sign over which Mercury rules. With Uranus, Mercury's mission is to enlighten us through the brow chakra with sudden, sometimes shattering, illumination and revelation.

Intoxicated wisdom, or foolish wisdom, is the challenge of the sixth chakra. When the third eye remains closed to spiritual illumination and sees only earthly reality, it becomes filled with a sense of the rightness of its own opinions and adjusts reality according to its own illusions. While the third eye is focused on such illusion, then intuition and inspiration, the heavenly twins that bless the vision of the third eye and activate the sixth sense, are prevented from sporting and playing in the field of its vision. The result is intoxicated (in the sense of inebriation and toxicity), or foolish, wisdom. Mercury in his lower aspects can also turn intelligence into silver-tongued, self-serving cunning, manifesting as guileful wisdom.

The lesson of the brow chakra is to hone our consciousness to the point where 'the eye of the vision ... in the soul' opens and commands the body and the five senses according to the new spiritual vistas opening up to its divine sight. Its job is to step up the vibration of physical reality and transform it from its mundane limitations into the limitlessness of the spirit. That is why the animal or creature of the sixth chakra is the hawk or the white eagle. Swift, high-flying and far-seeing, this bird is the Divine messenger of the Sun.

THE SEVENTH STEP – THE CROWN CHAKRA

We now come to the seventh stair of the pyramid. This corresponds to the crown chakra, whose mystery is contained within the stars of the constellation Auriga, particularly the star Capella, 'Little Goat', which reflects the constellation of Capricorn, thus connecting the last stair with the first.

If we think of the ecliptic, which is the annual path the Sun seems to take around the Earth and which represents the ring of the solar zodiac, we might imagine that this in itself is the crown chakra for the Soul of the World, the soul of all humanity.

In my first book, *Earth Magic*, I wrote concerning this idea:

> *There is a strange and beautiful night-time phenomenon, only occasionally to be seen in the Northern hemisphere, called the Zodiacal Light. In*

springtime, it is just a glow in the Western skies after the sun has set and gone. In the autumn, it can be seen in the East before sunrise, like a radiant mist with a pearly lustre set at its heart. But in the tropics its conical shape expands into a ring of light like a crown, some parts of it as brilliant as the stars.

For those who believe that life has meaning, and that no phenomenon is senseless or random, this haunting light may seem to be a celebration of the zodiac itself, its stars and planets, the Sun and Moon which majestically tread its course, and the unending and unfathomable significance it has for our beloved Earth, the exquisite centre-jewel of the universe as we experience it.

The zodiac, both the ecliptic and the sidereal (the actual constellations themselves) can be viewed from this perspective as the Earth's crowning glory.

The crown chakra of the individual human being is properly two centres, one at the top of the forehead at its midpoint, and one secreted in the middle of the brain. This shines from the crown on the scalp and is reflected in the Soul Star, the chakra above the top of the head, as our Earth Star is a reflection of the base chakra and exists below our feet.

The kingly or queenly crown of jewels is a symbol of these topmost chakras and illumines their form and purpose, which is to receive the divine illumination of the stars and the supernal glory which shines behind their physical manifestation, and to give forth the light of Christ Consciousness so that the individual can take his or her place among the radiant stars.

When the chakras are fully developed and activated, the door which is the *nous* opens like a great archway, and we become one with our divine spirit. When this happens, we do indeed become one of the great company of brilliant stars. We become independently radiant. This is the meaning of the eighth level of the pyramid, the apex above the base, which we reach by climbing the seven stairs – the ladder. Beyond the pinnacle are the starry heavens, our destiny and our destination.

Both of these chakras (the composite crown chakra), especially the one in the centre of the brain, are associated with the Moon. Influences from Neptune and Mercury also govern these centres. Their colours are as a mystical rainbow, every combination of colours that we know on Earth, and more beyond these. The one at the midpoint of the temples is where we attain cosmic consciousness. We become as 'the Woman Who Knows All'.

The chakra in the heart of the brain, which is a reflection of the *nous* or the mind in the heart and is so strongly linked with the full Moon, is also closely connected with hearing and listening. It is a receiving and reflecting station which feeds the diadem whose central jewel is the point in the middle of the forehead between the temples, the flashing gem of divine wisdom. This full Moon chakra is like a lake reflecting the light of the spiritual star, which shines above the head. It becomes as the Sphere of John-Shar-On and is linked with the Pole Star.

Whilst ever we are unable to activate our chakras and pass through the *nous* in full-moon consciousness, our being is like the Moon we see from the Earth – a beautiful shining entity which is gradually eaten by the darkness of the Earth, but which is always reborn out of the belly of the night. It signifies the in-breath and the-out breath, the flowing and ebbing tide, sleeping and awakening and the process of reincarnation – being drawn back towards the Earth.

When we attain our fully illumined state, however, the moon of our being remains imperishably full, just as we are one with the imperishable stars (the spiritual light of the celestial bodies). It is then that the chakra above our crown can be seen, pouring forth its effulgence in a starburst of rainbow colours, exquisitely radiant yet delicate, subtle, almost pearlized. The chakras take up the colours and each one spins in its own permutations of light, colour and sound, fabulous to behold.

Ann Napier (editor of *Cygnus* magazine) describes the development towards our 'fully illumined state' in the following words:

> As I see it, when the kundalini is raised in the divine way (as a result of the divine light spreading outward from the heart) this is how the process happens: the light emanating from the heart eventually reaches a level of intensity sufficient to stimulate the base chakra and the kundalini coiled within it. At the same time, it is also strong enough to open the crown chakra. Then, as the divine energy locked into the base of our spine (kundalini) rises from the base chakra in response to the call of the light in the heart, the divine consciousness above us descends via the crown chakra, and they meet and become consummate in the chamber of the heart – the wedding chamber – thereafter radiating outwards in unified glory. This consummation is also mirrored in the head – in the meeting and mingling of the purified energy fields surrounding the pineal and pituitary glands (the 'full moon' crown chakra), resulting in the activation of the 'unicorn's horn' crown chakra and the reflection in the mind of the divine wisdom in the heart. If you visualize all this, you will see the sign of the cross within the circle – the sign of the Earth, the sign of the heart, and the sign of divine consciousness.

The challenge of the crown chakra is self-righteous materialism, which manifests when a very narrow and bigoted sense of divinity is all that is allowed to develop, or when the ego mistakes itself for divinity, and pronounces its judgements (often only a reflection of its likes and dislikes and the restrictions of its viewpoint) as if on divine authority. Both of these states choke the motion of the chakras and cause their energies to stagnate.

The lesson of the crown chakra(s) is the attainment of cosmic consciousness through the development – in the heart – of love, wisdom and spiritual willpower (the will-to-good), which activate the chakras. The two animals connected with the two crown centres are (mid-brain) the dragon and (mid-forehead) the unicorn. Mary and Jesus symbolize these chakras. Intriguingly, the zodiacal sign of Capricorn is depicted in the Glastonbury Zodiac (*see* Appendix One) as a unicorn. The dragon is to be found there in the stellar mirror of Scorpio, symbol of Earth life and rebirth into the Spirit, the zodiacal sign into which Tamar, the Holy Grail, was born.

ADDITIONAL POINTS

It is a common teaching in the West that the chakras correspond to the colours of the rainbow, from red (the base chakra) to violet at the crown. This is a misconception. No such rigid system applies. The chakras do reflect the colours of the rainbow, but in a multitude of varying hues, many of which we have never experienced on Earth, and their source is the Soul Star, the Rainbow Seat, rather than the assignation of a colour by inherent design, although a system does loosely exist, taught by the Eastern mystics, which we have given.

The brief teaching on the chakras which is outlined in this chapter is similarly not intended in any way to be rigid, or to override the teachings given elsewhere, especially those in Joan Hodgson's *The Stars and the Chakras*, which uses a slightly different approach.

The chakras enshrine many secrets, and we have been advised by Mary that a much deeper and more extensive exposition is desirable. We are content to wait for this to appear in the fullness of time. Meanwhile, only a few pointers are necessary.

* Never stimulate the chakras by mental concentration. They must be allowed to develop naturally, through spiritual aspiration, which is conscious attunement to the highest good.
* You can open your chakras before commencing meditation by gently visualizing them spinning in a clockwise direction and emanating white light. Let your focus be soft and brief so that there is no danger of overcharging them.
* Drugs and excessive alcohol, as well as extreme emotional states and some forms of medication, overcharge the chakras to a damaging extent. Meditation will help to harmonize overcharged chakras. *However, do not relinquish medication before seeking advice from a doctor.*

* Always seal your chakras after meditation or similar activity. Use the symbol of a circle of light containing a bright silver equal-sided cross, and imaginally place it over each chakra in turn, starting at the top (the crown).

The seven tools we can use to help us attain soul ascension, described in Part III, Chapter Thirty-one, may also be applied specifically in the case of difficulty at the level of any particular chakra. For instance, if you are fearful and the world seems dark, this would indicate a need to overcome the challenge of the base chakra. Using the corresponding image (as listed below) when you sit for meditation may help. Of course, the implements are valuable in themselves, without forming part of a system, which should never be rigidly applied. The following is only a guideline. Descriptions of each instrument and how to use it are described in the preceding chapter.

1. The Rose – Smell – Base Chakra
2. The Breath – Taste – Sacral Chakra
3. The Star – Sight – Solar Plexus
4. The Chalice – Touch – Heart Chakra
5. The Silence – Hearing – Throat Chakra
6. The Rainbow Bridge – Sixth Sense – Third Eye
7. Meditation – Cosmic Consciousness – Crown Chakra (Balance)

CHAPTER THIRTY-THREE

The Fall of the Moon

We have studied how the aspirant seeking soul ascension must first of all free his or her consciousness from bondage to the Earth-plane and the powerful pull of the elements, and then climb the seven steps of the pyramid of being, ascending through the chakras and overcoming the Seven Manifestations of Wrath which comprise the fire element, the element that leads us upwards and that starts us on our path, because within it lies buried the divine light of heaven, the 'imprisoned glory' which we are seeking at the heart of our experiences in matter. The seven steps of the pyramid, when viewed as our chakra system, equate with the stars in the constellations of the zodiac and with the seven planets, connected to the seven rays of creation, according to the system of traditional Western astrology.

The order of the planets (which include the Sun and the Moon) was anciently organized according to their rapidity of motion; and in conformity with this concept, the seven planets start with Saturn at the bottom stair of the pyramid, progressing upwards through Jupiter and Mars to the Sun in the centre of the stairway, and then on again through Venus and Mercury until, at the top of the stairway and the apex of the pyramid, we enter the sphere of the Moon. We think that this full Moon represents the *nous*, for it is when we pass through the Gates of the Moon (as when we pass through the *nous*) that we are released from the bondage of Earth and step into the starry heavens. The Moon is the soul, the gateway through to our divine spirit. When we stand at the Gates of the Moon, our soul has earned its freedom and is ready to ascend into the beauty of the spiritual worlds. The Moon sphere is symbolic of the pinnacle of our achievement in freeing our soul from the elements of Earth and from the passions and forces of the lower mind.

We now need to study some truths which may seem strange, but which hold the key to our origins, to the great task of our time, and to our astonishing future, for, make no mistake, the future of humanity is marvellous and noble beyond our present conception. The first of these truths that Mary gave us was that our beautiful Moon is not the first Moon to have sailed the skies as Earth's satellite. It is in fact the fifth Moon.

Through the ages of the Earth (which are more numerous and of much greater duration than scientists believe), the ignorance, wanton power-seeking and cruelty of earthly human society has on four occasions reached such a pitch, despite the tireless and selfless efforts of angels and other spiritual beings to help us to turn away from our destructive path, that a global disaster occurred. Our civilization sent forth a note (for all the stars and planets, and the life on them, sound a note of harmony, or of discord, in the grand symphony of the cosmos) whose vibration brought the Moon (the soul) crashing down towards Earth. As the Moon approached very near to our planet, it exploded, leaving a ring of dust and solid matter that eventually collided with the crust of the Earth. It was this ring of rocks that caused large-scale fossilization to occur on our planet's surface.

From the cataclysmic waves, the seismic eruptions, the extremes of temperature, the atmospheric pressures and the disturbance of the Earth's tectonic plates caused by the Moon's explosion and impact, gaseous substances were released from within the Earth which joined the swirling mass of Moon dust and debris, still in our orbit, that had escaped the gravitational pull of the Earth. This ball of dust, matter particles and gas condensed in space over a period of no more than two years until it was once again the Moon, our beautiful satellite, but slightly diminished in size and luminosity. Our present, fifth Moon, is the smallest of all the Moons which have through the ages graced the Earth.

The very large, powerfully bright Moon which was the first to shine in our orbit was reflected in the Star of Bethlehem when, after the four stars had gathered from the 'four corners' of the skies, they formed a radiant white sphere like a huge full Moon which dropped a comet or serpent tail over the stable-cave in Bethlehem as Mary drew her first breath.

Is there any evidence for this seemingly bizarre history of the relationship between the Earth and the Moon? Some does exist. For instance, there are three recognized geological epochs, and it seems possible that each one might have been recorded in stone by the Moon's descent and impact. The fossilized remains that determine each one occur around the globe in ring formation. Moreover, scientists agree that the process of fossilization is very uncommon, and are unable to explain why the fossils which mark the three geological epochs have been discovered along a path which describes a circle on the surface of the Earth, or why there is such a high incidence of them along these paths. Of course, this theory does not support the idea of four geological epochs revealed to us through the fossilization created by four Moons, but only three eras and three Moons. However, we believe that the first Moon to fall on the Earth was so large, and created such devastation, that scientists have not yet been able chronologically to isolate the first great era of Earth life, the true Palaeozoic age.

According to this scheme of things, we have found evidence for the secondary, tertiary and quaternary geological periods and are currently in the fifth great epoch. As yet, we know nothing about the primary cycle, the first great age of the Earth, at the commencement of which the god-people settled in Eden around the North Pole and at the end of which they removed themselves to a nonphysical location above the Himalayas because of the appalling vibratory level given off by Earth's developing humanity, who had eventually begun to refuse their teachings and guidance. As each Moon approached the Earth, the planet's gravitational field was dramatically affected, and living things were able to attain increased size without the normal corresponding increase in gravitational pressure. Therefore, giant species of plants, insects, animals and Homo sapiens were able to develop. When the Moon finally fell, these giants disappeared, although some species and races, invested with a rapid rate of adaptation either biological or intellectual, remained in existence. It is not likely, because of the enormous dependence of Earth life on the presence of the Moon, that we were without her for long, perhaps only for a generation or two or maybe for an even briefer span.

The idea that a ball of gases and dust particles could solidify into a moon in just two years is supported by recent findings by a research team from the University of Colarado, in Boulder. They formulated 27 different scenarios relating to the origin of the Moon. In all of them, computer simulations showed that the particles and gases thrown (we say released) into orbit, agglomerated to form the Moon in less than a year. Our source assigns two years to this process (2 is the magical number associated with the Moon, as well as 8 and 9), so even allowing for the lapse of time before the next Moon was released from the Earth, it seems that the Earth's moonless state would have been measured in decades rather than in hundreds or thousands of years. Nevertheless, there exist very ancient Chinese texts, and an astronomical map from 13,000 years ago, found in the depths of a cave at the foot of the Himalayas in Bohistan, which seem to depict a sky without a Moon.

The giant god-people initiated the development of Earth's humanity, who were themselves much bigger than the human race is today. Ours was a new planetary colonization, comprising a new wave of souls breathed forth from the Godhead. The god-people were a group of highly advanced beings who came from beyond the stars as an act of love and sacrifice to help to get us started on our evolutionary path. We brought down the first Moon some time after the god-people had been forced to withdraw into the higher ethers in the Himalayas because of our refusal to heed their guidance. At a certain point in history, the falling Moons gave rise to two distinct civilizations upon the Earth. The first race was gigantic in size, and knew some of the secrets of the god-people. They had abandoned themselves to the forces of evil, however, and with their knowledge they threatened the survival of our Mother Earth herself. The second civilization seems to have comprised our ancestors, the much smaller race to which we belong. We believe this to have been the race that had established itself after 'the Flood' (the cataclysm caused by the last falling Moon) which was making an effort, even if rather primitive compared to humanity's past when it was still under the guidance and instruction of the god-people, to attune itself once again to its spiritual source.

Humanity at this juncture reached something of a turning point. It had to struggle to overcome the sinister giant strain of its race, an offshoot it itself had caused to arise through its own foolishness. If it had failed, humanity would eventually have destroyed itself and the planet. It was almost as if, in order to turn back once again to the light, humanity had to renounce its God-like status and become very little and humble, because in its former assumption of that God-like status, it had allowed itself to become unbalanced and polarized towards evil. A certain bloodline was being continued, link by link, so that one could arise who might achieve the final lap of the struggle. Abraham and Sarah, Rebecca and Isaac, Jacob, Rachel and Leah, Ruth and Boaz were among its guiding beacons.

Then came David, who slew the giant Goliath with stones from his sling. We think that this is symbolic of David destroying the vessel in which the race of evil giants could contain their consciousness. They had to leave the physical Earth and reassemble at the astral level of the planet, where they awaited their chance to reinfect the soul of humanity so that they might again assume bodies and rule on Earth. Having taken away their sovereignty, David became king in their stead. The decision had been made, the battle had commenced, and the 'little people' had won. Tolkien's richly symbolic tale of the hobbits defeating Sauron is reminiscent, in exactitude, of this victory. Now that humanity had, of its own free will, turned again to the light, Jesus and Mary, the avatars of the coming age, could descend down the bloodline, preceded by Solomon and the Queen of Sheba who bore Solomon a son. Tamar curtailed this divine bloodline, for its purpose (to earth the divinity of Christ in direct human form) ended with her.

We need to make it clear that the bloodline was not racial, and that anyone can be filled with the Christ spirit. That is the whole point of Jesus and Mary's mission, which was a healing mission. Healing means to make whole, and although this concept must be understood at the deepest and highest level of which we can conceive, we think it is true to say that, in the context of the times, there was a little mundane work to be done as well. By bringing down the Moon, creating a race of sinister giants, and then being required to eliminate their authority on Earth, humanity had managed to turn the tide of evolution backwards to a certain extent, and in so doing had scrambled some of the patterning of its DNA. For a full baptism of the Christ light such as the world had never seen before in its long, long history, some preparation had to be made as far as the three vessels which would contain it were concerned (Jesus, John and Mary, with Tamar expressing the 'hidden force' principle). Because of the nature of the times, as discussed above, special bodies had to be prepared. These bodies were entirely human, but they needed to be able to contain souls of an extremely high vibrational order, and the DNA available was not of the required resonance. Therefore, the bloodline was instigated, the bloodline which descended link by link in particular via the sacrifice and suffering of women, because these women were, in their deepest souls, of the essence of the Dragon Queens, the first and greatest of whom was Mary Magdalene; and in their hearts they knew they were working for the greater destiny of the whole human race.

When the bloodline produced Tamar, she mingled her parents' high-vibrational essence in her own body and being, and the DNA of humanity was restored, set once more on the right track, as it were. This healing influence was a part (we might say a very basic part) of the healing mission of Jesus and Mary. The death on the cross, and Mary's sacrifice, helped to bring about the correct orientation of the DNA, as did Tamar's birth. This is one of the reasons why Joseph of Arimathea and Mary caught Christ's blood at his moment of bodily death on the cross. The deeply mystical aspect of the ceremony helped to facilitate this reorientation as well as to enshrine and 'earth' a profound spiritual dynamic. As soon as the global healing of humanity's DNA took place, Tamar herself purposely ended the bloodline. By going to Rome, she knew she would end her life. First of all, she taught Paul the deeper mysteries. He preserved them and grieved deeply at her passing. Yet they both knew that negative higher forces wanted to make use of the bloodline so that through it they might descend to Earth, in particular the very strain of advanced but sinister giants whom the bloodline had been designed to help humanity overcome. We have been told by Tamar that she too felt profound grief in leaving the Earth so soon, as a young girl of 24. She longed for the union and companionship of a lover, and for children. She had to leave her beloved Earth behind in the springtime of her days, and the sacrifice was deeply felt.

The giant race did indeed manage to infect humanity's consciousness again after their initial downfall and banishment from the physical plane of the Earth, most importantly in the case of Nazi Germany, where Hitler told one of his colleagues: 'I will tell you a secret. I have seen the New Man. He was intrepid and cruel. I was afraid of him.' Not surprisingly, this 'New Man' gave Hitler orders to destroy the Jewish race, every last man, woman and child, even if a person was only distantly related by blood to a member of it. They clearly did not want to risk the danger of encountering the bloodline again, and seem to have harboured a demonic hatred towards the Jewish people who were responsible for ridding the world of them, through David. They detested and showed great fear towards the idea of Christ, David's prophesied descendant, Hitler often pouring scorn in private over the 'pity ethic' of Jesus.

The Nazis held great sway over the pope, to the point where a certain collusion developed between them. History has recorded this baffling situation as arising because the pope wanted to prevent the Vatican from being bombed. This is surely inaccurate, not only because any such act would have roused the instant hatred and enmity of one billion Catholics around the world – and Hitler was far too wily a politician to allow that to happen until his plan of world domination was much further advanced – but also because of the extremity of the times, which demanded a clear choice between good and evil such as humanity had not previously experienced since the Crucifixion. The world was being bombed around him, and it is inconceivable that the pope would have supported the Nazis because he was afraid of damage to a building, even if that building was the Vatican. He would surely have been much more likely to believe in the eventual triumph of the Christ-forces through willing self-sacrifice, such as sustaining damage to his headquarters.

Hitler was obsessed with finding the Holy Grail and had collected many rare relics, among them the Spear of Longinus, the blade which had pierced Christ's side at the Crucifixion. We believe that Hitler had been told something by his inner chiefs, the sinister giants dwelling on the astral planes who called themselves the New Men, with which he could hold the pope to ransom, backing up his claims with artefacts he had discovered – something that would have been ruinous to the male-dominated Roman Church.

We leave it to our readers to surmise what that might have been! One thing is certain, however: the Nazis would have manipulated any revelation to their advantage, and would have released only confusing half-truths. Their aim was not only the suppression of the Sacred Feminine, but its complete reversal (hence the swastika, which shows the life forces dancing backwards) and the harnessing and harvesting of these cruelly perverted energies. Within the hearts of the New Men lurked entire abnegation of Divine Mother – a situation which, thank goodness, has never yet obtained on Earth and will never be allowed to do so.

The concept of the Moon falling to Earth is not new, but we believe that what Mary further revealed to us about the Moon might indeed be unprecedented. The Moon down the ages has always been regarded by humanity as supremely important, even though its status appears to be no more than that of a little satellite. But, in fact, the Sun and the Moon together, activated and inspired by the Sacred Masculine and the Sacred Feminine Principles of Goddess-God, created our entire solar system. Geoffrey Hodson's angelic revelations, which follow in Appendix Four, will give the intuitive reader some idea of how such a project came into being.

As far as we are able to understand, the Sun and the Moon are truly one, a unity containing two Principles. The Moon separated from the Sun so that the dynamics between them would cause her to give birth. When she did so, she differentiated herself as female and divided the lower or infant spheres of consciousness into male and female, light and darkness, positive and negative so that physical life could come into existence (no such separation exists on the higher planes of being). She herself came from the heart of the Sun. She was breathed forth as the mysterious and holy essence within a sphere of fire-mist which solidified to become the Moon, pregnant with her children, the sons and daughters of the Sun and the Moon. She released their 'children', the planets, in the form of gases and fire-mist from the Sun which eventually solidified. This fire-mist contained the principles of the Moon and the Sun, the Divine Principles of male and female which on Earth became the intake of oxygen and the exhalation of carbon dioxide – the Sacred Breath.

However, the planet Earth was not released in the same way as the other planets. Our beautiful Earth was born in solid form from her mother, the Moon. And when this birth had taken place, the Moon remained hollow, emblematic of the Mystic Hollow or the Great Womb, the Mother. This means that the Earth is actually part of the Moon. Our planet is literally the inside of the Moon, the selfsame body. The people of our present Moon (for people do live there) dwell inside her sphere, not at the physical level of life, but deep within the exalted dimension whose symbol is the hollow sphere of the Moon. These people are spirits of great pulchritude and grace, with only healing and benignity in their hearts towards their earthly brethren.

Unfortunately, at the time of the Crucifixion, when the full Moon was blotted out in darkness – a supernatural darkness which cloaked the entire Earth despite her different time or sunlight zones and which was recorded by many ancient astronomers – a very powerful and magnificent nature spirit took flight from the Earth to the Moon. This nature spirit was by no means intrinsically evil, but she was heart-broken and wrathful because of the affliction of sorrow visited on the Earth by Earth's human children. She flew forth from her Mother Earth's tremors and ructions at the time of the Crucifixion – tremors and ructions caused by the Earth's agony at witnessing such an event – as an expression of the Earth's grief, and she became a curse to the Earth people. It is she who disturbs the equilibrium of humans and animals at full Moon, and who is especially associated with lunacy. She reflects our own mad disorientation in rejecting the Christ, which consists of our foolish ignorance about Mary Magdalene as well as the slaying of Jesus.

Whilst ever her essence is in negative mode, it will continue to work against the great gift of healing and brotherhood which Jesus and Mary worked so hard to procure for humanity. Her curse can and will be overcome, and she cannot do harm to anyone who follows Mary's lead in harmonizing themselves with the Moon, which will be explained later. Indeed, the nature spirit concerned is waiting for the people of the Earth to make such recompense, for then she will be healed and released. This process really comes about through the way we express the Law of Love in our individual lives, of course; nevertheless, the process of reconciliation can be helped by simple ceremony, which in its purest form is always an expression of the Law of Love.

There is a face on the Moon which many people are able to delineate. It is commonly referred to as 'the man in the Moon'. The poet Sylvia Plath says in her poem entitled 'The Moon and the Yew Tree' that its mouth is an 'O-gape of complete despair' and that the face is 'terribly upset'. In fact, the face is strangely similar to that of the figure in Edward Munch's painting *The Scream*. Interestingly, the inspiration for the painting came to Munch whilst crossing a bridge under which a slaughter-house operated, and it is of course the human propensity for slaughter and the unspeakable incident of it as demonstrated by the Crucifixion which caused the nature spirit to become an expression of outraged grief. She is the essence of the blight on the soul of humanity that it wrought upon itself when it decided to sacrifice to Wrath the Christ, the Light in the heart, rather than sacrifice its lower nature to that Divine and healing flame. The face on the Moon called 'the man in the Moon' is an impression of the nature spirit's reflection. It is an image of her face that we see looking down on us when we see 'the man in the Moon'.

There is much deeply intuitional imagery in Plath's poem, and there exists no other which so perfectly expresses the sinister nightmare horror of the nature spirit's trauma and sorrow.

When I was 19 or 20, I looked at the full Moon one night and observed 'the man in the Moon' (actually, the image is vague in its suggestion of gender, and reminds me more of a crone than a man). Something startling suddenly happened. The shapes that formed his face rearranged themselves in my mind and became, unmis-takably, the features of a young girl, sweet-faced and gentle, calm and contemplative, with the rumour of an ethereal smile playing over her face. Oak leaves or olive leaves girded her brow, with a jewel at its midpoint where the unicorn's horn chakra resides. There was no doubt that I was gazing on the face of the archetypal Virgin.

Since that night, the clear image has never deserted my vision. I see it on the Moon's face every time she is full, and it is difficult to persuade my mind to rearrange the dark shapes on the Moon's surface so that they once again form 'the man in the Moon'. Even when they do, I can only hold 'his' face in my vision for a moment or two before it reverts to the face of the Virgin. Many people have told me that what I see is 'vision' or 'imagination', but except for the fact that, of course, the dark shapes on the Moon are not literally a face, this is not so. Once the perception has recognized the Virgin, she is undeniably there, just as the more commonly recognized 'man in the Moon' face is also there.

I believe that the deeper reason for my recognition of the 'Virgin in the Moon' is that the Moon is continually confirming that the soul of humanity is still pure, intact and beautiful, if only we will embrace her sweetness and look upon her with wonder again. Four times have we brought her tumbling down from the summit of the pyramid to its earthly base, but still she sails the skies, sweet and serene, smiling down upon us with the eternal love and forgiveness of Divine Mother.

CHAPTER THIRTY-FOUR

Mary's Gift

*W*e might ask who it was that initiated our solar system, who it was that longed for the Earth to come into being and oversaw the project? The only answer must be that it was Divine Intelligence, Goddess-God working through the third principle of the Godhead – Christ or the Divine Child, the Son-Daughter of God – to bring about further aspects of creation. Who but the materialist would deny this? Yet there is more to the story. When a child is longed for by an earthly woman, she responds to an urge that rises from a mystical source within her to her outermost being. She herself, her own longing and response, is part of the equation. Under normal circumstances, no child would be born to her unless she first yearned for and sought impregnation.

This simple scenario leads to a much deeper revelation. Mary Magdalene as the Dragon Queen, so close to the heart of Goddess, had to long for the Earth to be born before the mystery which initiated the Earth's origins could begin with the dynamic which was set up between the star we call the Sun and the feminine mystery within it we call the Moon. It was her longing, her deep mystical desire, which brought about the birth of the Earth and her family, the solar system. The Moon is an expression of her womb.

The Moon is invested with the consciousness of the Dragon Queen and signifies ether, that fifth element purer and more refined than fire – a form of spiritual fire. Venus also perfectly expresses the spirit of the Dragon Queen, and between this beautiful planet, the Moon and the Earth, there exists a spiritual sisterhood, a pyramidal bonding of three. So the Moon is indeed our mother, and planet Earth is of her body. The Moon was Mary's gift to us, the gift of the vast soul known as the Dragon Queen, who came to the Earth in humble human form as Mary Magdalene to teach, bless, heal and inspire the consciousness of the sphere she had inaugurated.

The Moon, embodying the motherhood of Goddess via the Dragon Queen, is also the Soul of the World, the magical emblem of the Soul of Humanity in which our individual souls are combined. When in our foolishness we set in motion those destructive forces which are aroused once we, en masse, cease to follow the light, and thus brought the Moon crashing down from her rightful place at the apex of that pyramid which is the structure of our greater being to its base, the Earth, it was Mary who came to our rescue. Through her auspices, through the fathomless compassion, forgiveness and mercy of Mary or the Dragon Queen who reflects Goddess, the Moon was reborn from the Earth, and, four times over, set sailing in the starry heavens once again.

There is a body of opinion which posits that the Moon is an artificial object and, when one considers its many anomalies and puzzling features, such a conclusion is hardly surprising. The Moon is not, of course, unnatural or artificial in any way, but it was formulated on certain principles so that it could stimulate and nurture Earth life, in particular Earth's humanity. Spiritual engineering was necessary for this purpose in the case of the four Moons which followed the original Moon, although the process was essentially organic and co-operative in that angels and advanced nature spirits who comprise the secret organization within material objects carried out the necessary work. Nevertheless, the work was also directed by human intelligence from the Sphere of John-Shar-On, which is centred in the Pole Star. The Druids, Essenes and other esoteric brotherhoods-sisterhoods comprised the earthly representation of the mystic Sphere belonging to the Pole Star, and the Moon and Venus are also very closely linked with this spiritual centre. The entire Earth project was overseen by Mary. She was its guiding light.

As the Moon is so crucial to the origins of our solar system, why is her true status not recorded in the system of the zodiac, that all-important segmented ring which symbolizes the cycle of our lives and our soul-learning? The Moon is regarded as one of the planets in traditional astrology, and she is placed as the ruler of one of the signs – Cancer, the sidereal constellation or the ecliptic zodiacal tenancy signifying birth, origins and the ocean. So far so good. In the Glastonbury Zodiac (*see* Appendix One), Cancer is depicted as a galleon, the ship which carries the soul into earthly incarnation. Capricorn is the mystical point of ascension from the zodiacal wheel, the Omega, whilst Cancer is the mystical point of entry into it, the Alpha. But even so, the Moon is not bequeathed any status beyond that of the other planets, whilst the Sun is the centre of the universe and rules as supreme Lord of the zodiacal scheme. To assign the Moon her rightful place as supreme Lady in the scheme of things, we must look, not to the solar zodiac, but to the lunar zodiac.

This lunar zodiac is based on the Moon's annual revolutions around the Earth, by means of which the subtler vibrations of the zodiacal signs are reflected upon the soul of humanity. The signs of the lunar zodiac, of course, are the same as the signs of the solar zodiac – with one significant difference. Whilst the solar zodiac has 12 signs, signifying the 12 months of the year through which the Sun makes his annual round or, more correctly, the 12 divisions of the year that it takes the Earth to move around him, the lunar zodiac has 13, because there are (almost) 13 Moon revolutions in a year (approximately 13 periods of 28 days). What is this mysterious, 13th sign, and where does it lie?

It is the sign of Arachne, the Spider. It is situated between Taurus and Gemini, which are ruled by the planets Venus and Mercury, the two higher influences which are associated with the heart, throat, brow and crown chakras, and which seem to form a line of light leading from the heart up through the other three elevated chakras and out of the crown into the region of the starry heavens, or supernal consciousness, a line of light like the spider's cord or thread. This hidden, 13th sign takes its place upon the ecliptic between Taurus and Gemini, fitting into the last 5 degrees of Taurus and the first 23 degrees of Gemini; but its true place in the scheme of the zodiac is in the centre of the zodiacal wheel. Of course, this is where the planet Earth resides, because we see the zodiac as travelling round the Earth. Earth is the zodiacal heart (in the English language, whose deepest origins share a resonance with the first language spoken on Earth, 'heart' is an anagram of 'earth'), and it is in the centre, the throne, that Arachne sits, as if in the heart of her web, which we might see as the starry heavens – the cosmos itself. Arachne herself is a symbol of the Moon, but of course, now we know that the Moon gave birth to the Earth, and that the Earth and the Moon are literally one, this makes perfect sense. She is centred in the Moon/Earth and also in the starry heavens. The three centres are one, as we shall see.

The question arises as to who Arachne is. She is associated with the Spinning Goddesses (of which the Corn Maiden in Virgo, wielding her distaff and representative of Isis, is an example), who feature in almost every mythology and who have been associated in the ancient mystery schools with this veiled, magical 13th lunar sign throughout history. It is interesting that, as well as the idea of creating bodies for the spirit, starting with the soul and continuing through to the outermost or physical body by spinning and weaving 'clothes' or form, the idea of the Spinning Goddess and the mysterious spider also give us the idea of the clew or clue, the silver or silken thread which we follow through the maze of life when we heed the call of the spirit coming to us through our soul, the call which is in itself that clew or silver thread. Ariadne, another Spinning Goddess whose name, literally translated, means 'one who spins', gave Theseus a silken thread or clew to guide him through the Labyrinth when he undertook his quest to kill the Minotaur, or to overcome the elemental forces of the lower self.

Our source advises us that the story of Arianrhod, the Moon Goddess of the British Celts, will yield more of the mystery of the 13th sign than the Greek story of Arachne, after whom the sign has been named. Nevertheless, this must wait for a deeper study, although for the time being we may ponder on the fact that Arianrhod, the Lady of the Silver Wheel, was also associated with spinning. She drove her chariot around the heavens and her silver reins were the threads of light which guided human souls on their life-path back to their spiritual home. Although this spinning emphasis shows that the goddesses related to the Moon and the act of spinning were involved in weaving the destiny of mortals (recording and weaving their karma into their life-path) as well as giving them the guiding clew, it seems that the idea of spinning brings with it an insight into the nature of time. Planets spin, stars spin, and humanity along with them, as we live on the face of the rotating Earth. This concept of the spinning wheel or globe is related to the spinning wheel upon which the spinning goddesses create form from the white ether, the fifth element, and it is related to the cycles of time and the origins of the cosmos. At the heart of it lies the secret of the Dragon Queens.

The story of Arachne tells how she was a mortal maiden who could spin and weave with wonderful dexterity and inspiration. Her particular gift was the art of tapestry, and she took great pride in her creations. The goddess Athene would not believe that a mere mortal was capable of creating something more beautiful than a deity could, so she challenged Arachne to a competition to see which of the two might weave the most enchanting tapestry, the contest to be judged by the gods. Arachne's tapestry was considered by them to be the most beautiful, an outcome which made Athene so angry that she turned Arachne into a spider to punish her for her presumption. Arachne, in despair, hanged herself by her own silken thread, but the gods took pity on her and lifted her up into the starry heavens, bestowing immortality on her and assigning her the task of weaving humanity's karma into the individual tapestry of each life, with its threads of light which guide human souls on their path to the stars.

There is something that this story is not openly declaring. Arachne, tellingly, wove a tapestry for the competition which depicted the storyline pertaining to the 12 signs of the solar zodiac. But she also wove a 13th scene showing Jupiter pursuing Asterie. This goddess was born to Phoebe, daughter of Heaven and Earth (Uranus and Gaia). She (Asterie) gave birth to Hecate and her sister Leto gave birth to Apollo.

This is intriguing, because Apollo and Hecate can be seen as the Sun and the Moon. Hecate is the queen of witchcraft and darkness, but in the sense of things hidden and secret, veiled from the common view, rather than evil. Moreover, Phoebe was also known as a reference to Diana or the Moon. Apollo later took on the name of Phoebus, 'Shining One', in memory of his grandmother. Asterie was pursued by Jupiter until she came to the sea. She threw herself into the waters, and a magical island appeared, where she reigned in the midst of the ocean. This island gave sanctuary to her sister Leto, who came to her sister's haven to give birth to the twins Apollo and Artemis (again, the Sun and the bright Moon).

So Arachne's 13th sign was of a goddess (Asterie) whose name means 'of the starry heavens', whose mother was the bright Moon joining Heaven and Earth (her parents) and whose daughter was the dark Moon (the Moon in its fourth or dark phase when, after waning, it cannot be seen in the heavens for a night or two). Her sister Leto repeats the Sun and Moon theme, giving birth to Apollo (the Sun) and Artemis (the Moon). Asterie herself rules an island amidst the ocean waves.

Arachne clearly knew about the 13th sign, about its power, its mystery, its origins and its destiny. She knew its secrets. She showed it to the gods alongside Athene, who was goddess in a solar-orientated world (the consciousness of the ancient Greeks), and Athene's tapestry, which proved to all present that Athene was not aware of the true mysteries of the Sacred Feminine, and that her own realization of her spiritual mystery and power as an expression of the Sacred Feminine was maimed and constricted compared to that of Arachne. It is this which makes Athene so jealous and angry, to the point where she tears Arachne's work to pieces and turns her into a spider. But the idea of Arachne being taken up by the gods into the starry heavens where she then serves the Moon Mother can have been no unplanned outcome on Arachne's part. The story with its ramificatory threads has already been told in her tapestry.

It seems likely that Arachne purposely sacrificed herself in order to offer herself in service to humanity, working through the power of the Moon and the Sacred Feminine Principle to aid soul ascension. Athene and the solar influences may have held sway at the time, symbolizing the ordinary, everyday consciousness lived at the outer level; but Arachne knew that the time would come when human souls would once again long for their own mysterious depths and vision, seeking spiritual realization and the rays of inner light on the path to their Source, which at present lay in darkness. So she sacrificed her lower, mortal self and ascended to the stars, determined to help others to do the same. It is most interesting, in this sacrificial context, that the Minotaur, the 'bull' of the lower self whom Theseus overcame with the help of Ariadne the Spinning Goddess and her silken thread and who was contained in a maze or a web, was also called Asterius, 'of the starry sky'. In other words, in his two facets he represented the two major initiations of the great adventure of soul ascension: as the minotaur, he indicates the need to attain mastery of the four elements which comprise the base of the pyramid and, as Asterius, the mastery of the Seven Manifestations of Wrath, after climbing whose steps the soul is released through the Moon into the starry heavens – infinite life.

We might say that Arachne's story demonstrates that a 'mere' mortal woman, carrying within her and expressing the Old Knowledge concerning the Sacred Feminine, dared to challenge the male-dominated status quo and offer herself in sacrifice so that a balance might, in part, be restored. Her tapestry showed that she knew a secret which the gods could not deny. The supernatural agents (embodied by Athene, goddess of war) who sought to keep in place the solar imbalance for their own ends reacted in rage and aggression when Arachne so boldly threatened their domain (little to her consternation, as the story recounts that she was very unimpressed with Athene's many warnings not to challenge the goddess's authority).

But the deeper spiritual powers protected Arachne, accepted her sacrifice and granted her wish to serve. Her service was to Mary, who gave us the Earth and who was the true Moon Goddess, the goddess of peace, harmony and perfect balance, initiating the birth of humanity under the auspices of Divine Mother. We might indeed say that Arachne knew a thing or two. In her tapestry scenes depicting the 13 signs of the zodiac, she evoked the stories relating to the signs in such a way as to clearly reveal the unbalanced state of the Masculine and Feminine Principles and the injustices and abuses relating to it.

For instance, in the six portrayals of Jupiter, the dominant male god, he is shown in discreditable situations. As a bull he seduces Europa (Taurus). He pursues Asterie until she is so desperate she plunges into the ocean, the sea of our hidden soul-potential (the 13th sign), to escape him. As a swan he seduces Leda, who bears him twins (Gemini). He assumes the form of a spotted snake (Scorpio), and he seduces the daughter of the river (Aquarius). Of course we cannot judge the gods, those potentialities of the psychic and elemental life forces, in the same way that we judge human behaviour. Nevertheless, these pictures woven by Arachne show that the universal differentials which are the gods are creating unharmonized dramas in the human psyche, because of our human tendency to pursue power-seeking and selfish motives in our lives. They do not reflect the high ideals which are our birthright and our salvation. Even the gods themselves have to bow to the truth, the spiritual light from the one Source, and they elect Arachne as the triumphant 'spinner'. When she has to undergo the infliction of the backlash which is an inevitable result of challenging the dominant powers, the deeper spiritual forces within the gods unite her individual essence with 'the starry heavens', with Asterie herself, who is Queen of the Waters and who is mother to the dark (veiled and hidden) Moon and daughter to the bright Moon. (The Earth became mother to the dark Moon by releasing her in gaseous form, invisible for two years.)

Is Asterie the Earth, Earth's humanity, its consciousness itself, which includes the Moon's relationship with the Earth and the Earth's relationship with the Moon? Mary has told us that the Moon (bright Phoebe) gave birth to the Earth, and then, through drawing the Moon down to Earth (Asterie, as the Earth's soul – the Moon – plunging into the ocean because of the negative force of the unbalanced Masculine Principle, Jupiter, which 'pursued' her? – after all, three quarters of the Earth consists of the oceans), the Earth herself had to give birth to the Moon, although the deep truth that this situation conveyed was kept hidden and secret (Hecate, the dark Moon). To allow the myth to speak to us further, we might say that through spiritual attunement to the Moon (the Earth and the Moon in sisterhood) we would attain the perfect balance of the Sacred Masculine and the Sacred Feminine principles (Asterie's sister giving birth to Apollo and Artemis). This is in line with Mary's teaching, both in her gospel and her teaching of today; for if Asterie is the Earth and the Moon's relationship with the Earth, which we think she truly signifies, then she properly belongs to 'the starry heavens', not only the starry heavens through which the Earth is literally travelling, but the realm of the imperishable stars which is the starscape of spiritual enlightenment and freedom, waiting for the people of the Earth when they are ready to undertake soul ascension and express the Law of Love. It is our supreme destiny and destination. And so Asterie is revealed as, not the literal 'Earth' in our understanding of a physical planet, but the Earth which is the consciousness, the deeper being, the bright soul, of the Earth people – ourselves.

Is there any indication in the 13th sign itself of all this wonder and glory? It seems that there is. Near to the ecliptic, between Taurus and Gemini where Arachne lies, stretches the constellation of Auriga, the Charioteer. Here we begin to understand something of the nature of how Arachne the magical 13th sign, and the Moon, are connected to our soul origins, for in this constellation, which is the con-stellation belonging to Arachne, shine 12 stars, each one representing the 12 signs of the zodiac, the soul-path which must be trodden, its lessons deeply ingested, before we can ascend to the realm of the imperishable stars. In this sense, the entire solar system and Earth's soul consciousness is contained within the sign of Arachne, the sign of the Moon as Supreme Mistress of the cosmos. All is contained within this mystical womb, and all that there is issues forth from it. Arachne is the origin of the other 12 signs, and Auriga, her Charioteer, drives the wheel of the zodiac.

James Vogh, in *Arachne Rising*, the groundbreaking book which unveiled many of Arachne's secrets, asks if the secret of the constellation of the spider is 'a force connected in some way with the elemental forces of the stars?' And in *The Stars and the Chakras*, Joan Hodgson tells us that the Druids and many other ancient broth-erhoods preserved cosmic secrets in their stone circles which we have lost today. The mystical forces of the stars were actually impregnated in the sacred stones of these ancient circles. Many of them are aligned to Capella, 'Little Goat', the bright star in the constellation of Auriga which represents Capricorn in the zodiacal round, the mysterious star-gate through which Jesus and Mary were born onto the Earth and which is known as the Gate of Ascension. Capella has a beautiful crystalline, sometimes pearly, hue, and is a symbol of the Sea-Goat which is also a unicorn and which was venerated as a symbol of wisdom and liberation by those knights who were so intimately involved with the mysteries of Mary – the Knights Templar. A deeper exploration into these mysteries is needed, but for now we may briefly dwell on the importance of Arcturus and Capella.

Arcturus is the fourth brightest star in the heavens, and shines in the constella-tion of Boötes. It is deeply associated with the second ray of Love and Wisdom, one of the great Seven Rays underlying and informing all creation, the ray upon which we receive the spiritual vibration of the Mother, the Moon and the metaphysical essence of water. Arcturus has to do with the heart chakra, and it is sending us the energy of hope – wonderful, blissful hope that smiles in the heart and that cannot be destroyed by the shadows of the material world. Arcturus is shining a beautiful awakening into the patterns of our blood and the water in our bodily cells (which is akin to liquid crystal). It is attuned to Divine Mother and to the cosmic mysteries associated with Mary Magdalene. Arcturus is helping humanity to realize and express Christ Consciousness through the spiritual channel of Mary Magdalene so that we may balance it with the channel we know as Jesus. Arcturus is known as the Star of Gladness.

In *The Chakras and the Stars*, Joan Hodgson tells a truly marvellous story about a vision she had, relating to Capella, which seemed to be a past-life memory. The ceremony in which she took part was held at full Moon during the winter solstice, within a stone circle aligned to Capella. The druidical masters led all those assembled into the Silence, and, as they worshipped, the star Capella seemed to grow much larger and nearer, its rays touching each of the standing stones. Great angelic forms appeared, impregnating the stones with the spiritual energies of the Godhead, Will, Wisdom and Love, emanating from the Little Goat. It seems that the stones held the monumental strength and stability needed to earth these precious and unconscionably powerful spiritual rays, and from their kindly giant strength of containment the Druids were able to utilize the rays according to the capacity of fortification to which the people were attuned. (These rays were a consummate wonder in their essence, but their application required a sound and stalwart spiritual receptivity to withstand their impact.) The rays and the stones created a centre of light arranged like a Grail Cup into which the heavenly forces were poured, and from this centre cords of light arose which connected the consciousness of the people to the consciousness of the stars and planets of the entire cosmos. All knowledge could come to an individual so connected, through the attunement of the crown chakra at the top and in the centre of the forehead, the unicorn's horn of divine intelligence. These powers could also be misused, causing terrible destruction, which was why the lunar magic had to be hidden and suppressed until humanity had progressed beyond selfishness to an awareness of its own innate nobility and divinity.

The Greeks had no knowledge of the thirteenth sign or the lunar zodiac until the Hyperboreans – the British Celts – brought it to them via their priesthood, the Druids, who were so influential in the development of the thought and philosophy of Pythagorus. The Greeks did not fully embrace the Sacred Feminine but they accepted the new (or rather lost) knowledge. It was not stamped out again until after the fall of Arthur (540AD) when it was once more ruthlessly suppressed. If Arachne is the 13th sign, the sign of the Moon as Mistress of the Zodiac, our mother and linked with our soul origins, how is her link with the number eight, the eight-rayed being depicted by the spider and, as we know, indicative of an entire octave – a perfected harmonic or dimension of life – expressed in her sign?

Arachne's number is 13, the 'difficult' or illogical number of which so many people have an unconscious fear. At King Arthur's Round Table, the 13th seat was 'the Perilous Seat', where only the king, or a knight pure and true, could sit with impunity. Any falseness or adulteration in the sitter's soul would strike him dead if he sat on the Perilous Seat ('... You yourselves create (sin) when, as in the nature of adultery, you are unfaithful to your true nature and act within the habit of your corrupt nature ... That is why you become sick, and why you die.' The Gospel of Mary, page. 7, lines 19–26). We think that 13 is a half-symbol, incomplete because it needs the Mystical Marriage to restore it to wholeness. When the Moon broke away from the Sun to give birth to the solar system, her symbol became that of the half-circle, because she had separated the Two (unified) Principles of the Godhead into Night and Day, Feminine and Masculine. As the Soul of the World, a role taken on to birth us individually into supernal consciousness, she became the Mirror, the Reflector, which is the function of the soul.

If we take 13, and let it reflect another 13, we get the symbol ƐI13. If the two ones are pushed together, we get the staff. If the two mirror-opposite threes are pushed together from either side of the staff, we get the caduceus, with the two entwined snakes about it. The two entwined serpents create the number 8 – the Goddess number. The caduceus is the eternal symbol of healing, of opposites united and harmonized. The pyramid, with its base lines running in opposing directions but meeting in a point at the top, unifies division in the same way. When two pyramids, one upright and one downward-pointing, merge into one to form the three-dimensional star, the figure is invested with 6 Soltaire crosses (X) (*see* Appendix Two). It expresses the number 8 three times, and so the sacred 3 is linked with the number 8 via the highly significant structure of the pyramid. This mirror image of 13 making 8 can be carried further. The 1 and the 3 of the two 13s (13 reflecting itself to make a complete image), each add up to 4, which when put together make 8. Twice 13 is 26. 2+6=8, and so on. It is an intriguing game!

Within the number 8 is contained the secret of the Goddess and the secret of the Dragon Queens. It is the number of the Moon, as is 13.

CHAPTER THIRTY-FIVE

Calling Back the Moon

*S*cientists confirm that, in our present age, the Moon is gradually slipping away from the Earth. According to a solar-powered laser planted by the *Apollo 11* rocket in 1969, it is moving away from us at the rate of three centimetres each year. When the Moon gave birth to the Earth in solid form and became hollow, she also diminished in size so that she could enter our orbit (even so, she was much bigger and brighter than our present Moon, as has previously been discussed). This was because the infant souls incarnating onto the Earth in physical bodies needed the care, stimulation and nurture of an ever-present mother.

Although we believe today that we are a very progressive global society, this is not really so at all. We are advised that there are many planetary civilizations so much more advanced than ourselves that we are, in comparison to them, as insect life is to us. We are still infants, we still need the evolutional nurturing of our cosmic mother, but we are driving her away! There is a certain spiritual axis within us around which we are spinning in the wrong direction. We are moving away from the Moon because of our spiritual disorientation and lack of attunement. This throws out forces of negativity which are slowly causing alienation to occur between the Moon and the Earth.

Our source tells us that there cannot be a sixth Moon. There seems to be some correlation here between the number of elements and the possible number of moons that may serve the Earth. We have reached the 'quintessential Moon', and she must be our last. Mary's advice to us now is part of the great healing mission which she and Jesus brought to the Earth. Her teaching is to do with the expression of the Law of Love, with our origins and our connection to the Moon, the great themes of soul ascension. She tells us that we have to attain the point of attunement where our souls can ascend to the Moon, via the Silence, through the vision of the *nous*. Our souls need to connect with the group-soul of the Moon, as it is necessary for us to rise in spirit to the Moon in order to unite with our soul origins and to receive the love, blessing and healing of the Moon and her beings. We might also add forgiveness to this list, although we are already forgiven; but so far we have closed our hearts to the deeper gifts of the Moon, and have received them blindly, ungraciously and unconsciously.

Mary showed us three symbols – a square, a pyramid and a sphere – which were associated respectively with healing, the Silence and vibration. We feel that if those of us who are prepared to serve Mary by doing this work can learn to ascend in our soul state to the Moon (i.e., through the Silence), we will receive a vibration which will bring about healing for humanity. That is why, in the following chapter, we give a ceremony revealed to us by Mary and Tamar, which we can use to attune ourselves, in meditation, to the pure original energies of the Moon. Healing will come to us when we attune to the group-soul of the Moon – the symbol of enlightenment. When we connect with the Moon, we will attune to a beautiful spiritual magnetism which we will be able to give to one another. The key is to give it and share it from the heart, to be willing, like Arachne, to be servers in the great plan of soul ascension for humanity itself.

CHAPTER THIRTY-SIX

The Moon Ceremony

PREPARATIONS FOR THE MOON CEREMONY

A simple and pure ceremony is all that is necessary. If it is not convenient to take a bath before the ritual, wash the hands and face, the inside of the mouth and the feet (just wipe a washcloth over the feet if it is inconvenient to soak them).

It has been brought to our attention that a yellow cloth (of a bright, vivid yellow), clear quartz crystal points and natural white coral laid out on a little dedicated altar are most helpful in attaining attunement with Mary, the great guardian of this work. White coral is a protected species these days, but as it was once given as a luck-bringing gift, you may find a piece in second-hand and antique shops, or at flea-markets or car-boot sales. Nevertheless, if you are unable to procure these things, or would rather not work with any physical 'props', this is perfectly acceptable. All reality is within, and ultimately is not reliant on material objects.

Even so, it is interesting to consider the symbolism of the three items. Cloth, woven and spun with the knowledge which is sacred to the Spider Goddess Arachne, a profound symbol of the Moon and women's mysteries; its yellow colour, indicative of the mind or the psyche, which in its higher element is the soul itself; clear quartz crystal points which are symbolic of the purity and beauty distilled from the underworld, the Sacred Hollows of the Earth with which Mary is so strongly associated (consider her life in the underground caves in St Baume); and white coral, a manifestation of exquisite purity, beauty and grace gleaned from the mysteries of the ocean and the mysteries of death (signifying our Earth lives and, of course, the profound association of the Earth and the Moon, and the three Marys, with the sea).

ASCENDING TO THE MOON

Light a white or a gold candle and place it before you. If this is not possible, take the time to light the candle in imagination.

Using one of the images described in chapter Thirty-one, or some other visualization that you prefer, focus quietly on your breathing and find the *nous*, the point which leads you into consciousness of the light of the spirit. See the six-pointed star blazing with exquisite light in your heart chakra. Walk right into the centre of the star.

You are in your temple. Be aware of the floor and the walls, which are made of pure light. Look towards the altar.

The altar is a white spiral staircase, as if built of alabaster, yet the white substance has radiance in it, and lives. It winds away through the open ceiling of your temple into the starry heavens, where the full Moon hangs, a bright white sphere of magical luminescence. The spiral steps lead right up to the gates of the Moon, which form a great arch of pearly, crystal substance, flashing with jewels of light.

Up the steps you must go to pass through the shimmering gates, but you will not ascend alone. At your right side stands Michael, Archangel of the Sun, coruscating with brilliant light touched with gold. At your left side stands Gabriel, Archangel of the Moon, radiant with a light touched with brightest silver.

Each angel gently takes your hand, Michael your right and Gabriel your left, and guides you to the bottom of the staircase which forms the altar of the temple.

As you feel the touch of their angelic hands, you sense two beautiful currents of light rising from your heart, as if they were two plumes of perfume from the rose in your centre ascending your spine to your brow chakra, which now glows with a clear rose light. The current on the right is fostered and blessed by Archangel Michael, and is called Pingala; the current on the left is fostered and blessed by Archangel Gabriel and is known as Ida.

Feel these currents rising from your heart come together in your third eye, making your brow chakra radiant.

Feel yourself gently beginning to ascend, supported on each side by Michael and Gabriel. Your ascension is calm and serene, as if you were a feather floating on the breath of the Great Spirit.

Settle with grace upon the top stair, which lies before the threshold of the gates of the Moon. Michael and Gabriel are still with you, but they are now within you. Their presence remains, but they are invisible.

Focus once more on your breathing. As you breathe in peace and utter stillness, the gates will open. Take a little time and float gently on the magical rhythm of your breath.

The gates open, dissolving like mist. Walk inside.

This is the temple of the Moon. It is the Sphere of Silence.

Enter deeply into the Silence. Continue to focus on your breath. From the heart of the Silence, something is rising. It is a prayer.

Say the prayer:

I pray to Divine Mother and her angels, in the name of Mary the Great
One, in the name of the Christ, that I may by the Law of Love connect
with the Great Soul of the Moon, and enter into harmony with her
people.

As you breathe, focus on the silvery beams of the Moon. Breathe the peace and the beauty that flow from the Moon directly into your heart so that they begin to fill your greater being. Blend with the mighty magnetism of the Moon, blend with her rays of purest white light, feeling your mind and your soul fill with the flow of her infinite peace, her radiant beauty, and her all-encompassing love. Blend your soul with hers, and feel your spirit expand in the bliss of her embrace. Blend with the being of the Moon in the temple of your heart.

As you do this, feel your crown centres (one at the top of the forehead in the middle, one below the centre of your scalp) glowing with this perfect light, the light of the marriage of the Sun and the Moon, the light of the power of universal love. See the delicate rainbow colours hidden in the pure white light, pearlized angel colours, pour over your whole being in a rainbow fountain.

Now follows the part of the ceremony where you are enfolded deep, deep into the heart of the Moon, into the inestimable love of Divine Mother, and no method or ceremony can intrude. Go within, where the sacred Moon will unite you in loving brotherhood with the Moon beings and the origins of your soul.

When you emerge from this profound communion, the gentle Moon mother will have given you a blessing, and also a special power of blessing. Use this power to bless all humanity, holding it as a point in the heart of the Star, which blends the light of the Sun and the Moon, the white and the gold. Know that this Star is also your own heart as it is the heart of the universe.

Give forth the blessing in a great starburst of light from the heart-centre, yet let it be emitted tranquilly, in a calm and serene sea of peace. Let the blessing form the sacred shape of the six-pointed star. Remember that the point of the ceremony is to sound the note of love, for love is the heart, and the whole, of the teaching that Jesus and Mary brought to us.

Gently return to the mundane world, sealing each centre with the silver cross in a ring of light, and using your breath and the seven circles of spiralling light (from the left foot upwards) to root you into the Earth, seeing the head of the spiral of light descend like a rod of light through the chakras and down into the ground as soon as it has encircled your crown chakra.

*　　*　　*

Little ceremonies under the Moon, where you breathe in and blend with its rays, following the steps of the ceremony in a simple way, are also helpful, as are moments of contemplation upon the Moon, considering her huge importance to us as mother and nurturer, and as Mary's marvellous gift to us. Offer the Moon your love and honour her presence.

These short and simple ceremonies will help beginners in their efforts to meditate. The magnetism of the Moon herself aids us in absorbing and attuning to meditative energy. To guard against disorientation, always seal your chakras afterwards and, before commencing, see beautiful strong roots, like those of a great sturdy tree, growing from the soles of your feet and snaking far down into the heart of the Earth, where they find repose and absolute stability. To perform the ceremony in its entirety, try to select the night of the full Moon or a waxing (growing) Moon rather than the waning (diminishing) Moon, although, because this is a spiritual rather than a psychic ceremony, no condition is necessary other than heart-centredness and purity of intention.

Each time you perform the Moon-blending ceremony, either in full or in simplified form, you are helping to reawaken humanity's consciousness of its Soul, the Soul which, beautiful and radiant as the Moon, will reflect the light of the Spirit more and more into Earth life, until from shore to shore, from east to west and north to south, humanity will begin at last to fully express the Law of Love. When this joyful day dawns, the great Healing Mission of Jesus and Mary, initiated by them with such love and self-sacrifice so long ago, will finally be fulfilled.

In Memory of Margaret Ada, Dorothy and Kelly

The Camelot Connection

Prior to Margaret Bailey's first communion with Mary, she was led to Glastonbury, where a profound revelation was given to her which helped her to perceive the direct links between the history of Jesus and Mary's life in Palestine, Mary's arrival in Britain and the eventual rise of King Arthur and Camelot.

This revelation came to Margaret Bailey in the Lady Chapel in Glastonbury Abbey, England, contiguous to an area known as 'Galilee'. When we came to write our book, we received the intuition that Galilee and Glastonbury reflected one another, and that the waters of the pools of Glastonbury (then known as Avalon) and the waters of the lake or inland sea known as the Sea of Galilee were anciently considered to be holy waters, becoming so again when they were used in baptismal rites presided over by Jesus in Galilee and Mary in Avalon. We were excited to discover that the name Galilee means a moving ring or a turning wheel, and that the name Glastonbury can be interpreted as 'glass-castle' or 'crystal-castle', linking it to the revolving crystal castle of Ahrianrod, the Celtic star goddess who is associated with spinning and spiders and the number eight, all of which are Magdalene symbols.

The revolving crystal castle seemed to indicate our home, the Earth, a stable and fortified environment spinning on its axis in the cosmos and mirroring the starry heavens. Although the crystal castle of the British mysteries must also surely represent the reflective qualities of the soul, we were assured by Mary that Glastonbury itself could be considered as Heaven's Looking Glass or Heaven's Mirror. Shortly afterwards, we learned of the existence of the Glastonbury Zodiac, a great circle of ten miles across, laid out on the land itself, its zodiacal symbols sculpted by the mystic hand of nature and bearing traditional names which corroborate their identity.

At the crossover point between Pisces (the age of Jesus and Mary whose avatars they were) and Aquarius (the age we are currently entering) stands Glastonbury Abbey, built on the site of the first church to be raised in the name of the Christ. 'Kirk' or 'church' and 'circle' have a common root, and in considering this fact and its relation to the Glastonbury zodiacal circle, we were reminded of the Ring Dance of Jesus and his Apostles as recorded by St Augustine of Hippo, who presented it in his writings in every detail, exactly as it was given in the second-century Acts of John. In this dance, Jesus instructed the 12 disciples to form a ring and to link hands and dance around him, whilst he, in their midst, sang a hymn and created rhythm with

a sequence of chanting. The ring-dancing disciples responded with frequent into-
nations of 'Amen' ('so be it') on appropriate beats.

This wheeling dance, originating in ancient Egypt and comprising a healing or
integrating ceremony to impart wholeness of spirit, was initiated by Jesus shortly
before the dramatic events leading to his crucifixion began to unfold. Surely it was
an expression of the cosmic dance of the planets of the solar system around their
central sun, and of the wheel of the stars around that great central sun which vision-
aries and esotericists say is the radiant heart of the entire universe, reflecting the
eternal circle of light wherein all truth, justice and wisdom are to be found and
whose turning is a perpetual act of divine love.

Here we find the clue as to why it is so significant that 'Galilee' means 'a wheel
in motion', why 'Glastonbury' is a 'revolving crystal castle' and the 'Looking Glass of
Heaven', and why the first 'church' or circle dedicated to the Christ Being was raised
between Pisces and Aquarius within the ring of the ancient zodiac of Glastonbury
in Britain, the 'mystic isle'. The zodiacal ring, the turning wheel of stars, is the
heavenly ring within which our human consciousness is fostered, and we predict
that eventually esoteric astrology, which unveils its profundities (not the popular
rendition of it to which nowadays it has been reduced), will come to be considered
in the light of one of the major scientific disciplines. And yet, it seems that, even in
spite of the tradition of esoteric astrology, through the aeons we have lost the true
apperception that humanity itself and the stars are as one, and that human consciousness is an emanation of the mystical starlight.

This is the remembrance to which the teachings of Mary Magdalene seek to
reawaken us – that we are connected to the stars in our deepest essence as well as in
our constitution at the biological level of reality. There is a star shining within each
human heart and radiant upon each human brow which will dispel all shadows, all
confusion, all disharmony, and serve as infallible and undeniable proof that we are
all one, brothers and sisters linked together in the eternal dance of life who have,
through its medium, the natural capacity to geometrize exquisite formations of
creative joy. It is the most important teaching of the sacred zodiacal ring, the Holy
Twelve dancing around the central point of light which purifies and perfects their
consciousness. Mary will teach us to dance that dance of creative joy.

Mary's teachings on the chakras, those energy points within our own body
which simultaneously link us to the mystical emanations of the stars and to the
starlight within our own hearts which is divine consciousness, are secreted within
the confines of the breathtaking star temple that is the Glastonbury Zodiac. The first
stage of their unfolding is given in this book.

The establishment of Camelot (meaning 'curved light' or 'ring of light') upon
the Earth was an objectified expression of this star temple, the one which truly
exists within higher consciousness. King Arthur and his true consort (not

Guinevere), who because of obstacles placed in her way could be with him only in spirit, sat at the Round Table as the conjoined central sun, the 12 most famous knights comprising the 12 signs of the starry zodiac placed around this Christ-blessed pairing. Their aim was to live in brotherhood and self-sacrifice, led always by the light of the soul and the spirit, the true teachings of Jesus and Mary Magdalene. Their principles were starlit and keen as a sword, and their quest was heart-centred living – the Holy Grail, and the nourishing, vivifying mystery it contained.

The 'Holy Twelve' (the number of the perfect circle or ring) first came to Glastonbury as the disciples of Christ under the protection of Joseph of Arimathea, and their esoteric symbolism points to the revelation that there are actually 12 major chakras (and a hidden 13th) within the structure of human consciousness (so far we are conscious of only 7), waiting to be activated and to conduct the heavenly starlight into every aspect of our lives individually and corporately as they are expressed here below. This was the divine aim of Camelot, the New Jerusalem, the Celestial City come down to Earth. With regard to the five new chakras we are to develop, Mary has revealed that the chakras in the palm of each hand are of maximum importance, for we work, create, communicate through gesture, build, heal and caress with our hands. Developing the proper use of these chakras will bless, balance and make whole almost everything we do.

Was Camelot established only around Cadbury Hill and Glastonbury? This was its mystical heart, but the web of energy extended to Cornwall, to Wales, to Scotland, to Ireland, to France and to Brittany and other key places, ever expressing a 'seven' rhythm in harmony with the number of active chakras in the human body which would eventually have transmuted into that of 'twelve-thirteen', the esoteric dimensions of the sacred circle with the dot in the middle – the sigil of All That Is – coming forth from the Mother-Father Creator. Camelot, the faithful reflection of *Sarras* or 'Star City', the mythical wonder spoken of in the Grail legends, would eventually have mirrored itself in numerous foci across the Earth, sustained by the Holy Breath whose temple was Glastonbury or (anciently) Avalon. The result would have been a joyous, united planetary civilization expressing the principles of unalloyed brotherhood.

King Arthur's consort (she who was *not* Guinevere) was obscured and denounced and the brave mission was doomed to failure; but not real failure, because Mary Magdalene is bringing to us once again the vision that was lost, and every opportunity to realize it that humanity has abused in its bloody and woebegone past will be fully restored to us. And Camelot has by no means yet yielded up all its secrets and all its gifts. Its relevance is eternal, and Margaret Bailey and I have been promised that its hidden mysteries will be 'revealed to this generation'.

Mary Magdalene, intimately linked with the mystery of King Arthur and Camelot, and whose teachings are expressed in the design of the Glastonbury Zodiac, is associated with the phoenix, the dying-and-rising bird who shows us that, even though death on every level of experience appears to reduce us to ashes, in truth it has no dominion. The sign for Aquarius marked out on the Glastonbury Zodiac incorporates Glastonbury Tor and forms the effigy of, not the water-bearer in this instance but rather, a great bird in flight, enfolding Glastonbury in its wings. It is a dual symbol of a phoenix and an eagle: in one sense, Mary Magdalene and Jesus (Jesus is often envisioned as a hawk in carols, poems and images relating to the Christ mysteries); in another, Mary Magdalene and her brother John, whose sign is the white eagle, telling as if in bardic song of the coming of the new age of Aquarius, the New Age which Jesus prophesied, the Age of John and Mary Magdalene, and of another, whose story is yet to be told.

The head of the phoenix-eagle is Glastonbury Tor, indicating the divine consciousness of the Aquarius bird. Archaeologists consider that the tor itself was constructed by human hands, perhaps by Sumerians who lived in Britain several thousand years ago, although our sources reveal that the entire Glastonbury Zodiac is considerably more ancient. Here, indeed, is a model of a Chaldean ziggurat, its seven terraces tracing the Seven Manifestations of Wrath or the seven steps to perfection as they are outlined in Mary's gospel. Although the tor is its head, it is from here that the Aquarius bird takes wing – our soul freed and perfected, guided to its liberty by Mary's teachings which reflect the light of the Christ. And at the eighth level, the squaring of the circle by the sacred 4-4 which denotes perfection, there stands upon Glastonbury Tor the immaculate symbol of the Tower, the sign of Goddess and the image which correctly translates the name 'Magdalene' – the Tower, the Magnificent, the All.

Mary's Secret Sign and the Mystery of the Chakras

A secret sign indicating the deeper mystery of Mary Magdalene occurs on ancient manuscripts and on paintings and artefacts relating to her. It is the Soltaire, the X-shaped cross, revealed to St Andrew one day as he meditated in prayer upon blue skies, although this sacred symbol preceded St Andrew's era by untold aeons. It is the esoteric emblem of the Sacred Feminine Principle, the V or the Chalice reflecting itself in the waters of the soul – the mirrored pyramid.

It waits for the moment when the reflected reality (the upward-pointing pyramid with its base set on the earth, which represents human consciousness dwelling in matter), through an act of free will, love and wisdom, reaches up to the descending pyramid or V and allows itself to be penetrated. Thus the higher melds with the lower, the little nature of earth is subsumed into Divine Being and Christ consciousness occurs. The conjoinment of the two pyramids creates the mystic inner Star, the six-pointed Star which has no inner divisions, sign and symbol of the Aquarian Age. Intriguingly, the usual state of things is reversed in order to bring the Star into being, because the feminine V penetrates from above and the masculine Λ, the 'blade', becomes receptive.

When the Star is visualized in three dimensions, the sacred X appears on every facet. It is not a double V as at first it seems, but a four-square V, the base from which the mystery of the pyramid rises. It is the sign of the Soul of the World, the soul of humanity as represented by Mary Magdalene, whose image has been divided and dismembered by the blindness of the world but whose true being cannot be violated.

Virginal in the sense that she is inviolable, her essence of light invincible and impenetrable by the forces of darkness and ignorance, she is both spirit and its emanation – soul or purified consciousness which is First Thought, First Body, First Matter, matter pure and lovely in its descent as a projection from the Godhead, a perfect and exquisite receptacle for the mystic flame of Spirit. This beautiful matter is indeed soul itself, a sublime mirror which faithfully reflects the radiant spirit. When matter on its designated downward spiral is allowed by the arrogance of the human mind (which is the lower aspect of the soul) to fall into unconsciousness of its true self, it ceases to reflect the light of the soul and the spirit (for the soul gives forth light in the same way as the Moon). Then it becomes dark and full of confusion and, no longer able to see the Godhead, conceives a passion or love for itself. This self-love fuels the drive towards self-gratification and the mind of materialism, and all the ills that flesh is heir to begin to manifest.

The concept of this 'passion for itself' to which unenlightened matter gives birth (in the words of Mary's gospel) is what the ignorance of the world seized upon and held up as the alleged identity of Mary Magdalene throughout the centuries since her essence, her teachings and her truth were deliberately repressed and harlotized. It is the biggest lie of the last two millennia, an exact reversal of the reality, for the mystical being within the essence of Mary Magdalene is the personification of the unity of matter most bright and beautiful – the soul – and the ineffable spirit. She is the Lost Bride of which all secrets whisper, the obscured partner in the Mystical Marriage of the two fused human souls who made of themselves such perfect vehicles that they were able to bring the Christ to Earth. And because her image in the mirror of our consciousness has been veiled for so long, humanity has been unable to see its true reflection and thereby integrate and heal itself.

The great symbol of the Soul of the World as represented by the X is spoken of by Plato when in his tract *Timaeus* he refers to the two 'Great Circles' of the zodiac and the celestial equator. There are two zodiacs, one making an imaginary circle just above the Earth as though she wore a crown or a circlet (the ecliptic or the celestial equator) and the other a circle of star formations around the Earth which is much vaster than the little ring of the ecliptic. They can be likened to a small wheel within a big wheel.

The obliquity of the big-wheel zodiac (its calculation is 23 degrees to the plane of the equator) causes it to intersect with the celestial equator in the form of an interconnecting X. This X conjoins what we might call the heart-circle of the Earth (the ecliptic or celestial equator) with the starry, big-wheel zodiac. This is another reason why the X is associated with Mary Magdalene. It is the mystic sign that connects us to the stars, the Soul of the World suspended in the heavens and linking the Earth via purified ethereal matter (the Soul itself) to the wheel of the stars, symbol of the fiery light of the spirit. What more perfect realization of Mary Magdalene's true essence could there be than this?

We might think of the zodiacal ring within which human consciousness is fostered as the Star Temple or the World Soul, for the body or structure which contains the fiery spark of Spirit, destined to become a great and powerful Star within the heart of each one of us, is indeed the soul. At this moment in human development, the soul and the spirit have seven active chakras or centres with which to work. These are located in the physical body but actually link the material plane with the spiritual dimension. The seven chakras are associated with the seven rays of creation. The number of the zodiacal circle is 12, with its 13th point – the

Earth/Sun (the body containing the soul and the flame of spirit) – in the centre. Eventually, 12 chakras will become active. It also seems that a mysterious, hidden chakra, of which we presently know nothing, will also bring its secret forces to play within the innermost sanctuary of our being. Could this be a second and even deeper heart chakra than the one we use today? The idea of two heart chakras is already abroad, and as the crown chakra has two centres, and the heart and the crown chakras are of such sublime significance, and so deeply connected, it would seem to make sense that the heart should also have two. Just as is the case with the two crown chakras, the two heart chakras would surely reflect one another as two expressions of a mysterious unity, a Divine Oneness. It is interesting in this context that the New Testament phrase 'Only-Begotten Son' is more correctly translated as 'Child of the Oneness', an expression of the Oneness of the Godhead which yet contained its two aspects – Divine Father and Divine Mother. And so we see that the (possible) double heart chakras and the double crown chakras are an expression of Jesus and Mary Magdalene, or the Spirit and the Bride.

The important link between the number 7 and the numbers 12 and 13 is worth considering in the light of those chakras which are presently active in humanity (they can even be photographed!) and those which are waiting to be activated. We might meditate on the number 12 as the sacred number of the circle, with its 13th point as its centre, the mystic dot within the circle which is a timeless ideograph of creation and its Creator. From the dot within the circle come forth the 7 rays of creation, so the connection between 7, 12 and 13 is mysterious and holistic. In the spiritual science of numbers (numerology), 12 is an expression of 3 (1+2=3) containing 4 threes, and 13 is an expression of 4 (1+3=4), bringing us back to the sacred 8 or 4-4, which squares the circle. The energy pattern of 7 expresses in its completeness the numbers 3 and 4 (12 and 13 in another guise) because it is most perfectly divided by 3 and 4 (3+4=7). Therefore, 7 is an expression of 12 and 13 and will eventually manifest them.

This gives us an insight into why the mysteries of the 7 chakras are contained within the Glastonbury Zodiac as well as its 12 naturally occurring effigies, and why a complete understanding and application of Mary's teachings concerning them will help us to activate the remaining 5 (or 6) chakras.

It is interesting to consider that a well-known mathematician, who is actually able to perceive numbers as visionary expressions of specific qualities, sees the number 8 as a sign denoting water (the waters of life?). He sees the number 9, which is the ultimate expression of 3 and is also connected with the Moon and Mary Magdalene, as a monumental, overpowering number which is intimidating to the uninitiated – a number whose imagistic portrayal suggests a mighty tower.

The Ring of Hares

Immediately prior to Margaret Bailey's first conscious communion with Mary Magdalene, a symbol concerning the Sacred Feminine began to present itself to thousands of seers and spiritually attuned people across the world. They saw in their inner vision the emblem of three hares pursuing one another in a ring, their ears forming a pyramidal shape above the circle they created.

The appearance of the symbol of the ring of three hares directly prior to the event of Mary Magdalene's complete gospel and her secret teachings being given to the world is surely no coincidence. From east to west across the globe the hare is a sacred animal. In Buddhism, particularly that of China and Tibet, and in Celtic mysticism, the hare is revered as a sign of good hope, new beginnings and bountiful blessing. Mary Magdalene's special connection with Celtic mysticism and the Buddhist wisdom which her gospel reflects, as well as her direct link with the Great Mother Goddess who is symbolized by the hare, associates her unmistakably with the ring of hares. Moreover, the shape of a running hare can be discerned upon the face of the Moon, that mystical sphere which is the gift to Earth's humanity of the greater soul who took simple human form as Mary Magdalene in first-century Palestine.

We believe that the ring of hares especially depicts the pyramidal group of the three Marys, represented again by the three pyramids at Giza and their alignment to the three stars of Orion's belt and their association with the famous Great Triangle formed by the three bright stars Procyon, Betelgeux and Sirius. The three Marys, as the three hares, create the Orbit of Sharon, a spiritual sphere connected with the starry heavens whose mysteries are reflected in the beautiful teachings on the chakras which Mary has imparted to us.

Although the celebration of spring has long been marked by the application of special colours and symbols to eggs, Mary Magdalene is particularly associated with the giving and receiving of symbolic eggs at Eastertide. After the Crucifixion and her subsequent removal to her temple in Alexandria so that she could safely give birth to Tamar, Mary travelled to Rome with Joseph of Arimathea in one of his merchant ships in order to seek an audience with Emperor Tiberius, who had retired to Capri but at this time was on one of his occasional visits to the capital. She set sail in the early spring of 35AD, leaving her little daughter in the charge of her devoted friend and attendant, Sarah. Her mission was to reach the heart of Tiberius, who was a tyrannical emperor, and, to some extent, restore his soul. She also sought to sow a seed whereby the mighty Roman Empire, ruled by 'the prince of this world' – a world-view in harmony with the drives and desires of materialism – would eventually bend its haughty knee to the inner Christ, to the true life within the heart of humanity. The process certainly began after she had completed her mission. Some may say it never hit its mark, but it is important to bear in mind that that same process is still ongoing, and that its story is indeed not yet over. Worldliness and self-seeking values as symbolized by Rome and Caesar will one day be overcome by the enlightenment of the Christ within, and we believe that the arrival of that day is not far off.

When Mary Magdalene was ushered into the presence of the powerful and laconic emperor, she greeted him with the gift of a goose egg, explaining that it was an emblem of the Resurrection, and telling him of how Jesus had risen from death. Emperor Tiberius was touched by the sweet charisma of this beautiful and dignified woman who spoke with such quiet and gentle authority, but the legend tells us that he was unable to believe in the miracle of the Resurrection. He remarked to Mary that her story was as impossible as it would be for the egg that she offered him to suddenly turn red, upon which it became permanently suffused with a beautiful crimson colour before his eyes.

This miracle was similar to the one which Jesus performed with his mother at Cana, wherein the water was turned to wine. As on that occasion, the presence of the Sacred Masculine and the Sacred Feminine principles working in perfect unity was necessary for the spiritual truth of the life-blood of Christ, of the cosmos, to be revealed in physical actuality. In this instance, Mary Magdalene the feminine Christ worked the miracle with the aid of her beloved kinsman, Joseph of Arimathea, the Bridesman – he who cared for the Bride. It is appropriate to mention here that the pyramidal group of the three Marys, as symbolized by the three hares, was counter-balanced by the pyramidal group of Jesus, John the Beloved Disciple, and Joseph of Arimathea.

The heart of the emperor was pierced, his soul was enlightened, and the seed was sown. He soon fell into a decline and died (some historians say he was murdered) less than two years later, which was an objectification of his symbolic act of letting go of his worldly power and the source which fed it. Mary returned to Alexandria with Joseph, her mission of mercy accomplished. Although the dragon of the Roman Empire was roused into greater fury by the sowing of this seed, so that Mary Magdalene and her family, the disciples and Joseph of Arimathea's close kin had to flee to Europe soon afterwards, Mary remained sure and certain in her faith that eventually – perhaps in a little over 2,000 years' time – that same seed, planted in the heart of worldliness, would bear glorious and miraculous fruit.

The Gothic Arch

In *The Coming of the Angels* by Geoffrey Hodson, the author gives an unrivalled description of a teaching on the Gothic Arch imparted to him by angels. The Knights Templar initiated the establishment and the Gothic architecture of many of the great cathedrals of Europe, building them as soaring celebrations in stone of the Sacred Feminine and of the ineffable Mystery enacted in flesh by Jesus and Mary Magdalene. The following angel teaching tells us why the Templars, the original Night-Protectors who were linked to the esoteric order of the Children of Solomon (whose knowledge similarly guided the erection and design of Solomon's Temple) chose to express their homage and their spiritual messages to posterity in grand Gothic style.

> The two angels then began to 'converse'. In the upper portion of the blue angel's aura appeared a number of small glowing spheres arranged in three concentric semi-circles above his head. Each sphere was encircled by a broad white band, somewhat like the rings of Saturn in shape and position, and was spinning, with its axis inclined like that of the earth. A golden glow then rose from the region of the angel's heart and suffused the upper portion of his aura. The number of the spheres gradually increased, but without changing colour, which in the upper hemisphere was deep rose and pale yellow, whilst the lower half was a deep gold. Gradually the brilliance of the golden glow increased until it was almost blinding and the angel's form was hidden by it, as were also the original spheres; these were replaced by white spheres arranged in lines to produce various geometrical forms.
>
> One of these consisted of two wing-shaped figures, composed of four blades at right angles, like the feathers of a dart. These came to a point behind the angel's shoulders at a spot where conventional wings would be attached to a body. This design was followed by a large five-pointed star, perfectly formed, which in its turn changed to a circle round which the points of the star were arranged as triangular radiations like a conventional symbol of the sun. For the time being the teaching angel remained standing as a passive spectator, though his face was irradiated

with an expression of vivid and intelligent response.

The symbols now began to change with a rapidity quite beyond the author's power to grasp or to record. In fact this whole lesson presents extreme difficulties to the author's clairvoyant, recording, and literary powers. The result of his best efforts in these three directions are here offered, but he knows them to be inadequate.

Suddenly a further and marked change occurred. The angel's head and shoulders were once more revealed, surrounded by a clear and beautiful azure blue, his own natural colour. In this a number of small silver balls appeared, dancing and quivering like a glorious living headdress of pearls. The teaching angel also arranged a similar display in his aura, and the spinning spheres, each the size of a tennis ball, began to pass backwards and forwards between them with great rapidity and in large numbers. As they travelled, they created lines of light, which remained to mark their track. The two angels were thus linked by a system of connected geometrical forms of increasing complexity produced by the backward and forward movement of the spheres. They themselves somewhat resembled celestial jugglers keeping a hundred or more balls in the air at one time. There was, however, a definite system in the arrangement of the figures and in the relative position of the spheres at any time.

Suddenly all the balls rushed in a rising curve towards the centre, where they met and turned directly upwards in a stream; this movement then ceased, and the balls, together with the lines of force which marked their path, were united to form a beautifully proportioned Gothic pillar a silvery pearl-grey in colour, like some polished stone or marble on the outside, whilst a rich deep blue filled the hollow vault within. The silver balls took the place of gargoyles and other Gothic ornaments, while others danced in the air.

Slowly the pillar rose. Streams of coloured force flowed from the heads of the two angels to a point midway between, and from ten feet above their heads. They met directly under the base of the pillar, which they joined as if to support it. These streams were curved into a perfect Gothic arch, with the angels' bodies providing the uprights on which it rested.

The angels themselves then rose slowly into the air, bearing the pillar aloft and maintaining the perfect proportion and shape of the form which they had built. They rose to such a height that they appeared like two glowing stars, connected and crowned by a third, which was the pillar. They sang as they ascended, and other angel voices were heard chanting a hymn to the Deity to whose Altar beyond the author's ken was borne the votive offering which they had constructed in this classic Gothic design.

*   *   *

It is evident that there is a deep spiritual significance in the Gothic style of architecture, something of which was discovered when later the angel explained the day's lesson.

The fundamental idea behind the angel's communication was to display, and discourse upon, the relationship between the Logos and His system. This appears to be a favourite subject of meditation and discourse among the members of the higher levels of the angelic ranks. As on this occasion, such conversations frequently include a dramatic and symbolic enactment of the subject under discussion by one or more members of the gathering.

The blue angel had begun by representing himself as the Logos surrounded by His planets supported within his aura. The colour blue typified the early or virginal stages of manifestation, as did also the fact that the globes, though spinning, were stationary in space.

The angel then passed into a condition of meditation in which he endeavoured to unify himself with the Divine Mind so closely that the further symbolic expression of the subject would be ordered by It, rather than himself. Success in this endeavour produced a change of colour, and his aura became flooded with golden yellow, which completely veiled his face and shoulders. This symbolised the fact that he, as an individual actor, had temporarily disappeared. Under the influence of the power which he had contacted, the spheres, representing the globes of the system, began to move and their colour to change to a silvery, pearl-like hue. The Logos proceeded to 'play' with His heavenly 'toys', forming them into numberless geometrical patterns, each one represent- ing a fundamental spiritual verity or material scientific principle in Nature and evolving naturally from its predecessor.

As the Logoic morn passed on to midday, the sun itself appeared as the central glory of the universe and the globes arranged themselves as the rays which emanate from its effulgent splendour. Doubtless each triangle represented a scheme or chain of planets.

At this point the teaching angel joined in the discourse, agreeing to all that had been enacted by rapidly reproducing it within his own aura. He, however, played the part of the female aspect of the Logos, the receptive, gestatory principle in Nature. The process of balancing these two principles was then enacted, the spheres passing between the two actors as if in some celestial game of tennis. Many symbols were formed by this passage of the spheres and the line of force along which they travelled, each symbol representing a stage in the evolution of the solar system.

Gradually all the spheres were set in motion, held within the play of the positive and negative aspects of the Logos, till at last perfect equipoise was attained. As that culmination was reached the spheres gradually came to rest between the two angels, and the play of force between them gradually outlined the shape of another symbol of deep significance, that of the Gothic arch and pillar. This style of architecture was evidently intended to be a representation, in all its wonderful variety of decoration and embellishment, of the perfect product of the interplay of these two aspects of the divine life. The pillar rose, like the towering steeple of some medieval church, supported, as it had been formed, by the combined life of the two angel representatives of the Logos, who, standing perfectly still and upright, their arms at their sides, represented the walls upon which roof, tower and steeple were supported. Then, bearing this beautiful form aloft, they offered it on some angel altar on high.

The angel explained that the Gothic style expresses many fundamental truths, for it was partly inspired from the angelic kingdom, with which many medieval artists and architects were in contact. Despite the unreality of the paintings of angels of that and other periods, they represented the best of which the artists of the day were capable, and their inspiration was real in spite of their relatively low level of craftsmanship. Their visions were subjective rather than objective, for few of them led the life which would make the latter possible. In translating their visions they lost the sense of freedom, vividness, and ethereal beauty, as well as the non-human characteristics, of the angels, who played an important part in human affairs at the period of the Renaissance, and did much to stimulate the progress of learning and the growth of art.

The Secret of the Antioch Chalice

Whilst checking some details towards the completion of this book relating to the nineteenth-century American physician, Mary Jacobi, I came across a photograph of the Silver Chalice of Antioch, which appeared on the opposite page. As I studied its details I was struck with astonishment, because the figures it depicted seemed to tell, right before my eyes, the story that we have revealed in the foregoing chapters.

This silver chalice is an intricately designed and superbly crafted vessel dating from the first century, and was discovered in Antioch, Syria, borne there perhaps by Paul the Apostle, whose mission had connections with the city. A legend associated with it is that Joseph of Arimathea specially commissioned the creation of the chalice to commemorate the occasion of the Last Supper. Our intuitive investigation into this legend revealed a fascinating story.

According to our sources, Joseph of Arimathea did indeed commission the silver chalice. The work was entrusted to Joseph, the brother of Jesus. This brother was the love child of Joseph the father of Jesus. He had been born to a woman whom Joseph, for some reason pertaining to a form of tribal taboo, could not marry. Joseph the father's feelings of guilt concerning this matter, and his uneasiness regarding its impact on Mary the mother of Jesus, whom he met and married after this incident and whom he preferred to cherish instead of his former love, conspired to create emotional difficulties within him which led him to ignore the existence of his first son. As he grew up, Jesus took great pains to do all in his power to heal this unhappy situation, becoming very close to his half-brother and visiting him frequently, even though he had to travel many miles on foot to do so.

Joseph, the brother of Jesus, was a metal-worker by trade, and was well known to Joseph of Arimathea, Jesus's great-uncle, who of course was the Nobilis Decurio, the grand minister of metal mining. This link between the God-man and a metal-worker is continually affirmed throughout myth. Vulcan, the Smith, works alongside Zeus. Wayland, the elven metal-smith of Arthurian legend, serves Arthur the king and crafts Excalibur for his use, forging it from the most precious treasures and secrets of the Earth, which is his element. Brigid, the pure and exalted goddess of ancient Britain and Ireland is also a 'Smith-Woman', overseeing the Forges of Destiny. These are only a few examples of this deeply significant theme.

The craftsman or woman working alongside the deity is identified in mystical thinking as the 'Demiurge', literally, 'the craftsman'. Some traditions cite him as the 'Devil', but, more wisely, he may be seen as representative of the midpoint between pure spirit and the realm of the physical cosmos, connecting the two. He is a personification of the *nous* (*see* The Gospel of Mary in Part II) and, of course, symbolically, he is guardian of 'the treasure' that Jesus speaks of as residing at this sacred point. As his whole task is one of objectification, the craftsman's treasure is literal – the precious metals and gems of the interior of the Earth – the 'essence within'.

The Demiurge is subject to 'the cosmic powers and authorities' which Paul spoke of as being discarded by Jesus on the cross 'as a garment'. If he follows the light of Christ, the Demiurge becomes a light in himself. If he chooses to ignore the divine light, he becomes blind, like Bartimaeus the beggar, whom Jesus healed of his blindness 'on his way down from Jericho'. ('Jericho' means 'moon', and, as we have seen in Part I, certain paragraphs were removed from The Gospel of Mark, which relates this incident. Although the intention was to veil the identity of Lazarus as the 'Beloved Disciple' (John), we think that references to Mary Magdalene were also obscured at this point in the story, so that her link with the Moon as the feminine light of the Christ Being, which was one half of the potency that restored Bartimaeus's sight, might not be suspected.) Plato's *Timaeus* (Timaeus was the son of Bartimaeus) discusses the intriguing concept of the Demiurge – the mediator between divine spirit and the physical cosmos. (We can see how Joseph of Arimathea mediated between the pragmatic realities of the Roman and Judaic world, and that of the inner essence which is the Christ, in order to serve the Christ couple and smooth their path.) If this mediator responds to the light and follows the principles outlined in Mary's gospel, he will overcome the cosmic powers and authorities, stemming from the physical universe, which oppress his soul. As Paul taught his initiates: 'Did you not die with Christ (escape the grip of materiality) and pass beyond the reach of the elemental powers of the cosmos?'

And so the Demiurge is revealed as Everyman or Everywoman, applying themselves to the true craft of life, which is to master the downward pull of the elements, as Mary's gospel teaches. Of course, there is much more to the mystery of the Demiurge than this simple statement contains, and his-her depth of meaning is well worth meditating upon.

Joseph, Jesus's brother the craftsman and metal-worker who represented the Demiurge rooted in the material realm but with aspirations rising far beyond it, was therefore the natural choice of Joseph of Arimathea (who personified the Demiurge resonating at a higher octave) when he came to commission the Antioch Chalice.

Why are there two Josephs, two Demiurges? The answer seems to be that Joseph the brother symbolizes that wounded or shadowed part of ourselves which we are sometimes tempted to reject and ignore when we are working on the craft of forging our Soul Temple (as Vulcan is depicted as maimed and bearing an ugly face, and as the Smith-Woman is also that aspect of Brigid which manifests as a withered crone), not realizing that without it, and what we learn through its existence, we can never attain to the light. Jesus demonstrates this latter point for us when he embraces the existence of his half-brother (the shadow-half), and, with all respect and loving kindness, gives Joseph his rightful due of absolute equality with himself, the 'legitimate' or accepted brother. Joseph of Arimathea is the already healed, finely balanced Demiurge, who commands the elemental forces on their own terms and who is yet Joseph of Arimathea or Arimatheos, the man of Maria-and-God, Joseph of the Spirit and the Bride. Between them, Joseph of Arimathea and Joseph, Christ's brother, devised the design for the Antioch Chalice.

The figures on this beautiful open-work container are considered to be authentic portraits of Jesus and his followers, although we feel that the central portrait should not be taken literally. From the open mouth of the Lion of Judah on the viewer's right is given forth the 'true vine', also depicting the sacred bloodline. Jesus sits enthroned in a heart shape created by tendrils of this fruit-bearing vine. He is beardless; a dove perches above him directly in line with his crown chakra, and a lamb stands at his side, gazing upon his heart chakra. Below his feet the Aquarian eagle (the eagle of St John, which is also the phoenix, indicating the coming New Age of John and Mary Magdalene (*see* Appendix One)) stretches its wings. With one hand, Jesus wields a plate of loaves and fishes, looking down upon St Peter, who sits at his feet below the eagle, as if offering them to him. With his other hand he points towards St Paul, who sits underneath the heart shape opposite St Peter.

Surely this chalice, symbol of the Holy Grail, one of its earliest Christian forms in the mundane world, shows us, not Jesus (a beardless man from the culture of first-century Judea would have been almost unheard of, as Jewish people considered that a hairless face denoted prepubescence) but the fused being of Jesus and Mary Magdalene. Why else would the central figure be depicted as beardless, set in a heart shape created by intertwining vines and surrounded by symbols of the Sacred Feminine and the Sacred Masculine? And, significantly, the fused Jesus-and-Mary figure points to St Paul, the man who would at first have appeared to share St Peter's blinkered vision for the Church but who afterwards was initiated into the true mysteries of 'The Way' by Tamar, and entirely changed his stance even though he had to keep much of his knowledge secret and disguised. As if to confirm this, the Jesus-and-Mary figure creates a V with its pointing finger and thumb, the sign of the Sacred Feminine as a vessel containing divine wisdom, whilst St Paul sits quietly contemplating the open Book of Truth spread out on his lap.

St Peter, on the other hand, seems to fear the offered gift of the loaves and fishes (a perfectly balanced symbol of the Sacred Feminine and Masculine principles). The Sword of Truth points at him also, virtually hidden under the toga-like cloak that the Jesus-Mary figure wears (to denote royalty), bearing in its depiction an aspect of the 'true vine' from which Jesus and Mary emanate, and also reminiscent of the 'unicorn's horn', that part of the crown chakra that receives truth from the higher spheres. In order to shield himself from the proffered gift of the loaves and bread, Jesus-Mary's gaze and the shaft of energy from the Sword of Truth, Peter wields a squat, ugly little idol (the idols that were used in the worship of Ba'al, or materialism). The festoon of grapes above St Peter's head appears a little different, darker and more closely clustered, than the surrounding images of them. Could it be that these are the 'false grapes' frequently referred to in the Scriptures and also identified in the Old Testament as the Grapes of Wrath? These black densely-grouped berries were produced by the deadly nightshade, the poisonous plant that took over vineyards and destroyed them, producing grape-like fruits that were fatally toxic. If our surmise is correct, the reference to the 'false grapes' is ambiguous. It appears that these could be 'true grapes', if only Peter would stop hiding behind the idol and let go of Wrath! Perhaps this is a message for us all at this time. Universally, we have mistaken the false grapes for the true, and pursued empty shadows of materialism which ultimately bring us no happiness or fulfilment.

Sages, prophets and spiritual teachers predicted that something marvellous would occur in the last 25 years of the twentieth century which would change the world forever. During the 1980s, the first stirrings concerning the truth about Mary Magdalene began. Surely this truth, now coming to us in full spate, is the fulfilment of that prediction? And surely the great gift is coming – the gift that was secured for us by Mary and Jesus and which cannot be withheld from us unless we refuse it – the gift of a global baptism of light, dependent not on any religion or political faction or anything that divides and denies another's truth, but simply on our acceptance of the principles of universal love. With that acceptance, we confirm that our hearts will be open to receive their gift, and that we know we are children of the light, each one of us endlessly rich beyond compare when we draw upon the spiritual starlight secreted within the sacred vessel of the heart and give it forth to the Earth and to the human family as a similar gift of all-embracing love.

Further Reading

Cannon, Dolores, *They Walked with Jesus*, Ozark Mountain Publishing (USA), 2001

Cannon, Dolores, *Jesus and the Essenes*, Ozark Mountain Publishing (USA), 2001

Freke, Timothy, & Gandy, Peter, *Jesus and the Goddess*, Thorsons, 2001

Hodgson, Joan, *The Stars & the Chakras*, The White Eagle Publishing Trust, 1997

Hodson Geoffrey, *The Coming of the Angels*, Rider, 1935

Jowett, George F, *The Drama of the Lost Disciples*, Covenant Publishing, 2001

King, Karen, *The Gospel of Mary of Magdala*, Polebridge Press, 2003

Leloup, Jean-Yves, *The Gospel of Mary Magdalene*, Inner Traditions (USA), 2002

White Eagle, *Divine Mother: The Feminine, and the Mysteries*, The White Eagle Publishing Trust, 2005

White Eagle, *The Light Bringer: The Ray of John and the Age of Intuition*, The White Eagle Publishing Trust, 2001

White Eagle, *The Living Word of Saint John*, The White Eagle Publishing Trust, 2000

Index